THE ONLY THING WORTH DYING FOR

Also by Eric Blehm

The Last Season

P3: Pipes, Parks, and Powder

*Agents of Change: The Story of DC Shoes
and Its Athletes*

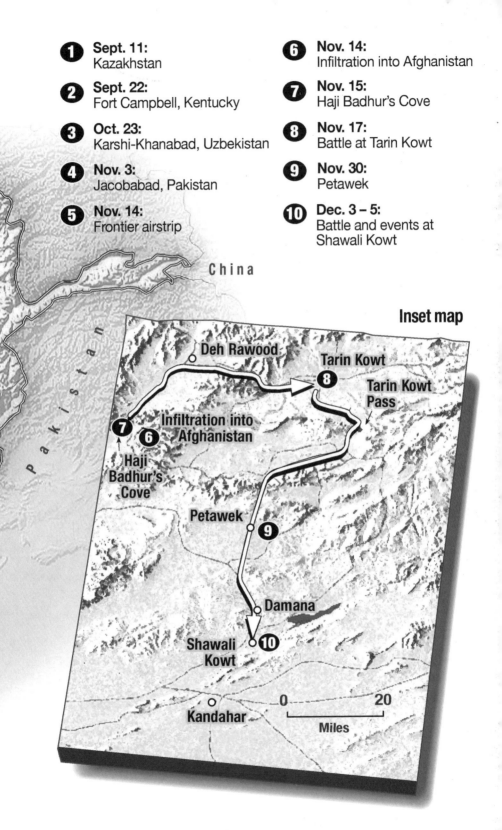

1. **Sept. 11:** Kazakhstan
2. **Sept. 22:** Fort Campbell, Kentucky
3. **Oct. 23:** Karshi-Khanabad, Uzbekistan
4. **Nov. 3:** Jacobabad, Pakistan
5. **Nov. 14:** Frontier airstrip
6. **Nov. 14:** Infiltration into Afghanistan
7. **Nov. 15:** Haji Badhur's Cove
8. **Nov. 17:** Battle at Tarin Kowt
9. **Nov. 30:** Petawek
10. **Dec. 3 – 5:** Battle and events at Shawali Kowt

China

Inset map

Deh Rawood

Tarin Kowt

Tarin Kowt Pass

8

Infiltration into Afghanistan

7 6

Haji Badhur's Cove

Pakistan

Petawek

9

Damana

Shawali Kowt

10

0 — 20
Miles

Kandahar

THE ONLY THING WORTH DYING FOR

**How Eleven Green Berets
Forged a New Afghanistan**

ERIC BLEHM

HARPER

An Imprint of HarperCollins*Publishers*
www.harpercollins.com

This story is dedicated to the men and women of the coalition forces who have fought in Afghanistan, and to their families and loved ones, many of whom have come to realize that not all battles end with the war.

HarperCollins books may be purchased for educational, business, or sales promotional use. For information, please write: Special Markets Department, HarperCollins Publishers, 10 East 53rd Street, New York, NY 10022.

FIRST EDITION

Designed by William Ruoto

Library of Congress Cataloging-in-Publication Data has been applied for.

ISBN 978-0-06-166122-8

10 11 12 13 14 OV/RRD 10 9 8 7 6 5 4 3 2 1

Ten good soldiers, wisely led,
will beat a hundred without a head.
—*Euripides*

Contents

★

Prologue

I met Hamid Karzai, the president of Afghanistan, at the Barclay Hotel in midtown Manhattan on September 23, 2008, when he was approaching the end of his five-year term as the country's first democratically elected leader. Since 1700, twenty-five of the twenty-nine rulers of Afghanistan had been dethroned, exiled, imprisoned, hanged, or assassinated.[1] That Karzai had survived multiple assassination attempts since taking office was a feat in itself. Even more remarkable, however, was the journey that had brought him to this presidency.

He greeted me in perfect English with a British accent, shook my hand firmly, and ushered me across the elegant room of his suite. Though it was Ramadan, when Muslims fast from dawn to sunset, he offered me cookies and coffee or tea, which I declined out of respect for his religion. Sitting opposite the president in a cushioned armchair, I handed him a stack of photographs. As he held them in his palms, he stared intently at the one on top: eleven American soldiers grouped tightly around him on a sandy hillside in southern Afghanistan. A smile spread over his face, and he began to nod as he flipped through the pictures chronicling the mission that had changed the course of history.

For nearly two years, I had been trying to interview Karzai so that he could confirm crucial details of his rise to power during the early days of the Global War on Terror, a war that Karzai and his staff—who had joined us in the room to hear their president tell his stories—called by another name: the Liberation. He transported us to the mud-walled safe houses of his insurgency, where, lit by kero-

sene lanterns, turbaned freedom fighters with AK–47s planned strat-
egy with U.S. Special Forces soldiers wearing camouflage. He led me
through the photos, which I had placed in chronological order, taking
us back to October, November, and December 2001.

I was concerned that he might not be able to recall details about
the men who had sacrificed so much for both America and Afghanistan in carrying out one of the war's most dangerous and secretive
missions. I wondered whether all that he had experienced in the ensuing years had erased or distorted his memories.

Then he held up a photo to his staff and pointed to an American
soldier. "Had there been *anybody* else, things would have gone terribly
wrong," he said. A mournful tone now entered his voice. "Oh, some
good men . . ."

"Very sad," he said about the next photo. "This is perhaps a day or
two before he died." Looking closely at the following photo, he said,
"This man is dead. And this man—he is also dead. And this man."

"When?" I asked. "Do you remember the date they died?"

"Of course," he answered. "How could I forget?"

The following is a true narrative account of modern unconventional
warfare as recalled by the men who were there. Some names have
been changed to respect the privacy of the individuals.

CHAPTER ONE

★

A Most Dangerous Mission

[H]e knew from experience how simple it was to move behind the enemy lines. . . . It was as simple to move behind them as it was to cross through them, if you had a good guide.

—Ernest Hemingway, *For Whom the Bell Tolls*

Late on the night of Tuesday, November 13, 2001, Hamid Karzai and his military adviser, U.S. Special Forces Captain Jason Amerine, walked briskly down a deserted road near their safe house in the Jacobabad District of Sindh Province, Pakistan. For Amerine, it felt almost as if they were walking along a country road stateside, the adjacent unplanted fields softly illuminated by starlight. In the distance, a half mile to the west, a dull glow marked more densely populated civilization, but here they were relatively isolated.

Karzai was unarmed and wearing the traditional Afghan *shalwar kameez*,* and his poise and flowing arm motions marked him as an orator. Tall and thin, Amerine had an M9 pistol tucked into the belt of his camouflage uniform. Above a coarse brown beard, his alert eyes never stopped scanning the dark fields while he and Karzai spoke in hushed tones.

"I just received confirmation," said Amerine. "Tomorrow is the night—have you heard any news from the tribal leaders in Uruzgan?"

---

* A long, loose shirt with pajama-like trousers.

"Yes," said Karzai. "I followed up with one of the local chiefs in War Jan. If the location we decided upon is safe, if no Taliban patrols are nearby, the signal fires will be lit as planned."

"Your men are ready?"

"They are—word has spread about Kabul. The Pashtun are ready to join the fight."

Earlier that day, allied U.S. and Northern Alliance resistance forces had liberated Kabul, Afghanistan's capital, from the Taliban. That was in the north; in the south, the home of the majority Pashtun ethnic group and the birthplace of the Taliban movement, things weren't going so well. Neither the CIA nor the U.S. military had been able to establish a presence, and there was no organized resistance like the Northern Alliance. The few Afghans who dared to oppose the Taliban had been imprisoned or killed.

For four weeks beginning in early October, Karzai had traveled the region unarmed, trying to persuade leaders throughout the Pashtun tribal belt to rise up against the Taliban. The CIA considered this undertaking so dangerous that it refused to put any men on the ground with Karzai, limiting its involvement to giving him a satellite phone so that a case officer could monitor his progress. By the end of October, Karzai and a small group of followers had been pursued by the Taliban into the mountains of Afghanistan's Uruzgan Province. Using the phone, he called for help on November 3 and was rescued by a helicopter-borne team of Navy SEALs.

Though he'd been chased out of Afghanistan, Karzai told the CIA that the Pashtun in the south were ready to rise up—if he returned with American soldiers who could organize and train them into a viable fighting force.

Only a few individuals were supposed to know that Karzai was now in Pakistan, so it had shocked and angered both Karzai and Amerine when U.S. Secretary of Defense Donald Rumsfeld disclosed Karzai's whereabouts to the media during a Defense Department press briefing earlier that week. Rumsfeld recanted what he called his "mistake" a couple of hours after he made it, telling the press that while Karzai *was* being assisted by U.S. Special Forces (Green Berets), he was somewhere in Afghanistan, *not* in Pakistan.

Amerine and Karzai feared that the Pashtun would interpret the news that Karzai was in Pakistan as a sign of weakness. Every village elder, Taliban deserter, and farmer who might otherwise support him could withdraw their backing or, even worse, turn on Karzai. In order to maintain credibility within the Pashtun tribal belt, he and Amerine would return to Afghanistan on the most dangerous and politically important mission thus far of Operation Enduring Freedom.*

Now, walking down the center of the gravel road, Karzai and Amerine were reviewing the plan for the following night's mission, when the eleven members of Operational Detachment Alpha (ODA) 574, Amerine's Special Forces "A-team," would be the first American team to infiltrate into southern Afghanistan. There, they would link up with the Pashtun tribal leaders and villagers who had promised Karzai allegiance.

The purpose of this mission was twofold: destroy the Taliban in the important southern city of Kandahar, where they were expected to regroup after the fall of Kabul; and unite the southern Pashtun tribe with the northern Tajiks, Uzbeks, and Hazaras. The Northern Alliance was on course to topple the Taliban, so unless the Pashtun joined the fight, they would be frozen out of the government that would rule after the Taliban. If this happened, Karzai was convinced that Afghanistan would descend into another devastating civil war.

Headlights appeared behind the two men, and Amerine quickly ushered Karzai to the side as a large flatbed truck passed by.

"There is something else, Jason," said Karzai, falling back into stride behind the truck's taillights. "Just an hour ago I received a call that my supporters in the town of Tarin Kowt are discussing an uprising to overthrow the provincial governor in Uruzgan Province."

"It's too early," Amerine said. "If they succeed, they won't be able to hold the town. The Taliban will slaughter them and fortify their position, which will make our job all the more difficult when we move on Tarin Kowt."

---

* The official name for the joint U.S., U.K., and Afghan military action that began in Afghanistan on October 7, 2001, as part of the Global War on Terror.

"I will call the tribal leaders when we return," said Karzai.

Nodding his approval, Amerine reflected back to the week before, when the name Hamid Karzai had meant little more than an obscure warlord. "You can't trust anything these guys say," Amerine's team sergeant, JD, had warned him. "They will smile and tell you exactly what you want to hear—but don't trust them to cover our backs." Amerine had been wary, and rightly so. As a thirty-year-old captain, he alone would decide whether Karzai's questionable southern rebellion against the Taliban was worth gambling the lives of American soldiers. His soldiers.

Karzai was not the warlord Amerine had expected. To the contrary, he was dignified, cultured, gentle. *Still*, Amerine had thought, *that doesn't mean he's trustworthy*. Nine days before, on the first of their nighttime walks, Karzai had posed some awkward questions: "Who will govern Afghanistan after the terrorists and the Taliban are defeated? What are the U.S. government's long-term plans for Afghanistan?"

Other than hunting down the terrorists responsible for the attacks on September 11, 2001, Amerine suspected that the United States had no comprehensive plan, military or otherwise. He wasn't obligated to answer Karzai's questions, but he did want to build a foundation of trust with him. "I don't know," he had admitted.

"My fear," Karzai replied, "is that the warlord generals of the Northern Alliance will use the momentum they've gained working with your American forces in the north, and take over the government as they move through the country reclaiming their cities."

He explained that the September 9, 2001, assassination of Ahmad Shah Massoud, the charismatic leader of the Northern Alliance, had spurred a bloodless battle among those warlords. The generals had managed to settle their differences—at least temporarily—enough to unite with the United States against the Taliban and the terrorists. "But even if one warlord rises to the top," said Karzai, "a much bigger problem will result." The majority ethnic group—the Pashtun in the south—would "never be ruled by a minority ethnic group leader from the north who *takes* control," he said. "Especially after the atrocities committed by both sides during the civil war.* A new civil war would be inevitable. Afghanistan would be ripe once again for the next Taliban or al-Qaeda."

Please don't tell me you want the power, Amerine had thought, anticipating the age-old solution to problems raised by a politician: the politician himself. Aloud, he'd asked, "What do *you* think would be best for Afghanistan? Who would be the right man for the job?"

"The best *person* for the job," Karzai had said, "is not for me to decide. That is for the Afghan people to consider. I want to see the people voting, as in the United States. My dream is to see a Loya Jirga—a grand council where the tribal leaders set down their guns and talk. For years I have been talking about this. Nobody has listened."

By now, on the eve of the team's mission, Amerine had determined—over the course of several walks the past nine days—that Karzai was neither a warlord nor a politician. Indeed, he seemed to be a visionary idealist, a gallant statesman whose quest in Afghanistan bordered on quixotic.

Amerine liked the man. More important, he felt he could trust him.

/

The following morning, the safe house was abuzz with activity as ODA 574 from the Army's 5th Special Forces Group prepared for that night's infiltration into Afghanistan.

The eleven-man A-team had gathered in their meeting room in the safe house, dressed in a mix of desert camouflage pants, dark civilian fleece or down jackets over thermals, Vietnam War–era boonie hats, and baseball caps bearing such logos as Harley-Davidson and Boston Red Sox. As a sign of respect for the Afghan culture, none had shaved for the past month, starting before they had even left Fort Campbell, Kentucky.

---

* The post–Soviet occupation civil war lasted from 1989 to 1992.

Amerine watched as his weapons sergeants, Ronnie, Mike, and Brent, laid out enormous piles of weaponry and ammo as well as two laser-targeting devices and began to discuss the distribution of their loads. The only non–Green Beret on the mission, an Air Force combat controller (CCT) named Alex, joined the communications sergeants, Dan and Wes, in making final checks on all radios, laptops, and batteries. Victor, the engineer responsible for the load plan, paced back and forth between the two groups of men and their piles, ready to re-weigh the equipment for the helicopters that would fly them in. Every passenger and every item they carried had to be weighed and logged. Assigned to the team at the last minute, Ken, the medic, was leaning up against a wall with the medical supplies organized in front of him, laying out small but ominous morphine injectors that he would issue to each man.

JD, the team sergeant and Amerine's number two, and Mag, the intelligence sergeant and third in command, placidly observed the scene. They were veterans of the Gulf War and had seen all this before.

By noon, the eleven men had double- and triple-checked their gear. Each would carry an M4 carbine,* an M9 pistol, grenades, ammunition, food, water, minimal clothing in shades of desert camouflage, a midweight sleeping bag, and a waterproof jacket. Each man would also carry gear specific to his job—communications equipment, medical supplies, extra weapons—that added another fifty-plus pounds per pack. They had no body armor or helmets: for this unconventional warfare mission, the team would share the risk with the guerrillas they would lead. If Karzai's followers did not have armor, neither would they.

The load was split between a bulging rucksack and a smaller, lighter "go-to-hell" pack of survival essentials, always kept on their bodies in case they had to jettison their rucksacks in a firefight or retreat. Together, the two packs weighed about 150 pounds (not including fifty pounds of radios, grenades, and ammo in their load-bearing

---

* A lightweight assault rifle with a telescoping stock.

vests, and a ten- to fifteen-pound loaded weapon), so heavy the men had to lie down on the ground to put on the shoulder straps, then roll over on all fours, and still needed help to stand up.

Extra team gear such as flares, computer equipment, and medical supplies for the indigenous population filled a half-dozen duffel bags that would be shuttled by vehicle or pack animal, both of which had been promised by Karzai.

An officer from Air Force Special Operations Command (AFSOC) arrived to brief ODA 574, as well as the men from the Central Intelligence Agency who would be infiltrating with them, on their flight and escape-and-recovery plans. As the officer spoke, Amerine felt an eerie connection to the three-man Jedburgh teams—considered the predecessors to both Special Forces soldiers *and* CIA agents—that had parachuted behind Nazi lines to assist the resistance fighters during World War II.[1] Those teams had received similar briefings. How many made it back alive? *Not many*, thought Amerine.

The CIA team, led by a spook called Casper,[2] sat beside Amerine's men as the officer explained that they would be flown by AFSOC pilots from a nearby airstrip to a clandestine one near the Afghanistan border on two MH-53 Pave Lows,[3] the Air Force's heavy-lift helicopters. There they would board five smaller MH-60 Black Hawk helicopters—piloted by the 160th Special Operations Aviation Regiment (SOAR), which specializes in clandestine low-altitude night operations—for the flight into Afghanistan.

Shortly before 3 P.M., ODA 574 was loading gear onto a flatbed truck for transportation to the helicopters when Casper drove up with three men in a Humvee, parked, and approached Amerine, shaking his head. "Change in plans, skipper," he said.

Here we go again, thought Amerine.

In the War on Terror, the CIA and Special Forces were working side by side, but with Special Forces running military operations, Amerine couldn't determine exactly what the CIA's role in Afghanistan would be. Casper's agenda had at times intruded during the planning of the mission, even though Amerine had been told that he and his men were in charge of the insurgency.

"These guys are coming with us," said Casper, motioning toward three Delta Force soldiers unloading rucksacks and weapons from the Humvee. "They're a recon team that's spotting for emerging al-Qaeda targets. We've got to come up with some seats in the helicopters. Task Force Sword* isn't going to let us fly without them."

Every seat in the helicopters, every ounce of weight, had been scrupulously allotted. Now, minutes before the team was to board the Pave Lows waiting on the tarmac, was the worst possible time to reshuffle.

"They expect us to bump our men to make room?" asked Amerine. "This is ridiculous."

"You're free to take it up with your boss," said Casper. "He can hash it out with Task Force Sword, but we don't have time to argue it now. We'll have to scrub the mission for tonight."

Amerine thought through his next move. He doubted Casper's story about being ordered to take the three Delta Force soldiers, and questioned his motives: Was he attempting to bring along bodyguards for Karzai? But if they postponed the infiltration, Amerine's commander, who had voiced reservations about the mission in the first place, might cancel it entirely. Maybe that was Casper's agenda: gum things up enough to scrub the mission and keep Karzai stranded in Pakistan.

All that really mattered was getting Karzai into Afghanistan.

"What's going on, sir?" JD asked Amerine as he joined them.

"SNAFU," said Amerine. "We've got those guys coming along." He pointed to the newly arrived soldiers loitering by the Humvee with their piles of gear. "We've got to lose some weight."

"I can leave two guys and you guys leave one; we'll split the loss," said Casper.

"We don't leave our guys alone," said JD; the Special Forces buddy system dictates that a Green Beret never leaves another Green Beret

---

* An elite special mission unit that was based primarily in Pakistan, comprising Delta, Navy SEALs, British Special Air Service (SAS), and Army Rangers. Its main role was to capture or kill high-value Taliban and al-Qaeda targets.

alone, even at a secure location. JD knew that whoever was left behind would be joining the team soon enough, and that meant another flight into bad-guy country. If that aircraft were to go down behind enemy lines, the buddy system was crucial. ODA 574 was already short one man, however, and losing two more would sap nearly 20 percent of the team's already less-than-optimal combat strength.

JD and Amerine made the decision to leave behind their engineer, Victor, and junior weapons sergeant, Brent—since Mag, the intelligence sergeant, was also a trained engineer, and they had two senior weapons sergeants, Mike and Ronnie. They knew the reorganization wouldn't sit well with anybody on the team, but it was the only alternative.

Casper strode off toward one of his fellow spooks, and Amerine walked in the opposite direction to greet the Delta Force soldiers. "I don't want to ruffle things up," one of them quietly told Amerine, "but you should know that Task Force Sword had nothing to do with putting us on this mission." He pointed his chin toward Casper. "*He* wanted us here."

As ODA 574 and the CIA team loaded into the cavernous cargo holds of the two Pave Low helicopters, JD paused for a moment beside Amerine. "Sir," he said, "you know, I've never been a big fan of some of the people in this part of the world—and warlords in general, the lack of respect for human life, we saw that in Somalia. Hell, sir. What those fanatics did to all those people in New York City and the Pentagon, those passengers on the airliners . . . it's hard to think about it still."

Stroking his beard, JD gathered his thoughts, then continued. "Karzai is either feeding us a load of bullshit or he is something different from the warlords up north. This is a good mission. Feels right."

They were interrupted when Air Force Lieutenant Colonel Steve Hadley approached. "You two are the last to load."

JD slapped Amerine on the shoulder and walked up the ramp and into the second Pave Low.

"Thanks for the ride," Amerine said while shaking Hadley's hand. "Sorry you're not taking us all the way in."

"You'll be in good hands with the 160th," said Hadley. "We've got your back, though. Just call if you need us. Anytime. Anyplace."

Over the noise of the engines powering up, Amerine yelled, "I'll remember that."

/

The two helicopters hugged the rolling hills of the Pakistani desert for an hour before coming upon an airstrip just south of the Afghan border, which appeared like a mirage on the horizon. They landed when it was still light enough to see squads of Army Rangers patrolling the perimeter. When the helicopter ramps dropped, some of the Rangers ran over to help the teams unload their gear, then the Pave Lows immediately lifted off, blanketing everyone in dust.

"Now we wait," JD said to Mag as the men settled on their rucksacks.

As the sun disappeared behind the mountains, they heard the *thump, thump, thump* of rotors beating against the wind, announcing the arrival of their next ride: five Black Hawks to carry the men in groups of four and five on a western heading into Afghanistan. The Rangers helped move the gear onto the helicopters, which lifted off into the night sky in a tight combat formation—staggered, with a distance of one rotor disk between them. Two more Black Hawks beefed up with heavy weapons flew on the flanks. Thousands of feet above, heavily armed jets escorted the formation. At the border of Pakistan and Afghanistan, the flock turned north. If all went well, they would cover close to two hundred miles before setting down on Afghan soil for a few seconds to unload their passengers.

In pitch darkness, the SOAR pilots used only their night vision goggles, known as NODs,* to fly ODA 574 deeper behind enemy lines than any U.S. team currently in Afghanistan. The ground signal the helicopter pilots would be looking for in the mountains was a configuration of wood fires: the same "all clear" signal that Allied pilots had often relied upon when inserting their Jedburgh teams into Nazi-occupied France.

---

* NOD, night observation device, or NVD, night vision device; commonly referred to as night vision goggles.

In the third helicopter, Communications Sergeant Wes McGirr—new to ODA 574 and at twenty-five its youngest member—was electric with anticipation. Looking down at the rugged mountains of Afghanistan, he realized that he was experiencing the same combination of euphoria and fear that the Jeds had felt when they'd crossed over the English Channel. *It's dark, and I've got more gear than I can possibly run with,* he thought. *Once we get dropped off, we're on our own. God, this is awesome. This is a war and we're live and we've got ammo and anything can happen from here on out: We're in enemy country.*

The flight held a northerly course toward the Hindu Kush mountains. Two hours in, during a midair refueling, Amerine's helicopter—first in the formation—filled with jet fuel fumes and, strangely, the scent of flowers. It wasn't the right season for poppies, and Amerine didn't know what poppies smelled like anyway, but the thought of flowers in the midst of all this firepower and modern military might brought a smile to his face.

A few moments later, the Black Hawk bucked and jerked in an evasive maneuver, and its right gunner squeezed off a burst of gunfire. Amerine looked at the SOAR mission commander, who shrugged. Whatever it was, they were apparently okay.

"What happened?" Ken asked, tugging on Amerine's sleeve. "What just happened?" Even in the darkened interior of the helicopter, Amerine could see fear in his medic's eyes.

Putting up his hand, Amerine waited for the mission commander to update him through his headset, then told Ken that the gunner had apparently mistaken the infrared laser-aiming beam* from his own mini-gun for ground fire.

"Sir," said Ken. "You need to keep us informed right away."

Amerine said nothing, but he thought, *I hope this isn't how he's going to react in combat.*

---

* A laser pointer built into a gun's target sighting system. It is invisible to the naked eye, so only those using NODs can see the beam or the "dot" that the beam casts on its target.

A half hour out from the landing zone, surveillance aircraft flying ahead reported no signal fires. Although Karzai had been confident that the landing zone was both remote and void of Taliban activity, no fires were to be lit if the enemy was thought to be nearby.

"Remote" was relative. The landing zone was only a couple of miles east of the Helmand River, where villages were regularly patrolled by the Taliban. Because of the anti-aircraft artillery known to be in the area, the Black Hawks could not deviate from the route or circle around for another pass: If the fires were not spotted soon, the team would have to cancel the mission.

The mission commander asked Amerine what he wanted to do.

"Press on," replied Amerine. "Let's give it another five minutes."

After five minutes, there was still nothing. Amerine shook his head and was about to tell his pilot to turn back when the pilot from the surveillance plane came on the radio.

"We see four fires. Say again—we see four fires."

⚔

The landing zone was in a small valley as long as a football field and slightly narrower—a cleft atop one of the taller broad-backed peaks in the region. As the helicopters swooped down into the rugged mountains, the fires marking the four corners of this smooth, barren patch of earth were extinguished so as not to blind the pilots through their NODs.

Less than two hundred feet above the ground, the five Black Hawks drifted gracefully into a straight line. Amerine's helicopter descended first, with the others following close behind like boxcars tethered to a locomotive. As the helicopter dropped, its powerful rotors stirred up fine sand and dust that billowed into the air like a volcanic eruption, creating a brownout that shrouded the landing zone and threw the tightly synchronized formation into disarray. Amerine's helicopter set down gently, its crew and passengers unaware that they were now invisible to the pilots above. Amerine, Alex, Ken, and a spook jumped out, dragging their rucksacks with them as the helicopter lifted off.

The second helicopter, descending quickly on top of Amerine's group, nearly collided with the cleft's rocky right wall. The men squinted up in disbelief as the mechanical monster seemed about to crush them—then it suddenly lurched to the left, regained stability, and landed gently as well.

The third helicopter dropped rapidly through the dust, its pilot determined to land despite zero visibility. The Black Hawk hit the ground hard. While Karzai, Casper, another spook named Charlie, and two of the Delta operators scrambled out, a gunner crawled underneath to inspect the landing gear. It was undamaged, and the helicopter lifted back into the air.

The fourth helicopter dipped into the enormous cloud. Inside, Mag, Mike, Ronnie, and a spook named Zepeda were choking on dust. The main rotor blades, throwing sparks from the static created by their proximity to the sides of the cleft, looked like giant sparklers to Mike, and he braced for a collision with the ground. Instead, he felt his stomach flip as the Black Hawk powered up and out of the brownout, banked away, and disappeared into the night.

Undeterred, the pilot of the fifth helicopter, carrying JD, Dan, and two spooks, set down without a problem.

Had the Black Hawk pilots been able to land in a row as planned instead of putting down wherever they could, the men would have dropped to the ground and remained in place, forming a single, cigar-shaped defensive perimeter about forty yards long.

Instead, they were scattered in small groups around the valley, each setting up its own defensive perimeter. And there was movement: a half-dozen armed Afghans milling next to a string of undersized donkeys a hundred yards away, near the eastern edge of the valley, and a solitary figure striding through the dust toward them.

Hamid Karzai, who was to make the initial linkup with the Pashtun tribesmen, had immediately sprung forward to meet them, the white leather tennis shoes he'd been given by the CIA in Pakistan practically glowing beneath his *shalwar kameez* and looking as if they were walking themselves through the darkness. The Americans aimed their carbines at the tribesmen, the beams from their lasers invisible to the Afghans.

If there are spies or assassins within the ranks, this is when they'll have his ass, thought Wes as Karzai reached the reception party. To Wes, Karzai's lengthy greeting of each man took an eternity. Finally, Karzai called out to the Americans: "Hello, hello! It's okay. It's fine. Come to me. Come to me."

Standing up, Amerine ran to Karzai, leaving the rest of the men lying prone beside their rucksacks, weapons still trained on the Afghans. "Friends of yours?" he asked.

"Yes, yes," said Karzai, "these are good men. We are safe."

Amerine radioed JD: "Get the men moving. Have them bring their rucks to the pack animals."

After the men from the ODA and CIA had dropped their rucks next to the donkeys, JD set them all in a tight perimeter, with every man lying prone and facing outward to form a circle half the size of a basketball court, with Amerine and Casper alongside Karzai at its center. Then he approached Amerine. "We're missing four men: Mike, Mag, Ronnie, and one CIA. Their helicopter must have headed to an alternate landing zone."

"What does that mean?" asked Karzai.

"Means we have men lost in the mountains," Amerine said.

"I'm going to need to get to higher ground to reach them," said Dan, holding up his radio's hand mic. "I'm not getting anything here."

Any Taliban patrols in the area would have heard the helicopters and would already be en route to the landing zone. They had to get moving.

"We need to find our guys," Casper said to Amerine, who then told Karzai, "We need to leave this valley and get to higher ground so we can reach our lost men."

Karzai rattled off something in Pashto to the tribesmen. They switched on flashlights, alarming the soldiers, who felt safer under the cover of darkness, and led their animals away. The men followed fifty yards behind the glow of the flashlights south for a quarter mile, then Amerine and Karzai guided the column of Americans a few hundred vertical feet up a steep slope and onto a ridgeline that rimmed the western side of the valley. On a small hillock that offered little cover but was the highest ground in the area, JD formed another security perimeter around Dan, who sat down on the hard dirt, assembled the sections of an antenna, and screwed it into his radio. The Afghans remained in the valley at the bottom of the ridge with the pack animals.

"They would like to keep the donkeys moving," Karzai said to Amerine.

Amerine looked at JD, who shrugged and said, "I wouldn't want to get in a fight in the middle of that pack."

Nodding, Amerine told Karzai, "Let them go. We'll meet up with them at the village."

Karzai called out in Pashto, and the tribesmen continued on into the night while Dan attempted to reach his missing teammates using ODA 574's call sign: "Any Texas element, this is Texas One Two, over . . ."

From a rucksack between Dan's legs an obscenely long antenna stuck up into the starlit sky. His bearded face was almost hidden beneath a black beanie pulled low to battle the cold wind that chilled his hands as they worked the radio's knobs. "I can hear them now—they're trying to reach us, but they can't hear me at all," he growled. "They need to get to higher ground."

"Keep trying," said Amerine.

The absence of gunfire was encouraging, but three of Amerine's nine men and a CIA spook were lost in the night, and until they too got to higher ground, there was little Amerine could do to find them. Then JD's rapid footsteps announced the arrival of more ominous news.

"Casper and Charlie sneaked off to try to find the missing men," he told Amerine angrily.

"If *we* don't have commo with our guys, *they* sure as hell don't," Amerine said. "Did they tell anyone their plan?"

"They left their commo guy behind and took only handheld radios, so they aren't going to be able to talk to anybody," said JD, looking out into the night. Distinguishing between friend and foe is often difficult during the daytime; at night it's nearly impossible, even with clear communications and a well-devised set of signals. The two spooks had neither.

"C-I-A, Children In Action," Dan said.

"Oh, it gets worse," JD said. "They took Karzai with them."

There was a pause as the men realized they had lost their guide, their only translator, and the one man whom Amerine trusted to muster the local Pashtun fighting force and, in doing so, possibly avert a civil war.

"We are so fucked," said Dan.

The fourth Black Hawk had drifted more than two miles west from the landing zone as its pilot searched for a suitable place to set down. In desperation, he briefly flicked on his spotlights, flooding the valley below in white light and prompting a resounding "What the fuck!" from the back of the helicopter.

"We better not fucking land right there!" yelled Mike.

As the Black Hawk crisscrossed the terrain for what seemed like forever, Mag, the highest-ranking sergeant present, went from being nervous about announcing their arrival with spotlights to being nervous that they weren't going to land at all. Finally the pilot said, "I'm putting it down right here."

He dropped the helicopter like a rock, determined to land before the dust storm could swallow the Black Hawk. They bounced hard, then settled on a massive shelf with mountains rising to the east. To the west, the flat terrain rolled off into either a sloping hillside or a cliff—it was impossible to tell which. Before Mag jumped from the helicopter, he told the pilot, "Radio my team with these coordinates so we can link up." The crew chief practically shoved Mag out as the pilot nodded mechanically and lifted off.

Squatting with his gear, Mag gripped his rifle as the engine noise from the departing Black Hawk faded away. He reviewed the situation: nighttime, foreign land, behind enemy lines, separated from the main group, no cover except low brush. *Oh God*, he thought. Then he flipped on his NODs, bathing the high desert terrain in familiar green hues.

The four lost men—Mike, Mag, Ronnie, and the spook Zepeda— had just set up in a 360-degree security formation when a light appeared in the distance. They hadn't been on the ground for more than two minutes.

"We've got movement," said Ronnie.

Unfuckingbelievable, thought Mag.

A couple hundred yards northwest, someone was sweeping a flashlight beam back and forth across the ground, slowly and steadily, as if searching for something. Leaving Ronnie and Mike with instructions to head for the mountains to their east if they weren't back in fifteen minutes, Mag took Zepeda and crept east in a straight line, searching for better cover. About eighty yards out, they practically fell into what would suffice as a fighting position: a depression at the base of a slight embankment. They hurried back to get the others, and the men concealed their gear as best they could in the bushes, then relocated to the depression with their go-to-hell packs.

Although the flashlight continued to flicker in the distance, here they felt sheltered enough to try to orient themselves. Unfolding the map produced a crackle that was, in this silence, almost as disconcerting as gunfire. *Jesus,* Mag thought, *might as well make some popcorn while we're at it.* But the flashlight didn't waver.

Using their GPS, they figured out that their position was below the valley where the main group had landed. The Helmand River and its Taliban-patrolled villages were more than two miles to the west, at the base of the mountains. Only one and a half miles lay between them and the rest of the team to the east, but on terrain like this it might as well have been fifty. Their best course of action was to stay put, avoid detection, and pray that they could make radio contact by morning.

As Mike continued trying to radio the rest of the team, one thing was certain: Pashtun tribesmen didn't normally travel around the mountains at night. Whoever was out there with that flashlight was not a goatherd looking for a lost kid.

★

CHAPTER TWO

The Quiet Professionals

It makes no difference what men think of war. . . . War endures. As well ask men what they think of stone. War was always here. Before man was, war waited for him.

The ultimate trade awaiting the ultimate practitioner.

—Cormac McCarthy, *Blood Meridian*

Two months earlier, on September 14, Captain Jason Amerine had been sitting in a hotel room in Almaty, Kazakhstan, writing in his journal, when his burly senior communications sergeant, Dan Petithory, knocked on the door. Dan was dressed casually in jeans, a T-shirt, and a Boston Red Sox baseball cap, but his normally jovial eyes were narrowed in an intense glare.

Amerine was immediately concerned—the last news Dan had delivered was that of the terrorist attacks on the United States three days before.

"Kazakhstan," said Dan, entering the room. "Shit. We're still only in Kazakhstan. I'm here a week now . . . waiting for a mission, getting softer." He began to pace. "Every minute I stay in this room I get weaker, and every minute Osama squats in a cave, he gets stronger. Each time I look around, the walls move in a little tighter." Dan threw a mock punch at a mirror.

Amerine laughed. He'd always admired the sergeant's ability to ease a tense situation by quoting the perfect movie line. Dan's spot-on impersonation of Martin Sheen's opening monologue as Captain

Willard in *Apocalypse Now* made light of the reality: The men of ODA 574 were restless, sequestered in this hotel killing time when all they really wanted to do was kill the terrorists responsible for the attacks on their homeland.

Picking up where Dan left off, Amerine said, "Everyone gets everything he wants. I wanted a mission, and for my sins they gave me one. Brought it up to me like room service. It was a real choice mission, and when it was over I'd never want another."

"Not bad, sir," Dan said with a chuckle. "You've got a Captain Willard thing going on without even trying. Anyway, your mission tonight is to get drunk with Colonel Asimov."

For the previous year, ODA 574 had been teaching counterinsurgency tactics to Colonel Asimov's airborne battalion, but during his five deployments to Kazakhstan during this time, Amerine had barely interacted with the high-ranking Kazakh army officer.

"No shit?" said Amerine.

"No shit, sir," said Dan. "Meet in the lobby at eight P.M. He's sending taxis for the whole team. Private dinner at some old KGB hangout . . . and sir? Don't forget your liver."

The aroma of savory beef-and-horse-meat stew wafted into the dimly lit dining room, where it mingled with plumes of cigarette smoke from the boisterous crowd. Dressed as civilians, the men of ODA 574 drew little attention as they followed a uniformed Kazakh officer through a doorway at the back of the restaurant.

In a private dining room at the top of a flight of wooden stairs, Colonel Asimov stood abruptly as the Americans entered, as did his twelve subordinates, whose blue-and-white-striped undershirts at the necks of their uniforms identified them as Kazakh paratroopers. The colonel was shorter than his men and markedly thin, with an emaciated, skull-like head. When he smiled, gold teeth glinted.

He waved Amerine to his side and beckoned the rest of the team to sit around the long table laden with traditional Kazakh and Russian dishes—flat bread, herring, and beet salad. Bottles of beer and soft drinks stood sweating at the center of the buffet, where they would remain. The Kazakhs assumed the Americans were off to war, and that called for vodka.

During the Cold War, as sworn enemies of the United States, the men in Asimov's unit had fought the U.S.-backed Mujahideen in the Soviet war with Afghanistan.* Now, little more than a decade later, Asimov offered a toast: "To our enemies, who are now our allies."

The men raised their glasses. The drinking began.

The Kazakhs quickly drained glass after glass of vodka. The Americans paced themselves, stalling as courses of food were delivered. When the colonel realized that they were nursing their drinks, he upped the number of toasts, shot after shot in honor of everything from John Wayne to the colonel's dog. As Asimov extolled the greatness of both American and Kazakh airborne, ODA 574 began shuttling glasses to the adjacent bathroom, where they replaced the vodka with tap water.

At last, Asimov lit a foul-smelling cigarette and launched into a rambling speech recounting the Soviet–Afghan War. With a drunken slur, he spoke of the Afghans they had killed, the men he had lost in the slow defeat of the Soviet army, and the multitude of walking dead who had returned home. He ended with a solemn warning to ODA 574: "Do not trust the Afghans. Do not trust your friends. Do not trust anyone except your enemies."

The colonel drained his vodka and set the tumbler upside down on the table. His dour expression turned into a grin.

"Time for bed for the young paratroopers," he said, standing up and nodding toward Junior Weapons Sergeant Brent Fowler, who had considered it disrespectful to his host not to drink vodka with every toast and was now passed out in his chair.

Amerine followed Asimov outside to his waiting sedan. While his driver opened the back door of the car, the colonel gripped Amerine's

---

* The Soviet invasion of Afghanistan began in 1979. Over the next decade of Soviet occupation, some 15,000 Soviet troops were killed, over 1 million Afghans were killed, and another 5 million Afghans fled to Iran and Pakistan. In 1989, the Soviets withdrew. The war in Afghanistan is often considered the Soviet equivalent of the United States' Vietnam War.

hand and looked him in the eye. "Captain Amerine," he said, "I do not believe that anyone can win a war in Afghanistan. Just try to bring your men home alive."

That same day at Fort Campbell, Kentucky,* Amerine's company commander, Major Chris Miller, strode across the block belonging to 5th Special Forces Group.

In 2001, 5th Group was one of seven Special Forces groups in the U.S. military, each focused on a different geographic area of the globe with the sole purpose of supporting the fifty-four ODAs assigned to it. There are six ODAs—each led by a captain—to a company, led by a major; three companies to a battalion, led by a lieutenant colonel; and three battalions to a Special Forces group, led by a colonel. This bureaucracy serves one purpose: to provide support to the elite ODAs that do the actual fighting in order for them to accomplish their missions.

Thirty-five-year-old Miller had done his time as an ODA captain, and now, as much as he would have loved to parachute into Afghanistan and shoot Osama bin Laden in the face, his duty was to oversee and support his six Alpha Company ODAs. The only team of Miller's not at Fort Campbell on 9/11 was ODA 574, and Amerine had been badgering his major since the terrorist attacks for information about the role Special Forces would play in the military response. Miller hoped to have something concrete for Amerine following the morning meeting with his boss, 3rd Battalion's commander, Lieutenant Colonel Queeg. Queeg wasn't his real name, but Miller—and most of 5th Group—likened him to the eccentric, sometimes tyrannical Captain Queeg from Herman Wouk's 1951 novel, *The Caine Mutiny*. Like the fictional Queeg, the commander was notorious for melodramatic speeches, angry outbursts, and being difficult to work with.

Since 9/11, Miller and the two other company commanders in 3rd

---

* Fort Campbell is located on the Kentucky-Tennessee state line.

Battalion had been attending three mandatory meetings a day—up from the usual one per week. At first, when Queeg had told them, "Hey, let's not jump to conclusions; I've been through this kind of thing before," Miller had exchanged looks with the two commanders. They were all thinking the same thing: *How the hell has he been through something like* this *before?*

At this morning's meeting, Queeg had them hold hands as he led them in prayer, which was disturbingly out of character. The more he talked, the more he seemed to feel in control, but Miller got the distinct impression that he wasn't.

Man, thought Miller, *this guy does not have a clue what we're fixin' to do.*

Shortly after the prayer, the commander of 5th Special Forces Group and Queeg's boss, Colonel John Mulholland,[1] strode into the room.

"I need to talk to Major Miller," he said to Queeg. "Can I borrow him for a minute?"

Having taken command of 5th Group just two months earlier, Mulholland knew few of his men personally, but he had worked with Miller planning some classified missions over the previous two years and considered him a resourceful and reliable Green Beret.

The two stepped outside the office and faced each other in the empty hallway.

"Chris, I was just notified that they're having a planning conference in Tampa at SOCCENT* starting this Monday," Mulholland said. "I want you to go down there and get us into the fight."

/

In Quetta, Pakistan, on September 15, Hamid Karzai was having tea with a group of close friends in a café near his home.

In 2001, the forty-three-year-old Afghan was unknown on the

---

* United States Special Operations Command Central is responsible for planning special operations throughout the U.S. Central Command area of responsibility, which includes, but is not limited to, the Middle East, Central Asia, and Africa.

international stage.[2] But in this café he was nobility, a direct descendant of Ahmad Shah, founder of the Durrani dynasty, which had ruled Afghanistan for more than two centuries. Hamid's father, Abdul Ahad Karzai, had served in the Afghan parliament in the 1960s and had been the chief of the Popalzai, a distinguished subtribe of the Durrani clan, itself a part of the Pashtun ethnic group—the dominant majority in Afghanistan from which the Taliban arose.

The Afghan expatriates sipping tea with Karzai respected him, not only for his lineage but also because he had not used the privilege it afforded him as a shield from danger. During the Soviet occupation, Karzai's five brothers and one sister had emigrated to Western countries while he finished his master's degree in international relations and political science at India's Himachal University. In 1983 he returned to Afghanistan, where his knowledge of English, French, Dari, Pashto, Persian, Urdu, and Hindi helped him to channel funds and weapons to the Mujahideen in their war with the Soviet Union.

After the Soviets retreated in February 1989, Karzai, then thirty-one, served the newly established Mujahideen government as deputy foreign minister. In that post, he watched helplessly as the rival factions of the Mujahideen dragged his beloved Afghanistan into a brutal civil war. Hundreds of thousands of civilians were killed in the lawlessness that plagued the country until a one-eyed former Mujahideen foot soldier named Mullah Muhammed Omar and his Taliban brought stability in the mid-1990s.

Omar's Taliban movement was sparked by the rape and murder of two young boys at a checkpoint on a road outside Kandahar in June 1994.[3] Mullah Omar, then the imam of a mosque in the Maiwand District west of Kandahar, led a band of armed students from his small madrassa to the checkpoint, where they killed the checkpoint commander and his men. He became a national hero, and his students of Islam, or *Taliban*, grew into an organized fighting unit. Composed overwhelmingly of ethnic Pashtun, mostly from the Durrani clan, the Taliban retaliated against brutality, extortion, and other injustices throughout the southern provinces of Helmand, Kandahar, and Uruzgan, and were hailed by Afghans for restoring a degree of safety they had not experienced in many years.

It was during this time that Hamid Karzai, who shared the movement's early vision of peace and stability, joined the Taliban as a spokesman.

In November 1994, just five months after its inception and now backed by Pakistan, the Taliban took the city of Kandahar; within a few months, Mullah Omar controlled twelve provinces across southern Afghanistan. The country's other twenty-two provinces were controlled by regional warlords, the majority belonging to the Northern Alliance, a coalition of minority tribes including Tajiks, Uzbeks, and Hazaras and backed by Russia, India, and Iran. In the ensuing two years, the Taliban moved north and in September 1996, Omar captured the capital city of Kabul. Though Kabul would remain Afghanistan's official capital, the Taliban continued to rule from Kandahar, their spiritual home.

At first Karzai believed the Taliban leadership to be honest and honorable, but by 1996 he began to notice that their priority was shifting from Afghanistan's welfare to maintaining political power. He suspected that Taliban policy was being heavily influenced by Pakistan and by Arab terrorist groups—including Osama bin Laden and his al-Qaeda network—that were permitted to operate freely in Afghanistan. Karzai also became increasingly wary of the Taliban's fanatical interpretation of Islam. That year, he shunned the Taliban when he refused an appointment to become Afghanistan's ambassador to the United Nations. As a result, he was no longer welcome in his own country, and he left to join his father in Quetta, Pakistan, where they began quietly to champion an anti-Taliban movement, petitioning foreign governments to intervene. Even though Hamid was not his eldest son, Abdul Ahad Karzai named him the heir to his position as chief of the Popalzai tribe—a decision uncontested by Hamid's brothers, who had no political aspirations.

The younger Karzai visited the embassies of the United States, Great Britain, France, China, and other countries to warn of the suffering the Taliban was inflicting in Afghanistan and the growing number of terrorists using it as a base of operations. Over the next few years he became more vocal in his denunciations. These "dark years," as he called them, were branded by gross human rights violations committed by the Taliban, which caused the international community to impose heavy-handed sanctions on the already oppressed Afghan people. When Taliban assassins gunned down the elder Karzai on his way home from a Quetta mosque in 1999, Hamid became chief of the Popalzai tribe and defiantly escorted his father's body on an overland burial procession from Quetta to Kandahar.

On July 20, 2000, Karzai testified before the U.S. Senate Committee on Foreign Relations about the terrorist organizations flourishing in Afghanistan. He warned that the Clinton administration's response to the August 7, 1998, suicide car bombings of the U.S. embassies in Nairobi, Kenya, and Dar es Salaam, Tanzania—firing cruise missiles at terrorist training camps—was not enough. "Bombings or the threat of bombings," he said, "will not remove terrorist bases from Afghanistan. Such actions will only add to the problems and prolong the suffering of our people and, worst of all, solidify the presence of terrorist groups. I call upon the international community, and particularly upon the government of the United States. . . . [T]he time to watch is over and the responsibility to act is long overdue."

Karzai spent hour after hour in meetings with Western ambassadors and intelligence officers. If he could convey the severity of the looming threat posed by the terrorists the Taliban had welcomed into Afghanistan, he reasoned, perhaps the Western powers would help defeat them and, in the process, oust the Taliban. Karzai believed that the Afghan people would embrace a more moderate political and religious environment, such as the one before the Soviet occupation, when Afghanistan's diverse factions each had a voice at the ruling Loya Jirga.

On September 11, 2001, Karzai was in Islamabad, Pakistan, preparing for meetings at Western embassies scheduled for the following day. The attack on the United States resulted in cancellation of those meetings and also conveyed, in a way that could not be ignored, the need for the regime change Karzai sought. In the days that followed, conversation among Karzai's fellow Afghans at the café in Quetta turned to speculation about the U.S. response that was sure to come. Everyone knew that al-Qaeda operated training camps in Afghanistan—Karzai had been warning about it for years. He felt that the people of Afghanistan had had enough of the Taliban's fanatical rule: the public executions, the closing of schools, the mistreatment of women, the ban on music and games. Rather than wait for the United States to act, however, Karzai decided to launch his own insurgency.

"The time is right," he told his friends. "Let us move back into Afghanistan. The eyes of the world are upon us."

/

Armed with credentials and passwords, Major Chris Miller entered the Special Operations Command Central (SOCCENT) bunker—a shelter used by B-52 crews during the Cold War—at MacDill Air Force Base in Tampa, Florida. Once past the entrance guards, he made his way underground through several cipher-locked doors to the office of Major Robert Kelley. It was Monday morning, September 17, and for the past six days, Kelley, who was SOCCENT's chief of plans, had been attending the highest-level meetings to plan a military response to the terrorist attacks. Only a few people on the planet knew precisely what military options the United States was considering in the hours and days following 9/11, and Kelley was one of them.

Kelley looked up from his computer screen. "Chris!" he said, surprised to see his friend and fellow Green Beret in the doorway. "Who let you in here?"

"I cracked the codes on the cipher locks," Miller joked. "Actually, Mulholland sent me over to make sure Fifth Group gets in the fight."

Over the previous decade, the thirty-nine-year-old Kelley had watched incredulously as top military leaders downplayed the importance of the Special Forces' primary mission of unconventional warfare (UW).* He had noted massive cuts to the Special Forces budget as other Special Operations units that specialized in direct-action

---

* "Unconventional warfare, or UW, is a broad spectrum of military and paramilitary operations, predominantly conducted through, with, or by indigenous or surrogate forces organized, trained, equipped, supported, and directed in varying degrees by an external source. UW includes, but is not limited to, guerrilla warfare, subversion, sabotage, intelligence activities, and unconventional assisted recovery (UAR)." See Field Manual 3-05.20, Special Forces Operations, June 2001.

missions were given increasingly more funding; UW training had been significantly downscaled, and certain UW skills, such as understanding foreign languages and cultures, were losing value in a military that was able to dominate adversaries with speed and devastating firepower. In February 1998, Peter J. Schoomaker, the commander in chief of U.S. Special Operations Command, told Kelley, "Unconventional warfare is not a viable mission for Special Forces. The only reason you train for it is because it is the best vehicle for maintaining your Special Forces skill set."[4]

In other words, why put men in harm's way to organize and train dissidents against regimes such as the Taliban when we can overwhelm them with superior firepower?

Kelley found that line of reasoning shortsighted. He had studied the occupation of Afghanistan by the Soviets, whose conventional army and air force, in spite of overwhelming firepower, were still defeated by the Afghans. Unconventional warfare was the way to go in Afghanistan, he believed, but there was a vast military hierarchy that needed convincing before a single soldier would touch Afghan soil.

Offering Miller a seat, Kelley began to brief him on the first "Crisis Action Planning" meeting that had taken place just hours after the Twin Towers fell, when key planning officers from all branches of the military assembled on the other side of the air base at CENTCOM* to figure out how to go after the terrorists.

"We had nothing preplanned for Afghanistan," Kelley told Miller. "The Army looked at the geostrategic situation in Afghanistan and said, 'Whoa, that damn country is landlocked; we'll have to think on this one . . .' The Marines said, 'Whoa, that country *is* an isolated bitch. No freakin' ocean. But we'll go in lighter and get there before the Army.' The Air Force said, 'Let's bomb the fuck out of them.' The Navy said, 'We'll help the Air Force bomb the fuck out of them.'

"Finally, I proposed UW on behalf of Special Operations. I said we should avoid a repeat of the Soviet Union's 'experiment'—randomly

---

* In 2001, United States Central Command was responsible for planning and executing all U.S. military operations in the central area of the globe, located between the areas of the European and Pacific Commands. This included the Middle East, Central Asia, and Africa.

bombing the population and invading with large armies. Instead, we'll use some of the same guys who just kicked the Soviets' asses to defeat the Taliban and al-Qaeda."

"What was the reaction?"

"Silence," said Kelley. He stood up and motioned for Miller to follow. "I kid you not, there were guys at CENTCOM who didn't know what UW stands for. I mean, damn, they're going forward with a plan to start bombing the shit out of the most destitute country on the face of the earth, where the targets are all holed up in caves. It's not gonna work."

"So how can I help?" asked Miller.

"Let me introduce you to the guys and I'll think about it," Kelley said, ushering Miller into a small conference room where three men looked up from a table cluttered with documents around a map of Afghanistan. "These are my partners in crime, the True Believers."

He walked Miller around the table, introducing him to each man. "Lieutenant Colonel David Miller's focus is the interagency aspects of the planning—CIA and whatnot. Chief Warrant Officer 3 Bret Brown and I focus on connecting tactical reality to strategic vision; I have the strategic piece at CENTCOM and Bret focuses on the ground-level considerations. Retired Chief Warrant Officer 3 Ron McNeal is our conduit into CENTCOM's inner workings—he knows how to get our ideas onto General [Tommy] Franks's desk. All four of us have been pushing for unconventional warfare while everybody else charges forward with direct-action mission planning and bombing."

"What we need," Kelley said, "is to make sure Fifth Group is prepared to do something never done before." The rest of the True Believers nodded their agreement.

"What's that?" asked Miller.

"If we can make this work, Fifth Group will lead a large-scale campaign with unconventional warfare as the main effort."

"Not a supporting role."

"Nope," said Kelley. "In Afghanistan, not the supporting side-show. The Agency [CIA] is moving fast, but they really have no plan beyond putting small teams of guys on the ground with lots of money and some comms [communications equipment]. Fortunately, they know they need Special Forces to accomplish anything of military significance. On the other hand, General Franks is the one who will actually command this war, and he has no plans beyond bombing and a conventional invasion."

/

On the morning of September 19, Miller was walking from the parking lot outside SOCCENT when he saw Kelley—in a rare moment above ground—standing near the steps that led into the bunker. For the past eight days, Kelley had been sleeping on the floor of his office, or leaving after dark and returning before the sun came up.

For the first time since Miller's arrival, Kelley was grinning as he explained that they had figured out a back door into the war. An air campaign would require combat search-and-rescue (CSAR) teams to be in the region, on standby to rescue downed pilots. ODAs were qualified CSAR teams.

"So I can get Green Berets into the region as search-and-rescue," Kelley told Miller as the two men walked into the bunker. "Then, when somebody wakes up and realizes the only way to get to the terrorists is by unconventional warfare, we'll have ODAs ready to go."

"Great idea," said Miller, "but how in the hell are you going to make it happen? Lots of other units do CSAR."

"I know the fellow putting together the force list over at CENTCOM, a Navy SEAL. I told him we *have* to be on that list."

"What did he say?"

"'I can't do that.' So I told him he was the first SEAL I'd ever met who said 'I can't.'"

Miller laughed. "Where did it end up?"

"We're on the list. Rumsfeld and the Joint Chiefs don't have to sign off, but they will. They can't authorize the air campaign without checking that box."

"You're a genius," said Miller as he rushed off to a meeting about the formation of the Joint Special Operations Task Force (JSOTF),[5] the Special Operations command center for the war.

He entered the conference room and took a seat in the back just as a SOCCENT officer was asking, "Any nominations for who's going to run the JSOTF?"

Recalling that a JSOTF had something to do with commanding Special Operations forces, Miller immediately spoke up. "We got it," he said.

"And who are you?" asked the officer.

"Fifth Special Forces Group, representing Colonel Mulholland."

Within the hour, Rear Admiral Albert Calland, the commander of SOCCENT, approved the nomination, and Miller called Mulholland to relay the good news. "Sir! Got us in the fight! We're going to be the JSOTF."

There was a long silence, then Mulholland said, "You're joking, right?"

"No, sir. You're the JSOTF commander."

More silence.

"*We* don't do that, Chris," said Mulholland. "*Generals* run JSOTFs. As a group commander, I'm supposed to fall under the JSOTF—not run it!"

Oh shit, thought Miller.

"I've got to get down there and do a face-to-face with Admiral Calland," Mulholland said. "I'll be there tomorrow." He hung up.

Jesus, thought Miller, *we've gotta get out of this thing.*

/

With commercial flights to the United States grounded after 9/11, the men of ODA 574 spent ten agonizing days in Kazakhstan, unsure whether they would remain in the "Stans" as part of an invasion force or get back to Fort Campbell and find they'd been left behind. Once flights resumed, the team was ordered to return home. The country they knew had changed in their absence. Driving home to Clarksville, Tennessee, after landing in Nashville on Saturday, September 22, Amerine watched low-flying Apache attack helicopters patrolling Fort Campbell's fence-line perimeter. Stern-faced guards stood at hastily erected sandbag-and-concrete barricades in front of each gate.

There was no welcome home for Amerine. Before his last deployment, he had helped his ex-wife move her belongings out of their Clarksville house. On his first night back, he spread a blanket on the floor beside the fireplace—it would be days before he could bring himself to sleep alone in their bed. The following day, as the men on his team stepped back into their other lives—went to church, had barbecues, cuddled their children, made love to their girlfriends or wives—Amerine awoke on the hard floor of his living room, laced his boots, and drove the nine miles to Fort Campbell, which felt more like home than his own house.

Amerine had grown up a *haole*—a white kid—in Honolulu, Hawaii, surrounded by the freethinking academics and legal eagles who were friends of his anthropologist father, Ron, and his lawyer mother, Carol. When Amerine was ten years old, Ron introduced him to the writings of Marcus Aurelius and the Stoics, which instilled in him the belief that life was short and fickle so he'd better make it count for something. Amerine read widely, and his heroes were mostly the dreamers and madmen who clung to idealistic notions about the way the world ought to be—the Don Quixotes of literature. Few of them had happy endings.

During his freshman year of high school Amerine met a retired Green Beret and Vietnam veteran named Howard Noe; talking with Noe about his combat experiences, Amerine became hooked on the idea of the military as a career and joined his school's Junior ROTC program. He wanted to see the world, explore exotic cultures, and commit his life to something important. At seventeen he enlisted in the Army Reserves at the same time his JROTC instructor, Sergeant Major Kenneth Ching, ordered him to apply to the U.S. Military Academy, in West Point, New York. Carol was reluctant to embrace her only son's military aspirations, having seen too many of her friends die young in Vietnam, but she ultimately supported his decision. "You've always been an idealist," she told him at his high school graduation, "and following your ideals is the only thing worth dying for. Just remember that: Don't ever put your life on the line for something you don't believe in."

Now thirty, Amerine had worked on five continents and led

two Special Forces teams, ODA 572 for a year and a half before moving to ODA 574, 3rd Battalion's military free-fall team, whose specialty was high-altitude, low-opening (HALO) parachute insertions behind enemy lines—the most dangerous way to infiltrate a hostile area.

On September 11, Ron had thought immediately of his son. While most of the world was shocked by the attacks, he was certain that for Jason, they were also a calling.

/

After a short stack at G's Pancake House, where Amerine reveled in the Americana of diner coffee, the smell of bacon frying, and a waitress who called him "honey," he drove onto Fort Campbell. He parked in a half-full lot that was usually empty on Sundays, and walked onto the 5th Group block past the ZPU-4 anti-aircraft artillery gun that ODA 523 had captured in Kuwait City during Operation Desert Storm.

Fifth Special Forces Group (Airborne) began operating in Vietnam in 1962, a year after being activated at Fort Bragg, North Carolina. In 1988, after its focus shifted from the jungles of Southeast Asia to the deserts of the Middle East, Central Asia, and East Africa—the CENTCOM area of responsibility—it relocated to a block on Fort Campbell that was a far cry from the high-security compounds of the other units in Special Operations: Rangers, Delta Force, and SEALs. The men of 5th Group didn't care. Their decrepit barracks, built in the 1940s for the infantry of the 101st Airborne Division, served as a reminder that their profession was intended to keep them away from Campbell.

"We don't fuck around with giant fences and restricted airspace," a sergeant major had told Amerine about their modest home base. "We don't create cloak-and-dagger nonsense as if our every waking moment involves a classified operation. We do our job, go home to our families, and look forward to the next deployment. Special Forces is an elite unit. Some of the other Special Operations units are *elitist* units."

Amerine made his way to the Trees of the Dead, located on Gabriel Field*—the parade ground. As he walked onto the lawn beneath parallel lines of sugar maples, their leaves just beginning to take on the yellows and oranges of autumn, he thought about the two months in 1992 when he was assigned to ODA 512 for an internship while still a cadet at West Point.

That summer, a senior noncommissioned officer (NCO)** named Dennis Holloway had brought Amerine to the field and told him that each of the twenty-one maples memorialized a Special Forces soldier from 5th Group killed in the line of duty. Holloway had introduced Amerine to some of the "men" he had known, represented by more than half of the trees.

"I prefer the heat," Holloway had said, moving out from under the maples. "I hope you never have to look at these trees and see the faces of the men they represent. But if it ever comes to that, you will find comfort knowing that they died for something larger than themselves. You will know in your heart that they died doing something that makes a difference. They will have died because they strived to make the world a better place."

Almost a decade later, Amerine could recall Holloway's words as they had walked away from the maples that day: "Too much damn shade on this field."

/

---

* On April 8, 1962, Specialist 5 James P. Gabriel was shot in the chest during a Vietcong attack upon his four-man advisory team and a group of Civilian Irregular Defense Group trainees near Danang, Vietnam. Critically wounded, the twenty-four-year-old Green Beret continued to defend their position and radio for reinforcements until his position was overrun. He was captured, then fatally shot, before reinforcements arrived. His sacrifice is considered the ultimate testament to the dedication of Special Forces soldiers.

** In the U.S. Army, commissioned officers wear the rank of second lieutenant or above. NCOs, always junior to commissioned officers, are enlisted soldiers who have earned the rank of corporal through sergeant major. They have managerial responsibility over enlisted soldiers, and usually act as advisers to seasoned officers and informal mentors to inexperienced officers. Special Forces is unique in that there are no junior enlisted men such as privates on the ODAs. All members of an A-team are senior.

In the 3rd Battalion building, at the end of a long hallway of doors belonging to the six ODAs of Alpha Company, Amerine stepped into the stale air of his team's room. Nobody had been in this space, the size of a two-car garage, for the past two months.

A wall of twelve lockers to his left represented a full-strength ODA, but currently carried only eight names. Amerine, the captain, was from Hawaii; the team sergeant, thirty-nine-year-old Jefferson Donald Davis, or JD, was from Tennessee; the engineer, Victor Bradley, twenty-nine, was from South Dakota; weapons sergeants Mike McElhiney, thirty, Ronnie Raikes, thirty-seven, and Brent Fowler, twenty-seven, were from Missouri, Tennessee, and Utah, respectively; the thirty-eight-year-old intelligence sergeant, Gil Magallanes, Mag, was from California; and the communications sergeant, Dan Petithory, thirty-two, was from Massachusetts. After five years with ODA 574, the warrant officer and second-in-command, forty-one-year-old Lloyd Allard, had just been promoted to the company B-team (which oversees the ODAs, the A-teams) under Major Chris Miller, leaving four vacant lockers. If JD and the battalion's sergeant major couldn't figure out a way to get ODA 574 more bodies, the team would be severely undermanned.

Desks lined the other three walls, and a large planning table stood in the center of the room. Amerine's desk, along with those of the second-in-command and the team sergeant, were squeezed into an adjacent office. Amerine had just opened the windows and settled in his chair when Allard walked in.

"Sir," he said. "What are you doing here?"

"Came in to clear my head before the shit storm," said Amerine. "How about you, chief? Shouldn't you be with your family?"

"I was getting up to speed for my new job. Ran over here to clean my desk out."

"Well, you'll be in a good position to keep an eye on us," said Amerine. "You can make sure we're operational: We're short a medic, a junior communications sergeant, a junior engineer, and now a warrant officer since you're bailing on us."

"Shit, sir," Allard said with a grimace. "Don't make it any harder than it already is."

"So, what's going on down the hall? When is Miller coming back from CENTCOM?"

"Should be any day. Big news is Colonel Mulholland is going to be the JSOTF commander for the entire war effort. They're giving him the ball. Everybody is pumped up to go kill terrorists, but there's no plan yet. You didn't hear this from me, but we've got a few teams in isolation now, set to do CSAR when we start bombing. Bad news is General Franks seems to be leaning toward a conventional approach."

"Worked so well for the Soviets," Amerine said.

The men of ODA 574 assembled in their team room on Monday, September 24, to prepare for a war they knew little about—and might never fight.

With Allard gone, Master Sergeant Jefferson Davis, the team sergeant, was now second-in-command. A proud southerner from a small town in Carter County, Tennessee, where he grew up fishing, camping, and playing football, JD was married, with two children. Nearing forty, he was a veteran NCO and the oldest member of ODA 574. The Kazakhs had called him Gray Wolf because of the gray hair at his temples, and the name had stuck with his own team.

The role of Special Forces team sergeants is often described as a tough "father," while the team medic acts as the gentler "mother." As JD was also a trained medic, he was able to shift his personas to fit the situation. His most important duty, however, was to serve as the conduit between Amerine and the NCOs who made up the rest of ODA 574.

To maintain momentum and synchronize their preparations for war, JD would be calling team meetings twice a day. He would also hand out endless "to do" lists that included packing personal gear, taking inventory of team gear, and requesting mission-specific gear; prepping weapons, radios, and optics; attending classes on new equipment; scheduling live-fire exercises; and preparing the men's families for a long separation.

/

Over a week and a half of fifteen-hour days, Major Miller had watched the True Believers trying in vain to persuade the powers at CENTCOM that unconventional warfare was the way to go in Afghanistan.

During a break on September 26, Miller and Kelley were in Kelley's office, watching a television interview that a British reporter in Afghanistan was conducting with a Mujahideen commander of the Northern Alliance. Holding an AK-47 rifle, the fighter stood on a ridgeline overlooking the Shomali Plain and pointed out the Taliban's front lines. Journalists had invaded Afghanistan before the U.S. military.

"How come," Kelley said, "it's this easy for a reporter to go in and have a conversation with the Northern Alliance—within view of enemy positions, no less—and we can't convince anybody that sending in Green Berets to conduct UW with the Northern Alliance is the best way to fight this thing?"

An hour after the program aired, Kelley was meeting with his boss, SOCCENT commander Admiral Calland, when the admiral was urgently summoned away. Two hours later, Calland returned, looking distressed. "General Franks just got his ass chewed by Rumsfeld," he said. "What can we do to get some guys in with the Northern Alliance?"

Kelley all but slapped his forehead. For two weeks the True Believers had preached this precise course of action, but it was a news broadcast that finally sold the secretary of defense.

The True Believers requested five days to plan; the Joint Chiefs gave them three. Word got around, and the True Believers were inundated by requests to brief CENTCOM planners on how UW worked. The detailed explanation was confusing to most, so Kelley whittled the plan down to its key elements, testing his CliffsNotes version late one night on a two-star general:

"We're going to put small teams of Special Forces guys on the ground in Afghanistan. If CENTCOM gives them two broad powers, then all the complicated tribal nuances, shifting allegiances, tactical reality—they will work it out, and they will win.

"One, we need to give the teams the power to make a radio call and bring great death and destruction from the sky. Instantly, 24/7, no matter where they are.

"Two, they need to be able to make a radio call and at the next period of darkness, we have to be able to deliver from the sky shelter, medicine, lots of weapons, munitions, and explosives for guerrilla fighters.

"If we give them those two powers, the Green Berets will make it happen on the ground."

On September 30, the True Believers briefed General Tommy Franks in his CENTCOM office, spelling out the advantages and disadvantages of four potential courses of action for conducting UW in Afghanistan.* Franks ultimately chose the True Believers' recommendation, to begin in the north and ally with the Northern Alliance, which was already fighting the Taliban, despite the potential for civil war if the Northern Alliance took power.

"You talked to me in terms I can understand," said Franks. "Okay, do it."

/

On the morning of October 5, Amerine walked to the end of the hall, where the B-team was headquartered, and found Lloyd Allard talking with the company commander, Chris Miller.

"Must be strange to see how the country changed while you were gone," Miller said as they shook hands.

"It's like a police state at the airports," Amerine said. "And one-hour waits just to get into Campbell. Tell me you have some good news."

---

* Proposed Courses of Action: 1) Start in the south. Advantages: Pashtun majority, can't win the country or the war without winning in the south. Disadvantages: Extremely risky, no allies/rebels in the south, Taliban stronghold. 2) Start in the north. Advantages: The Northern Alliance is already fighting the Taliban, best chance for killing terrorists. Disadvantages: Politically risky, Northern Alliance is minority tribes, potential for civil war if it takes power. 3) Simultaneously begin operations in north and south. Advantages: Prosecute war as quickly as possible on multiple fronts. Disadvantages: Very risky in the south. 4) Never put U.S. boots on the ground; train and equip guerrillas in an adjacent country and provide air support to them. Advantages: Lowest risk. Disadvantages: Would take a long time, operations could not be directly overseen, lowest chance for success.

"First of all, you probably heard that I volunteered Mulholland to command the JSOTF. I had no idea what a shit sandwich that job is. Mulholland tried to bow out gracefully, but Admiral Calland wouldn't budge. He flicked the booger on Mulholland and now he's stuck with it."

"Mulholland's leaving tomorrow," Allard added. "His staff is saying he's overtasked."

"That's an understatement," said Miller. "Fifth Group doesn't have the personnel, the equipment, or the background to stand up a JSOTF, and Calland, who should be running the show, is giving jack shit for support or guidance. It's a mess, but Mulholland will figure it out. He's a Green Beret."

"About that good news?" Amerine said.

"Oh, I don't want to spoil the surprise," Miller said, waving him off. "I'm going to get the company together in a little while."

The Alpha Company Green Berets had lined up along the walls outside their team rooms, and now Miller walked purposefully from his office to the middle of the hallway, nodding at his men as he went. Usually, Miller would ease into meetings with small talk, but today he got right to his announcement.

"All right!" he boomed. "I just got off the phone with SOCCENT. The Joint Chiefs of Staff have approved the war plan in Afghanistan. Let there be no doubt in anyone's mind: Everyone here is going to war." He held up his hand to stifle the beginning of a cheer. "You might not be going today, you might not be going tomorrow, but we're going to be moving out of here. Every single person in this company is going to do what they get paid to do, and it's coming soon!"

Pulling a scrap of paper from his pocket, Miller said, "Now I give you Rudyard Kipling. He spent a fair amount of time in the region we'll be operating in and reminds us that if there is a time to be at our very best, that time is now. Because if you fuck up and," he read,

> . . . you're wounded and left on Afghanistan's plains,
> And the women come out to cut up what remains,

Jest roll to your rifle and blow out your brains
An' go to your Gawd like a soldier.

There was a roar of laughter.

ODA 574's senior weapons sergeant, Mike McElhiney, turned to Kevin Moorhead, his hunting buddy from another team, and said, "Looks like we're not going hunting this year."

"Yes we are," responded Moorhead. "We'll be hunting for man."

⟋

That afternoon saw two new faces at ODA 574's standard end-of-day meeting.

Sergeant First Class Wes McGirr was a twenty-five-year-old Californian with intense eyes but a laid-back attitude, who introduced himself and explained that his former team, ODA 582, had just been "ghosted"—temporarily disbanded because too many positions were vacant. Its members and equipment had been shuffled around to fill the needs of the other teams in the battalion. "It's good to be here," he said with the brevity of a good communications sergeant. "I'm ready to go to work."

A native of Tennessee, Sergeant First Class Ken Gibson was in his mid-forties, Amerine guessed, and out of shape: The medic didn't look as if he belonged in the Army, let alone the Special Forces.

"I know I'm fat," Ken said by way of introduction, "but I promise I can keep up with you guys. I really want to go on this deployment—and I'm good at my job."

Amerine thought Ken, who had been sent over from 3rd Special Forces Group to fill a medic slot at 5th Group, conveyed an air of superiority as he gave his teammates an overview of his background—he was a Gulf War veteran with extensive medical skills—but his attitude also suggested that he probably *was* good at his job. Even though any Green Beret medic who had been at it as long as Ken had to be competent, Amerine still sensed that the man was "ROAD," a pejorative acronym for Retired on Active Duty.

After the meeting, Dan took Wes out for a beer, telling Amerine the following morning that the new junior communications sergeant was "gonna work out just fine. But I keep thinking about the medic. I've got a major problem with him."

"What's that?" asked Amerine.

"He's not Cubby."

Thirty-two-year-old Sergeant First Class Tim "Cubby" Wojcie-howski had been ODA 574's medic since 1996. While the team was in Kazakhstan, Cubby had been attending the Advanced Noncommissioned Officer Course at Fort Bragg, North Carolina, where, after 9/11, he, like many Special Forces NCOs, was checking off career boxes. To his frustration, he was ordered to complete the course rather than rejoin his team. ODA 574 was family to Cubby; Dan had been both his roommate and best friend on the team.

"We'll miss Cubby," said Amerine. "But we have to be thankful we got a medic at all. They're in short supply."

"Yeah, I know," said Dan. "But it still doesn't feel right going to war without him."

/

On October 7, 2001, the United States sent fifteen land-based bombers and twenty-five carrier-based fighter bombers to attack Taliban targets in northern and southern Afghanistan. U.S. ships and British submarines in the Arabian Sea launched fifty Tomahawk missiles, targeting Taliban compounds, command centers, and airfields. In the first hours of Operation Enduring Freedom, the small—forty combat aircraft—Taliban air force was destroyed, along with its supply of anti-aircraft surface-to-air missiles.[6] This offensive kicked off the air campaign, with bombing raids continuing both day and night.

Two days later, Miller and his B-team staff, including Lloyd Allard, were in the Alpha Company command office watching the morning Department of Defense briefing on television when a reporter asked Secretary Rumsfeld to verify the rumor that pilots flying the bombing missions were running out of targets.

"We're not running out of targets," Rumsfeld said. "Afghanistan is."

The remark that drew laughter from the crowd at the press conference reminded Miller of Kelley's prediction: CENTCOM would quickly run out of targets. "The enemy is not stupid," Kelley had told Miller. "Once the bombing starts, we'll take out their air defenses in short order, then the Taliban will hole up in caves. We need small teams of Green Berets teamed up with the Northern Alliance, and together they will assault Taliban positions, driving them out of their caves and making them vulnerable to airpower. Without men on the ground, we'll be pounding sand."

The men in Miller's Alpha Company command office began to discuss an e-mail being forwarded around 5th Group, written by a pilot who had been ordered to rebomb targets that had already been destroyed. "This is such bullshit," he wrote. "If the rubble of two walls forms a 90-degree angle on imagery, my orders are to drop a precision-guided munition on it."

"You won't see that quote on the news," said Allard as Major Kurt Sonntag entered the room.

Sonntag had two announcements. First, Lieutenant Colonel Queeg, their battalion commander, had deployed forward with Colonel Mulholland, so Sonntag was now in charge of 3rd Battalion. Then he said, "The battalion is isolating. Tell your teams to say good-bye to their families and report to the ISOFAC* on Sunday."

When Miller relayed the news to the team leaders later that day, he wasn't certain what pleased them more: their impending missions or Queeg's departure.

/

Late on the morning of October 8, four men riding tandem on two clunky motorbikes approached the Afghan border from Pakistan.

---

* An isolation facility where Special Forces are sequestered from the outside world to plan their missions in a secure environment. Inside the building, teams are isolated from each other in apartments; if a Green Beret is captured, he will thus have no knowledge of other teams' locations or missions.

Without weapons or even the most basic military training, Hamid Karzai and his friends were armed only with their faith that the Pashtun people were ready to rise up against the Taliban and take back their country.

The week before, in Islamabad, Karzai had met with his CIA case officer, a man named Casper, and assured him that his tribe was prepared to revolt. Casper had given him a satellite phone, his own phone number and those of other Pakistani-based CIA operatives, and instructions to call once Karzai had raised an army in Afghanistan—the Agency's way of saying "put your money where your mouth is." Those in the higher echelons of the CIA seemed to consider Karzai's quest an impractical dream at best; he might be helpful down the line in forming a post-Taliban government—if he survived.

To Hamid Karzai, that satellite phone symbolized hope.

CHAPTER THREE

To War

There was tremendous pressure from the Secretary of Defense to do something. [We] went forward with a plan, and I believe that most of the senior officers at CENTCOM did not believe it was going to work and that it was just to buy time.

—Lieutenant Commander Philip Kapusta, Joint Strategic Plans and
  Policy staff, Special Operations Command Central, 2001[1]

The two-story brick building surrounded by a simple chain-link fence looked like a cross between an industrial warehouse and an Econo Lodge, not a state-of-the-art Special Forces isolation facility. On Sunday, October 14, the A-teams chosen by 5th Group to isolate for Operation Enduring Freedom arrived one by one to the ISOFAC—located not far from the 5th Group block.

Some brought family members to their team rooms for a private good-bye before heading over to the ISOFAC; others opted for a public farewell in the parking lot. Most maintained smiling composures to alleviate their families' fears. All of them knew of Afghanistan's reputation as "the graveyard of empires," where invading armies had been routed since the time of Alexander the Great.

After taking leave of their families, the men of ODA 574 entered the self-contained, electronically pimped-out "Bat Cave" and were greeted by Sergeant Bob Webb, half of ODA 574's two-man administrative support team, or AST. Each team member had the shadow of a beard that would thicken during isolation, which could last anywhere from five days to several weeks. During this period of time, Webb would serve as a twenty-four-hour on-call link to the outside world, procuring anything the team might need: a piece of intelligence, a weapon diagram, a photo of a warlord, or a New York–style pizza. Now he led ODA 574 to one of twenty-four isolation dorms, a two-story apartment opening onto a central hallway where the Special Forces motto, *De Oppresso Liber,* was posted. The phrase, which means "to free the oppressed," wasn't exactly resonating with the men. News channels were still looping footage of the airliners striking the World Trade Center, and the country was still mourning. The people living under Taliban rule certainly qualified as oppressed, but 5th Group's core mission was to avenge the United States of America.

Inside the apartment, the décor was "military clinical": gray and white, concrete and metal. Even the dull desert camouflage worn by the men added color to the drab interior. A double-wide door with small square windows led outside to a fenced cement "yard," and a stairway in the corner led to the bunkroom and communal bathroom upstairs. Walking in, Dan Petithory shouted out, "All right! Where's the keg?!" Then he and Wes wired their laptops into the ISOFAC's secure network at desks along the walls of the cavernous planning room. Mag headed upstairs to claim the lower bunk in the quietest, darkest corner of the room before returning to stand quietly at Amerine's side.

Only his aunt Olga called Sergeant First Class Gilbert Magallanes, the team's intelligence sergeant and third-in-command, by his first name; to everyone else he was Mag. Raised in Livermore, California, Mag had cruised around Oakland as a teen, Mexican machismo coursing through his veins and the chest-out-shoulders-back-stand-tall posture to match. After high school, rather than join the family tile business, he enlisted in the military, where he became a Ranger-qualified Green Beret and earned a reputation as the type of guy you wanted at your side in a firefight—"the strong, silent type," as a fellow NCO put it, "minus the word *silent*." Like JD and Ken, Mag was a Gulf War veteran; during the war he'd been tasked with photographing the atrocities committed by Saddam Hussein's forces upon the Kuwaiti people.

Amerine seemed entranced by the map of Afghanistan taped to the wall.

"There she is," said Mag.

With a wry smile, Amerine said, "Here there be dragons."

"Yeah," replied Mag, "but not for long."

The room was silent. The half-dozen A-teams, including ODA 574, that were gathered in the ISOFAC briefing chamber had been warned not to talk outside their teams, and nobody wanted to get blackballed from a mission for violating this order. Major Kurt Sonntag, standing next to a white screen onto which was projected a PowerPoint briefing, began to speak.

"This morning we are going to tell you everything we know, which frankly isn't much. Be patient and don't beat up your ASTs for information that none of us have. This is not going to be your typical isolation. We will go over your likely mission and discuss what has been going on in Afghanistan since the first ODA tried to infiltrate four days ago. A storm forced the helicopters to turn around, and bad weather has been keeping them grounded, but they should get in very, very soon. We'll keep you posted."

Excited whispers filled the room. Their fellow Green Berets from 5th Group were already pulling missions—it was really happening.

Breaking protocol that called for complete secrecy from one team's mission to the next, Sonntag explained that teams already in place at a forward operating base in Uzbekistan were preparing to link up with warlords of the Northern Alliance. "You won't be conducting classic unconventional warfare," said Sonntag. "You won't be recruiting, organizing, and training the Northern Alliance soldiers—they've been doing this for years. We'll be working alongside them and supporting them. They will guide us to the enemy."

Seated beside JD, Amerine scribbled notes for the next hour while intel and operations officers took turns briefing the men, but as Sonntag had warned, the information was thin. There was little beyond a general outline of Northern Alliance safe havens and the names of both Northern Alliance and Taliban leaders.

"What do you think?" JD asked Amerine as they returned to their apartment.

"Get all the guys together in the planning bay. I have an idea how to tackle this," said Amerine.

"Those are the scariest words a captain can say."

"It gets scarier."

While Amerine suspected that this was going to be a long war, he knew that only a few teams were going in right away, which meant they were all competing for a limited number of imminent missions. He had to be creative with his concept for a plan—and ODA 574 needed to lay it out flawlessly. Back in the planning room, he hastily wrote bullet points on an easel before assembling the men.

"Okay," Amerine said to his team. "Our mission is to 'conduct unconventional warfare in order to destroy al-Qaeda's safe haven in Afghanistan.' Instead of traditional guerrilla warfare, CENTCOM thinks our teams will be linking up with the standing armies of the Northern Alliance in their safe havens to call in air strikes and advise the warlords. That isn't too hard to plan, so we aren't going to do it."

Amerine registered the puzzled looks with a smile.

"We are going to plan an unconventional war from scratch, from making friends with happy little villagers to organizing them as an army of killers and taking them to war. I intend for us to pull a plan out of our asses in five days that will make us marketable for just about any mission they throw at us. With any luck, that will get us out the door first."

Amerine's "broad concept" plan proved difficult to construct. The men needed a big-picture analysis of the Taliban and al-Qaeda, their current numbers and locations, leadership structures, and weaponry. If ODA 574 was going to foment a rebellion among the locals, the team would also need detailed reports on Afghanistan's ethnic geography.

The book *Taliban* by Ahmed Rashid provided the best information on Afghanistan under that regime. *The Other Side of the Mountain,* a study of Mujahideen tactics compiled by the Marine Corps Combat Command, outlined, among other lessons learned, how the Soviets were repeatedly ambushed at the same locations. As the team sorted through piles of pseudo-intelligence, most of it dredged from Soviet military archives, it became clear that there was barely enough information to write a high-school history report.

JD floated among the men spread out around the room, some seated at desks, others on the floor, assisting when he could. He had compiled a list of questions about Afghanistan, but there were no resources to consult for the answers.

"You would think," he said to Amerine, "that with Osama bin Laden identified as our greatest terrorist threat, the CIA, DIA, or some alphabet agency would have files on the country where he operates."

"You'd think."

"If the intel existed, we'd have it by now, right?"

"I'm thinking the channels are open," Amerine said. "There's just nothing to push through."

On the third day of isolation, Amerine briefed Sonntag, who was impressed with ODA 574's unique concept for a full-scale unconventional warfare campaign—especially in the absence of hard information. The other teams had chosen to focus their plans on linking up with the standing armies of the Northern Alliance. He told Amerine to press on.

By the fifth day of isolation, the planning room walls were plastered with large sheets of butcher paper bearing the handwritten step-by-step notes that were the blueprint of their plan. By noon the men were ready to deliver a finalized brief when their AST entered the room.

"Congratulations," said Sergeant Webb. "You don't need to brief Major Sonntag; you're already at the top of the pecking order. You can prepare for deployment to Uzbekistan."

This news elated the team. The men knew their plan was based on spotty intelligence, but—being the "tip of the spear" for the ground forces—they assumed they would receive better intel at a forward base. The metaphor implies a first-offensive thrust followed by a larger force, but in this case there was no planned follow-through.

General Franks had begun the war as an air campaign. When he committed to unconventional warfare, Special Forces became the main effort, and the other units in all the branches of the U.S. military were directed to support them. The Army and Marine Corps were still working on developing a plan that would get large numbers of their conventional forces into the country, but at this time ODA 574 and the rest of 5th Special Forces Group were not just the tip of the spear, they were the entire spear.

Meanwhile, General Franks appeared to second-guess the plan he'd okayed. While Colonel Mulholland was trying to get the first Special Forces teams into the north, Franks openly voiced his doubts to his subordinates. He was confident the Green Berets could buy some time and thus get Rumsfeld off his back, but he directed the Army and Marines to press forward with their plans.

The idea of large-scale reinforcements was comforting to some in Special Forces; others were troubled by the implication that they would be necessary.

Late on the night of October 19, the men of ODA 574 were busy packing gear and sorting through planning materials when the door of their apartment swung open.

Amerine and JD looked up from folding maps at the table to see their AST standing in the doorway, grinning. They could hear chatter from the usually quiet hallway, then a muffled cheer before Webb slammed the door shut behind him.

"What's up?" asked JD.

"The first teams are on the ground in the northern mountains," said Webb, "and the Rangers just completed a raid at an airstrip in the south near Kandahar."

"Damn," said JD. "Any casualties?"

"No. The Rangers got out clean."

"Did they nab anybody?" asked Amerine.

"No, but I don't think they expected to. It was a symbolic strike, a 'fuck you' showing the Taliban we can drop into their backyard and kick them in the nuts. Meanwhile, two ODAs slipped into the north and are with the Northern Alliance."

Before this, ODA 574 had been skeptical that they would actually have the opportunity to execute missions, but the knowledge that two other A-teams were on the ground sobered the men as they completed their final task before leaving for Uzbekistan: death letters.

Even before he entered isolation, Dan had written a lighthearted letter to his parents and given it to Lloyd Allard to deliver in the event of his death. He had quickly asked for it back and torn it up, saying that his folks would kill him if that was the last they ever heard from him.

Here in the ISOFAC, he began a more serious letter: "Dear Ma and Dad. So sorry you have to be reading this letter today. I guess we can never tell when our time is coming."

Mike McElhiney wrote three letters, one to his wife, Judith, another to his twelve-year-old daughter, Maria, and the third to his eight-year-old son, Michael Jr.: "I hope Mommy has explained where I am and what I had to do. This war and what has happened to me is for you and all children of your age. I have gone and suffered this fate so you don't have to. You are now the man of the house and I know this is a big responsibility but when you grow up you will understand. Take care of your mother and sister and I will be watching over you from heaven. I love you always. Your Daddy."

Mag was too superstitious to write a death letter, especially to his teenaged twins, Shaun and Brittany, who spent summers with him. As toddlers, they had sneaked a blue teddy bear with pink paws into his rucksack, and he always brought it along on deployments to remind himself to be good and be careful. His most precious talisman—the four-leaf clover Brittany had found and given him when she was four, just before he'd deployed for Desert Storm in 1990—had recently gone missing, and he was unable to shake the feeling that something unlucky was going to happen on this mission. As Mag packed for the ISOFAC, he had set out on his bed favorite pictures of his kids, one of him and his girlfriend, Sherry, and some portraits of himself in uniform. That act—acknowledging that he'd been thinking about his loved ones and selecting the photographs he would want displayed at his funeral—was as close to writing a death letter as Mag got.

Amerine didn't write a letter. "Dad, I'm not going to die over there," he had told his father, Ron, on their last phone call before isolation. His only fear was losing any of his men.

/

On October 22, the night before ODA 574's scheduled departure after nine days of isolation, Cubby knocked on the back door. Amerine had asked Allard to buy a "BFK"—a Big Fucking Knife—to present to the guerrilla leader they would link up with, and Cubby was delivering it along with a prewar toast: a couple of six packs of beer and a bottle of Jack Daniel's, "Tennessee's finest," in JD's honor. Alcohol was forbidden in the ISOFAC but it was tradition for teams to have a nip on their way out the door.

As the men said good-bye, Dan—Cubby's best friend on ODA 574—gave him a rough hug. "Don't worry, Cub," he said. "You don't want to go on this one anyway. We aren't doing anything big. It's going to be boring."

"You'll probably link up with us in-country later," JD added. "We'll see you then."

By the next morning, their gear was packed and waiting on pallets to be loaded onto a C-17 transport plane. The team had "sterilized" the apartment by placing in a burn bag all the sensitive planning materials they were leaving behind.

Amerine double-checked the isolation bay, pausing to read one last time the printout of an e-mail he'd received from his father before heading into isolation:

Jason Luke,

With the reality sinking in of your likely imminent departure for a war zone, I found myself at work tonight contemplating the burdens you are shouldering, and how much physical, emotional, moral, and intellectual strength they will require of you. I hope you'll remain confident of your strength, intelligence, and highly developed skills as a professional warrior, whatever ordeal you find yourself facing. I hope you'll find inspiration in the fact that, in response to a terrible evil, your country now looks to you to help deliver it from danger. I will be thinking of you every day that you're gone, and hoping fervently for your safe return.

And then I hope you live a very long, happy, and peaceful life, taking pride and satisfaction in having helped secure peace and safety for your country in one of its most trying times.

To millions of Americans you represent the best of us, entrusted to lead and defend us. As you know, though we're a country of hundreds of millions, we grieve for even one loss among those who represent and serve our nation. I hope, then, that as you confront danger you'll know that the prayers of many, many others are with you.

So I hope it's not simply an awful experience, Ole' Son, though most wars, for most people, have been just that. You're enough of a realist to prepare for that; but I'm enough of an optimist to hope . . . I'm hoping you'll come through it triumphant, and then regard it with some degree of satisfaction for the rest of your life. You're strong, you're skilled, and unlike many of your foes, you agree with Patton that you should make the other poor bastard die for his cause. I'm sure you'll temper courage with prudence, especially because you want to bring all your men home.

I'm with you in my thoughts, and I remain awfully damned proud of you.

Trust your luck, Luke, it's always worked for you in the long run.

Love,
Dad

Crumpling the letter, Amerine tossed it into the burn bag and joined his men outside.

Twenty-four hours later, around three in the morning Uzbek time, the C-17 touched down on a crumbling Soviet-era runway. Bleary-eyed American staff officers checked in the members of ODA 574 while Uzbek soldiers looked on, then Sergeant Tom Conrad, the team's new AST, led them down a gravel road and onto the air base at Karshi-Khanabad or "Camp Stronghold Freedom," better known as K2. Here, Colonel Mulholland had set up a large tent to house JSOTF-North, dubbed Task Force Dagger, from where he would oversee the Afghan theater of operations until JSOTF-South was established and ready to take over the lower region of the country—roughly south of the Hindu Kush mountains. Until then, Mulholland was responsible for the entire country.

As they walked, Conrad checked off the inconveniences the men were likely to encounter at K2, including floods, electrical outages, and heater malfunctions. Ideally, they would have remained isolated in a high-security location within the base, but there was a dearth of manpower and building material this early in the war. The "isolation area" was just a handful of tents with a single strand of concertina wire running around their perimeter, and the teams could hear each other planning through the thin fabric walls.

Starting at daybreak, it rained for the next seventy-two hours, flooding the camp. The men of ODA 574 had to empty their planning tent in order to shovel out the mud, and they struggled to protect electronic equipment from both standing water and leaks in the sagging roof. But the soldiers of 5th Special Forces Group were accustomed to austere living conditions and took pride in the hardships of their profession.

Stateside on October 26, smoke continued to rise from the smoldering ruins of the World Trade Center, the threat of another terrorist attack loomed large, and parents debated whether they should let their kids go trick-or-treating. In the White House Situation Room, a National Security Council meeting was in progress.

President George W. Bush sat with his principal advisers—Chief of Staff Andrew Card, Secretary of Defense Donald Rumsfeld, Secretary of State Colin Powell, CIA Director George Tenet, and National Security Advisor Condoleezza Rice—as they briefed him on the status of the war. Three ODAs had successfully infiltrated northern Afghanistan: ODA 595 had linked up with Northern Alliance general Abdul Rashid Dostum and split into two six-man teams south of Mazar-e-Sharif; ODA 555 had joined Northern Alliance generals Fahim Khan and Bismullah Khan at an old Soviet air base they controlled at Bagram, near the Shomali Plain; and ODA 586 had linked up with another Northern Alliance general.

These thirty-six men—grainy photos of them in Afghan garb and riding horseback alongside Northern Alliance soldiers had appeared in newspapers around the world—represented the extent of the U.S. invasion force one week into the ground campaign. These few Americans were critical in directing pilots to enemy positions if the United States hoped to avoid bombing and bombing again the same charred rubble. In one eighteen-hour period, they had called in close air support that destroyed more than eighty-five enemy vehicles, including armored personnel carriers, twelve command positions, and a large munitions storage bunker.

There had been no combat casualties, in part because the Northern Alliance generals were very protective of the Green Berets, forbidding them at first to even approach Taliban positions. "Five hundred of my men can be killed," General Dostum told the men of ODA 595, "but not one American can even be injured or you will leave."[2]

In contrast to the action going on in the north, Condoleezza Rice told the president, the south was still "dry": There were no U.S. soldiers or intelligence agents on the ground.[3]

While the CIA had nurtured a few friendly relationships within the Northern Alliance over the years, the Agency had failed to recruit any effective operatives within the enemy ranks of the Taliban in the south. George Tenet *was* familiar with two Afghans, Hamid Karzai and Abdul Haq, Pashtuns who had been exiled by the Taliban and who felt there were sufficient gaps in the Taliban armor—and enough popular resentment in the south—to initiate an insurrection. Karzai had sneaked back into Afghanistan in the beginning of October; Haq had entered the country a couple of weeks later, traversing the mountains on a white horse, with nineteen armed supporters riding with him.

Both Haq and Karzai were attempting—independently—to rally Pashtun tribes in the provinces surrounding Kandahar, an endeavor considered so dangerous by Tenet and the CIA that he was not willing to put Americans on the ground with them. The CIA had limited its involvement to offering both men satellite phones in order to monitor their progress and gather intelligence, and dangling the carrot of American support if they could create a fledgling Southern Alliance.

Haq, a well-known Mujahideen war hero, had refused the satellite phone.[4] He was reportedly offended that the United States was supporting the Northern Alliance with soldiers and arms while offering him only a phone that he believed could be used by his enemies to track him. Karzai had accepted the phone and kept in touch with the CIA as he traveled through the south.

The conversation in the White House returned to the north, with President Bush asking when more teams would be joining those already on the ground.

"We have five teams in Uzbekistan waiting to get in," said Rumsfeld.

The math was sobering: thirty-six Green Berets in-country, close to sixty ready to infiltrate from K2, and a handful of Delta Force teams. This was the extent of the force mustered by the United States to conquer the Taliban and hunt down Osama bin Laden and his al-Qaeda cronies.

/

The following day at K2, Conrad entered ODA 574's tent to find the entire team lounging on their cots after lunch.

"Something is brewing," he said to Amerine, who swung his feet down and stood to face the AST. "It's sounding like a real UW mission—building a resistance from scratch. I'll tell you more when I know."

Amerine thanked Conrad and then, for the hell of it, fished for a little more information. A warlord's name, perhaps? A location? Anything?

The AST waved his hand over the lower portion of the map of Afghanistan unfolded on the table and jabbed his finger. "Somewhere down here. Kandahar."

The tent went silent. Kandahar—the spiritual capital of the Taliban movement—was a well-defended stronghold where the Taliban would likely make its final stand. Kandahar Province was part of the Pashtun tribal belt, and the Pashtun were thought to be fiercely loyal to the Taliban. For an American soldier, the south was no-man's-land. There were no established armies with whom to ally and no warlord fiefdoms in which to seek refuge if they had to retreat. And while history has branded all the tribes of Afghanistan for their proficiency at routing foreign invaders, the warlike, ruthless, and vastly numbered Pashtun have been particularly adept at the enterprise.

British General Andrew Skeen, who faced a similar military mission in 1939, wrote, "When planning a military expedition into Pashtun tribal areas, the first thing you must plan is your retreat. All expeditions into this area sooner or later end in retreat under fire."[5]

Conrad returned a short time later with a dossier on Abdul Haq. The team crowded around the table to pore over this latest clue to their mission: Haq was trying to garner support among the Pashtun in southeastern Afghanistan, which could only mean that he had a serious following, serious firepower, and serious cojones.

Two hours later, the AST poked his head inside the tent. "Bad news," he said. "Abdul Haq is dead."

After only four days in-country, Haq and his men had been ambushed by Taliban soldiers at a village in Logar Province, north of Kandahar.[6] Word was that Haq, once surrounded, had used his personal satellite phone to call his supporters in Peshawar, Pakistan, who in turn desperately sought help from the U.S. embassy. This plea was relayed to the CIA, which sent an unmanned drone to launch a Hell-fire missile at Haq's attackers. The response had been both insufficient and too late: Haq had been taken to Kabul, tortured, and then hanged within the ruins of a building destroyed by an American bomb.

For Amerine, this news generated a new set of questions: *If Haq was important, why hadn't the CIA provided him with more support? Why hadn't an SF team been with him?* Haq's death signaled either a grievous breakdown in communications or the profound peril of operating in the area. Or both.

The men continued to wait. Rumors at K2 were passed via the Piss Tube Information Exchange System—the plastic-pipe urinals that served the same function as the office water cooler—and the latest was that all A-teams entering Afghanistan would be joined by an Air Force forward air controller[7] to help them direct air strikes from Air Force and Navy fighter jets and bombers. Soon enough, ODA 574 got theirs.

Tech Sergeant Alex Yoshimoto, an Air Force combat controller (CCT)*—who, like Amerine, was thirty and had grown up in Hawaii—said little as he shook the hands of his new teammates. Putting his rucksack next to the last open cot, he immediately pulled out his laptop and started reading a technical manual. He'd been with ODA 574 only a few hours when the teams in the isolation area were ordered to dress in their desert camouflage uniforms and "hide" while a VIP from Uzbekistan visited the camp. The men huddled in their tents until the second comical part of the order came through: await the signal, then run to the command center "for a treat." General Tommy Franks, who had flown in from CENTCOM headquarters in Florida, was there to deliver a going-to-war speech to the Green Berets.

A couple of hours later, the 10th Mountain Division soldiers posted

---

* The Air Force had two different types of forward air controllers, often called battlefield airmen: CCTs and TACPs (tactical air control party). Both air and ground forces often refer to CCTs or TACPs simply as JTACs (joint terminal air control).

nearby were baffled to see a hundred bearded men dashing across the dirt road that separated the ISOFAC from headquarters. Inside the "big tent," they stood shoulder to shoulder but were forbidden to speak to one another. After thirty minutes of waiting, they were whispering among themselves. After an hour, loud conversations and laughter filled the cramped space.

Finally, General Franks walked in, greeted the Green Berets, and embraced a soldier in the front row, saying, "That's from the president." He spoke for just fifteen seconds before reaching the climax of his underwhelming speech: "Aw, fuck. Go get 'em!" Perplexed, the men looked at each other as Franks posed for a photo with Mulholland in front of the 5th Group colors on his way out of the tent.

That's it? thought ODA 574's junior communications sergeant, Wes McGirr. *We wasted three hours for that?*

Conrad was used to a warm welcome—or at least good-humored ribbing about being the team's gofer or ISOFAC "bitch"—but when he entered the tent around noon on November 3, there was hardly a glance in his direction until he rustled some papers and said, "Anybody here interested in a mission?"

Immediately, the men were looking over the three sheets of paper. "Hamid Karzai" was the name, but there was no photo, and the sparse details led the team to believe he was just another warlord.

"This guy is trying to start a Southern Alliance, I guess," said Conrad.

"Like Abdul Haq?" asked JD.

"Yeah. He's also a Pashtun, like Haq, and it seems that a living, breathing Pashtun who opposes the Taliban is quite a commodity. We're going to see about helping him out. How many days will you need before you can brief the colonel?"

"We can be ready in three hours," Amerine said.

Conrad thought Amerine was confused. "Hours? Three *hours*?"

"That's all the intel you've got on him?" asked Amerine. It wouldn't take long to incorporate the new information into the plan for unconventional warfare they'd prepared back at Fort Campbell and had continued to refine since their arrival in Uzbekistan.

"That's it."

"We'll be ready in three hours."

Two hours had passed when the AST walked back in and said, "You're not going to believe this, but Karzai is dead."

Amerine shook his head in disbelief. "Next time you want a G-chief* killed, just assign him to us. He'll be gone before we hit the ground."

Two hours later, Conrad returned. "New intel. It's back on. Karzai is alive after all. The Taliban have him cornered in the mountains."

This time nobody jumped up.

"No shit," said Conrad. "There's a QRF [quick reaction force] from Task Force Sword going in to grab this guy. This one's for real. You're still going to be ready to brief in an hour, right?"

Colonel Mulholland had been running Task Force Dagger out of K2 for nearly a month. Long hours, high stress, and inadequate sleep had left dark circles under his eyes. Usually clean-shaven, the colonel had a week's worth of stubble on his cheeks and a thick, wiry mustache. As he faced the men of ODA 574 inside Task Force Dagger's mission planning tent, he looked exhausted.

Mulholland didn't know the members of the team, but, as a Green Beret who had commanded his own A-team in the mid-1980s, he knew that they'd been trained to cope with the danger they would face. Gary Schroen, the agent who had led the first CIA team (code-named Jawbreaker) to infiltrate friendly territory held by 20,000 fighters of the Northern Alliance two weeks earlier, called that mission the most dangerous assignment in his thirty-five-year career.[8] The mission Mulholland was currently considering for ODA 574 would be the first in southern Afghanistan, a uniquely precarious area de-

---

* Special Forces slang for guerrilla leader.

lineated by the Hindu Kush mountains to the north and the Pakistan border to the south that contained far more unknown variables than any of the missions he'd authorized in the north.

Amerine had to demonstrate to Mulholland how ODA 574 would accomplish its mission without the most basic intelligence, such as the names of the villages, roads, and waterways in the area or where they would infiltrate the country.

For more than an hour, Amerine and his team briefed Mulholland, laying out how they would link up with Karzai, help organize and train his guerrillas, provide them with weapons and other supplies, and take them to war. Once the force grew to three hundred men, they would, per Special Forces doctrine, coordinate for a company B-team to arrive with additional A-teams, at which point they would continue the mission under the B-team's command. One by one, every member of ODA 574 provided details of the plan, including updated intelligence estimates, anticipated phases of the campaign, logistics, even a rundown of individual equipment and the weight each man would carry.

The brief concluded when Amerine said, "Sir, ODA 574 is ready to execute the mission."

Mulholland's face betrayed his grave misgivings as he considered whether to authorize the mission. He let out a long, contemplative breath.

This shit's grim, thought Mike, sensing that the colonel wasn't telling them everything he knew.

Moving from man to man, Mulholland looked each one in the eyes and asked, "Are you ready for this?"

"We need to get him out of here," JD whispered to Amerine, who knew he had to get between Mulholland and his men before the colonel killed their morale.

Amerine was trying to figure out how to do this when Mulholland said, "Good brief. We'll keep working with our CIA counterparts to figure out when and how to put you on the ground."

Following Mulholland out of the tent, Amerine reassured his boss that the team was ready. The men back inside heard Mulholland's response: "Well, if it gets really bad, if it's looking like it's going to be really bad, just kill as many of them as you can."

Oh fuck, thought Mike. *We're not coming back.*

When the men walked back to their tent, the mood was as dark as the cold, damp night. The situation was ripe for a one-liner from Dan, but even he was silent.

Amerine returned a short time later and whispered something to JD, who immediately perked up.

"Listen up!" JD shouted. "I'm posting a timeline for the next eighteen hours. We're on standby to infiltrate tomorrow night, so get your shit packed up!"

Working through the night, ODA 574 packed rucksacks and boxes and sanitized the work space. The following morning, JD yelled from the tent entrance, "Initial precombat inspection in one hour!" eliciting a renewed flurry of activity, during which Mike paused to write a quick last letter home. He cast a vote on Maria's request for her own phone, asked about Michael Jr.'s progress in hockey, and sent Judith his love and thanks for holding down the "fort" as a full-time parent and pre-med student, reminding her that she was his hero.

After sealing the envelope, he double-checked the only personal items he would carry with him into battle—a tiny crucifix and a two-inch-by-three-inch American flag—and tucked them into a split seam on his uniform, a secret pocket that he hoped would remain undetected if he was captured. For Mike, the American flag stood for more than just duty, honor, and country. It represented family and would bring him both comfort and resolve if he fell into the hands of the enemy.

Sergeant First Class Mike McElhiney's mother, Tammy, was a Daughter of the American Revolution: She had traced her family's roots back to a Revolutionary War soldier, and in her research, discovered that both her relatives and those of Mike's father, Bill, had fought in nearly every war since then. Bill retired from the Navy after serving in Vietnam but remained active as an MP company commander in the local Army Reserve in Kansas City, Missouri. As a child, Mike often accompanied his father to the armory, where the sergeant in charge would show him around and let him handle the weapons. He could stare at the rows of guns for hours.

Mike's neighborhood squad waged war in the woods behind Westridge Elementary School, constructing elaborate battlefields complete with foxholes, trenches, and forts. Bill McElhiney made wooden models of a Thompson submachine gun with a drum magazine and an M60 machine gun with blanks glued onto its stock. During the summer, the boys would drink Kool-Aid out on Mike's porch while they polished their "guns" for battle just like real soldiers.

"Shit," Dan said as Mike was addressing the envelope. "Don't forget to fill up your water bottles."

How the hell did I forget that? thought Mike.

As the men continued to prep their gear, their AST walked in, accompanied by Captain Glenn Thomas, the team leader of ODA 594.

"Change two," Conrad said to Amerine. "The old plan just got thrown out the window; have fun with this new one. Mulholland decided to make this a two-team mission. You're going to hook up with Captain Thomas's team and go in together. And Mulholland is sending Lieutenant Colonel Mark Rosengard to keep Task Force Sword from fucking with you."

For the next half hour, Amerine and Thomas reworked ODA 574's original plan.

"This actually makes things much easier," Amerine said. "I was trying to figure out how to work with the G-chief while leading my men in combat operations. With you and your men coming, I'll park my ass beside the G-chief. He'll be my focus, and you can lead both our teams."

"Sucks for you," Thomas said, "but sounds like a good way to handle it."

"It's the right thing to do," said Amerine. "I'll advise the G-chief while you lead from the front."

Five hours later, Conrad came back to the tent and pulled Amerine aside. "Change three. You and Thomas each need to pick two guys from your teams. You're heading to Pakistan with Lieutenant Colonel Rosengard in half an hour to sort all this out."

Every member of ODA 574 was ready to go. Uncertain how to

break the bad news, Amerine said a few words to JD. Then he quietly told Mag, "Be ready to walk out of here in five minutes. You and Alex are heading out."

The three men retrieved their already packed equipment from the foot of their cots. Once they were out the door, JD called out behind them, "Okay, change in plans: Colonel Mulholland wants a leader's recon to sort things out in Pakistan, so he's sending the team leaders with a couple guys each. Mag and Alex are going with the captain."

As he walked away from his teammates' curses of frustration, Mag was chuckling on the inside. For the first time in weeks, he felt lucky.

★

CHAPTER FOUR

The Soldier and the Statesman

It is the ODA commander who will internalize the implications of acting or failing to act and the ultimate impact on United States foreign policy. The burden and responsibility for sound decision-making under such circumstances goes way beyond the normal expectations of a United States Army Captain. But this is a Special Forces officer, and he will be held to a higher standard.

—Colonel Gerald Schumacher, U.S. Army Special Forces (ret.), *To Be a U.S. Army Green Beret*

Shortly after two in the morning on November 4, Lieutenant Colonel Mark Rosengard, Captain Jason Amerine, Captain Glenn Thomas, and their subordinates walked off the ramp of the Special Operations MC-130 transport airplane and onto the tarmac at Jacobabad Air Base (known as J-Bad)[1] in Pakistan. U.S. forces had the run of the base but occupied a cordoned-off section near the halfway mark of a two-mile-long airstrip—where Hamid Karzai and seven Pashtun tribal leaders had disembarked from helicopters only hours earlier. Access roads were barricaded and guarded by Marines, creating an enclave of whitewashed adobe administrative buildings, bombproof jet fighter shelters, metal storage containers, and a massive, camouflage-painted hangar.

As Rosengard led the Green Berets to the hangar, he explained that despite his higher rank, he was there only to oversee, a laissez-faire command style that indicated his confidence in Special Forces captains. "You two do your jobs," he told Amerine and Thomas, "and don't worry about me. I'll advise as needed."

Lights flickered a third of a mile to the west, where a town edged up against the base's perimeter fence. The side of the hangar facing the town was barricaded by steel Conex shipping containers stacked on top of each other.

"The locals in that urban sprawl over there weren't too happy when we got here," announced J-Bad's deputy commander, Air Force Lieutenant Colonel Steve Hadley, nodding toward the containers as he strode out from the hangar to greet them. "They weren't very good shots, but we wanted something to stop the bullets from coming in where we're sleeping."

Forty-six-year-old Hadley, one of twelve pilot-physicians in the Air Force and the only one with a Ranger tab, was known to his men as a human Swiss Army knife, as sharp as they come both physically and mentally. In the fluorescent light coming from the hangar, Hadley's thick mustache was prominent against his wind-chafed, sunburned cheeks. Amerine could just make out his West Point class ring, while Mag honed in on the bumpy rash covering the lieutenant colonel's forearms.

"Mosquitoes," said Hadley with a grin. "This was a bare base when we got here. Had some standing-water issues that started a whole eco-system for a while, but things are better now."

This was hard to believe, judging by the smell. The influx of Air Force personnel—some 250 were living in the hangar like refugees in a high school gymnasium—had overwhelmed the septic system, and there was standing sewage on the low ground surrounding the buildings.

"That's your place out there, on the other side of what we call Lake Jacobabad." Hadley pointed across the sewage runoff pond.

The men piled into the back of a waiting cargo truck and were driven seventy-five yards to a modern-looking flat-roofed structure, about two hundred feet long and fifty feet wide, which was their "safe house." They unloaded their gear and carried it beneath an unlit balcony and past darkened windows, stopping in front of the building at a sliver of light shining through the crack at the base of a closed door.

"That's where a Pakistani general keeps regular office hours," Hadley said, referring to a smaller building standing by itself fifty yards to the west. "He's watching over us—making sure we're not mounting an invasion." He winked.

"Do the Pakistanis know Karzai is here?" asked Amerine.

"Negative. Besides you guys and the spooks, only four people at this base know Karzai is here. The Agency wants to keep it that way. The general over there—he *definitely* doesn't know."

Mag asked Hadley about the base's security.

"There are two hundred and fifty Marines living in holes out there in the dirt, providing security for the base. Bless their hearts— we barely know they're here. I'll just ask that you guys stick to the roads in the neighborhood of your safe house."

Hadley opened the door, and the Green Berets followed him down a hallway of white-painted bricks and cracked tile floors to the only open doorway. Inside, two scruffily bearded men dressed in khaki pants, fleece jackets, and hiking boots straight out of an L.L.Bean catalog sat talking together on metal-framed beds topped with thin mattresses and sleeping bags. *Spooks,* thought Mag as Rosengard introduced Amerine as the military adviser who would be working with Karzai.

"Good to meet you, skipper," said the more muscular man, "Casper," who looked to be about forty-five. The leader of the CIA's only Pakistan-based Jawbreaker team with the intent to operate in southern Afghanistan, Casper had accompanied the Navy SEALs who'd evacuated Karzai from Afghanistan only hours before. Casper introduced the other, older, spook, "Charlie," then told the men about the rescue and Karzai's current status: asleep, with his seven support-ers, at the other end of the safe house. "We're here to facilitate your work with Karzai," Casper concluded. "We've scheduled for you to meet him and his men tomorrow morning at ten."

Facilitate? thought Amerine. *What the hell does that mean?*

It was still dark when Amerine awoke the following morning, put on desert camouflage pants and a brown T-shirt, and wandered down the long hall of the safe house to orient himself, take a peek outside, maybe find the kitchen. A door suddenly opened up ahead and a thin, balding, middle-aged man with a neatly trimmed beard and a blanket wrapped around his shoulders stepped into the hallway and began to head in Amerine's direction, seemingly deep in thought. As soon as he realized he wasn't alone, the man straightened his posture, smiled, and continued toward Amerine, his hand outstretched. "Hello," he said. "I am Hamid Karzai."

"Good morning, I'm Jason Amerine," said the captain, surprised at the Afghan's appearance. In fact, Karzai looked more like Ben Kingsley in his movie role as Mahatma Gandhi than Amerine's notion of an Afghan warlord.

"Very nice to meet you, Jason. We will be meeting again later this morning, I suspect?"

"Yes, ten A.M. I'll see you then."

With a smile and a slight bow, Karzai continued down the hall.

Amerine watched him walk away, thinking about the Big Fucking Knife in his rucksack and sensing that Hamid Karzai was not the kind of man to whom you would present a BFK.

Back in ODA 574's room, Mag had just woken up when Amerine returned.

"How's it going, sir?" asked Mag, shoving his sleeping bag into a stuff sack.

"Good," said Amerine. "I just met our guerrilla leader."

"Is he a badass?"

"Well . . . not exactly."

Standing together in the conference room of the safe house, the Green Berets were a wall of camouflage and big smiles as the Afghans, led by Karzai, filed into the room. Each wore a well-tailored robe of a different color—tan, gray, midnight blue, burnt orange—while their feet were bare or strapped into severely worn sandals. To Mag they looked like biblical characters.

One had hennaed hair, the rusty color accentuating streaks of gray at his temples. One was heavyset and exuberant, grinning cheerfully at everyone. Another handled a string of beads and stared at the ground. The youngest man and the last to enter stood out to Amerine: His jaw was set, his arms were crossed, his eyes were penetrating and fierce. He appeared to be in his late thirties, with a slender physique that wasn't commanding, but Amerine suspected that in this group of tribal leaders, he was the one warrior.

The eight Afghans and six Green Berets settled onto plastic and metal chairs arranged in a circle while Rosengard remained in the background with Casper and two other spooks. Karzai introduced "Captain Jason" to his men in Pashto—the language of the Pashtun tribe—and Amerine greeted the Afghans, nodding to each, then directed his attention to Karzai and said, "We're here to learn what it is that you want to accomplish in southern Afghanistan and how we can support you."

Closing his eyes, Karzai raised his chin, drew in a deep breath, and exhaled. "That," he said, opening his eyes, "is something I have waited a long, long time to hear. I am honored." He nodded to each American in the room, coming back to Amerine.

"I would like to begin by telling you that without these men"—Karzai motioned to the tribal leaders—"I very likely would not have survived my journey from exile back into Afghanistan. I would not be here to humbly tell my story and convey to you some of the great hardships my country has suffered under the Taliban and the foreign terrorists who have made our country their home.

"There were four of us on two motorbikes, and none of us had a gun, or any weapons." He described how they had pulled over to the side of the road as they neared the border and prayed. "We all knew the dangers, but I was the reason they were there, and so I felt that I needed to ask them if they were ready to be captured or killed. I told them that our chances to survive were much less than our chances for death.

"And these men, all of these men"—he again indicated the assembled Afghans—"watched their elders die and spent their own youth fighting the Russians for a land that no longer exists."

Karzai spoke of his childhood memories: riding horses, flying kites, playing games, eating grapes—"oh, the grapes in Kandahar are like no other grapes in the world"—then, coming out of his reverie, said, "These have been troubling times for Afghanistan: the foreigners, the terrorists, and the bad Taliban. . . . You have to understand that not all the people in the Taliban are bad. There are good men still among them, many who were forced to join the regime out of fear. If a young man refused recruitment, his family was killed, their bodies hung in trees on the streets where they lived. It did not take many examples like this to grow their army. These young men will be the first to lay down their weapons and join us.

"The Taliban began as a Pashtun movement in Afghanistan, then spread into Pakistan. Now the Pakistani Taliban have earned the reputation as the most cruel in the Afghan villages I visited. In Afghanistan, they are away from their own homes and villages and seem to carry out their atrocities more readily. They are trained to be terrorists in the most fundamental sense of the word: to become legendary for the creativity of the horrors they're able to commit."

Lowering his voice, Karzai said, "The Pakistani Taliban will be the last to lay down their arms, along with the foreign terrorists—they would all rather die."

For nearly two hours Karzai recounted the story of his recent weeks in Afghanistan, evading the Taliban as he moved from the border town of Chaman northwest to Kandahar, then farther north to Tarin Kowt, stopping in villages along the way to hold secret meetings with tribal leaders and mullahs. In Tarin Kowt, the capital of Uruzgan Province, just north of Kandahar Province, he had stayed at the home of a mullah he knew from their years spent fighting the Soviets. The mullah had gathered four influential tribal leaders, one of whom asked, "Do you have the Americans with you? Are they behind you, as they are behind the Northern Alliance?" Karzai had shown him the satellite phone and said he had been promised support, though whether that meant ground forces or just supplies and weapons, he did not know.

Another tribal chief had held up leaflets dropped by American planes across Afghanistan, urging the populace to rise up. One was a cartoon of an Arab walking a mullah on a chain as if he were a dog, with the caption: "Who really runs the Taliban? Expel the foreign rulers and live in peace."

"You have a phone," the leader had said. "Have the Americans bomb the Taliban command here in Tarin Kowt—we can tell them which buildings."

"I cannot do that," said Karzai.

"Then you will never win," retorted the leader.

The mullah told Karzai that the Pashtun needed proof that the United States was behind them before they would rebel. "The people are sick of the Taliban; they will stand behind you. But the Taliban will fire their cannons, crush our homes, and send the flesh of our women and children into the trees. Our lives are not good—it is not the Afghanistan we remember—but it is still *life*. Get the Americans to come, and we will fight."

The word of a mullah could be trusted, Karzai informed the Green Berets. "But pieces of paper do not stop bullets and rockets. Paper promises that fall from the sky cannot be trusted." He explained that the Afghans were well aware of what happened in Iraq during the Gulf War, when the Shiites and Kurds believed the leaflets the Americans dropped urging them to rise up against Saddam Hussein. They did, and the Americans did not come. Saddam's forces had retaliated by massacring the insurgents. "The Afghans in the south fear the same fate—they need to be assured that a powerful friend will stand with them and fight."

Karzai spoke in English, translating his words into Pashto as he went around the circle, praising each of his countrymen. When he reached the man Amerine had pegged as a warrior, Karzai said, "Bari Gul is the youngster in this group, but do not consider his age a reflection of his experience or bravery. This man saved my life. As the Taliban pursued us into the mountains north of Tarin Kowt, it was Bari Gul, with just a few men, who covered our escape. When I called and you sent your helicopters to pick us up, he did not wish to leave the mountains of Uruzgan—he felt that he and his men could have kept fighting the Taliban off. He is the lion here, stuck in his cage, but he represents the Pashtun population."

Karzai paused, as if catching his breath.

"Tarin Kowt is the capital of Uruzgan Province," he said at last. "It is very remote but is considered the heart of the Taliban movement. Liberating Tarin Kowt will strike a demoralizing blow to the Taliban. If they cannot control Uruzgan, their credibility will unravel all the way to Kandahar. If we take Tarin Kowt, we rip out the heart of the Taliban."

As Karzai spoke, Amerine began to wonder why the man had not received more support from the United States from the beginning. Osama bin Laden had been identified as the greatest threat to the United States years before 9/11, so it seemed that the CIA should have been laying the groundwork for an insurgency in anticipation of war, then stepping aside for the Special Forces teams to do their job as the combatants running the revolution. Unable to establish effective contacts inside the Pashtun tribal belt, however, the CIA had focused almost exclusively on the Northern Alliance. Now, out of desperation, the Agency had essentially procured a warm Pashtun body and was passing him off to the Green Berets to create a revolution from scratch.

For the first time, Amerine fully understood the magnitude of his mission: There was no master plan for Afghanistan. The entire military campaign for the southern half of the country had to be shaped by the first Americans to infiltrate the region—he and his fellow Green Berets from 5th Special Forces Group.

Two days after Amerine, Mag, and Alex left for Pakistan, the rest of ODA 574 was in purgatory at K2, having heard nothing from the captain. All Conrad would tell them was that Amerine and the others were still in Pakistan, which meant that JD, sick with a bad cold, was in charge. He was feeling nostalgic for home when Conrad offered him and the other men on the team a "morale call": two minutes for a personal phone call, under supervision in order to protect operational security.

Since meeting his wife, Mi Kyong, in 1985, when he was on his first overseas assignment as an Army medical specialist at Camp Howze in South Korea, JD had been deployed an average of seven months out of the year. For the two years before ODA 574's most recent deployment to Kazakhstan, however, he had taught at the Special Forces Selection and Qualifications Course at Fort Bragg, working normal hours and living in the nearby town of Hope Mills, North Carolina, with his family. He was able to coach his seven-year-old son Jesse's flag football team and bonded with his eleven-year-old daughter, Cristina, over long talks on their porch. For the first time the Davis family experienced what life would be like once JD retired from the military.

Still, Mi Kyong was used to being alone with the kids for long stretches. She wasn't used to receiving calls from her husband while he was deployed, even in peacetime, so she was shocked to hear his voice after she picked up the phone.

She immediately gave the phone to Jesse, beginning to cry when she saw how happy he was to hear his father on the line. When Jesse handed the phone back, she tried to suppress the trembling in her voice as she asked JD if there was anything he needed.

"Besides you," he said, "I sure would love some Rice Krispies Treats."

Mi Kyong spent the morning making the bars, wrapping them in wax paper, foil, and plastic, and packing them into a box with beef jerky, cold medicine, a Harley-Davidson magazine, and the most recent family photo she could find. Then she drove the package to Fort Campbell and hand-delivered it to a warrant officer at 5th Group, who promised her that it would be shipped to JD as soon as possible.

In Uzbekistan, JD returned to the team's tent and finally wrote his death letter to his wife and children.

/

For two days the Green Berets holed up in the safe house in Pakistan, learning from Karzai about southern Afghanistan and formulating a workable plan to take Tarin Kowt—a town of 10,000 located approximately seventy-five miles north of Kandahar.

Situated in a high desert valley rimmed by mountains, the town's only access to the outside world was a dirt track, barely a thread on the map. Karzai called this segment of the Kandahar Road an "appalling journey," so treacherous to navigate in places that it took at least fifteen hours to drive the distance. A few other roads branched out from Tarin Kowt through mountain passes into even more remote districts. The town, which relied upon its few trade routes to supply the populace with the staples of life, had experienced a recent drought that greatly reduced the productivity of the little farmland was still irrigated from the receding waterways. All of this information contributed to the Green Berets' basic plan to disassemble the Taliban in the south: The region was ideal as a base from which to start a guerrilla war to seize Kandahar.

The plan was to infiltrate near Tarin Kowt, raise a guerrilla fighting force big enough to close off the surrounding mountain passes, and put the town under siege; the Taliban defending it would ultimately surrender, and additional A-teams would be brought in. Under the direction of the Green Berets, Karzai's guerrillas would then occupy Tarin Kowt and continue to grow Karzai's army with recruits and volunteers from the citizenry.

This "Southern Alliance" of Pashtun clans, along with their Special Forces advisers, would branch out, seizing all the major features—roads, waterways, and mountain passes—in Uruzgan Province. Taliban-held and Taliban-sympathetic villages would either surrender or fall as Karzai's movement continued south into Kandahar Province, where they expected the Taliban to make its final stand.

Once Karzai's army reached Kandahar, there was a good chance that the Taliban leadership would want to negotiate a surrender with him, a fellow Pashtun. If Karzai's campaign failed, there was almost no chance the Taliban would surrender to the Northern Alliance or the U.S. military, which the Taliban had vowed to fight to the death in the streets of Kandahar.

The success of the plan hinged on Karzai's support base, and nobody present could say how big that would become. That he had required rescue meant whatever support he currently had was not enough. Since his "infiltration" a month earlier, Karzai's following had increased from three men on motorbikes to the fifty who were chased on foot into the mountains. Amerine and Thomas, ODA 594's team leader, concluded privately that Karzai's fledgling resistance did not require, nor was it worth risking, two ODAs, each capable of training and leading a force of three hundred.

The two captains approached Lieutenant Colonel Rosengard, who was standing in the safe house's conference room with Casper, studying a large table map of southern Afghanistan. They told Rosengard that only one team was needed on the ground to see if Karzai had indeed raised a credible fighting force.

"I agree with sending fewer men," said Rosengard, "but on that note, considering what little we know and how vague the situation on the ground is, I'm thinking this might even be a split-team mission—maybe five or six men."

Amerine couldn't argue: ODAs were designed to be broken down into "split teams" if the situation called for a leaner, faster unit.

"You're thinking of going in with just six guys?" Casper said with what sounded like trepidation.

"Initially," Amerine said. "That's how we operate."

Amerine had been told by higher command that for this war, the spooks were "tourists and cashiers," there to observe and dole out cash. The CIA had no authority over the Army's campaign, and Casper had made it clear that, though armed, he and his men were leaving the combat operations to the ODA.

"Well, it's your fight," Casper told Amerine.

/

That evening, as Rosengard was preparing to return to Kazakhstan with Captain Thomas, he told Amerine to make sure both of his split teams were fully operational. "The way things are stacking up," he said, "another mission will emerge. Limit what you tell your guys when you break the news that you're splitting the team. You don't want to blow their chance for a mission and bench them as ASTs by telling them too much."

Now Amerine had to decide which men would join him in Pakistan and which would stay with JD, the leader of the other split team. Since Alex, with his extensive communications background, was already in Pakistan, Amerine would bring the junior commo sergeant, Wes, and leave Dan, the senior commo sergeant, with JD. Mag was an engineer, so the other engineer, Victor, would stay with JD. JD was a medic, which freed Ken to join Amerine. That left the weapons sergeants—Ronnie, Brent, and Mike—and Amerine could take only one more for his split team. Ronnie and JD were pretty tight, and Brent was the junior weapons sergeant, so Mike would come to Pakistan and Brent would stay with the more senior team members.

In Uzbekistan, Conrad told JD, "This has become a split-team mission. Amerine gave me a list of team members to send to Pakistan. They need to prepare immediately for a flight."

Trying not to sound disappointed, JD passed along the order as emotionlessly as possible to the men. "Pack your bags," he said to Ken, Mike, and Wes. "You have a plane to catch. The rest of you just sit tight."

Mike started to pack immediately, the silence in the tent reminding him that those staying behind must have felt as if they'd just been kicked in the balls.

When the three men arrived in Pakistan just before midnight on November 6, the first thing Mike said after shaking Amerine's hand was "The rest of the guys aren't very happy, sir."

"I know," Amerine said with a shrug. It wasn't his job to make his men happy; it was his job to complete the mission—and bring them home alive. "There is no such thing as a beloved captain in Special Forces," his mentor Dennis Holloway had told him. "But you can take care of your men, lead from the front, and they'll respect you for doing what's right."

/

At the Department of Defense press briefing on November 6, Secretary Rumsfeld announced that an Afghan named Hamid Karzai, who had been attempting to stir up a rebellion in southern Afghanistan, had been extracted from that country by the U.S. military and taken to Pakistan. During the six years Karzai lived in exile, his warnings about his homeland had been buried in the foreign-update sections of the world's newspapers. Now, when it was crucial that Karzai remain in the shadows, Rumsfeld had pushed him into the spotlight.

That same day, ABC's Dan Harris reported the same information on the evening news broadcast, adding that Karzai was in Pakistan consulting with U.S. Special Forces.

ABC then played an audio clip of a telephone interview with Karzai, who was forced to "correct" Rumsfeld and Harris. "No," he said, "I am in Afghanistan."

The Americans working with Karzai in Pakistan understood the need for this deception. "Retreating" to another country would have been considered a terrible sign of weakness to the Pashtun, threatening the meager support Karzai had built over the past few weeks.

The news segment concluded with Harris saying that "there is a lot of confusion" at the Pentagon regarding Karzai's current location. "There is no disagreement, however, about the importance of Karzai's mission, called pivotal to the success of the war."

In fact, there was plenty of disagreement as to Karzai's importance.

On November 8, CIA Director George Tenet—who had been receiving daily updates from Casper—reported to Rumsfeld, Powell, and other principal White House advisers that Karzai's tangible following was not as robust as they had originally thought. "We don't have anything working in the south," he said, "and we have nothing to put on the table."[2]

That same day, in Pakistan, Amerine's split team was close to finalizing a plan for infiltrating the south. In the Air Force mess hall, Amerine sat down to eat breakfast with Mag, who pulled a *Wall Street Journal* editorial from newspapers piled at the end of the table.

"Check this out," he said, handing the article to Amerine.

In the editorial, "The Tragedy of Abdul Haq: How the CIA Betrayed an Afghan Freedom-fighter," Robert McFarlane—national security adviser to President Reagan from 1983 to 1985—wrote a scathing account of CIA dysfunction and lack of foresight in Afghanistan, outlining what had happened to Abdul Haq: "Even the best force in the world will fail without solid intelligence. The CIA cannot provide it; it has utterly failed to do its job. But the military can. By working together, the Pashtun commanders and our special operations forces can win in Afghanistan."[3]

Amerine had been unaware of this parallel between Haq and Karzai, both of whom had asked the CIA for support and had been denied meaningful backing. Barraged by such negative press after Haq's death, the CIA had gone to great lengths to rescue Karzai—the only anti-Taliban Pashtun attempting to stir up resistance in the south—when he'd called for assistance. Had Karzai been the first to call for help, Amerine and his men might be planning a mission with Haq now, and it would be Karzai's name in the obituaries.

Back in the safe house, Karzai showed Amerine, Mag, and Alex a short list of villages he and the tribal leaders were considering as their base of operations; all of them were east of Tarin Kowt and hugged the Helmand River where it ran through a valley alongside formidable mountains.

"Almost two years ago," Karzai said, "I met with Massoud* in the Hindu Kush mountains to discuss a southern rebellion against the Taliban. He advised me to find someplace in the south that would be like his Panjshir Valley in the north. This was one of the areas that Massoud agreed would be appropriate."

"We'll look at these carefully," said Amerine. Having a plan that bore Massoud's fingerprints was a good omen. It also increased his respect for Karzai: He had been planning this southern rebellion for far longer than Amerine had imagined.

Alex and Mag headed off to the operations center in the hangar to check out the locations on "Big Mama," the Air Force's powerful

---

* Ahmad Shah Massoud earned the nickname "the Lion of Panjshir" after the region from which his guerrilla tactics drove the Soviets in 1989. He was the commander of the United Islamic Front for the Salvation of Afghanistan (the Northern Alliance) until he was assassinated on September 9, 2001, by suspected al-Qaeda agents.

computer system that turned high-resolution satellite imagery into three-dimensional maps, allowing them to "fly" the terrain within Afghanistan, not unlike a flight simulator.

"I think we've found our base," Mag informed Amerine that afternoon when he stopped by Big Mama.

Sitting in front of the massive screen, Amerine zeroed in on the point where Helmand, Kandahar, and Uruzgan provinces meet. In the mountains just north of this intersection he swooped over the easily identifiable Kajaki Reservoir, a massive body of water created by the Kajaki Dam, built in 1953 by American engineers on the Helmand River for irrigation and hydroelectricity. He followed the river downstream eight miles to War Jan, a mountain town of approximately 1,500 Pashtun that was 3,600 feet above sea level and set in a deep, water-carved canyon that protected it on two sides. The canyon bottom was a fertile river valley wide enough for low-altitude air supply drops and helicopter landing zones. The most likely attack routes, along the river, were easily monitored and very defendable. And according to Karzai, the nearby villages were friendly to his cause. Amerine made sure there was a viable escape-and-evasion plan in case they needed to retreat from War Jan, then called Casper over from the safe house to show him the plan.

"Skipper," said Casper, "that's a big town to hold in the middle of Taliban country."

"Not really," replied Amerine. "Hamid is saying the people who live in the immediate vicinity are friendly to our cause. The terrain is compelling. It's perfect."

"I think we're going to need more men. At least a platoon of Rangers."

The comment reminded Amerine of Roy Scheider's line in the movie *Jaws*: "You're gonna need a bigger boat." It also ran against the tenets of unconventional warfare.

"We don't want a bigger footprint," he said. "We'll be fine."

Twenty-four hours later, Amerine checked the team's secure e-mail account and learned from an intelligence report that in the north, more than 4,000 Northern Alliance troops in concert with approximately thirty U.S. Special Forces soldiers had conducted a massive assault on the country's fourth-largest city, Mazar-e-Sharif, home to 300,000 Uzbek and Tajik Afghans. They had run thousands of Taliban out of the city.

The next e-mail was from Mulholland's staff at Task Force Dagger, who informed Amerine that the CIA team working with Karzai had requested a Ranger platoon to be added to the mission. "Request was denied," read the message.

Why the hell is Casper pulling this shit? thought Amerine.

The message continued: "However, the commander does not want your team to infiltrate unless Karzai can assure you he has at least 300 fighters."

Amerine had been trained to make decisions based on his analysis of what was happening on the ground and, if need be, without consulting higher command. This Special Forces philosophy and the term "Operational Detachment" (fully operational even when detached from leadership) had been born of necessity during World War II, when teams were unable to communicate with their superiors. In 2001, even with modern communication technology, most ODA captains felt that the spirit of this operational independence remained, although a gray area existed as to how far a captain could take it.

Special Forces captains have been known to bristle at orders handed down from higher command, not because of a problem with authority but because they know more about what is going on from the intelligence they have gathered themselves: the battlefields surveyed, the working relationships forged with indigenous fighters and leaders, and the instincts honed while immersed in a mission.

Amerine knew that Karzai did not have three hundred men, but having spent almost a week with him and his most loyal tribal leaders, he believed his claim that the Pashtun populace was behind him—but only if Karzai returned to Afghanistan with American soldiers. Karzai needed ODA 574 on the ground in order to rally support; Mulholland now required demonstrated support in order to green-light ODA 574's infiltration. Though frustrating, this new order, Amerine assumed, was issued with the best of intentions: the safety of his team.

For the rest of the day, Amerine contemplated Mulholland's order. He was envious of his fellow captains working with thousands of hardened Northern Alliance soldiers in the north, while Karzai was having a hard time guaranteeing a couple hundred guerrillas. Then again, Amerine was confident that the man he was allying with was not a violent, unscrupulous warlord. Nearly all the Northern Alliance generals had been accused of human rights violations, but Karzai had no blood on his hands.

The victory at Mazar-e-Sharif was a good indication that the Northern Alliance, with the support of the U.S. military, would continue south, reclaiming Uzbek, Tajik, Hazara, and other ethnic-minority territory from the Taliban. If the Northern Alliance were to attack the Pashtun tribal belt, civil war was inevitable. The ensuing lawlessness would create a ripe environment for the next Taliban—and a haven for the next al-Qaeda.

ODA 574 had to infiltrate with Karzai; the consequences of abandoning him, Amerine decided, were too dire. *Now,* he thought, *is the time to help Hamid rally the Pashtun—before the Northern Alliance moves into the southern provinces.* But to do that, he would have to work around an apparently overly cautious CIA officer and convince his own 5th Group commander that it was necessary.

That evening Amerine wrote in his journal, "It's a fucked-up war when you are more worried about fighting your chain of command than the actual enemy."

The fall of Mazar-e-Sharif was good news for Operation Enduring Freedom, but it increased the urgency of the work of James Dobbins, a former U.S. ambassador who had been appointed envoy to the Afghan resistance only ten days before. He had built his reputation as a diplomat specializing in crisis management and "state-building" in Somalia, Haiti, Bosnia, and Kosovo. The State Department had told him that in Afghanistan, the military operation was gaining momentum but "the political track was not keeping pace." While the Taliban regime would certainly be defeated, Dobbins later wrote, there was "no clear idea of what group could be put in its place or how to do it."[4]

Dobbins had identified three key milestones essential to stabilizing Afghanistan after the war. First, all six of Afghanistan's neighboring countries would have to agree on the successor to the Taliban and the interim government. Second, Dobbins needed to identify Pashtun leaders who were untainted by association with the Taliban and remained popular in the Pashtun tribal belt. Third, he must convince the Northern Alliance leadership, which represented minority ethnic groups, to share power with this figure.

In Dobbins's estimation, the Northern Alliance and the supporters of former king Zahir Shah* were the two most significant opposition groups in Afghanistan, but he was having trouble bringing them together for a meeting. The leaders of the Northern Alliance were in no hurry to share power with Afghan émigrés who controlled no forces on the ground—they were too busy winning a war.

During their customary stroll that night, Amerine informed Karzai that the infiltration was scheduled for November 14—five days away and the darkest night in the current lunar cycle. They reconvened for tea afterward in the safe house meeting room, where Amerine told Karzai of his dilemma: Mulholland's order that he not infiltrate until a force of three hundred Afghans was ready to join them.

"The support is there," Karzai insisted. "The people will join us. They will rise up."

"I know this, but . . ."

"Then we will make our own way back into Afghanistan," Karzai said, uncharacteristically interrupting Amerine.

"No, Hamid," said Amerine. "What can we do *now* to bolster your numbers?"

---

* Mohammed Zahir Shah was the last king of Afghanistan. He reigned from 1933 until he was dethroned in a 1973 coup. He went into exile in Rome, where he headed an organization of émigré Pashtun that came to be known as the Rome Group, which lobbied for Pashtun representation in a post-Taliban government.

"I should return to Uruzgan immediately with the tribal leaders. I have been absent too long already."

"I don't believe that would be a good idea," Amerine said. "We need you here."

"Then I will discuss this with the tribal leaders," said Karzai, who stood and left the room.

He returned an hour later. "They are ready," Karzai said. "Bari Gul is already packed and waiting at the door. They will go to Uruzgan while I remain here to complete the plan. They will have your three hundred men."

Karzai held Amerine's eye without a blink or a twitch to reveal any misgivings. *This man would make a hell of a poker player,* thought Amerine.

The plan had always called for the tribal leaders to return to Afghanistan in advance of Karzai and the American infiltration, but not this far in advance: The longer these Afghans were on the ground, the greater the chance that the infiltration plan might be leaked or accidentally disclosed to a Taliban spy or sympathizer. But now they needed this additional time to rally more recruits. Amerine coordinated with Casper and Hadley on the spot, arranging to insert the tribal leaders back inside Afghanistan the following night.

"In the meantime," Amerine told Karzai, "you should sit down with Alex and identify any villages in need of humanitarian aid. He can coordinate the airdrops. If you can contact the leaders, let them know that you personally requested the aid."

On November 10, Amerine's split team at J-Bad went "Christmas shopping" for the insurgency. The U.S. military and the CIA had settled on Russian weaponry in large part because the AK-47 was the iconic weapon of the Mujahideen, originally supplied by the United States in great numbers during "Charlie Wilson's War,"* when the

---

* Charlie Wilson was a Texas congressman who led Congress to support Operation Cyclone, the CIA's largest covert operation, in which the United States secretly supplied the Mujahideen with weapons to fight the Soviets during their occupation of Afghanistan.

CIA could not afford to be linked to the weapons it supplied to Afghan freedom fighters during their insurgency against the Soviets. Many Afghans had lovingly maintained the rifles, adorning them with engravings and bright paint and passing them along to their sons.

The weapons list read: 300 AK-47s; 150,000 rounds of ammunition; 300 ammo pouches; 5 PKM Russian machine guns with 200,000 rounds; 100 rocket-propelled grenades (RPGs). As the weapons sergeants finalized what would be their first lethal weapons airdrop once ODA 574 was in War Jan, Wes received a message from Task Force Dagger.

He found Amerine at the hangar, flying the terrain on Big Mama in preparation for that night's mission to deposit the tribal leaders back in the Uruzgan Mountains. "Task Force Dagger is sending the rest of the team over," Wes said.

"Good news," Amerine said. He assumed Mulholland or Rosengard decided that training three hundred guerrillas warranted a full-strength ODA 574, and though Amerine looked forward to seeing the rest of his men, he was certain that all was not forgiven for having ditched them at K2.

Wes continued to hover.

"Something else?" asked Amerine.

"Yes, sir. The guys, we wanted to have a little powwow with you about tonight, when you get a chance."

Wes left, and a civilian entered the room. "She's a beauty, isn't she?" the man said to Amerine, looking at Big Mama over his shoulder. "Really purrs."

"Yep," said Amerine, who presumed that the man was CIA and had the clearance to be there. "Well, I just wanted to introduce myself," the man said, handing Amerine a business card. "I'm making sure everything is working for you guys. But give me a call if your command at Fort Campbell wants to drop in on something like this. I can fly out, give you a demo."

Amerine glanced at the card before throwing it in the trash. *Unbelievable*, he thought. Here he was, getting ready to go to war at a high-security, supposedly secret base, and he had gotten pitched by a civilian software salesman.

/

Mag was waiting for Amerine when he walked into the safe house late that afternoon.

"Sir, about tonight. I'm ready. Bring me along."

"No, Mag. I'm going on this one alone."

"You're not going to take me? You're not gonna take your pit bull?"

Amerine laughed.

"Sir, you gotta stay back," Mag said as they entered the team's room. "Something happens to you, you get shot down, they'll scrub the mission."

"One of us should go with you," added Mike, who was waiting just inside the door.

"Is that what this is all about?" Amerine looked around at the rest of his split team. "This isn't about me getting my feet wet first," he said. "This is about showing good faith, an officer going in with other officers. Hamid isn't too happy that we don't have weapons for them yet. These guys are his officers—the highest-ranked leaders he's got. Casper's going, the aircrews, and the guerrillas. There's no more room. It will be in and out."

The men were quiet. At last Mike said, "Sir, we could give the guerrillas some of our frag grenades. So they've got something to fight with."

"Good idea. Can you put together what we can spare?"

"Roger that," said Mike.

Every member of the split team—Alex, Ken, Wes, Mag, Mike—looked concerned about their captain. Or maybe they were just tired: Sleep was minimal and stress levels were high.

"All will be well," Amerine told them. "I'm going to start prepping to leave. Mag, get the rest of the guys situated when they arrive. I'll brief them first thing in the morning."

/

Casper entered the room as Mike was delivering the sack of fragmentation grenades to Amerine.

"I don't think that's a good idea, skipper," said Casper, eyeing the weapons.

"We're dropping our guerrillas into a location where they could get into trouble," said Amerine. "They're my men, they deserve a fighting chance, and they are crucial to the completion of the mission."

"That's fine, just don't hand them out before the flight."

"Does he think they're gonna go suicidal?" asked Mike after Casper left. "Blow up the helicopter?"

"I'm not sure *what* he's thinking," Amerine said. The CIA team seemed solid, and ODA 574 respected them, having heard about some of their previous missions. But Casper's comment about the grenades and his request for a Ranger platoon, made behind Amerine's back, worried the captain. Casper would have little authority in the ground force campaign once they were in Afghanistan, but here in Pakistan, he seemed to have enough pull to get the mission canceled. It was imperative that Amerine keep the peace until they were in-country.

Amerine, Casper, and Karzai's seven tribal leaders boarded an AFSOC Pave Low helicopter shortly after nightfall. Watching Casper closely, Amerine thought the spook seemed edgy, his eyes more alert and his mannerisms more deliberate as they flew to a barren airstrip flanked by flat grids of farmland less than fifty miles east of the Afghan border.

There they loaded onto two Black Hawks, sleek helicopters that flew low and fast on a northern heading into Afghanistan. Amerine smiled at the tribal leaders, and they responded in kind; toothy grins were their only visible features in the darkness. "Welcome to Afghanistan," said the air mission commander once they entered Afghan airspace.

Amerine knew he should have been excited, but he dreaded leaving these men, whom he now considered his guerrillas, in the desert at night while he returned to safety in Pakistan. If the mission was called off, he feared he would never see them again.

It took two and a half hours to reach their landing zone in Uruzgan Province. Stepping off his helicopter, Amerine felt a surge of adrenaline in his legs. Quickly he scanned the surrounding area through his NODs. All appeared clear, and he got the tribal leaders out of the Black Hawks and made sure they were crouching safely on the ground. He gave them the bag of grenades, and took two additional fragmentation grenades out of his ammo pouch and placed them in Bari Gul's hands before climbing quickly back through the open side door, the helicopter lifting off before he was even seated.

The Black Hawks gained elevation, dropped their noses, and screamed across the landscape, the familiar pull of G-forces tugging at Amerine's stomach as his pilot navigated the mountainous terrain. Casper was in the other helicopter, and it felt strange to Amerine to suddenly be alone in the back of the bird. He ate a sandwich that he had surreptitiously taken from a bag of food beside one of the pilots, then lay on the floor with his go-to-hell pack under his head, the banking of the helicopter rocking him to sleep.

/

The absence of city lights made for pitch darkness as Amerine waited on the tarmac the following evening to meet the other half of ODA 574, whose arrival at J-Bad had been delayed by a day. He heard the MC-130 land and experienced a feeling of vertigo triggered in part by fatigue—he'd slept just two hours since returning from the drop-off in Afghanistan.

The roar of the props grew, then died down as the massive airplane taxied, stopped, and lowered its ramp to reveal JD, Dan, Ronnie, Victor, and Brent in the dim light of the cargo hold. Amerine's exhaustion evaporated when he saw his men. Heavily shadowed by the lighting, their expressionless faces made them look ghostly as they silently descended the ramp, JD giving a brief nod to Amerine, who had to stifle a chuckle. Were these seasoned Green Berets actually pouting? But he couldn't blame them. Had he been in their boots, he would have been pissed off, too.

"Have them throw their bags in the truck and we'll get moving," Amerine said to JD. "Mag will show you to your rooms. Drop your bags, then join me in the meeting room. I want to get you guys caught up before you go to bed."

Still silent, JD, Dan, Ronnie, Victor, and Brent filed into the room and sat down on the chairs Amerine had arranged to face a map of southern Afghanistan. It bothered Amerine that Mag and the others followed in a second group: ODA 574 was one team, and he had to bring it back together.

"Welcome to Pakistan," Amerine said, noting that most of the new arrivals were slouched down in their chairs, studiously avoiding eye contact with him. "For the last seven days, we have been working with Hamid Karzai to develop an unconventional warfare campaign to start an insurgency in the Pashtun tribal belt. Hamid is the only tribal leader in southern Afghanistan working with the United States. Our mission is to support him in starting an insurgency from the ground up in Uruzgan Province, the birthplace of the Taliban movement.

"Hamid believes, and I agree, that the Taliban regime should be removed only by fellow Pashtun. The campaign in the north is going well, but we cannot allow the Northern Alliance to come south to continue the fight once they finish retaking their land; if that happens, the country will descend into civil war. Our team's job is to lay the groundwork for Hamid and his followers to seize southern Afghanistan by themselves."

Amerine paused, scanning the faces of his men, who now sat upright, all eyes on him. "Their numbers are currently fewer than a hundred."

The hostility in the room immediately dissipated. Now, the new arrivals were excited, a little scared, and definitely listening.

"On November 14, our eleven men will take Hamid and infiltrate Uruzgan along with a nine-man CIA element. We will establish a guerrilla base in the mountains of eastern Uruzgan and grow an army for the next four to six months. Once we have the manpower, we will lay siege to Tarin Kowt, capital of Uruzgan. From there, we will continue to expand our force, fighting our way south to Kandahar. When Kandahar falls, the south will fall, and this stage of the war will be won.

"I know you were ticked off about being stuck in K2," Amerine said. "Now get over it and get some sleep."

He left the room quickly, his dour expression giving way to a smile once he cleared the door.

That got their heads in the game, he thought.

The night of November 12, less than forty-eight hours before the in-filtration, Amerine was going over last-minute details with Karzai as they drank tea in the safe house when the statesman's satellite phone rang. Amerine had grown accustomed to standing quietly by as Karzai spoke to journalists from the BBC, CNN, and Al Jazeera, tribal lead-ers, foreign dignitaries, and family members, including his wife and brother in Pakistan. He seemed to have boundless energy for these calls, which he conducted fluently in several languages. This one, in Pashto, lasted five minutes.

"I have news," he said to Amerine, calmly putting down the phone. "That was Mullah Omar."

"You were speaking with Mullah Omar *personally*?"

"It was his protégé, though I suspect Omar was nearby."

The intermediary had probed Karzai for his location and intentions. "What do you think you are going to accomplish?" he'd asked. "How do you see this conflict ending?" Karzai had reiterated the demands of the United States: unconditional surrender of the Taliban regime.

"We will talk again," Omar's intermediary had ended with.

Mullah Omar had not reached out to anybody in the United States or the Northern Alliance—in fact, he had scoffed at the demand for surrender when it was delivered through Pakistan. He also had re-fused to hand over Osama bin Laden.* This phone call to Karzai could

---

* The last confirmed sighting of Osama bin Laden occurred on November 7, 2001, when he gave an interview to a Pakistani reporter somewhere near Kabul. The U.S. government also concluded that Osama bin Laden was present during the Battle of Tora Bora in December 2001, when U.S. and British forces conducted a series of air strikes against al-Qaeda fighters in the White Mountains of eastern Afghanistan.

mean any of three things: 1) Omar viewed Karzai, a fellow Pashtun, as someone with authority; 2) Omar was opening the door to negotiations; or 3) Omar thought that Karzai was a chump who could be easily played.

"What do you think?" Karzai asked Amerine.

"If they are willing to negotiate," said Amerine, "then maybe you should talk to them further. Once the Taliban collapses in Kandahar, many of them are going to keep fighting as insurgents if you can't find a way to achieve some kind of reconciliation."

"Rumsfeld expects unconditional surrender," Karzai said, "and so does the Northern Alliance. I might be able to calm the Northern Alliance, but I can't risk alienating the U.S. by negotiating with the Taliban. What do you think, Jason? How do you feel about these unconditional demands?"

"Regarding Osama bin Laden, there is no question. He needs to be turned over unconditionally. Period. But as far as the Taliban goes . . ." Amerine felt himself veering into a gray area he wasn't certain he should discuss. "Let me put it this way," he continued. "It is much easier to be an insurgent than to defend against an insurgency. Ask yourself, Hamid: Once the Taliban are defeated, do you think they will go away? Or do you think they will regroup and do exactly what we are doing—against the government your Loya Jirga elects?"

Karzai laughed. "Jason, you have answered my question with more questions. You could be a diplomat."

Amerine laughed too. "I'm not sure it is my place to provide the answers, but tell me this. You say there were good people in the Taliban?"

"Yes. There were, and there still are."

"Would it make sense to negotiate with them, bring them into the Loya Jirga process? Or should we just kill them all?"

"We could never kill them all," Karzai said, shaking his head.

Amerine smiled and said nothing. Karzai was impressed. *The U.S. military has done a good job training this one*, he thought.

"I need to contact my chain of command and let them know about this phone call," Amerine said, excusing himself. He hurried down the hall of the safe house to the communications area and instructed Wes to send a situation report (SITREP) to Task Force Dagger with the subject line "Mullah Omar" and a summary of the exchange: Omar had reached out to Karzai, perhaps hinting that he was willing to negotiate. "Request guidance," it ended.

Hours later, Task Force Dagger responded: "Acknowledge receipt of SITREP. Keep us informed."

That's it? thought Amerine. *I guess we're on our own.*

Though Karzai had assured Amerine that his tribal leaders would be able to recruit three hundred men, he could offer no proof of their numbers.

Casper's suggestion to Amerine was for Karzai to call the tribal leaders on the ground and have them gather the group at a prearranged location. He could then send an unmanned Predator surveillance drone to the site, and the "pilot" could take a photo and count heads.

This proposal seemed like a roadblock for the mission, and Amerine had advised against it, saying it was not only heavy-handed but also unrealistic. The guerrillas would remain scattered until the Americans arrived. To gather three hundred men for a "Karzai's Rebellion" class photo would never happen—even if Karzai did have these numbers, which, Amerine privately suspected, wasn't the case.

Now, the day before the scheduled infiltration, Amerine had to address this problem. He walked from the safe house to the AFSOC headquarters, sat down at an open desk, took a deep breath, and dialed Colonel Mulholland on a secure line. Mulholland had been clear: Karzai had to have three hundred men already assembled, not arriving eventually, *Insha'Allah.* Amerine would not lie to his commander—that went against everything he stood for as an officer—but abandoning Karzai went against everything he stood for as a Green Beret.

Someone picked up on the other end.

"This is Captain Amerine. I need to speak to Colonel Mulholland."

"He isn't available. Would you like to speak to his deputy?"

"Please."

The deputy commander, an Air Force colonel currently assigned to Task Force Dagger, came on the line.

"Sir, this is Captain Amerine. I command ODA 574. I'm preparing to infiltrate my team into southern Afghanistan. Colonel Mulholland's guidance was not to execute until I could confirm I would link up with an element of no less than three hundred tribal fighters. The situation is that I cannot confirm that and will not attain those numbers unless I infiltrate with my tribal leader and commence operations. I am confident, however, that we will attain that number. I am seeking permission to infiltrate tomorrow."

"All right," said the deputy commander. "You have the go-ahead. I'll pass this on to Colonel Mulholland."

"Thank you, sir," Amerine said.

After hanging up, he paced the floor of the AFSOC headquarters, rubbing his beard. It had been too easy—almost as if he had just played Mom against Dad to stay out past curfew—and he considered calling back to clarify that the permission he'd been granted was valid.

Then he made a decision. "Fuck it," Amerine said, attracting strange looks from nearby Air Force personnel as he strode out of the hangar to inform his men.

The mission was on.

CHAPTER FIVE

The Taliban Patrol

All men dream: but not equally. Those who dream by night in the dusty recesses of their minds wake in the day to find that it was vanity; but the dreamers of the day are dangerous men, for they may act their dreams with open eyes, to make it possible.

—T. E. Lawrence (Lawrence of Arabia)

On November 14, in the mountains of Uruzgan Province, the single flashlight had been joined by three others, each beam sweeping across the landscape, moving closer. Mag, Mike, Ronnie, and the CIA spook Zepeda, lying prone in the darkness behind their go-to-hell packs and tracking the movement through their NODs, could now make out four men, each wearing a *shalwar kameez* and carrying a Russian assault rifle over his shoulder. Garbled voices could now be heard in the distance. The Afghans had been there too long to just be passing through.

"If they come over this way," Mag said, his weapon trained on the men, "I'm gonna light them up."

Mike noted a tension in Mag's voice he'd never heard before. This was a situation, sure as hell: separated from the rest of the team and unable to establish communications. What had been incomprehensible chatter became shouts that Mike, who spoke Farsi, recognized as Pashto, and the flashlights suddenly appeared to stop. It took Mike a moment to realize that they hadn't stopped—they were coming directly toward them.

"Shit," whispered Ronnie.

Shifting slightly, they steadied their aim at the group 150 yards away and closing. Infrared laser dots from their carbines covered the chest of the lead man, several yards ahead of the other Afghans, an easy kill. "Dead man walking," whispered Mag.

"Let him come in," said Ronnie. The Americans held their fire, allowing the group to advance. Their training had taught them to anticipate the worst and engage the enemy only if they had the upper hand, and these four men might be only a foot patrol sent out from a much larger Taliban force close by. A single gunshot would reveal the Americans' position. For now, their only advantage was to remain invisible.

High in the mountains to the west, separated from Mag, Mike, Ronnie, and Zepeda by roughly one and a half miles of steep, rugged terrain, the main group of ODA 574 were still trying to reach their missing comrades while Karzai and Casper wandered around somewhere in the darkness.

The team had halted on a bald hillock, a bump on a ridge located at the far end of the valley where they'd landed an hour before, while the donkey train carrying most of their gear continued on toward War Jan along with the majority of Karzai's supporters. JD had placed Wes, Alex, and Ken, along with the remaining CIA spooks, in a defensive perimeter around Dan, who, taking advantage of the high ground they occupied, continued his mantra over the radio: "Any Texas element, this is Texas One Two, over . . ."

Amerine had chosen this high position to provide his senior communications sergeant the best radio signal vantage overlooking the mountains that spread out below them like a starlit relief map. Kneeling beside Dan on the cold, hard, wind-scoured ground, he said, "I sure am glad you're here instead of patrolling the Massachusetts Turnpike."

Dan paused. "You heard that I almost got out?"

"Yeah, I heard."

A fourteen-year veteran commo sergeant, Dan had recently considered leaving Special Forces to become a state trooper so he could live in his hometown of Cheshire, Massachusetts, near his parents, big brother, and little sister. He had been talked out of it by his fellow soldiers. Dan was known around 5th Group as the "funny guy," but that came second to his reputation as a master in his field. In 1994, on a training mission in Pakistan, he had established a high-altitude communication outpost when a blizzard hit, trapping all six of Alpha Company's A-teams on a mountain. Ordered to hunker down for the storm, the men weathered an exhausting siege inside crowded, smelly tents that were in constant danger of collapsing under the weight of the snow. The situation became even more perilous when avalanches began to roar down the mountain in the dead of night. That was when Dan announced over the radio: "Donner Party, your table is ready."

Every half hour, Dan would check in on the teams with a joke, getting them through until the next morning, when the men began to post-hole with their heavy packs through waist-deep snow and deeper drifts. It took them five hours to move just over a kilometer, carefully picking their way over you-fall-you-die terrain.

"This is Rockin' Dan Petithory comin' at ya live from the Swat Valley's number one radio station!" came over the men's radios. "Taking requests all day long! If we got it, we'll play it!" Dan proceeded to play rock songs by request over the air by holding down the push-to-talk button of the radio, which he held next to his Walkman.

Here, in Uruzgan Province, Afghanistan, as Dan turned back to his radio and reached out over the airwaves, there were no light-hearted antics.

"Any Texas element, this is Texas One Two, over," he repeated, letting out a low growl in response to the static.

"Don't take it personally," said JD, who stood next to Amerine. "If Dan Petithory can't reach them, they can't be reached."

/

The missing men anxiously scanned their flanks and rear, wondering if the slow pace of the patrol in front of them was simply a decoy, allowing the enemy to pin them down.

Four Afghans were now between the Americans and their gear, about sixty yards away and closing in; each of the Afghans was tagged by a laser dot from an American carbine. Mike alternated aiming from the head to the chest of his designated man, which helped to steady his nerves as the minutes crept by.

Suddenly, one of the men yelled "Don't shoot!" in Farsi, and Mike heard another shout "Americans!"

The group had paused at forty yards out and were shining flashlights at the boot prints in the sandy soil. They kept their assault rifles over their shoulders. In fact, the more commotion they made, the less they seemed like a patrol on the hunt.

"I think they might be friendlies," Mike whispered.

"That's what I'm thinking too," said Mag.

"They're going to find us here," said Ronnie. "We should initiate, before they get here."

"All right," said Mag. "Mike, you know Farsi. You go forward a bit, away from this position. I'll be right behind you. Everybody else, cover us. I've got the lead man. We'll be back in a hurry if this goes bad."

Mag and Mike double-checked the accessibility of their grenades—which they would use in the event of a rapid retreat—and with carbines aimed, crawled forward, carefully avoiding the shrubs that crackled when crushed. "I'll be right with you," Mag told Mike. "If my guy so much as raises that rifle, I'll light him up."

Thirty yards away from the Afghans, Mike yelled out in Farsi, "Are you a friend of Karzai?"

If the men were startled, they didn't show it. Nobody raised a weapon. Someone answered in a dialect Mike couldn't understand, though he thought he might have heard the word *Hamid*.

Two additional armed men appeared behind the others.

"Are you a friend of Hamid Karzai?" Mike shouted again in Farsi.

The response was jubilant. "Yes! Yes! We are friends of Hamid Karzai!"

"Where is Karzai?!"

"We can take you to him. It is not far!"

Mag and Mike had no way of knowing whether these strangers were telling the truth, but there was no better option than to follow them. They returned to Ronnie and Zepeda, went back to their gear cache, and strapped their go-to-hell packs on top of their rucksacks, except for Mike, whose pack held the bulk of the shared team equipment from the last-minute reorganization and was too heavy to carry. The four men concealed the pack, as well as the extra duffel bags containing equipment and medical supplies for the local population, and wrote down the GPS coordinates; the Afghans assured them that Karzai would send for the gear soon.

For an hour, they lugged their rucks over loose talus, powdery sand, uneven goat trails, and, at one point, a field of gopher tunnels where their legs punched through the surface every few steps. After a mile, Mag's muscles were burning. He wondered if he could continue much farther carrying a 200-pound load, equal to his own body weight, and immediately chastised himself for the thought.

The only time Mag had quit anything was in the late 1980s, during the dreaded crossover exercise of the qualification for a Special Forces scuba team: Students, exhausted from a full day of physical training, separate into two groups at opposite sides of a pool, don their diving equipment—mask, fins, weight belt, air tank—and hold their breath while crossing back and forth underwater and trying to avoid running into each other. "Shark" instructors stand by, waiting to wrestle students to the bottom if they attempt to catch a breath or lose a piece of equipment. Pushed to the point of delirium, Mag, like many others, gave up when he felt he was just shy of drowning, and his sergeant kicked him off the team, saying, "I don't have room for quitters." Mag swore then that he would never quit anything again.

Two years later he was in Pakistan with ODA 573—a mountain team—learning high-altitude mountaineering at 21,000 feet when a teammate developed pulmonary edema. Another had cerebral edema, and both were medevaced out of the country. Suffering severe dysentery himself, Mag dropped from 200 pounds to 150 pounds in three weeks. Though sick, he crossed a glacier to aid a civilian mountaineer with pulmonary edema and fell into a crevasse on the way back. He was able to extricate himself but was hypothermic by the time he staggered into base camp. Through it all, he refused to be medevaced. "I will not quit until we complete the exercise, sir," Mag told his superior. "I'll die before you get me off this mountain."

Back in the mountains of Uruzgan, Ronnie grunted. "Fucking hell," he said. "This is the last klick [kilometer] they're getting out of Junior."

"I hear that, brother," Mag replied.

Ahead of them, Mike halted. "We've got some lights."

Mag and Ronnie lowered themselves onto their knees to ease their loads and watched as dots of light from distant flashlights bobbed down the mountain, traversing the slope in their direction.

Their guides moved forward until they were thirty yards from the approaching group, while the Americans found cover behind a rock pile. They heard yelling, then one of the Afghans returned to Mike and said in Farsi, "We have found your friends. There"—he pointed—"is Hamid Karzai."

Mike studied the other group of men, searching for weapons. A pair of white shoes glowed through his NODs, then he saw the two Western-dressed CIA spooks, Casper and Charlie, farther back.

"That's him," said Mike. "That's Hamid."

Karzai came toward them. "Hello, hello!" he said. "Welcome to Uruzgan."

When Mag asked about the equipment they'd left behind, Karzai spoke a few words to the Afghans, then said in English, "They are from the same village where we are going; they know where it is and will bring it to you."

"They can be trusted?" asked Mike.

"They can be trusted," replied Karzai.

"You know," Mike said with a lowered voice, "we thought these guys were Taliban."

"Hmmm," said Karzai. "They might be."

/

A few minutes after meeting up with Karzai, Mag heard Dan's voice through the static on his radio.

"Texas One Two," Mag radioed back, "your lost sheep are coming in. Don't open up on us."

Nearly three long, tense hours had passed since the infiltration, and now, with the missing Americans on their way, everybody became restless, uneasy about lingering so close to the landing zone.

"It will be good to get the hell out of here," said Dan a moment after sending Task Force Dagger a SITREP.

"The funny thing is that this is pretty much how bad it goes in training," Amerine said.

"Yup," said JD. "They say to train as you fight. I think we got it backwards."

Forty-five minutes later, the glow of flashlights announced the arrival of the men.

"Stay close to Hamid," JD said to Amerine. "And don't let those knuckleheads pull that shit again," he added, referring to the CIA spooks running off on their own.

"Roger that," said Amerine. He eyed Casper as he rejoined his men, but this wasn't the time for a confrontation. They needed to get moving.

No more than two minutes after the arrival of Mag, Mike, and Ronnie, who received some pats on the back, ODA 574 and the spooks moved out as a group, following Karzai and his Pashtun tribesmen—the first of his supposed three hundred guerrillas—down off the ridge toward the southern end of the narrowing valley. There, the gently sloping trail plunged into a steeper ravine, a drainage of loose rocks and boulders that elicited grunts and growls from the Americans trying to keep pace with the nimble guerrillas, whose flashlights flickered like fireflies as they glided across the rough terrain. For the team, the lights acted as a point of reference from which to read the terrain and anticipate an ambush, which would likely come uphill from the Afghans.

After a knee-jarring two-hour descent in a southwestern direction, the lights ahead paused in a group. Carefully walking forward to join the guerrillas, Amerine saw that they were at the end of the trail, or so it seemed. He peered over the edge of a cliff, seeing nothing but a black void that appeared impassable without ropes and climbing gear.

The guerrillas, having stopped just long enough for the Americans to catch up, continued on, squeezing through a small cleft marked with miniature rock cairns. Amerine could hear the men shuffling downward.

"We have to keep moving," said JD. He edged himself past Amerine farther over the rim of the cliff, then came back. "I can make out some vehicles below."

"How far below?" asked Dan, third in line.

"Pretty damn far."

"I'm going to be really pissed if I fall off this fucking cliff," said Dan as the men began to move down a two-foot-wide trail chiseled into the rock. It was dusted with patches of gritty sand that slid like ball bearings under their boots, throwing off their top-heavy balance. At one point someone shouted "Rock!" and a loose stone fell down the face above them, bounced once on the narrow ledge, and after seconds of silence clattered onto the ground below. Even though JD remained up top, using the Americans at the end of the line to maintain security, they were horribly exposed.

It took nearly forty-five minutes for the entire team to reach the bottom, where the Afghans waved for them to get into the two waiting vehicles—a truck and a minivan.

"We can't fit seventeen of us in there," said Ronnie.

Amerine looked at his map and GPS. They were about three miles north of War Jan and needed to get farther away from the landing zone as fast as possible.

"What are we doing?" JD asked Amerine.

"No choice," he said, glancing at his men, then at the truck and the minivan. "Get them inside, however you can fit them."

"We're screwed if we're attacked," said Mike.

"I know. But we're just as screwed if we stay here," said Amerine.

All seventeen Americans crammed into the vehicles, with Dan slithering into the minivan last atop shoulders and gear, his body tight against the roof. Amerine sat next to the Afghan driving the minivan and wondered if he was making the worst tactical decision of his career. Their fate was completely in the hands of these guerrillas, whom they knew only through Karzai. If they hit a checkpoint, ODA 574 would be executing every battle drill in the book—assuming they could get out of the vehicles in the first place.

They drove west down the rutted mountain track a short distance, then turned north on a better-maintained road that paralleled the Helmand River. The GPS in Amerine's hand indicated that they were moving away from War Jan, their intended destination. Karzai, the only translator, was in the other vehicle. *Another mistake,* thought Amerine. *I should have stayed with him.* He glanced to his left. In the light from the dashboard, he could see that the driver was smiling as he hunched over the steering wheel, peering through a windshield fogged up from body heat. After two miles, Amerine saw the dull glow of lights ahead. His M9 was holstered; he preferred his carbine, which was resting on the floorboard, barrel pointing downward, sending vibrations from the road into his arm.

Amerine had never felt so inept or so vulnerable.

The vehicles stopped in front of a mud wall, their headlights illuminating a doorway that was opening before the engines shut down. A man wearing an Afghan turban, known as a *lungee,* and holding a long-barreled rifle in one hand leaned out and smiled.

Stove fires and kerosene lanterns behind the wall painted the enclosed adobe-like buildings in soft light. The Taliban barricade Amerine had imagined was just a mountain hamlet, its main street lined with traditional Afghan homes such as this one—compounds composed of a central courtyard and one to several buildings surrounded by an exterior wall.

Mag crawled out of the dank interior of the minivan into the cold air, recognizing what he called "yeti," the odor that made him nostalgic for past 5th Group assignments: a hint of city dump, a pinch of campfire, and a dash of sewage. He inhaled deeply and thought, *Smells like a mission.*

The rest of ODA 574 followed suit, surveying their surroundings as they lugged gear into the compound. They'd all "flown" the streets of War Jan on Big Mama and studied the maps meticulously while formulating their plan. They'd plotted out locations for air-drops, designated rally points, and strategized avenues for retreat, *all pretty fucking major things*, thought Mike as it dawned on him: *This is not War Jan.*

Mike walked over to Amerine and said, "Sir, this isn't—"

"Yeah, I got that," Amerine cut him off. "I'm going to go see what's going on."

Tired but on edge, the Green Berets went about their individual tasks. JD immediately assigned Mike, Mag, and Ronnie to security, and Mike and Mag headed straight to the compound's far wall, both of them checking for the same thing—a back door. There wasn't one. *Okay*, Mike thought, *if these fuckers turn on us, how are we going to defend ourselves?* He stood on a crate and peered into an adjacent compound. *I'll toss a grenade over this wall; if they come in the front, there will be somebody covering the back.*

Setting up satellite antennas, Dan, Alex, and Wes linked into the U.S. military's secure communications network and sent an en-crypted SITREP to Task Force Dagger. Ken watched over ODA 574's gear while Ronnie kept an eye on the half-dozen armed Afghans mingling near the entrance to the narrow courtyard, and Mag walked around shaking hands with every Afghan with a gun, sharing cigarettes and seeing if his "street sense" picked up any bad vibes. Unarmed men began to enter the courtyard, seating them-selves around its walls.

Inside a twelve-foot-square room with an open stove exposing hot coals in the corner, Amerine, Casper, and Karzai sat on brightly col-ored hand-woven carpets with a group of tribal elders. A young man offered tea and something that looked like bread pudding from a clay pot; Amerine followed Karzai's lead in accepting both. The smell of what Amerine would come to call Afghan shepherd's pie—flat bread soaked in broth and layered with a stew of meat, lentils, and raisins—was tantalizing, and he ate it heartily, much to the pleasure of the man seated closest to Karzai, whom he introduced as Haji Badhur.

"This is Haji Badhur's village," Karzai said. "He has agreed to let us stay here; this will be our base."

"So we aren't going to operate from War Jan?" asked Amerine.

"No," said Karzai. "This is near the outskirts of War Jan. Haji Badhur thought this was a better location for us."

With Casper's earlier misgivings about War Jan, Amerine wondered if the spook had somehow orchestrated this change in plans. Not wanting to seem ungrateful for the hospitality, however, he asked no more questions. Instead, he smiled and thanked Haji Badhur. "I look forward to seeing your village after the sun rises," he said, speaking directly to the man, who he sensed would appreciate a BFK as a gift.

"And he looks forward to showing you Uruzgan," translated Karzai in return.

Sipping cup after cup of tea for an hour, Amerine felt as if his bladder was ready to burst, yet more and more men streamed into the room, having surreptitiously made the trek from neighboring villages in the middle of the night to lay eyes on Karzai and the Americans. When he finally emerged from the meeting, dawn was less than a couple of hours away. Mag was pacing the courtyard, so wired from nicotine and caffeine that he couldn't sit down for more than five minutes, and it wasn't even his shift. Some of the guys were lying awake in sleeping bags on the hard earthen floor of the hut they'd been given. Mike sat against a wall, shivering beneath a paper-thin survival blanket from his go-to-hell pack and hoping his rucksack would show up soon.

Nobody slept.

At daybreak the team saw that the village was situated at a sharp bend on the Helmand River, which created a pocket of calm gray-blue water. They dubbed their new guerrilla base Haji Badhur's Cove.

Karzai greeted ODA 574 while the village was still in the shadow of the mountains they had landed in the night before. Across the river to the west, farmland that butted up against more mountains was catching the first rays of sunlight. Other than a few compounds built on the floodplain and a road they could see only by the dust kicked up by an occasional vehicle, it was wide-open terrain.

"The villagers have arrived with clothing," Karzai said. "To help you blend in." The gate to the compound opened and a stream of young men entered, carrying piles of clothes.

Everyone in Haji Badhur's Cove knew, or would soon know, that the soldiers were there, and Amerine thought that dressing up would only make them look like dressed-up Americans. Even though they'd all grown beards, their physiques, for the most part, gave them the appearance of a pack of football players next to the sinewy Afghans. From a distance, however, the local garb might provide some degree of disguise from a Taliban patrol.

"Listen up," JD said, displaying a set of *shalwar kameez*. "Don't go completely native—find one of these long shirts, with a vest or whatever, and wear it over your DCUs [desert camouflage uniforms]. Don't bother with putting on the pants. Grab a hat, have fun."

While ODA 574 rummaged through the piles like shoppers at a garage sale, two other young Afghans carried in the limp shell of an American rucksack and a couple of duffel bags.

Instantly, Mike knew that his once-bulging pack had been plundered.

"I'm missing everything," he said, opening it. "Dan's extra laptop, the SOFLAM,* a couple of claymores, all my clothes, my sleeping bag, my food, every goddamned thing. Wait a minute. They left me this." He pulled out a Ziploc bag holding his toothbrush and two travel-size bottles of mouthwash.

The duffels full of medical supplies to treat the locals were also missing.

Karzai closed his eyes for a long moment. Turning to the Afghans who had delivered the gear, Karzai spoke in the firmest tone the Americans had heard him use. The two men looked scared.

"They say they are just delivering it," Karzai informed the team. "I will speak with Haji Badhur and get to the bottom of this. These two are not responsible."

---

* A Special Operations Forces Laser Acquisition Marker is used to designate targets usually intended to be bombed from aircraft, or to obtain the range or coordinates of a position or target.

Mike was fuming. The Afghans who had seemed so friendly ten minutes earlier now appeared sinister. He thought he caught one checking out his knife, and imagined the man's thoughts: *When you get killed, I'm taking that off of you, and that, and that . . .*

Sensing Mike's anger, Amerine said, "Why don't we recon the village?"

"Yeah," said Mike.

Haji Badhur's Cove looked like the American Southwest a hundred years ago: no electricity, not even the hum of a generator, a communal well that supplied drinking water, and single-story mud-walled homes. Amerine and Mike kept their weapons under their long Afghan shirts as they strolled the streets among the locals, some of whom made a show of ignoring them while others, especially children, didn't hide their curiosity. The Green Berets smiled at the people, all the while analyzing the surrounding mountains, getting a feel for how they would defend the village and where they would go if a battalion of Taliban rolled in.

Returning to the compound, Amerine and Mike found Haji Badhur standing beside Karzai, explaining to the team that the remaining gear was delivered exactly the way it had been found. According to Haji Badhur, strangers must have stumbled upon the cache—which had been left in the middle of nowhere at a location known only to Haji Badhur's men.

"Tell Haji Badhur that the weapons drop will be delayed unless he finds our gear," said Amerine.

Karzai translated the words as Amerine and Haji Badhur stared at each other. Haji Badhur's gaze intensified, then he cracked a grin and said something in Pashto.

"He will speak with leaders in neighboring villages," Karzai said, "to try and get to the bottom of this."

That afternoon, Karzai told Amerine that Haji Badhur was giving the Americans their own compound a few "blocks" down the street. According to Haji Badhur, the first compound was too crowded for ODA 574, the CIA, *and* Karzai. Trusting Karzai, who seemed okay with the decision, JD and Amerine went along with the move for the time being, though neither of them cared for the idea of being separated from Karzai.

The new compound was similar in size to the previous one, but had just one large building attached to the western wall. The team opted to sleep in the courtyard while Dan set up his commo equipment in the building that would be used as ODA 574's headquarters.

Once they had settled in, Amerine returned to Karzai to reiterate that the team had to have its equipment back. He went down the list: The SOFLAM was required for calling in air strikes and was useless to anybody else; the laptop was needed for communication. Karzai promised he would have another conversation with Haji Badhur.

A few hours later, some of Mike's gear, including the SOFLAM, was brought to them by a villager who "discovered" it under a bush at the side of the road. The laptop and his clothes and sleeping bag, among other things, remained missing.

As darkness fell, JD met with Mike, Ronnie, and Wes, whom he had tasked with running the drop zone for the first weapons drop. Their job was to vector in the aircraft to a narrow strip of farmland between the Helmand River and the mountains. If the plane didn't hit its mark, the weapons could land in or across the river—something that happened frequently with their Northern Alliance counterparts. "Let's not fuck this one up," JD told them.

The four Americans rode with twenty guerrillas in four trucks, parked at the edge of the drop zone, and marked its center with four infrared strobe lights visible only through NODs. Right on schedule, the MC-130 swooped down out of the starry night and into the river valley like a shadow. It glided low, rapidly ejecting several containers, then climbed into the sky and disappeared while the containers drifted slowly down on parachutes.

Amerine had asked Karzai to choose guerrillas with "strong leadership" qualities—that is, men who wouldn't steal any more supplies—to stand by at the drop zone and retrieve the containers. They were to keep everything together so that it could be properly divided among the tribal leaders scheduled to arrive the following day.

Instead, when the containers hit the ground, the Afghans charged across the field and tore into them as if they were birthday presents. Some contented themselves with the parachutes and harnesses, balling up the unwieldy items and dragging them away into the night.

Others—in groups of two or three—attempted to manhandle heavy crates that had been loaded onto the aircraft with forklifts.

From the sidelines, the Green Berets watched with bemusement as the operation descended into chaos. At last, the more senior guerrillas ran onto the field, shouting and pummeling their frenzied comrades until they were helping to load the waiting trucks.

"How did it go?" Amerine asked when JD returned to the compound.

"Total mess," said JD. "From now on we get control of the items first and hand them out later. The next drop is going to include food and water for us, so we definitely can't let them near it."

"I hope there isn't going to be a riot tomorrow," Amerine said. "Hamid is concerned about inventorying everything so he can show he isn't playing favorites."

Dan hurried up. "We got something going on across the river," he said. "The guerrillas are pretty freaked out. Looks like a bunch of headlights."

Amerine and JD followed Dan up a ladder and onto the mud roof of the building, where they lay prone alongside several Afghans. Alternating between his NODs and binoculars, Amerine counted the headlights of eight trucks parked in an open field a couple of miles away.

"They're a long way off," said JD.

"It might have nothing to do with us," Amerine said.

Casper and Charlie joined them on the roof. "What do we have, skipper?" Casper asked.

"We're sorting it out. Bunch of trucks way out there." Amerine offered Casper his binoculars.

"Is there any air cover available?" Casper asked and took a look.

"I'm sure. But I plan on sitting tight."

"They aren't bothering us, so we shouldn't bother them," said Dan.

"Yeah," said Amerine. "I don't think their lights would be on if they thought a threat was nearby."

"All the same, you should get air standing by," said Casper.

"We'll get it if we need it," said Amerine. "We don't even know if they're Taliban."

"The guerrillas seem agitated."

"They shouldn't know any more than we do at this point. I'm going to talk to Hamid about it."

"I can do that," said Casper, climbing off the roof.

"Thanks, but I was heading that way," Amerine said, following.

Amerine didn't think his men had noticed the subtle tug of war between himself and Casper, and he hadn't shared with them Casper's request for a Ranger platoon or told them that the spook was the reason they'd been forced to leave Brent and Victor at J-Bad to make room for the Delta Force soldiers. He *had* discussed all this with JD, and they'd agreed that involving the rest of the team would only create an unnecessary distraction.

As Amerine grabbed his weapon and go-to-hell pack for the walk to Karzai's compound, JD walked up and quietly said to him, "CIA is still looking for a job, eh? They want to be our link to Hamid."

"Looks that way."

"You're handling Casper just right. Keep ignoring the power play and carry on with business as if they aren't here."

Amerine thanked him and shouldered his pack. "I'll be gone for twenty minutes and I'll bring along Mike. Contact me immediately if those trucks come near the river. Judging from the map, it would take them hours to get to a crossing point upriver or downriver and reach this village. I'm more worried that they're a sign of something bigger going on in this area. Regardless, if shooting starts, I'll bring Hamid back here and we'll be returning on the street, probably hauling ass, so *don't* shoot us. If we're cut off, you know the rally point."

Unbeknownst to the Americans, there *was* something bigger going on in Uruzgan Province that night—something that could jeopardize their entire mission. Thirty miles to the northeast, the citizens of Tarin Kowt were in the process of storming the "palace" of the Taliban's provincial governor. If the people were successful in their coup, Tarin Kowt would be theirs—temporarily. Holding the town when thousands of angry Taliban arrived en masse for a brutal retribution would be another matter altogether.

CHAPTER SIX

The Battle of Tarin Kowt

It is the greatest houses and the tallest trees that the gods bring low with bolts and thunder: For the gods have to thwart whatever is greater than the rest. They do not suffer pride in anyone but themselves.

—Herodotus, *The Histories*

It was November 16 and the first day of Ramadan, the ninth month of the Islamic calendar, when Muslims fast from sunrise to sunset. It is a month dedicated to worshipping Allah, giving to charity, mending troubled relationships, and finding forgiveness for others.

In Haji Badhur's Cove it was a day to divvy up hundreds of rifles and thousands of rounds of ammunition. It was the day to arm Karzai's rebellion.

ODA 574 awoke with the sun. They had increased the number of men on security the night before, but the vehicles across the river had done nothing except rob the team of sleep.

Dan started the day with a hot mocha—one of Ken's coveted "tea" bags of instant coffee, twice used, steeped in a cup of hot cocoa—while downloading a few dozen encrypted messages from higher command.

"Get a load of this," Dan said to Amerine after converting the files to readable text. "Has our commander in chief always sent out Happy Ramadan cards?"

"You're kidding," said Amerine, looking over Dan's shoulder at the computer. Sure enough, there was an e-mail titled "2001 U.S. Presidential Holiday Greeting."

"I'm guessing he didn't send one of these to the pope," said Dan, who cleared his throat and started reading the letter in his best George W. Bush imitation:

. . . *We send our sincerest wishes to Muslims in America and around the world for health, prosperity, and happiness during Ramadan and throughout the coming year* . . .

When Dan finished, Amerine jokingly applauded the performance, copied the letter into one of his black journals so he could later read it to Karzai, and headed out into the courtyard.

Standing on the roof of ODA 574's headquarters, Mike raised his binoculars to examine the craggy mountains to the east. Morning light revealed new details of the formidable cirque that rose behind the village like an amphitheater, with the seats facing west, toward the Helmand and adjacent farmland. Caves dotted the rock face a hundred feet above the floodplain; the team would be able to observe the entire valley if they could reach them. Calling Amerine up onto the roof, Mike pointed out the caves and said, "This place will definitely suffice as a guerrilla base."

"I think we're going to be here with Haji Badhur and his pirates for a while," Amerine said.

"Pirates is right," grumbled Mike, still bent about his missing gear. "Froze my ass off again last night."

Turning their attention to the river and the road running next to it, they watched Haji Badhur's men load weapons from the lethal-aid drop onto trucks outside Karzai's compound. A truck carrying what appeared to be a farmer and his boys pulled up; they emerged armed with rifles and drove away. Would-be guerrillas arrived on foot and by donkey, carrying away tightly rolled carpets that concealed an AK-47 or two. Arming the Afghans was the first step in building the insurgency, and it gave Karzai a chance to inventory his gathering forces.

By twelve, business was booming at what Dan dubbed the grand opening of Uruzgan's "McWeapons" franchise, and most of ODA 574 had climbed onto the roof of the largest building in their compound to observe the rush.

"They're coming out of the woodwork," said Mag.

"It's a good sign," Amerine said.

"Any idea how many guys so far?"

"Not certain, but more than a couple hundred," said Amerine. "Some of them might be coming solo to arm a group. Might be a lot more."

"You know," said Mike, "they're just coming and going. I'm not seeing much of a force gathering behind Hamid."

"I noticed that, too," said Amerine. "Either his clout is still in question, or they're just too wary to stick around. I'll feel out the situation when I meet with him in a bit."

JD and Ken climbed up.

"Got some news," said Ken. "Miles, one of the Delta operators, has a bad case of dysentery—fever, cramping, can't eat, and liquids are pouring out of him as fast as we can pump them in."

"Are we talking medevac?" asked Amerine.

"He says no way," said JD. "He wants to gut it out."

The men laughed, then paused as a young Afghan crossed the courtyard, reached up, and handed Amerine a folded piece of paper.

"Well," said Mike, "we've got a long way to go before we're ready for any kind of combat operations. If you're gonna have the shits, this is a good place for it. We're not going anywhere for a while."

"Not so sure about that," said Amerine, holding up the paper. "Just got word from Hamid that there was an uprising at Tarin Kowt during the night."

"Wait a minute," said Dan. "Isn't that supposed to be *our* job?"

"Exactly. Somebody jumped the gun," said Amerine as he climbed down off the roof. "Consider this a warning order: We might be rolling out of here."

"Rolling out of here on what?" said Mike after Amerine had left to talk to Karzai.

"I will *not* get inside another meat box like the last one," said Ronnie. "I'll ride on top if I have to."

Amerine entered Karzai's compound, where four simply dressed old men sat on the ground admiring the AK-47 assault rifles cradled in their laps. Toward the back of the courtyard, more than a dozen Afghans wearing colorful long shirts or embroidered robes mingled round an opened crate of machine guns. Standing a few feet from them, Karzai was speaking with Casper.

Karzai smiled broadly when he saw Amerine. "Jason," he said, "you received my message?"

"Yes," said Amerine, nodding at Casper. "Is the news reliable?"

"Yes. These men"—Karzai motioned to the large group—"are elders from Tarin Kowt. They report that the Taliban governor—a very bad man— and his personal guard were killed in the uprising last night. The governor was hung in the street. Other Taliban have been driven out. The citizens are guarding the city. They wish for me to return with them and break the fast of Ramadan tonight with leaders from the rebellion."

Amerine studied Karzai's face. If the coup had taken place against Karzai's orders, he would have been angry. He recalled Karzai's phone call with his supporters in Tarin Kowt a few days earlier, in which they'd told him that the people there wanted to rise up. Amerine had strongly advised against it.

"They could wait no longer," Karzai said.

Amerine decided then that Karzai must have known all along that the people of Tarin Kowt were going to revolt. He must not have understood the repercussions—that the Taliban would send forces to recapture the town and likely increase their presence in Uruzgan. Or perhaps he was alarmed at the Northern Alliance's succession of victories in the north and feared they would beat him to Kandahar. Regardless, the more dire issue was that ODA 574's long-range plan, to take Tarin Kowt themselves once the team had built up and trained a guerrilla force of hundreds, was now back to the drawing board.

All Amerine could read when he made eye contact with Karzai were good intentions. *Still*, he thought, *he has no idea how fucked we could be because of this.*

"What do you intend to do?" he asked Karzai.

"I must join them in Tarin Kowt."

Amerine had expected to maintain a low profile for weeks, if not months, during which time ODA 574 would arm, organize, and train

Karzai's followers. Did Karzai not understand that a battle was imminent in Tarin Kowt?

He asked to speak to Karzai in private. Casper followed them into the house.

"There will be a counterattack," Amerine said away from the other Afghans.

"Yes," said Karzai. "But I must go to the governor's palace and meet with the leaders of the uprising right away."

Amerine understood that Karzai had, after all, been lobbying for the anti-Taliban Pashtun to rise up. What kind of a message would it send if he now left them to face the Taliban's reprisals alone?

"Okay," Amerine said. "Do we have vehicles?"

"Not at this time," said Karzai. "But we will have transportation."

"How many men can we expect to join us?"

"Those who took weapons today returned to their homes. There are a few remaining, but Haji Badhur's men will accompany us on the drive. We will have many men in Tarin Kowt."

"Translators?"

"Not yet," said Karzai. "But in Tarin Kowt that will not be a problem. I will translate in the meantime."

After nearly an hour of planning, Casper leaned into the conversation. "Skipper," he said to Amerine, "we have to get moving."

Since the spook wouldn't be involved in the fight, Amerine didn't even acknowledge the comment. He did, however, note the paradox: Risk-averse throughout planning, Casper seemed suddenly gung-ho about engaging the enemy.

/

"Gather around!" JD bellowed to ODA 574 when Amerine returned to the compound. "Captain has some information to put out."

The men stopped what they were doing and formed a circle around Amerine.

"All right," said Amerine. "I know we were just getting settled here, but we're leaving in three hours. The people of Tarin Kowt killed their Taliban governor last night, so that speeds things up for us. We're going to help the locals hold the town. Karzai is getting vehicles—it's a four-hour drive, and there are some twenty villages on our route that *should* be on Hamid's side. That said, Alex, let's get some air to escort us."

"Question, sir," said Alex. "What *is* the route?"

Unbuttoning the flap of a cargo pocket on his pants, Amerine pulled out his survival map,[1] which he'd folded so that Uruzgan Province was on one side and Kandahar Province on the other. He traced the route with his finger for the team to see.

"Hamid says we'll head north along the river to Deh Rawood and then cut east through these mountains to Tarin Kowt. All our maps are fucked—we don't know if these roads still exist, so we'll play it by ear, but this is the basic route. I expect a counterattack in Tarin Kowt within twenty-four hours. Hopefully we'll get there before that happens."

Mike said, "What happened to the hundreds of guys who picked up weapons today?"

"They disappeared back into the mountains," said Amerine. "It was understood that some of them were being armed to protect their villages, but it appears that Hamid is still lacking credibility or there would be *some* guys hanging around looking for something to do. Hamid says he's been promised all the men we need in Tarin Kowt once we get there."

"That sounds familiar," said Dan.

Amerine checked his watch. "Okay, it's 1500; Hamid says he'll have vehicles at 1700."

While the men got to work, Amerine huddled with JD and Mike to look over the proposed route. With a mechanical pencil, Amerine drew a circle around Haji Badhur's Cove and wrote K in the center, for "Karzai."

"This is where we fall back to," said Amerine. "Right now it's the only place that we're sure is backing Hamid. The rest of the south is a question mark."

They looked at the dime-size circle.

"Damn," said JD. "Pretty lonely down here."

By sunset, a ten-vehicle convoy of 1970s-style station wagons, 1980s minivans, and modern Toyota trucks, plus one small shuttle bus, lined up on the main street of Haji Badhur's Cove. Two pickup trucks that had arrived from Tarin Kowt and were full of guerrillas armed with RPGs and assault rifles would lead the convoy back to the capital of Uruzgan.

Amerine, Mike, and Alex piled into a Toyota king cab pickup behind the guide trucks; behind them, Karzai and the CIA team—including Miles, who was kitted out for combat while hooked to an IV—boarded the bus, and Ronnie climbed on top of it. Behind them, · the rest of ODA 574 crammed into another king cab.

Karzai told Amerine that the Afghans talking in a group nearby owned the vehicles and intended to drive them, a detail that didn't bode well with the Americans: Nobody trusted the drivers to react calmly if they drove into an ambush or were stopped at a Taliban checkpoint. Amerine balked, but Karzai explained that there was no other option—in Uruzgan, vehicles are hard to come by and the Afghans would not relinquish theirs. The team could have bought its own trucks in Pakistan and had them airlifted with the weapons the night before, but Karzai had wanted to be as inconspicuous as possible and promised to acquire trucks for ODA 574 in-country.

Now, with no choice but to take what were essentially taxis—and without time to recon the route—the team drew up a plan. In the event of an attack, the Green Berets would commandeer these vehicles, fight off the enemy, then retreat with Karzai back to the last rally point. After regrouping, they would retreat to the relative sanctuary of Haji Badhur's Cove, which they suspected would eventually be overrun by a large enemy force. They would call in airpower to defend the village while preparing to be extracted from the country.

While going over this plan, the men reminded each other of the agreement they'd made back in Uzbekistan regarding the "never leave a fallen comrade" creed. In JD's words: "If I'm killed and we're going to be overrun, don't die trying to bring back my body. Save yourselves and tell the story."

To avoid that outcome, ODA 574 had enlisted the help of a pair of F-18s to fly the road ahead of the convoy. At 30,000 feet the planes were invisible from the ground, but their advanced optics could identify approaching vehicles and roadblocks.

The route followed the Helmand River fifteen miles north to Mullah Omar's hometown of Deh Rawood. There the convoy would turn east and drive for another thirty miles across a small mountain range to Tarin Kowt. Karzai estimated that it would take them four or five hours to travel this distance, an indication that the roads in Uruzgan would live up to their reputation as the worst in Afghanistan.

Once under way, Amerine began to identify rally points—a hill, a *wadi*,* a stone hut—every mile or so, relaying the information to the other team members via radio and entering their coordinates into his GPS. For the first hour, just as Karzai had told them, there were no checkpoints or traffic. The recon jets spotted nothing up ahead, and the convoy advanced unimpeded over the narrow, spine-jarring roads. Soon after dark, they followed the river past the rusted-out remains of a Soviet tank that had been pushed onto its side and was now part of the earthen wall flanking the dirt road. "Mines," muttered the driver of Amerine's truck in a rare use of English as they pulled off and drove next to the road for a quarter of a mile. They passed other remnants from the Soviet army, detoured around landslides, and dodged loitering goats that didn't flinch at car horns or the sound of bullets fired into the air.

After two hours, the road took them into Deh Rawood, past neighborhoods, shops, and restaurants with small wooden tables and chairs stacked in front. It was early in the night, yet the town was almost completely dark, as though windows had been covered to black them out. Scanning the road ahead with their NODs, the men saw no one—not even a dog or a goat.

Amerine read the town's name on his GPS, savoring for a moment the depth of their infiltration and feeling the hair on the back of his neck tingle. *Just cruisin' through Mullah Omar's hood*, he thought. *Ain't no thang.*

---

* A ravine or channel that is dry except in the rainy season.

The convoy continued east out of Deh Rawood, through villages where the vehicles' headlights shone on rectangular metal signs bearing the stenciled names of past humanitarian projects—a well dug by UNICEF, the ruins of an abandoned Red Crescent clinic. Finally they crossed the mountains that formed a giant ring around Tarin Kowt Valley. Even though it was 11 P.M. as they rolled into the capital of Uruzgan Province, Tarin Kowt seemed almost too quiet, appearing to be as deserted as Deh Rawood.

Everything was desert-colored, brick and adobe. From one block to the next, it all looked the same. The string of vehicles zigzagged over narrow dirt roads through a honeycomb of mud-walled compounds, deep into the town where they finally saw life: a young man holding a kerosene lantern. He pushed open the metal gate of a compound and ushered in the two trucks carrying the Americans and the shuttle bus, while the two escort vehicles remained idling on the road outside.

Ronnie slid off the top of the bus and, with the rest of ODA 574, formed a perimeter around it, weapons at the ready. JD had Mike and Mag check the place out, as they'd done their first night in Haji Badhur's Cove, but in this case they were near the center of a much more populated area, with blocks and blocks of neighborhoods linked by a maze of roads. They couldn't just toss a grenade over a wall and run into the mountains.

Karzai said a few words to one of the four armed men in the compound, then led Casper and Amerine into the dwelling. He quickly showed them the two rooms their teams would stay in, then the three men returned to the driveway, where the Americans were unloading their gear from the trucks.

"Now I must leave you to go to the former Taliban governor's palace to meet with the local resistance," Karzai told Amerine.

"When can I meet them?"

"I must go to this meeting alone, Jason. I will send for you."

Not at all comfortable in their new surroundings, Amerine said, "Please keep me informed *immediately* of any developments."

"Of course," said Karzai as he got into a truck and was driven away.

By the light of kerosene lamps, ODA 574 and the spooks lugged the gear into their rooms, the mood remaining tense as the Green Berets settled into the claustrophobic space. Rolling a wire out the window, Dan and Wes set up the antenna for their radio. "I'm going to send up a SITREP," said Dan to Amerine. "Anything special you want me to say other than 'A massive Taliban force is on its way to try to kill us; be ready to help'?"

"You might want to tone it down a bit," said Amerine. "But I think that sums it up quite well."

Forty-five minutes after Karzai left, two guerrillas arrived at the compound with instructions to bring Amerine and Casper to Karzai.

"We'll be back in an hour," Amerine told JD, holding up his radio. "I'll update you once I know what's going on."

"You should bring somebody with you," said JD.

"No need," said Amerine. "If it's a trap, we're dead. You get the men out of here."

The guerrillas drove Amerine and Casper up a residential street, turned right at an open-air market shut down for the night, and entered a small business district where shop windows were full of medical supplies and automotive goods. Amerine noted every detail, down to the height of the compound walls, and replayed the route in his head so that he could make it back to the team's new safe house on foot if he needed to. A pair of rusted-out Soviet BMP armored infantry carriers, flanked by rows of sad, leafless shrubs, stood before an iron gate guarded by four Afghans with machine guns that was barely wide enough to admit their truck. Dozens of trucks were parked along the wide dirt driveway leading to a modest concrete building: the governor's palace.

As Casper hurried ahead, Amerine hung back and followed their guerrilla driver past smiling guards and into a large room dully lit by gas lamps in its corners. The Afghans seated along the walls also regarded them with friendly smiles, but Amerine remained vigilant even when Karzai emerged from the darkness to welcome him. "These are the tribal and religious leaders who took part in the uprising," Karzai explained. "And I have news from them."

These men looked more like well-manicured diplomats than revolutionaries, more polished than the tribal leaders Karzai had brought with him to Pakistan.

"A large convoy of Pakistani Taliban is on its way from Kandahar to retake Tarin Kowt," Karzai continued. "There are reports of one hundred trucks carrying one thousand men."

"When will they arrive?" asked Amerine.

"They left this morning," said Karzai. "The roads are difficult, like what you saw today. So they could arrive anytime tomorrow."

Kandahar was only seventy-five miles away across wide deserts and over mountains that would take some time to cross. Still, there was much to do in order to create the initiative Amerine's small team would require to make a stand against such a large force, and Amerine had to assume the attack could occur before tomorrow. He glanced at the door; the infantryman in him had already begun to plan their defense.

"So we must eat," said Karzai, smiling. "They waited for us to arrive before breaking their fast for Ramadan. Sit down and eat, then we can discuss this further."

"Please thank them, but I have to return to my team and make preparations immediately," Amerine said. "I need you to ask them to send us every man they can to defend the town."

Karzai's brow furrowed. "Are you certain there is not time to eat?"

"Yes."

"Then I will have men with trucks at your compound in two hours."

Amerine paused in the doorway of ODA 574's makeshift command post, feeling safe in the presence of his team. It was almost 12:30 A.M., and in his absence the men had lined up their rucksacks along one wall of the ten-by-twelve-foot room. In one corner, Dan was using his go-to-hell pack as a low desk for his laptop, and Wes was running a second antenna wire outside through a small window. Standing just inside the door beside Ken, JD was testing the flame on one of the two hissing gas lamps hanging from metal hooks in the wall, while Mike, Mag, and Ronnie were taking inventory of the grenades, claymore mines, and ammo clips piled on the cement floor. JD glanced at Amerine, who gestured for him to step outside.

"We've reportedly got a thousand Taliban in a hundred trucks coming to retake Tarin Kowt," Amerine told him. (See map on p. 352)

JD smiled. "Okay, so . . . what now?"

"Only thing I can think of is we find a good hill to climb and bomb 'em before they get here. Any better ideas?"

When JD shook his head, Amerine said, "It's going to be a long night and a longer day."

They went back into the room.

"Listen up!" JD shouted. "The captain has some info to put out."

Every member of ODA 574 immediately stopped what he was doing; the ensuing silence unsettled Amerine, who would have preferred the usual banter to calm his nerves about the terrible odds they faced.

"Hamid's people have reports that the Taliban launched a counterattack from Kandahar to retake this town, as many as a thousand men," Amerine said. "After what these people did to their governor, we can count on them sacking the town if we can't stop them. We have to be in position to defend Tarin Kowt before dawn. I need Mag, Mike, Ronnie, and Brent to do some quick terrain analysis and look for likely enemy avenues of approach, then find us some high ground with a good view to direct air strikes on the most likely route. Dan and Wes, get commo with Task Force Dagger and tell them that we'll probably be in the shit tomorrow, if not sooner. Alex, get us some aircraft and let's look for the bad guys. JD, figure out a timeline. Hamid is sending as many guerrillas as he can to help us, so we need to have a solid plan in about seventy-five minutes. We'll have a status brief at 0130. We depart at 0300."

Every inch of available floor space was soon covered with maps, with half of the men on their hands and knees studying them.

Alex got out his radio, laptop, and cipher book and within minutes announced that two F-18 fighter planes were inbound for reconnaissance. Amerine went next door to brief the CIA team on ODA 574's plan, telling them to be prepared to evacuate Karzai if the Taliban couldn't be stopped. If that happened, they would regroup at Haji Badhur's Cove.

"Good luck, Jason," Charlie said. "Make sure you take the car keys from those guerrillas so they don't leave you behind."

Amerine returned to his team's room, laid out his map on a small wooden table, and attempted to visualize the coming battle. Even though he had no appetite, he forced down an MRE, not knowing when he would next be able to eat. His eyes were drawn to that small circle he'd drawn around Haji Badhur's Cove. They'd driven through several villages on the way to Tarin Kowt, but they still didn't know whether their inhabitants backed Karzai or had merely allowed them passage.

With his pencil, he circled Tarin Kowt Valley and put a question mark in its center. He glanced at his team: JD was listening in on Mike, Ronnie, Brent, and Mag, who were kneeling over their maps in the center of the room, bouncing back and forth opinions of the positions they might occupy. Dan, Wes, and Alex were seated on the ground along one wall, leaned over their radios and laptops, sending up spot reports to Task Force Dagger on their situation and talking to aircraft overhead. Ken sat against another wall, drinking coffee and observing the men, his aid bag packed beside him. After almost an hour, Amerine stepped out into the courtyard hoping to see a group of armed men awaiting instructions, but it was just the same smiling guards.

At the 0130 status update meeting, Mike indicated on the map the only major route into the valley, tracing it through a narrow mountain pass. The high ground beside this pass looked like the best place to establish an observation post from which to direct air strikes on the enemy.

Mike's description was interrupted by Alex. "Sir, the F-18s spotted eight trucks heading north from Kandahar. Are they cleared to engage?" Immediately, Dan and Wes plotted the location of the convoy on the map while Amerine looked over their shoulders. The trucks were twenty miles away, and the team agreed that this must be the lead element of a larger force.

The room went quiet. Every man looked at Amerine. He visualized the valleys and roads, pictured the mountains and what the pilots were seeing. According to Karzai, a force like this coming north could only be Taliban. If a thousand men were closing in, they had to slow them down to gain time for Karzai to rally his men. These air strikes would also be crucial to defending Tarin Kowt. Without further consideration he gave the order: "Smoke 'em."

Alex keyed his hand mic. "Cleared hot," he told the pilots. The men resumed their conversations, easing the tension slightly, but they remained tuned in to Alex.

"I'm going up on the roof to watch for the explosions," said Alex.

"I'll come along," said Amerine, feeling for an instant his remarkable detachment. He'd just ordered his first kill, probably dozens of deaths, and the words he had chosen were as casual as if he was telling his men to swat flies.

Outside, Amerine steadied a ladder for Alex as he climbed up on to the roof.

A thousand men are coming for this place, Amerine thought. Horrible odds, just as there had been during Operation Safe Haven[2] when he was a second lieutenant fresh out of West Point, stationed in Panama on the first assignment of his career.

On December 8, 1994, Amerine's superiors had sent five twenty-five-man infantry platoons plus fifty Air Force security police to quell a riot in a Cuban refugee camp in Panama. In spite of his and other platoon leaders' objections, his commanders had denied their request to bring shotguns and teargas, and provided them instead with batons and face and body shields. Once the platoons were inside the fenced camp, approximately 1,000 refugees attacked the 175 soldiers with softball-size cobblestones that rained down on the Americans, breaking shields and bones with a never-ending supply of projectiles.

Reinforcements were sent in, but by day's end more than two hundred U.S. servicemen (including Amerine and his men) had been wounded, some critically. Though the incident would never be recognized by the Army as "combat," the level of violence was far worse than anything most of the men had experienced. The United States closed the camps two months later.

Amerine vowed that never again would he let men under his command bleed for nothing, but here he was almost seven years later, putting his team in harm's way despite major reservations by the CIA and his chain of command over the viability of the mission. He questioned his motives for pushing ahead. He'd had no doubts in Pakistan that his mission then was noble and righteous. *Why the misgivings now?* he asked himself. Was it his desire to set things straight, a belief that somehow succeeding here would reconcile the catastrophe in Panama that had haunted him all these years? He wondered if it was his ego that had brought him—and his men—into harm's way.

After a couple of minutes on the roof, Alex called down, "They're dropping bombs!" Amerine scrambled up the ladder and scanned the horizon, but could see no flashes nor hear the rumble from the explosions. Alex listened to the radio and reported: "Sir, they engaged the convoy. Five kills. Three got away when they ran out of bombs."

Amerine looked at the night sky stretching before them. Here, far from city lights, the constellations and the Milky Way were exceptionally bright, reminding him of childhood walks at night with his father, who'd taught him the stories behind the constellations. Orion—the Hunter—had always been Amerine's favorite, and tonight he could see it clearly, shining over the battlefield.

Karzai returned from the governor's palace moments later. He was pleased when Amerine informed him of the F-18 attacks, and apologized that he had not been as successful: He had mustered only thirty men with four trucks, plus two trucks with drivers for ODA 574.

"When will they arrive?" asked Amerine, not at all surprised.

"Within the hour," said Karzai.

"Is Bari Gul among them?"

"No, Bari Gul will not arrive until tomorrow."

"That's unfortunate," said Amerine, showing Karzai on the map where they would make their stand twelve miles outside town. As he did this, Alex announced that aerial reconnaissance had continued its hunt all the way to Kandahar and found no other signs of a convoy heading their way.

Amerine, Karzai, and Alex discussed what this meant.

Worst case: The Taliban had already arrived in the mountains surrounding Tarin Kowt Valley and were amassing there for an attack. In mountainous country, they could park under overhangs and alongside ridges and cover their vehicles with mud, making it difficult for aircraft to spot them—something the enemy had been doing in the north.

Best case: Karzai's original information about one hundred trucks had been flawed.

Amerine planned for the worst. "If Tarin Kowt gets overrun, my team will come back for you," he told Karzai, tracing his finger along the highlighted route. "But if we can't, Casper will take you back to Haji Badhur's village."

"And your team?" said Karzai.

"We will meet you there—"

"—God willing." Karzai completed Amerine's sentence.

The thirty guerrillas arrived an hour late, at 4 A.M. ODA 574 quickly loaded its gear—including a couple of heavy machine guns, plus ammunition, hand grenades, and RPGs—onto two trucks. Followed by the other two trucks packed with guerrillas, they tore out of the compound.

Every member of ODA 574 had marked the compound's location on his personal GPS, but Wes doubted he would be able to find his way back: All the compounds looked the same. After two sleepless nights he felt as if he were traveling through a dream. Sixty hours earlier they had landed in Afghanistan, expecting to remain concealed among the populace for months. Now they were rushing into battle.

On the edge of town they stopped at a gas station, where Amerine watched with concern as his driver, a frail-looking man named Qasim, began to fill the tank with the engine running. He laughed. Blowing up at a gas pump was the least of his worries, though pausing to top off the tanks did slow them down. Then the drivers got into an argument with the old man running the pumps over who was to pay. They invoked the name "Hamid Karzai" multiple times, but the man would not relent and Amerine surmised that Karzai's name didn't hold enough clout to act as credit. Begrudgingly, the drivers paid with cash from their own pockets.

Just past the gas station a twisted metal pole blocked the road, two armed Afghans asleep beside it. Qasim honked his horn. One man groggily raised the barrier, and the trucks left Tarin Kowt through the rows of connected buildings that formed the outer wall of the town— *like exiting a protective reef into the open ocean*, thought Amerine.

Their route descended from Tarin Kowt's sloping plateau into a cluster of ridges and hills, as if the skin of the desert had wrinkled, creating a maze of passages that became dead ends or goat trails or looped back on themselves. The road through this hilly labyrinth was dotted with simple compounds and led to Tarin Kowt Pass, a gash in the mountains twelve miles to the south. That's where ODA 574 would park, conceal their vehicles, and lie in wait, ready to call in air strikes on the enemy convoy they expected to arrive on the road below. On the map, the location seemed perfect, but Amerine knew that terrain analysis is much more art than science: It depends upon intuition and eyes-on consideration. Until they got out there and looked around, nothing they'd seen on the map was certain.

Five hundred yards outside town, the trucks' headlights shone on Tarin Kowt's graveyard: a hillside dotted with hundreds of slender wooden stakes, their colorful cloth streamers fluttering in the breeze, like a pincushion covered with threaded needles. Then they entered the labyrinth, heading toward the high ground they'd identified on the map.

As they sped through the twisting turns of the labyrinth, Amerine began to feel anxious. *Maybe there isn't a good observation point*, he thought. *Maybe these hills roll all the way to the gap in the mountains.* If that was the case, they would have a very difficult time striking the enemy before it reached the town. And if ODA 574 let the Taliban reach Tarin Kowt, the battle would be lost—airpower would be useless. Dawn glowed pink on the eastern horizon, the start of another blue-skied, temperate winter day. Time was up: the Taliban could be arriving at any moment. The team had to find cover and establish their observation post immediately.

The road began to climb, a subtle ascent not apparent on the map, then steepened and suddenly rose up onto a ridge running east to west, where the trucks pulled to a stop before an enormous valley—at least four miles south to the mountain pass and seven miles wide. Amerine's dread turned to excitement. They would not have to drive all the way to the mountain pass. They would make their stand right here, eight miles from Tarin Kowt.

He jumped out of the truck and ran ahead to where the road rolled over the ridge, turned sharply to the left, and traversed the slope down to the valley floor a couple hundred feet below. There it veered right and ran straight across the valley to Tarin Kowt Pass; it appeared to be the only route up this steep ridge, which formed a natural two-hundred-foot barrier from which they could easily spot enemy vehicles below.

We can set up the guerrillas along this ridge, thought Amerine, *and hit the Taliban with heavy machine guns and RPGs after they cross the valley, as they try to ascend this ground.*

The road narrowed as it climbed off the valley floor, too narrow for even a small car to turn around on and too steep to drive off. *Whatever vehicles survive our air strikes out in the valley will try to make it up this ridge. We'll attack the lead vehicles, clog the route, and keep the rest corralled in the valley. They'll have to retreat to the pass, and our pilots will pound them all the way back to Kandahar.*

"This is it," he called back to JD. "Get us a perimeter, and I'll tell you what we're gonna do."

Mike jogged forward from the lead truck to see the most perfect kill zone he could imagine: wide-open terrain below them for miles. Two of the guerrillas had leaned their AK-47s against the side of their truck and were smoking hashish from a small pipe; others were taking in the view and awaiting instruction. Anticipating Amerine's orders, Mag and Ronnie began to place the Afghans into fighting positions along the ridge. Alex announced that three F-18s had just checked in; they were overhead at 30,000 feet and standing by.

Mike was still shaking the stiffness from his legs when a glint in the notch of Tarin Kowt Pass caught his eye. "Looks like something parked in the pass," he said, looking through his binoculars. Dan stepped up beside him. "Is that a . . . BTR?" Mike asked, referring to the Russian-made armored personnel carrier with mounted machine guns.

"Nah," said Dan, "but something's there."

"That is, no shit, a fucking BTR," said Mike. "Sir," he said to Amerine, "does that look like a BTR in the pass?"

"Might be," he said, after peering through his binoculars.

"I think it's moving," said Dan.

Amerine looked again and saw a trail of dust. Whatever it was, it was moving fast. "Shit. That's them," he said. "Alex, let's get to work."

The eight trucks the F-18s had engaged a few hours earlier must have been the *tail* of the convoy, not its head. The lead element had already arrived in the mountains and prepared for a morning attack. *We're in deep shit,* Amerine thought. *If there are a hundred trucks on the other side of the pass, we don't have enough bombs to stop them all. Once they reach our ridgeline, we'll either stop them here or we'll have to retreat back toward Tarin Kowt.*

"Are they cleared hot?" Alex called to Amerine.

"Roger," Amerine answered. "Clear them all."

The convoy looked like a snake slithering out of the pass. There seemed to be no end; it just kept coming, its numbers obscured by the dust storm it created as it advanced across the flat desert floor. A hundred yards into the valley, the column of dust became three when some of the vehicles veered out into the open desert from behind the lead trucks and pressed forward on opposite sides of the road in an arrowhead formation.

"Bombs away," said Alex.

A large explosion kicked up dust and flame a few hundred yards ahead of the vehicle at the front, the sound reaching ODA 574 a couple of seconds later. Almost immediately, the same vehicle exploded as a second bomb found its mark. The team let out a cheer.

JD noticed that the guerrillas had gone silent. In fact, they were no longer on the ridge. After the first bomb had missed, they'd run.

/

"The G's are getting in the trucks!" yelled JD.

Amerine turned to see the few guerrillas not already sitting in the trucks facing off with Mag and Ken, who had blocked their retreat but weren't able to turn them around. The trucks were slowly rolling back toward Tarin Kowt, their drivers gesturing emphatically to the Americans to get in.

There was no interpreter to explain to the guerrillas what was going on. They had never witnessed American airpower, but they knew all about the atrocities the Taliban were capable of committing. For them, it was an easy decision. Yet the people of Tarin Kowt would be slaughtered if ODA 574 didn't stop the convoy.

"What do you want to do?" JD shouted to Amerine.

We cannot stay without trucks, Amerine thought, tightly gripping his M4 carbine. *The only way to stop them is to kill the drivers . . . I would kill them to prevent a massacre in Tarin Kowt . . . but that would be the end of Hamid's movement; we would never be trusted again. This position is lost.*

"Get everyone loaded," Amerine ordered.

Alex had to be pulled up from kneeling beside his rucksack as he continued to direct aircraft. "What the fuck is going on?!" he yelled. "We're just getting started!"

"They're running," said Amerine. "Get in the truck."

Amerine's pickup was the last to leave; the driver looked at him with panic as he pinned the accelerator to the floorboard and hit a rut that almost threw Wes out of the back. "Slow the fuck down!" Wes shouted, pounding on the roof with his fist. He continued to pound, frustrated that they'd just been forced to give up front-row seats to the Super Bowl of aerial ambushes.

/

When the first bombs hit the lead trucks, the Taliban drivers might have considered the explosions to be lucky hits from old Soviet mortars the townspeople were firing from somewhere up ahead. They did not know they were being targeted by American soldiers. The first contingent of F-18s had dropped its small complement of bombs and left to rearm, creating the illusion that the artillery barrage had ceased. Unable to hear or see the aircraft high overhead, the convoy drove faster, racing along the road on the valley floor past the burning wreckage of four vehicles toward the ridge abandoned by ODA 574.

The Taliban trucks converged back together once they crossed the valley and began to slowly climb the road ascending the ridgeline and into the labyrinth. Impatient drivers again split off to the east and west to form two new columns, searching for another way up and into the labyrinth.

Through the dust, the F-18 pilots were able to provide the team a rough estimate of what they were up against. They reported at least fifty vehicles, with more coming through Tarin Kowt Pass. One large truck appeared to be towing a cannonlike artillery piece.

/

While the frantic driver of Alex's truck negotiated the labyrinth, sliding around corners, bouncing up onto embankments, and accelerating through the ruts in the road, Alex somehow managed to continue directing the aircraft. He shouted out to Amerine, "I called in 'troops in contact.' Everything in theater is headed our way!"

Across the theater the word was out: A lone team of Green Berets was in contact with hundreds of Taliban fighters. Flights were diverted from other missions in Afghanistan and aircraft were scrambled from their carriers in the Arabian Sea, all of them heading to Tarin Kowt.

"How long will it take for them to get here?" Amerine asked.

Alex shrugged.

Slamming his fist against the dashboard, Amerine yelled, "These G's just pulled defeat from the fucking jaws of victory!"

In another truck, Mag was shouting at the guerrillas, who couldn't understand a word: "What the *hell*?! They were *miles* away! We had *minutes*! *Long fucking minutes!*"

Mike and JD were holding on tight, trying not to get tossed from the back of the truck they were in and nervously eyeing the RPG rounds bouncing around like popcorn in the bed. One had lost its safety cone. *That thing's gonna blow the fuck up*, Mike kept thinking. *We're gonna die.*

The trucks sped into Tarin Kowt, the town's gatekeepers lifting the flimsy metal pole barely in time. Men, women, and children bolted to the sides of the road and pressed up against buildings as the trucks flew past, not slowing down till they screeched to a stop in front of the team's compound.

Standing at the gate with a large group of armed Afghans around him, Karzai looked confused. "What is happening?" he asked Amerine.

"These guys ran," said Amerine urgently. "My team is taking the trucks. We need to get back in the fight."

"Okay, yes. Go! Go!"

Karzai uttered angry words in Pashtun to the panicked guerrillas as Amerine grabbed the keys from his driver and tossed them to Wes. "You want to drive?"

"Hell, yeah!" said Wes.

JD commandeered the second truck and yelled, "Drive 'em like you stole 'em!"

"I think we just did!" Wes shouted back.

✦

The Americans raced back through Tarin Kowt, then parked their two trucks side by side on a knoll just outside the town's gate. Amerine considered turning the vehicles around to face their escape route through town, but he wanted to appear confident. Once the Taliban came within view of Tarin Kowt, the two trucks might give them a moment's pause if they believed reinforcements were close behind.

Alex, perched on top of gear in the bed of one truck, continued to direct the U.S. aircraft arriving from all over the country: F-14 Tomcats, in their final months of military service, joined their replacements, F-18 Hornets, all staying above 30,000 feet. Below them, the pilots saw dust clouds from the Taliban convoy approaching Tarin Kowt along three roads through the labyrinth. They appeared to be converging on the pair of trucks sitting just outside town.

"Roger—I see two friendly victors [vehicles]," one pilot radioed to Alex.

"That's us," Alex replied.

"You mean that's all you've *got*?!"

The pilots described to Alex what they were seeing: The smaller western and eastern columns of the Taliban attack were moving at a slower pace than the main force approaching in the middle.

"Put it all on the center column for now," ordered Amerine. "That's the immediate threat."

Alex noted the number of planes as they checked in, via radio, when they arrived overhead. Amerine calculated how much firepower they had available: three aircraft, carrying a total of eighteen bombs, to take out at least fifty vehicles coming their way. Not enough.

Explosions echoed in the distance, and a few plumes of black smoke rose into the blue sky. Alex cleared another flight for the center column, marking the location of the air strikes on the map. The Taliban were halfway through the labyrinth, still coming on strong.

"Can you get an estimate on how many Taliban are left?" asked Amerine.

After conversing briefly with a pilot, Alex turned to Amerine. "Lots."

They exchanged grim smiles.

As more planes arrived, an F-18 pilot informed Alex that he was Airborne Forward Air Control–qualified and could help direct aircraft from the sky. Directing one airplane from the ground is relatively easy; directing dozens of aircraft attacking scores of moving vehicles is extremely difficult. Aided by the AFAC, Alex was able to coordinate multiple simultaneous air strikes. Yet the center column continued forward relentlessly. Each time the lead vehicle was hit by a bomb, the trucks behind it would pass the wreckage and continue to advance, while the outer columns, moving more slowly than the center, proceeded unchecked. If the outer elements flanked Tarin Kowt, ODA 574's escape route would be cut off.

"When you get a chance," Amerine told Alex, "get a SITREP on the progress of the western and eastern elements."

Dan was helping Alex direct aircraft, and Wes was firing off SITREPs to Task Force Dagger. The rest of the team could do little more than scan the ridges to the south and listen to the cross talk between the pilots, Alex, and Amerine. They began to tally the black clouds rising above the labyrinth. One dozen and counting—each representing a truck packed with up to twelve men—which might mean a hundred dead, but still the Taliban pressed forward.

And then the people of Tarin Kowt began to arrive.

It started with four townsmen, who timidly joined the team to listen to the bombing. More followed, speaking a language no one on ODA 574 understood. Soon twenty men had gathered, then small children and women ventured out and a mob of forty people was pressing up against the trucks, shouting their approval with every distant explosion.

The AFAC told Alex that, in spite of the multitude of burning trucks littering the labyrinth, the three prongs of the attack were continuing to close in on Tarin Kowt. Worse, the aircraft were out of bombs. The AFAC had remained until he was fuel critical—now he had to return to base.

Alex relayed the news to Amerine, who looked at his men. Mag and Ronnie—strapped with triple loads of grenades and ammo—had been putting the few locals carrying weapons into a rough defensive line on opposite sides of the trucks. The majority of the crowd was unarmed, and they would be the first gunned down by the Taliban if ODA 574 retreated.

"We gotta get these people out of the streets," Amerine said to JD.

JD had heard Alex's latest report, and he understood what Amerine was saying. The two glanced around at the Afghans, focusing on the children. "We still have some time," JD said.

"Yep. We'll stay as long as we can—then we have to get Hamid out of here."

"Mag, grab Ronnie and Mike and clear the crowd out of here!" JD shouted, moving the hand of a teenager playing with the pockets of his go-to-hell pack.

As the three Green Berets politely but firmly pushed the crowd back from the trucks, they realized that there were more than just a few armed men among them.

"We got a lot of guys with guns here," Mag called out.

"Well, put them to work," said JD.

More people arrived—carrying everything from AK-47s to bolt-action rifles that likely predated World War II—and Mag grabbed them by their shirt collars and put them in the defensive line. Ronnie was doing the same, spreading the men out on either side of the trucks, when Mag said to him, "Brother, you're gonna have to cover me, 'cause I've got a jumper at the door." Ronnie said, "Brother, you can cover me while I cover you." They ran to the nearest compound door, knocked, and—when there was no answer—Mag said, "Sorry about this," and kicked the door in. Hurrying to a back corner of the deserted compound, they faced each other and dropped their drawers.

Meanwhile, Mike watched two Afghans pull a canvas tarp off a rusty Soviet anti-tank weapon, set back between two buildings. To his amazement, it appeared to have been maintained. The parts moved, and another man carried some large rounds out of a nearby shed, loaded up the gun, and cranked it to point toward the labyrinth. Mike gestured at the weapon and gestured around, "Any more like this?" The men shook their heads and held up one finger. This was the extent of the town's heavy defenses.

Three or four men showed up with RPGs, and Mag and Ronnie, now back at the trucks, sent them to the rooftops on either side of the main street, pantomiming that they should stay there and fire at anything that came toward them on the road.

/

"Texas One Two, we are going to get permission to drop below altitude restriction and commence strafing runs," radioed one of the pilots.

This was bad news for ODA 574. Due to the perceived air defense threat from the Taliban, the pilots weren't allowed to fly at lower altitudes. They were now seeking permission to strafe—the most dangerous method of attacking ground troops—because they had nothing else left and didn't want to abandon the team and the town until they were completely out of ammunition.

Suddenly an F-14 swooped toward the center convoy, white smoke erupting from its nose. Its six-barreled Vulcan Gatling-style cannon fired sixty rounds of 20 mm ammunition per second, making a belching sound as it strafed the trucks and depleting in ten seconds all 676 rounds the aircraft carried. A single RPG arced upward from somewhere in the labyrinth and missed the plane by hundreds of yards, coming harmlessly back to earth in the desert to the west. One by one, jets dived down over the labyrinth, firing the last of their ammunition before returning to their ships to refuel and rearm.

For several minutes, the men watched the smoke from smoldering wrecks in the labyrinth, aware that their enemies were getting closer and they had nothing to throw at them. "We may be in trouble," Dan said under his breath.

As if on cue, a second wave of fully armed aircraft checked in. Alex quickly directed them to strike the middle column. After their first run, marked by a rumble of explosions, the pilots radioed some welcome news: "The victors in the middle group are starting to turn around."

"Let's work the western column, then the eastern one," Amerine said.

The smaller eastern column had stopped when the strafing began, and the lead vehicles were retreating back through the maze. Alex told the pilots to let them run and focus instead on the larger western column, which was still advancing.

"You're cleared hot," said Alex. "Give them whatever you've got."

As the 500-pound bombs began to explode on the western column, more fighters announced their arrival to Alex, who was controlling so many aircraft that he had to keep them in a holding pattern high overhead.

"I got one truck trying to hide in a draw," radioed a pilot. ". . . Not anymore." An explosion echoed across the valley.

Now under attack, the western convoy pressed forward, some of the trucks breaking away and speeding past the burning wreckage of their cohorts.

"I see 'em!" shouted Mike, pointing at a truck a mile to the west, the first of the Taliban to have made it through the labyrinth.

Amerine grabbed JD and whispered in his ear, "Get all the guys close to the trucks."

Machine-gun fire erupted at the western edge of town.

"Can we go over there?" asked Ronnie.

"No—stay here," said JD.

It soon became evident that the gunfire was coming *from* townsmen shooting at the lone Taliban truck, which abruptly turned around and sped away to the south. Sporadic gunfire persisted in the west, but the team couldn't see what was happening.

"The western column is turning around!" said Alex.

"Let's get as many as we can before they escape," said Amerine.

The aircraft continued their runs, dropping bombs on the retreating trucks. The sky had gone brown, hazy from dust and smoke from the destroyed vehicles. The columns of black smoke reminded the Gulf War veterans—JD, Mag, and Ken—of the burning oil fields in the Kuwaiti desert.

The rest of the men had seen those same scenes on television and the covers of *Time* and *Newsweek*. But this was their war, and ODA 574 had just won its first battle.

★

CHAPTER SEVEN

Credibility

The giants he sees are nothing but windmills . . . [but] only a man who sees giants can ever stand upon their shoulders.
—Ian Caldwell and Dustin Thomason, *The Rule of Four*

As the aircraft pursued the fleeing convoy down the valley, the now exuberant crowd of locals moved back in closer to the team.

"Look at that!" Ronnie shouted, pointing into the boisterous throng of Afghans.

Amerine and Mag clutched their M4s instinctively and spun around, eyes darting.

"That guy has a nickel-plated AKS,"* Ronnie sputtered. "Brent would love one of those. Let me see how much he wants for it."

"You can buy Brent a gun later," Amerine said with a laugh.

From the direction of town, a red truck approached, crawled through the mob, and pulled up next to ODA 574. Casper and Charlie were in the backseat of the king cab, being driven by a member of Karzai's guard.

"How's it going?" asked Casper, gazing out at the black smoke in the distance.

"Convoy is retreating," said Amerine. "I'm going to push the team out and get ready for a second attack."

---

* A snub-nosed, or "short," version of the AK-47.

"I'll send up a report briefing what your team did—what happened here today," said Casper.

Amerine nodded, then turned to Charlie and said, "You were right; we should have taken the keys."

Shaking his head with a smile, Charlie said, "I told you so."

JD was standing beside Alex at their truck, the Afghans crowding them while Alex listened to reports from the pilots. Walking up, Amerine set his weapon atop the gear piled in the truck bed and removed the light gray Afghan shirt he'd been wearing over his uniform since Haji Badhur's Cove.

"They know we're here now," Amerine said to JD, who took off his own charcoal-colored top. "We don't need to bother with these costumes anymore."

The rest of the men were stripping back down to their DCUs when a car horn started blaring and the townspeople scrambled off the road to allow an SUV full of armed Afghans to pass. When it hit the open road, it sped up in pursuit of the retreating Taliban.

"Good for them," said JD. "Alex, you'd better keep our pilots from bombing him."

"I'll do my best—but if he goes too far forward, there isn't anything I can do."

Five more trucks followed the first. "We need to get down there and see if we can reoccupy the ridgeline," Amerine said to JD. "We have to assume the Taliban will be back. We surprised them today. Next time they'll be smarter."

The team loaded into their vehicles while at least thirty more trucks with armed men streamed south out of Tarin Kowt. ODA 574's two trucks merged with them, hitting a traffic jam where the road entered a gully at the beginning of the labyrinth. They edged forward a hundred yards into the labyrinth and could see smoke rising ahead. "They almost made it to Tarin Kowt," Amerine said to Wes, pointing at the remains of a Taliban truck.

The truck bed was gone and the cab torn in half, a smoldering body slumped over the steering wheel. Body parts and charred clothing were scattered on the ground. A Taliban soldier—his intestines spilling from his abdomen—lay moaning in the ditch beside the road.

While the locals offered the man water, Amerine looked down at him from the passenger seat of the lead truck, feeling no remorse or pity, just a cold triumph. In the second truck, Mike and Mag felt the same: This dying Taliban who had been on his way to murder innocent civilians now represented little more than the cause of this traffic jam.

They got moving again, just to hit another jam as friendly trucks attempted to maneuver around more wreckage blocking the road. In fifteen minutes, they'd traveled only a quarter of a mile into the labyrinth. Ken, who was sitting in the bed of Amerine's truck, suddenly shouted when they slowed to a stop at another bottleneck.

Amerine stuck his head out the window. "What?"

"You're going to get us killed if we keep going!" Ken yelled. "There are cluster bombs* all over the road!"

"We didn't drop any cluster bombs," Amerine snapped, swinging open the cab door. He had never seen a Green Beret lose his cool this way, and he approached his medic with a mixture of anger and disbelief.

In the same truck as Amerine and Ken, Wes, who respected both men, felt like a kid listening to his parents bicker. From the truck behind, Mag and JD watched Amerine step toward the rear of the truck and get in Ken's face.

"Looks like the captain is about to go at it with Ken," said Mag, "This is not the time or place for this bullshit. We gotta roll!"

"I'm on it," JD said. He jumped out and ran forward. "Get in my fucking truck, Sergeant," he ordered, and Ken hopped from the truck's bed and walked to the other vehicle, shaking his head.

"What's going on?" JD asked Amerine.

---

* Cluster bombs release dozens of mini bombs that cover a large area, and are used to clear minefields and large concentrations of ground troops. A small percentage of the mini bombs fail to explode on impact and are notorious for blowing up as personnel move through the aftermath of a bombing raid.

"Ken is losing it. Says we're all gonna get killed if we push forward."

The dirt road ahead of them was congested with trucks from Tarin Kowt. Armed townsmen were creeping up embankments, searching for surviving Taliban.

"Looks like it might get nasty," said JD. "I don't think we should push forward with a scared medic and all these townsfolk confusing things. Why don't we let them do the initial sweep, and we'll get a translator and some guerrillas to clean up tomorrow. We can lay up somewhere around here tonight."

"Let's pull up onto that ridge and set up an observation post," said Amerine. "That will give us a decent perspective of the approach from the pass." With a nod, JD returned to his vehicle. The two trucks drove off the road heading east and climbed the highest ridge, about a mile and a half into the labyrinth. Though ODA 574 had an unobstructed view back to Tarin Kowt, their view to the south, where the Taliban had entered the valley through Tarin Kowt Pass, was limited by the rolling hills. With Alex monitoring hourly recon flights, however, this would do as an observation post for the night.

While Mike, Ronnie, and Mag took up positions at the three points of a triangular perimeter with the trucks at the center, JD and Amerine sat down away from the rest of the team to discuss Ken.

"We can try to have him medevaced," Amerine said.

"Do you want to risk an aircrew to get him out of here?"

Amerine shook his head. "I just don't know."

"It could be PTSD," said JD. "I heard him tell a story once about helping a Saudi unit that was hit by friendly fire in the Gulf War."

"They were hit by cluster bombs?"

"Yeah," said JD. "Let me talk to him. You stay out of it for now. I'll keep him close to me. Any of this shit happens again, we'll send him home."

"That means you would have to double as team sergeant *and* team medic."

"It's okay," JD said, smiling. "I'm a damn good medic."

"We'll be fine here for tonight, but I want to push out to our original observation post, with the view of Tarin Kowt Pass, tomorrow. I'm going to grab Mike and Wes and ride into town to talk to Hamid about getting us some men."

/

Back in Tarin Kowt, the streets were packed with pedestrians, many waving Afghan flags in lieu of the white flags of the Taliban. Shops were open. An old man stood in the center of an intersection wearing a tattered police uniform, directing traffic with a whistle and animated hand signals. Parked vehicles lined the streets outside Karzai's headquarters when Amerine, Mike, and Wes pulled up; inside the compound courtyard were groups of Afghan men, all in conversation, their voices echoing off the walls.

A very tall teenager, dressed in a bright aqua robe, greeted the Americans. "I am Seylaab," he said, carefully and loudly enunciating each word. "You want to see Hamid Karzai?"

"Yes," said Amerine. "Are you our translator?"

"No, I am Mr. Karzai's assistant. Rahim will translate for you. He is a pharmacist from this town. You will meet him later."

Leaving Wes and Mike near the entrance, Amerine followed Seylaab across the courtyard, ascended two concrete steps, and entered the compound's "guest room"—the room designated in Afghan homes where visitors are received by the head of the house, take their meals, and sleep.* Karzai was sitting on the floor in a large circle of cross-legged tribal leaders. He motioned toward Amerine, and the man next to Karzai gave up his seat.

Another Afghan served Amerine tea.

"Do you want sweets?" asked Karzai.

"Please," said Amerine, taking nuts and raisins from a tray. "Have you been out on the streets? It's very crowded. There's even a police officer directing traffic."

---

* During Karzai's youth, his father, as chief of the Popalzai, had used the family's guest room almost entirely for local politics. Afghan culture dictates that all guests—even enemies— receive hospitality and protection while in a home.

"Ah," said Karzai. "There is a story behind that man. He is one of many who have been released from the prison where he was held by the Taliban for years. I was told that he went home, saw his family, put on his old uniform, and wanted to go back to work. Nobody is paying him."

"The crowds and traffic are from all around the area," he continued. "The local mullahs from Tarin Kowt, some from Deh Rawood, even one from Helmand, came to visit me this afternoon. I thought they might be angry about the fight, maybe angry that all of you are here. Instead, they thanked me for bringing you—the ones from Tarin Kowt said they would be dead if you had not come."

Amerine looked around the room. "Are any of these men mullahs?"

"No, they have already departed," said Karzai. "These are local tribal leaders."

"Are they bringing men?"

"Oh, yes. After today we will have no problems."

"That is good news," said Amerine. "Tonight I'll keep my team south of town to watch for the Taliban. Have you heard anything about their intentions?"

"Not yet. I think it is good that you keep watch."

"I still need men. I need them right now. My eight men aren't very secure where I have them."

"Bari Gul is coming tonight or tomorrow morning with his men," Karzai said. "I will send him directly to you."

"Seylaab says you have a translator for me?" said Amerine.

"Yes. I will send Rahim with Bari Gul."

Amerine remained in the circle and listened, through Karzai's translation, while the Afghans discussed the anticipated arrival of tribal fighters and how they would be fed and quartered in Tarin Kowt. As much as Amerine needed guerrillas, the most important aspect of this meeting was the simple act of sitting and listening to the tribal leaders. If he was going to take their men into battle, they had to be as comfortable with him as they were with Karzai.

"They are concerned about more attacks from the Taliban in retribution for joining our rebellion," Karzai told Amerine. "There are villages across Uruzgan that will follow Tarin Kowt and denounce the Taliban, but they fear reprisals. Can we get them more weapons?"

"Yes. I will work on getting more weapons dropped in Tarin Kowt," replied Amerine. "You should put the word out that they'll arrive here in the next day or two."

"Good. That will help."

"Have there been any other reprisals by the Taliban in Uruzgan?"

"Not yet," said Karzai. "But they will come."

After an hour, Amerine excused himself to meet with Casper at the compound on the other side of the street that he had procured for his CIA team and ODA 574. Casper escorted Amerine to a large team room across the courtyard from the CIA. Karzai had a small room between them that he could use for sleeping or as a refuge from the constant flow of visitors.

"We have a helicopter arriving tonight with our three men," said Casper, referring to one of his spooks and to Victor and Brent, ODA 574's engineer and junior weapons sergeant.

"That's good to hear," said Amerine. "Can you drive them out to me tomorrow morning? It would be better not to move anyone tonight."

"Worried we might get lost in the dark?"

Amerine laughed.

Early that evening at the observation post, Alex sat in the soft glow of his laptop on the tailgate of the truck, explaining to Amerine and JD the method he had developed to recon the three major avenues of approach from Kandahar to Tarin Kowt, which he designated on the computer map with red, green, and blue lines.

"I'll get us recon flights down these roads every three hours," he said. "That should give us more than enough time to spot convoys."

Amerine relayed to the men that they were going to bottle up Kandahar by preventing the Taliban from sending convoys north out of the city and into Uruzgan. This would serve two purposes: it would protect the villages that defected to Karzai and it would undo the Taliban grip on the province.

The problem—especially from 30,000 feet above—was differentiating Taliban from civilians.

"I proposed the following rules of engagement to Hamid and he agreed," Amerine said. "We can freely engage convoys moving north that are composed of five or more trucks, or any containing tanks or troop carriers. Everything else we let go. We aren't going to see large numbers of trucks unless they are full of people fighting for our side or theirs. Hamid offered three as the magic number, but I wanted to err on the side of caution."*

"The mountain passes cause bottlenecks," Alex said. "Any vehicles are going to bunch up and travel in packs that might look like enemy convoys."

"We'll just monitor them, see if they stay together or disperse when they're out of those bottleneck areas," said Amerine. "It will be a judgment call. We'll watch them for as long as we can. If there is any doubt, we let the convoys go. I'd rather let a small force through than risk killing noncombatants."

That night, half the team stood watch at all times, with Alex (who had an uncanny knack for waking up when new sorties of recon aircraft arrived), Dan, and Wes rotating on the radio. An hour before sunrise, JD, Mag, and Mike woke up the others, and each man covered his sector of fire with his M4. They were practicing "stand to," short for "stand to arms," an Army tradition since World War I trench warfare, when soldiers on both sides announced their preparation to defend against attack each morning by ceremoniously firing their weapons at each other. Over the years, the practice was refined,** but modern soldiers still ready themselves for attack at dawn and some still refer to it as "the morning hate."

---

* Amerine devised this system based on the dearth of vehicles in Afghanistan and questions he asked Karzai regarding driving habits of the locals. In the current climate of war, Karzai and his tribal leaders confirmed Amerine's conclusion that trucks driving in convoys of five or more were Taliban military, except in specific instances. Each case would be individually scrutinized.

** Modern soldiers no longer announce their "stand to" readiness with gunshots, which not only wastes bullets but also enables the enemy to locate soldiers' positions, count enemy forces, and take other advantage of a tactical tipping of one's cards.

It was Sunday, November 18, their fourth day in-country. After sunrise the team reduced security to 30 percent and ate an MRE. At 6 A.M. a recon flight reported twelve trucks bumper to bumper in a mountain pass on the blue route, halfway from Kandahar. Alex estimated that if the trucks were headed for Tarin Kowt, they would be there in seven hours, and Amerine considered whether to order a strike: Being too conservative risked allowing a Taliban force to attack Karzai's allies along the way; being too trigger-happy could kill civilians. Alex plotted the location on the computer and, viewing the satellite imagery, saw that the area the convoy was passing through was mountainous—far from Tarin Kowt and not approaching any villages. The tension knotting in his stomach, Amerine continued to monitor the recon reports. One word and everyone in those vehicles would be incinerated.

After nearly two hours, the bottleneck dissipated and the trucks began to pass one another, spread out, and turn onto side roads. Amerine then made an announcement to ODA 574: "I'm the only one authorizing air strikes from here on out. I know we usually delegate that responsibility among the team, but I'm not appointing anyone unless I am completely out of the net for some reason, or you're under fire and need close air support. I apologize for micromanaging this, but I want to be the only one who has to live with killing a truckload of innocents if any mistakes are made."

He knew from the expressions on his men's faces that they didn't like this order, but no one protested. He assumed that JD would hear the complaints later. *C'est la guerre.*

The sound of engines laboring uphill broke the morning's silence as three trucks arrived at the top of the ridge and Bari Gul stepped out of the lead vehicle, followed by an older man in a white robe. Walking over, Amerine greeted them in Pashto: "Salaam alaykum."

Bari Gul's scowl broadened into a wide grin, and he returned the greeting. The other man, who introduced himself as Rahim, translated Bari Gul's next words: "He says that they heard all about the battle yesterday. He says they are here to fight with you."

"Tell him that it is good to see him again, and we are honored to be joined by him and his men," Amerine said.

Bari Gul's nineteen guerrillas spread out around the Americans as an outer layer of security, concealing themselves behind rocks or sitting on the ground, their weapons at the ready. Feeling confident that these men knew what they were doing, Amerine, along with Wes and Mike, went back to Tarin Kowt, where he received a warm greeting from both Karzai and the now familiar faces in the circle of elders.

"Sit, Jason," said Karzai. "We can talk. Did your friend Bari Gul find you?"

"He did," replied Amerine. "Can you tell me more about him?"

"He is a Popalzai chief, from Deh Rawood—very reliable. For a long time I thought that he was with the Taliban, but I learned when I was still in Quetta that was not so. He came and joined us in the mountains when the Taliban attacked. Remember, he wanted to stay and fight the Taliban. But Jason, Bari Gul, just like these men sitting here with us, could be Taliban or against the Taliban; it does not matter. God, family, and tribe are what matters. These things *are* Afghanistan to Bari Gul.

"That is why we need the Loya Jirga, so all of these tribes can see that they are part of a bigger tribe, so the Pashtun, the Uzbek, the Tajik, all the tribes will call themselves Afghans as readily as you call yourself an American."

Amerine pulled his map from his pocket and flattened it on the floor before them. "Could you give me an update on where your support lies in the tribal belt?"

"Many villages have pledged support," said Karzai. "I believe it is safe to say this one, and this, and this . . ."

Pointing out the locations, Karzai rattled off names of more than a dozen villages that had sent representatives to promise their allegiance. There were still a few, however, even some very close to Tarin Kowt, aligned with the Taliban. "But," said Karzai, "these are remote and do not wish to fight against us. They fly the Taliban flag, but they remain neutral for now."

Amerine began to draw circles—some of them overlapping—

around the areas backing Karzai, adding a K to each. Next to the villages Karzai deemed neutral, Amerine wrote the letter N.

"I'm told there are small *jirgas* [councils] taking place across the tribal belt," said Karzai. "All the way to Kandahar, tribal leaders are discussing which side to take."

"So this battle really stirred things up," said Amerine.

"It was as I've told your government for years. Most Pashtun have not been happy with the Taliban, but could not defeat them. Now they see an opportunity. The question they have now is whether or not your military will stay to finish the job."

"I can't make any promises," said Amerine. "I know we intend to stay until the Taliban fall and al-Qaeda flees the country. I don't know the plans for reconstruction. Afghanistan is going to take decades to rebuild."

Satisfied with Amerine's candor, Karzai nodded. Three Afghans approached, each handing him a few sheets of paper, and he glanced at the writing, then signed the documents with a flourish. The men thanked Karzai and left the room.

"These letters they asked me to sign," said Karzai, "they grant safe passage as they travel to Helmand Province."

"Who are they?"

"Young men who have snuck away from their Taliban units in Kandahar and are going home."

Amerine had read about these chits in Ahmed Rashid's book *Taliban*: Mullah Omar had provided letters of safe passage as his movement swept across the land, his signature serving as a stamp of protection. Now Karzai was receiving the same respect.

"That is a big deal," Amerine said.

"It is how things are done here," Karzai responded.

/

When Amerine, Mike, and Wes returned to the observation post, Brent and Victor had arrived and were settling back in with their team. Ronnie was telling Brent about the nickel-plated AKS, and Mike immediately began going through a new rucksack that Victor had brought him, full of replacements for his stolen gear.

"Thank God," Mike said when Victor tossed him a sleeping bag. "I have been freezing my ass off."

"Any news?" JD asked Amerine.

"The tribal belt is in complete upheaval. We don't have everyone on our side, but most of the villages between here and Kandahar are rethinking their allegiance."

"Not bad."

"Yeah," said Amerine, "but I think we should give it one more night out here. Hamid agreed."

Dan walked over. "Task Force Dagger wants us to provide battle damage assessment [BDA] with digital photos of the enemy vehicles we destroyed," he said.

"Are they worried about the effectiveness of five-hundred-pound bombs on Toyotas?" said JD.

"I think they're worried that we're still in Pakistan and just making all this up," replied Dan.

"Okay, so we'll take a drive around the battlefield, then camp on the ridge for the night," said Amerine.

Through Rahim, Amerine briefed Bari Gul, who nodded. Rahim, on the other hand, shook his head as he spoke. "I'm sorry," he said, "but I cannot go with you."

"Why is that?" asked JD.

"I am here to translate, not to fight," he said, expressing his concern that there might still be Taliban in the area. "I will return to the headquarters now."

"We need a translator," said JD. "Karzai said you're our man."

"I will send Seylaab. He is young," said Rahim, appearing pleased that he had solved the problem. He climbed into the passenger seat of one of Bari Gul's trucks, closed the door, and stared through the windshield. A guerrilla climbed behind the wheel, and the truck headed back toward Tarin Kowt.

Amerine looked at Bari Gul. Despite the language barrier, as long as this warrior was around, Amerine felt that ODA 574 was in good hands.

It was an hour before the truck returned, and the six-foot-four Seylaab, still wearing his aqua robe, stepped out; he was carrying an

AK-47 upside down, one hand gripping it awkwardly by the barrel.

"He's all yours, sir," said JD.

The team laughed as Seylaab hurried to Amerine's side. "Mister Jason, I was told that I am to assist you."

Amerine nodded to Bari Gul, who walked to his truck, which was packed with his men. Seylaab lingered, awaiting his next order. "Hop in, Seylaab," said Amerine. "We have to go."

Dashing ahead, Seylaab held open the door to Amerine's truck. "You don't have to do that," said Amerine. "Just get in."

"Yes," said Seylaab. "Yes, Mister Jason."

The five trucks moved slowly in single file along the same dirt road that had been gridlocked the day before. They had traveled no more than fifty yards south into the labyrinth when Bari Gul's lead vehicle turned off-road and ascended a ridgeline a short distance to the west. At the top, Bari Gul, Amerine, and Seylaab got out of their trucks. Staring across the labyrinth, Amerine realized that this piece of high ground, just across the road from the one they currently occupied, was a far better observation post. *He knows what he's doing*, thought Amerine.

Bari Gul spoke, looking at Amerine, not Seylaab.

"He says the people are angry here," said Seylaab.

"At us?" Amerine asked. "Or the Taliban?"

Unable to explain in English, Seylaab shrugged. "He says the people came and buried all the bodies yesterday. There are still angry people here; we must be careful."

"They are angry at us?" Amerine motioned to himself and his men.

"Yes," said Seylaab. "All of us."

Seylaab could not put into words the difference in sentiment between Tarin Kowt, where the Americans and Karzai's supporters were welcome, and the area just outside the town, but Amerine determined that the locals must have been sympathetic to the Taliban. From the ridge, he could see two dwellings in the distance, one with a truck parked beside it, but no people.

"Did the people of Tarin Kowt search the homes in the area for Taliban yesterday?" asked Amerine.

"Yes, maybe," Seylaab translated for Bari Gul.

"Yes? Or maybe?" said Amerine.

"Yes." Seylaab grinned. "Maybe."

Amerine laughed. They would remain vigilant.

Back on the main road, they continued south, but their route was soon blocked by the burned-out hull of a truck, with two others smashed up against it as though they had rear-ended the lead vehicle as it was hit by a bomb. The team dismounted to take a look—everyone but Ken, who sat stone-faced in the back of JD's truck.

In a single day, scavengers had picked these trucks clean of salvageable parts, leaving behind only their molten, twisted skeletons. Beneath each blackened pile of metal was the brown stain of burned gasoline. RPGs were incinerated in the remains and scattered on the ground. Mag took out his camera and started photographing the wreckage.

"The graves are there," said Seylaab, pointing to piles of rocks beside the road. Sticks, burned-up ammo clips, and wreckage were planted among the piles as headstones, and pieces of ammo vests were draped over them in lieu of the iconic upside-down rifle stuck into the ground—functioning weapons were too valuable a commodity to leave with the dead.

The rock piles varied in size, the larger ones marking whole bodies and the smaller piles, Bari Gul pantomimed, holding only pieces.

"How many pictures do we need?" asked Mag.

"I don't know," said Amerine. "I've never done this before."

After taking two or three shots of each destroyed vehicle they encountered, as well as a panoramic of the graves, the men got back in their trucks and rode silently past the wreckage. *We did this* was the collective realization. The shallow burials and the efficiency with which the locals had cleared the battlefield unnerved many of the Americans.

Amerine experienced a sort of warrior's remorse. Even though he had been responsible for the deaths of those buried here, he had not fought them in direct combat. In retrospect the battle seemed unfair, the antithesis of the more noble face-to-face combat he both dreaded and desired.

They rose out of the labyrinth and parked on the same ridge from which they had spotted the convoy the day before.

As they stared out across the enormous valley toward Tarin Kowt Pass, most of the wreckage was not discernible. With binoculars, though, the black specks on the desert floor became the remains of Taliban trucks.

"I think I see something," said Brent, looking east through binoculars. "There's a large truck pointing some kind of gun this way."

About a mile away, the vehicle appeared intact and definitely carried some sort of artillery piece. The men continued to drive along the backside of the ridge, remaining out of sight in order to get to a closer vantage point, and then patrolled ahead on foot to peer over the edge. This overview provided a side profile of the vehicle, a quarter of a mile distant, and the team could now tell that it was a flatbed truck—destroyed by a bomb—with a massive, cannonlike anti-aircraft gun mounted on the back that had remained intact.

"One last picture for the BDA," said Dan. "Team photo?"

They drove down to the valley floor and walked through the charred debris littering the sand toward the flatbed, crowding in close to the gun. Bari Gul and his guerrillas looked on until JD waved them over to get in the second photo. The only one not joining them was Ken, who refused to leave the truck.

Returning to their vehicles, the men headed back up the ridgeline to their observation post, where JD set up a defensive perimeter with the weapons sergeants and Bari Gul's men. To the west, the setting sun turned the horizon red, while the eastern sky was an encroaching pool of inky blackness.

While Mike, Brent, and Ronnie fortified the team's perimeter with claymore mines, Alex caught Amerine's attention and said,

"Pilots spotted six trucks heading north from Kandahar." He indicated the position on the map. "Open road, no bottlenecks anywhere.
Looks clean."

Alex waited as Amerine studied the map.

"Clear them hot," Amerine said in a low voice.

A minute passed, then Alex said, "Convoy destroyed. BDA is six
burning vehicles."

Amerine's stomach tightened. He wouldn't know if they had
hit an enemy convoy until word filtered through Karzai's network,
which would take at least half a day. Six trucks, eight to twelve men
in each: They may have just killed fifty to seventy men. What if he
was wrong? What if they were civilians? On his own map, Amerine
illuminated the approximate location of the destroyed vehicles with a
small flashlight, and used a pencil to mark the spot with an X.

Like the rest of ODA 574, he had been too busy to notice the me-
teors streaking across the sky. November 18 marked the beginning of
the greatest show the Leonid meteor shower had put on in thirty-five
years, and now there were dozens blazing across the sky simultaneously. As the night wore on, the men on guard duty were mesmerized
by the spectacle, forgetting for a time that they were deep in Afghanistan, defending a town against a force of thousands and attempting
to defend an entire province with a handful of guerrillas and a few
reconnaissance aircraft.

Overnight, Hamid Karzai's credibility in the Pashtun tribal belt was
established. Reports came in of villages throughout the south taking
down the white flag of the Taliban and replacing it with the black, red,
and green vertically striped Afghan flag, now recognized as Karzai's
battle flag. The stories were spreading, too: tall tales that put Karzai in
the middle of the action, defending Tarin Kowt from annihilation.

A local tribal leader claimed that Karzai had beaten back the Taliban with a thousands-strong Pashtun militia. In Pakistan, Ahmed
Karzai told reporters that his brother's eight hundred loyal soldiers
were engaged in heavy fighting with the Taliban along a main road

to Kandahar.[1] Most villages in the south were without modern communications equipment, and Afghans often relied disproportionately on such rumors. The Taliban estimated Karzai's troop strength by his support in the tribal belt and his ability to rebuff their own fighters; according to deserters, after the battle at Tarin Kowt, the Taliban believed that Karzai was as mighty as any of the Northern Alliance generals.[2]

The morning after the meteor shower, the team returned to Tarin Kowt and moved into their new compound, where they immediately noticed that some of the guards had shaved their beards off in defiance of the Taliban. Amerine joined Karzai in his meeting room, had tea, and then pulled out his survival map.

"Last night we hit a convoy of six trucks in this area here," Amerine said.

Karzai stared silently at the X on the map.

"Have you heard anything from your people about it?" asked Amerine.

"Nothing yet," said Karzai.

"Would you hear if there was a problem?"

"I believe yes."

"Good," said Amerine, feeling slightly relieved. "Please let me know whatever you learn. In the meantime, we need men as quickly as you can get them to man all the checkpoints around Tarin Kowt in these locations," he said, pointing them out on the hand-drawn map that Karzai kept. "I have recon planes flying operations twenty-four hours a day to spot for enemy convoys, but a single miss could be disastrous."

"How many convoys have you hit?"

"Only that one so far. Now that I'm back in town, I'll be talking to you before we engage anything. I will run the air operations from our compound across the street."

Just as Karzai began to update Amerine on new pledges of support, the Afghan's satellite phone rang. It was the Northern Alliance's defense minister, with whom he spoke for two minutes before ending the call.

"That was Mohammed Fahim," Karzai said to Amerine. "He

called on behalf of the Northern Alliance to congratulate me on our victory."

/

Two days after the Battle of Tarin Kowt, James Dobbins[3] was en route to Kabul from Uzbekistan. He was flying in a private jet with representatives from the CIA, the Department of Defense, and the Joint Chiefs of Staff, and a small contingent of Afghans, including Dr. Abdullah,* a protégé of the Northern Alliance's recently assassinated leader, Ahmad Shah Massoud.

This flight to Kabul—six days after the capital city was liberated by the Northern Alliance—represented the first U.S. diplomatic mission to Afghanistan in more than twelve years, as well as Dobbins's first face-to-face meeting with representatives of the Northern Alliance. He was hoping to make strides toward the three goals he'd identified two weeks earlier as being paramount to the success of a post-Taliban government: the cooperation of the six neighboring countries; the identification of Pashtun leaders not tainted by ongoing Taliban affiliation; and the Northern Alliance's willingness to cooperate with those individuals in the successor Afghan government.

In the past week, Dobbins had made contact with envoys from all of Afghanistan's neighboring countries, as well as Turkey. The Turkish emissary was the first to suggest, on November 14, that Hamid Karzai might be a good candidate to head the new Afghan government; the day after, a representative from Pakistan also suggested that Karzai would be an acceptable choice. Before Dobbins had been named envoy, he'd never heard of Hamid Karzai, but now he was heartened that the name had come up twice—and without prompting.**

---

* Dr. Abdullah uses only one name, though he has been widely referred to as Abdullah Abdullah. He was the foreign minister of the Northern Alliance from 1998 forward.

** While the United States was known at this time to be backing Hamid Karzai's anti-Taliban rebellion militarily, it was also backing various Northern Alliance generals in their rebellion. Thus Dobbins considered these genuine votes of confidence for Karzai.

The pilot of the jet invited Dr. Abdullah and Dobbins to join him on the flight deck for a view of Afghanistan's majestic Hindu Kush mountain range. Away from the other passengers, the two spoke privately for nearly two hours, the doctor giving Dobbins a crash course in Northern Alliance politics, personalities, and the challenges he would face. Abdullah also surprised Dobbins when he suggested that Afghanistan's next leader should be a Pashtun from outside the Northern Alliance but *not* the aging King Zahir Shah.

"We need more than a figurehead," said Abdullah. "We need someone who will be able to deal with the terrible challenges Afghanistan now faces."

"Do you have anyone in mind?" asked Dobbins.

Without hesitation, Abdullah replied, "Hamid Karzai."

It was more than forty-eight hours since the battle, and the Taliban still had not retaliated against Tarin Kowt. Amerine had authorized the bombing of one more convoy of six trucks, but these small, probing efforts appeared to be the extent of Taliban intrusions into Uruzgan Province.

ODA 574 used this time to receive another weapons drop, to set up an early warning system of security checkpoints on all routes coming into the town, and to "nest," a process ingrained from basic training. Assign a soldier a tent, a bunk, or a three-by-seven-foot section of dirt in a mud-walled compound in Afghanistan, and he or she will make it a home. The men had turned their central courtyard into an open-air living/dining room, using boxes of MREs, ammo, and other supplies as furniture. Each evening, a young Afghan man prepared a stew of potatoes, onions, goat or mutton, and a cube of the animal's fat, boiled in a cauldron over an open fire, and served it to the Americans with rice and flat bread. The team had seen locals foraging through the garbage for their half-eaten MRE packages, and they understood the significance of these simple but hearty meals.

Frequently, the men converged in the courtyard, sipping away Ken's stores of coffee. On occasion, Karzai would join them, as he did on the morning of the 19th when he asked Amerine: "What is next? What of Kandahar?"

"What of vehicles and men?" Amerine said. "And translators?"

Before they could discuss the topic, Karzai's phone rang, and he stepped away from the team to answer. "I'm sorry," he said to Amerine when he returned. "May we discuss this later?"

"What of Kandahar?" said Dan after Karzai had left. "Hamid doesn't look tough, but he's got the spirit. You watch, he's gonna be running this joint before he's finished."

After an hour, Amerine decided to follow up with Karzai, who was, as usual, in a large circle of Afghans, sipping tea.

"Jason," he said, as Amerine entered the room. "Come, sit. I was just going to send for you. I would like you to meet this gentleman." Karzai gestured to a darkly tanned and deeply wrinkled man of perhaps fifty sitting beside him. "He walked here from his village in Kandahar Province—a two-day walk—after learning of our victory. He came to meet you."

"Me?" said Amerine.

"Well, word has traveled, and he came to meet the U.S. military commander here in the south."

"I'm honored."

Karzai said a few words to the man, who nodded fervently with a wide smile, which contradicted eyes that looked as though they were about to brim with tears.

"This man would like you to know that seven of his children were killed in their home by an American bomb three weeks ago."* Karzai translated while the man stared into Amerine's eyes. "There was a Taliban command post nearby, but it had been abandoned."

"I'm sorry," Amerine said. "I'm very, very sorry."

---

* Though Americans were not on the ground in the south at the time, the air campaign had been in full swing, hitting Taliban targets based on satellite imagery and air reconnaissance throughout Afghanistan.

"He does not want you to be sorry," said Karzai. "He says that he would not mind losing the rest of his children, provided you liberate Afghanistan."

Amerine found it difficult to maintain eye contact with the man. He wasn't one to hand out promises, but he was positive that the Taliban government would be defeated. "Please tell him that his children did not die in vain. We will remove the Taliban from power."

The man stood, and with him, Amerine and Karzai. After saying a few words in Pashto, he bowed his head and left the room.

"What will he do now?" asked Amerine.

"He is returning home."

"Can you offer him a ride? Somebody driving that direction?"

"I did," said Karzai. "He said he preferred to walk. I believe he is fearful that a vehicle might be attacked. Or bombed."

Seating himself again, Amerine broached the topic he had come to discuss. "You asked about Kandahar earlier."

"Getting fighters is not going to be a problem," said Karzai. "The difficulty will be feeding them. We cannot maintain a large garrison here. I have to keep the fighters dispersed until the right time, so they can be fed by their own villages."

"Having large numbers of tribal fighters from outside Tarin Kowt would probably wear out our welcome pretty fast."

"Would you rather move on Kandahar with a force of a thousand undisciplined men or several hundred of our best fighters?" asked Karzai.

"We need discipline to avoid alienating your supporters," Amerine said. "But a few hundred men will not be able to take Kandahar."

"I believe Kandahar will be surrendered to us," said Karzai. "We just need to get our army to the outskirts of the city so we can talk to the Taliban leadership face-to-face."

Amerine's gut told him the quickest move was the best move. This was the time to make a run for Kandahar—before the Taliban realized how disorganized Karzai's forces really were and could retaliate.

"How quickly can you get your men assembled?" he asked.

"I will try to get them here so we can leave by November 28, or sooner."

In the meantime, U.S. planes would continue to monitor and protect friendly villages and bomb enemy convoys. Karzai and Amerine agreed that the Taliban would wise up and begin to travel in smaller groups. They would be better able to blend in with the populace, but these smaller forces would also be easier to defeat on the way to Kandahar.

Over the next nine days, Karzai would collaborate with local chiefs and cherry-pick the best fighters (such as Bari Gul and his nineteen men) until he had three hundred good men. Karzai also needed to purchase vehicles, something that wouldn't be difficult with CIA cash. Once these guerrillas were organized, ODA 574 would mold them into some semblance of a military battalion that would then move toward Kandahar in a convoy.

The team had realistic expectations. This would not be organized, mechanized-maneuver warfare—they would have no armored vehicles, not even Humvees; just station wagons, minivans, and Toyota trucks. The mob of guerrillas they would be attempting to harness would most likely behave more like a herd of wild horses, with the Green Berets just trying to hang on. But with air cover and a little luck, they would be able to ride hard, shrouded in the dust storm of Karzai's perceived power.

What seemed a reckless move was perhaps the safest way to victory. Who would think anyone was crazy enough to march on the thousands of Taliban waiting in Kandahar with just three hundred men?

CHAPTER EIGHT

★

Madness

There's a great deal of talk about loyalty from the bottom to the top. Loyalty from the top down is even more necessary and is much less prevalent. One of the most frequently noted characteristics of great men who have remained great is loyalty to their subordinates.

—General George S. Patton Jr.

The truck carrying Mike, Brent, Bari Gul, and a couple of his men was parked in a cloud of hashish smoke wafting from a security checkpoint seven miles outside Tarin Kowt. It was late morning on November 20.

While some of their teammates were content to hole up in the compound, Mike and Brent couldn't sit still. The two weapons sergeants were obsessed with ODA 574's security—nobody placed much confidence in the local forces that the team had positioned in concentric layers of security, from their compound to miles outside town. With Alex, Dan, and Wes monitoring the reconnaissance aircrafts' nonstop "pinging" of the countryside, a large force wasn't likely to sneak up on them. Still, Mike and Brent were eager to do something other than sit on their rears and drink coffee.

At this checkpoint, close to Tarin Kowt Pass, they discovered a single Afghan sitting on an old Soviet ammo crate, so stoned on hashish that he didn't seem to notice them until they were getting out of their trucks. Out of the Afghan's reach, a few AK-47s and a couple of RPG launchers were leaning against the checkpoint barricade.

Through their translator, Mike and Brent learned from the man that the other guards had gone into town for some food. Bari Gul stood back and observed, displaying his dissatisfaction with a grimace as Mike questioned the Afghan. "What if the Taliban come?" he asked, pointing toward the road. "How will you warn the town?"

The Afghan smiled, walked over to his AK-47, and fired a burst of rounds into the air.

"Gotcha," said Mike.

"We gotta get these guys radios," Brent said.

"And get them to lay off the weed," said Mike.

Back in the compound, Mag and Charlie had just finished the CIA's first interrogation of the mission: a young Taliban who had deserted outside Kandahar. Charlie had given Mag, who was a fairly new intelligence sergeant, the job of making the deserter feel at ease—smiling a lot, offering water—while the spook asked questions about enemy movements and the locations of key al-Qaeda and Taliban leaders.

Now, in the warmth of the afternoon, Mag noticed he was beginning to smell like "yeti." Grabbing a bucket of water, he stripped down to his boxers in the sunniest corner of the courtyard. As he soaped up, the man he'd helped interrogate walked over to the other side of the bucket and began to take his clothes off.

"Whoa, hold on there," said Mag. "Interrogation's over." The Afghan continued to strip. "Only one bucket of water here, amigo," Mag said.

Now naked, the man sat down cross-legged on the concrete, reached into the water with a cup, and started bathing, grinning up at Mag as if he were an older brother.

"Looks like you've got yourself a little buddy," Ronnie hollered from his seat on a box of water bottles in the living room. "Maybe he'll scrub your back, big fella."

Mag casually waved his middle finger in Ronnie's direction.

Amerine was also in the courtyard, writing in his journal and enjoying this camaraderie between his men before he had to return to Karzai's side. He glanced up when Dan emerged from the command post carrying his laptop, which he handed to Amerine.

A message had just arrived from Task Force Dagger. Amerine read it, then slowly wrote one word in his journal: "Madness." He looked at the Green Berets around him: men who had saved a town; men who had done everything right by their country and by their mission; men who, by doctrine and by damn, did not need to be babysat. He could not recall a single instance in the history of Special Forces when a *battalion headquarters* had joined an ODA on the field of battle. Now Colonel Mulholland was doing just that, sending a fifteen-man battalion headquarters staff, called a C-team—which normally commanded three company B-teams who themselves oversaw six A-teams each—to co-locate with ODA 574.

Fifteen headquarters guys to oversee a team of eleven? thought Amerine. He envisioned senior officers tripping over each other, fighting for a way into the war, and shook his head in disgust. Madness.

The two pickup trucks Amerine had in his possession were barely enough to move his team, Karzai, and the CIA—if they ditched all their equipment. Bringing in the C-team meant they would all have to stay and fight and die if the Taliban was able to overrun Tarin Kowt's pitiful defenses.

He hoped Task Force Dagger would pay close attention to his return message:

> Acknowledge intent to infiltrate 15-man battalion HQ SOCCE [Special Operations Command and Control Element]. Request delay of infiltration for the following reasons: 1) ODA does not possess sufficient vehicles to transport ODA/CIA and additional PAX [passengers] from SOCCE. 2) Tarin Kowt defense is precarious. As per previous SITREPs, Karzai's usable forces number fewer than 100 and counterattack is likely. In the event of retreat, we would not be able to transport all personnel. 3) ODA 574 is doctrinally capable of conducting operations without additional personnel at this time. 4) Karzai does not want any more Americans on the ground because it might jeopardize his credibility among the tribal leaders whom he is negotiating with. ODA 574 requests delay until additional vehicles are acquired and defenses better established and Karzai's credibility is further established.[1]

Mag was looking over Dan's shoulder when the response from Task Force Dagger came in a few minutes later: ". . . SOCCE will infiltrate as planned."

"The captain is taking care of this situation just fine," said Mag. "We don't need the brass in here—they're just going to get in the way."

The men of ODA 574 were unaware that Colonel Mulholland had been pressured by his superiors to get higher-ranked officers on the ground in Afghanistan. On October 23, only three days into the ground campaign, General Franks had received a phone call from Secretary of Defense Rumsfeld.

"Are you sure those Special Forces teams have senior-enough officers in command?" Rumsfeld had asked him. "It seems to me the Northern Alliance generals won't really listen to young captains and majors."

"Mr. Secretary," said Franks, "in a few weeks the warlords will think of those captains and majors as their sons. Our youngsters are very good at what they do."

"You are the commander," Rumsfeld said. "But keep an eye on it." [2]

General Franks had immediately leaned on Colonel Mulholland, telling him to infiltrate higher-ranked officers into the ODAs' positions with the most important leaders of the Northern Alliance, or Franks would bring in generals from the conventional Army.[*]

Mulholland knew it would be a disaster if conventional Army generals started getting in the way of his A-teams, so he appeased

---

[*] Placing higher-ranked officers on the ground with the important leaders of the Northern Alliance and Karzai was at best symbolic, a political ploy. There was not a single report of an anti-Taliban leader complaining about either the performance or rank of the captains assigned to work with them, nor about the NCOs on the ODAs. For example, Northern Alliance General Dostum raved about the ODA assigned to him, telling *National Geographic Adventure* reporter Robert Young Pelton, "I asked for a few Americans. They brought with them the courage of a whole Army."

Franks by sending in 5th Group's three battalion commanders, with one significant caveat. Though called Special Operations Command and Control Elements, these SOCCE headquarters elements would act primarily as liaisons and military advisers to the guerrilla leaders, while Mulholland, still in Uzbekistan, would retain ultimate control over the A-teams.

Mulholland did grant the SOCCEs tactical control (TACON) over the ODAs, which meant that the SOCCE lieutenant colonels could adjust the physical locations of teams to prevent "battle space" issues, such as two teams ending up in the same valley or attacking the same target. They did not, however, have the authority to intervene in the teams' missions. Thus the ODAs would continue to operate semi-independently. Regardless, placing a battalion headquarters element with an A-team upset a time-honored Special Forces doctrine and went against its very purpose. ODAs are composed of experienced, mature operators sanctioned to run campaigns far from the flagpole, with minimal bureaucracy injected only when absolutely necessary.

When Amerine learned of this novel command structure an hour after his "request for delay" had been denied, he couldn't decide whether it was genius or lunacy. At the very least, the presence of a lieutenant colonel who outranked him but had no operational control over his team would be very awkward.

Dan carried his laptop back over to Amerine, who was sitting on a crate across from JD, musing over this turn of events and dreading the possibility that it would be Lieutenant Colonel Queeg joining them.

"There's more," Dan said. "We're getting Second Battalion's HQ—Lieutenant Colonel Fox."

At least it's not Queeg, thought Amerine.

"Fox will assume the role as Hamid's senior military adviser," Dan said. "Looks like you can take off one of the hats you've been wearing. They want you to focus on organizing the guerrillas and doing the fighting. No offense, sir, but no more sipping tea with the tribal leaders. It's back to instant coffee and dirty water with the rest of us."

Amerine laughed, but he also felt a pang of sadness. In the past month, he and Karzai had become friends. They trusted each other.

Together they had risked their lives and the lives of their men and, thus far, they had succeeded. Amerine would continue to come to Karzai for clearance on air strikes and to discuss ongoing guerrilla operations, allowing him to maintain the momentum of the mission, which was paramount not only for Karzai but also for the war. And he had always known that additional A-teams and a B-team would arrive after Tarin Kowt fell—yet this still felt like a premature end to their partnership.

/

Amerine sat down on the floor of Karzai's modest receiving room and, borrowing one of Karzai's favorite lines, said, "I have news."

He briefed him on the new command structure and told him a little about Lieutenant Colonel Fox, who would take over as Karzai's military adviser.

"What does this mean, Jason?" asked Karzai. "Are you leaving? Is there a problem?"

"No, I'm not leaving, and this is a very good thing," said Amerine, keeping his reservations to himself. "Task Force Dagger is increasing its support to our campaign in the south. It means we'll get all the resources we need to end the Taliban."

"What will your role be?"

"I will focus on my team and your guerrilla fighters, but I'll consult with you regularly on all air strikes and guerrilla operations. We will maintain this momentum."

Karzai nodded. "I also have news."

Karzai's spies had told him that Mullah Biradar, the Taliban military chief overseeing operations in five of Afghanistan's southern provinces, including Uruzgan, Herat, and Kandahar, had dispatched assassins from Kandahar to kill Karzai and his U.S. supporters. He had offered a bounty of 5 million Pakistani rupees (around $55,000) for any American, double for Karzai.

"Good to know," said Amerine.

"There is also talk in Kandahar of another large force of Taliban preparing to come and retake Tarin Kowt."

Amerine raised his eyebrows. "How large?"

"Ten thousand men," said Karzai with a smile, doubting the intelligence himself.

"I think by now the Taliban have learned they cannot roam the countryside in large convoys. Do your spies report any movement? I haven't heard anything from our reconnaissance reports."

"It is all talk right now."

"We'll increase reconnaissance," said Amerine. "Just in case."

From Karzai's command post Amerine went to the CIA's house to inform Casper of Lieutenant Colonel Fox's arrival.

"I don't know how we're supposed to move everybody," Amerine said. "We don't even have enough vehicles for our two groups; add another fifteen men and we're in trouble if we need to get out of here in a hurry."

Casper shook his head. "Do your superiors realize the situation?"

"I conveyed it to Task Force Dagger. Nothing we can do about it. They're coming in, so we'd better find a place for them to sleep."

Amerine stepped toward the door, then turned back around. "Hamid tell you the latest?"

"The assassins?"

"Yes."

"Five million rupees," Casper said, pausing for a long beat. "Not bad."

/

ODA 574's team room looked like a rudimentary Internet café, with Alex, Dan, and Wes all busy working the war on their laptops. The men's faces glowed blue in the darkness.

Amerine sat down beside Alex. "Anything going on?" he asked.

"Actually, yes. F-18s spotted a very large camp north of Kandahar," said Alex, indicating an icon on the digital map glowing from his computer.

"I wonder if that could be related to the ten thousand Taliban that Hamid just informed me are rumored to be coming our way to retake Tarin Kowt."

Uncertain whether the captain was serious, Alex cocked his head sideways and told Amerine that a JSTAR* had also reconned the camp and reported what the pilots thought was a helicopter.

"A helicopter?" said Amerine.

"Well, take it with a grain of salt. Even JSTARs aren't really great in this kind of terrain with single objects like that."

"Any way of knowing if it was one of ours?"

"I checked as best I could, and nobody knows of any operations going on in the area."

Amerine stared at the screen. "If a helicopter landed there, then something weird is going on. See if you can get a B-52 to those coordinates and have it stand by in the area. I'll go talk to Hamid."

A concentration of troops like that didn't come around often; it could be a very stupid move by a Taliban commander. By now the Taliban should have learned that large gatherings of men or vehicles made excellent targets for American bombs. Or it could be noncombatants. Refugees, perhaps, fleeing Kandahar. But with a helicopter? *If* it was a helicopter. There had been zero reports of Taliban movements via air, and if one *was* parked somewhere, Amerine felt that it would have been completely camouflaged.

Walking back across the street, Amerine reentered Karzai's command post and took his seat beside Karzai. "We spotted a large camp," Amerine said, referring to his map, "approximately ten miles north of Kandahar, near this mountain range. The weird thing is that a helicopter was spotted there by one of my recon aircraft. It wasn't a coalition helicopter. And I'm pretty sure we knocked out all of the Taliban air force early in the campaign. Always a chance, though."

"That is strange," said Karzai. "I will send men to find out what is there." He issued a series of commands to a messenger sitting near the door, who jumped up and left the room.

It was nearing dusk when Karzai summoned Amerine back to his compound. "I sent two men with a satellite phone and they spotted nothing."

---

* The Air Force's $250 million Joint Surveillance Target Attack Radar System, integrated into the shell of a Boeing 707.

"The camp is definitely there," said Amerine. "Are your men still in the area?"

"Yes."

"Have them look around some more."

Alex had located a B-52 that had been on the way to bomb a cave complex in the north—not an urgent mission—and diverted it to a holding pattern over the camp, where the plane had been circling for over two hours. Back with Alex, Amerine told the airman, "Release that B-52. Karzai's people couldn't find the area, and we need better confirmation."

Alex nodded, and the bomber continued on its previous mission.

Early the following day, Karzai showed up at ODA 574's compound. He seemed concerned.

"I received word from my men north of Kandahar," he told Amerine. "They did not reach me until just now."

"Yes?" said Amerine.

"They found the camp. They reported no helicopter, just refugees—mostly families from Kandahar, running from the bombing and anticipated fighting in the city. They have camped near a group of Bedouin from the Kuchi tribe."

"We did not engage the target," said Amerine, goose bumps rising on his arms. Something hadn't felt right about the encampment; had they struck it the night before, many civilians would have been killed.

"That is good news," said Karzai, visibly relieved. "Thank you."

Later that morning, Dan received another e-mail from Task Force Dagger: "Acknowledge your concerns. SOCCE delayed temporarily. Pax are reduced to three: Commander, plus two. Stand by for infil date."

"Hmmm," said Amerine. "I wonder why the change of heart?"

Unbeknownst to Amerine, Casper had called his CIA superiors, who contacted Task Force Dagger and told them that there were not enough vehicles in Tarin Kowt to transport the men already on the ground. By sending a headquarters staff, they were putting Americans at unnecessary risk unless they could bring along their own vehicles.

The message apparently had more bite when it came from the upper echelons of the CIA. The SOCCE had been scaled back from fifteen men to three, with Fox's arrival now scheduled for November 26. The remainder of the SOCCE had to procure vehicles and coordinate an airlift, which would take more time.

Once Amerine had left to update Karzai, Dan speculated that Amerine had somehow manipulated Casper into blocking the headquarters infiltration. "Captain knows how to work it," he told Mike.

/

The next day, November 22, was Thanksgiving, and the teams in the field had been promised a turkey dinner with all the trimmings—code-named Operation Turkey Drop. Nobody was more excited than Dan Petithory.

Thanksgiving was one of his favorite holidays, and he hated having to miss his mom's spread on Turkey Day—the stuffing, gravy, buttery mashed potatoes. When the men opened up their airdrop and found that it contained a couple of magazines, some bags of Starbursts, a few cans of yams, and a frozen-solid ham, Dan thought it was a joke. Then reality sank in: Nothing else was coming.

"This is bullshit," he muttered, and stomped away from the cooking area of the courtyard. He returned with his laptop.

"Sir," he said to Amerine, "permission to bitch to Task Force Dagger for this pathetic holiday meal?"

"Sure, give them what for."

They went inside the command post, where Amerine watched Dan type a SITREP titled "You've Got to Be Kidding Me." The first line read: "So, what are you eating for dinner tonight?"* Amerine laughed.

"You trust me?" asked Dan.

---

* ODA 574 received an apology from Task Force Dagger the following day. They had supplied turkeys to the teams consolidating in the north, but had run out before the airdrop to the one team operating behind enemy lines in the south.

"I trust you," Amerine said.

"Then you better walk away. This might get ugly."

/

On Sunday morning, November 25, Dan's mother slid out of bed, careful not to wake her husband, Lou. Barbara Petithory removed the cotton gloves she'd worn over a thick coating of moisturizer for the night—a prescribed treatment for the stress-related psoriasis that had sprung up after 9/11. From the moment she'd received a call from Danny in Kazakhstan, she'd known he was going to war.

While coffee brewed, she stepped onto the front porch of their Cape Cod–style home in Cheshire, Massachusetts, to check the thermometer and adjust the American flag draped from its angled staff near the front door. Tidying up the flag each day was like fixing Danny's collar on his way out the door to school—she could not pass a flag without thinking of him.

Then she sat down at the kitchen table with a cup of coffee and wrote a letter to her son, as always adding the outside temperature and time—54 degrees/8:09 A.M.—in the upper corner.

My Dear Son,

Everyone is sleeping here, Dad, Nicole, and I guess even the cat. Dad, Nic, and I had a small Thanksgiving dinner Thursday. Mike came down for sandwiches and pie. We watched Charlie Brown's Christmas on video. Again! All of our prayers and thoughts were on you, Dan. Did you, I hope, have some kind of Thanksgiving dinner?

We love you so very much, Dan, and are really proud of you, please be careful. We know you have been trained well and have good common sense. I guess it's like driving a car, you gotta watch out for the other guy!

I'll write again soon. XXXXX OOOOO
Love, Ma!

The same day, at Mazar-e-Sharif, three hundred miles north of Tarin Kowt, Taliban and al-Qaeda prisoners had seized control of the Qala-i-Jangi prison.[3] The men of ODA 574 didn't yet know it, but the headquarters staff of their battalion commander, Lieutenant Colonel Queeg, had responded to the uprising and were in combat with the prisoners, who had overpowered the guards and accessed a huge cache of weapons.

Casper and his men monitored the situation, receiving word of one of the first American casualties in the War on Terror: CIA case officer Mike Spann had been killed. It was a somber evening for the Americans sequestered in Tarin Kowt, and an especially dark night for the spooks.

Five Special Forces soldiers had been wounded during the uprising, Dan heard over the radio a short time later, but none were from ODAs. They were all staff personnel. "So, what happened?" Amerine asked him. "Could you figure out how all these staff guys got hurt?"

"I couldn't tell," said Dan, "but I got some other weird news for you. Sir, the Marines are here."

"What?!"

"Remember the airfield the Rangers raided last month?"

"Rhino?"

"Yeah. The United States Marine Corps just seized it with seven hundred men in order to establish a base there.* They want to know what our intentions are for Kandahar and how they can be integrated into our plan."

"What the fuck?" said Amerine. With each new development, another military convention was tossed out the window.

"I'm sure it took a while to plan," Dan said. "Task Force Dagger should have told us this was coming."

---

* The Marines flew almost four hundred miles overland from ships in the northern Arabian Sea to land at what they dubbed Camp Rhino, an event they later touted to the media as historic because it was the longest recorded amphibious "assault" landing in naval history. The lone airstrip was deserted at the time of the "assault."

"If they even knew about it. This kind of cowboy shit can get someone killed: two friendly armies running around without talking to each other."

"Another thing . . . there is an Afghan named Sherzai coming northeast from Pakistan with several hundred Pashtun fighters accompanied by an ODA. They seem to be following the Marines north toward Kandahar."

"I gotta see this on the map," said Amerine.

The two men stood over the captain's map plotting locations, then Amerine studied it in silence. He noted that Karzai and all of the towns, villages, and districts he was courting to join him were north of Kandahar.

Camp Rhino was fifty miles south of Kandahar, but as far as Amerine was concerned, that was too close. He wondered if the massing American Marines at the doorstep of the Taliban's spiritual capital would rally the Pashtun to fight off the invaders. The one thing Afghanistan's tribes seemed to hate more than each other was an invading army—the seven hundred Marines at Rhino could put Karzai's plan of driving to Kandahar and negotiating surrender at serious risk.

"I have to go talk to Hamid," said Amerine. "We could really be fucked if we don't rein these guys in."

He found Karzai seated on a wooden chair on the sunny side of his courtyard, satellite phone to his ear. Once he was off the phone, Amerine informed him of the situation.

"The Marines? Outside Kandahar?" Karzai said.

They discussed the implications: Karzai and his guerrillas were achieving what all the Marines on the planet couldn't do—persuading moderate Pashtun to leave the Taliban and join his revolt. While ODA 574 was essential to Karzai's success, this foreign "army" of Marines could actually help Mullah Omar rally his remaining Taliban troops.

"What do you suggest?" asked Karzai.

"We weren't advised they were coming," said Amerine, "but they are requesting guidance. You can request that they stay in place well south of the city, while we continue to work things coming in from our position here in the north."

"Okay. Then please tell your commanders to have them stay in place. Let them know that the Pashtun are on the verge of collapsing the Taliban."

"What about Sherzai?"

"I will be in touch with him over the phone," said Karzai. "Gul Agha Sherzai was the governor of Kandahar Province before the Taliban. He should be helpful."

/

While the Marines were digging in at Camp Rhino, Major Chris Miller was in Uzbekistan trying to get his B-team, ODB 570—which included ODA 574's former chief warrant officer, Lloyd Allard, and medic, Cubby Wojciehowski—out of isolation at K2 and into the war.

Cubby had to laugh when he recalled Dan's parting words—that ODA 574's mission would be boring. ODA 574's "boring" would be a marked improvement over rotting away in Uzbekistan, where they had been for the past three weeks. To kill time, he'd learned to juggle with grenades.

ODB 570 had watched as the Army's 10th Mountain Division prepared to leave K2 to back up the Green Berets and help evacuate the wounded at Mazar-e-Sharif.

"Green Berets should be helping Green Berets!" Allard said to Miller. "Let's make ourselves a quick reaction force. Maybe that will get us in the war."

"Now that sounds like an A-team mission, soldier," Miller said, impersonating John Wayne. "We're a B-team. But it just might work."

He took the proposal to the Task Force Dagger command, and Mulholland bought the argument that if a Green Beret was in trouble, a Green Beret should go help him. The team began to practice quick reaction tactics and made sure they were ready to infiltrate on fifteen minutes' notice. This new sense of purpose was a little sunshine for ODB 570, whose men were part of K2's growing community of bored, sometimes disgruntled B-teams and their respective A-teams—men who watched their C-teams, their battalion staffs, infiltrate ahead of them to do *their* jobs.

As medic, Cubby refreshed the men on their medical skills, reviewing the basics of battlefield triage,* tourniquet placement, and amputations. He was grateful for the distraction, but in the back of his mind he dreaded the prospect of being called upon to save the lives of his friends.

⚔

Late on the afternoon of November 26, automatic weapons fire erupted on the street outside ODA 574's compound in Tarin Kowt, where the team was lounging around the "living room." Brent jumped up from his seat on an MRE box and grabbed his carbine, which was propped up against another crate.

Wearing his Harley-Davidson cap, JD was leaning against the wall, looking out at the street through the compound's entrance. He signaled "stop" with his hand and said, "They're celebrating something."

They learned later that the locals were celebrating the liberation of Kunduz, the last Taliban bastion in the north.

⚔

Around 2 A.M. on November 27, a Pave Low helicopter flew over the mountains north of Tarin Kowt. Inside, the commander of 5th Group's 2nd Battalion, forty-two-year-old Lieutenant Colonel Dave Fox, felt a hand tapping him on the shoulder—a member of the flight crew giving him the one-minute warning.

Fox gripped the webbing near the rear ramp and looked at his second-in-command, Major Don Bolduc, thirty-eight, who gave a quick nod. Across the hold, their young communications sergeant, Nelson Smith, was just getting up onto one knee when the helicopter touched down hard, knocking Smith flat as the air filled with swirling, chalky-tasting dust. "And that's what we call a controlled crash,"

---

* A system of sorting and assigning the wounded priority for medical treatment based on urgency and chance for survival.

said the crewman, nudging Fox toward the ramp. The three Green Berets turned on their NODs and walked off the helicopter to where a figure wrapped in a blanket stood in the rotor wash, beckoning to them.

The dust settled, slowly revealing three trucks and nine heavily armed Afghan guerrillas and American soldiers.

Amerine stepped forward. "Hey, Colonel," he said, shaking Fox's hand. "Welcome to Tarin Kowt."

"It's been a hell of a trip getting here,"[4] said Fox.

As they walked to the trucks, Fox told Amerine he realized his presence on the mission violated Special Forces doctrine. "When I was briefed about this," he said, "the first thing I said was, 'This is a B-team mission.'"

"What did Mulholland say about that?" said Amerine.

"I never even saw Mulholland. When we were at K2, he was here in Afghanistan, up north at Bagram. Which was where I thought I was going before we got diverted down here to join you and Karzai. You heard about what happened at Mazar-e-Sharif, right?"

"Bits and pieces."

"I heard that Lieutenant Colonel Queeg's battalion called in close air support," said Fox, "and a five-hundred-pound laser-guided bomb missed its mark and slammed into their command post, killing and wounding dozens of Northern Alliance fighters and seriously wounding five of Queeg's staff."

"Any ODAs involved?" Amerine asked.

"Not that I know of."

"So the headquarters called the bomb in on themselves?"

"Looks like it," confirmed Fox.

By 9 A.M., Amerine had briefed Fox and Bolduc on the events of the past two weeks, including insights into Karzai's character, his background, and his strengths and weaknesses—respectively, diplomacy and understanding of military affairs. He detailed the complicated but highly successful aerial reconnaissance system Alex had developed to protect the friendly villages and to scout their route to Kandahar. He told them about the untested and untrained guerrilla fighting force, as well as the team's plan for moving south, scheduled to begin the next day. Fox left the brief satisfied with the way ODA 574 was performing its job.

Now everybody was hanging out in the "living room," drinking coffee.

"Is everybody here, Sergeant?" Bolduc asked JD.

"We're up," said JD, confirming that all of ODA 574 was present. "Okay, Major Bolduc has a few announcements."

Nelson Smith winced inwardly while his superior spoke to the casual gathering in loud bursts, as though he were formally addressing a battalion: "The commander and I understand that our being here has deviated from doctrine. I'm here to tell you that this all came as much as a surprise to us as to you. Our main function is to militarily advise Hamid Karzai. What this means is that we are here to give you top cover. We are here to facilitate. We are here to advise and assist and relieve some of that burden from you so you can focus on small-unit tactics, organizing, advising, and assisting the anti-Taliban forces. We'll hold meetings to update the commander daily at 1630 while we're here in Tarin Kowt. Any questions?"

There were none.

After the meeting, Fox and Bolduc followed Amerine across the street into the courtyard of Karzai's compound, where Amerine nodded at the two guards, both holding AK-47s. Up on the roof, another guerrilla with an RPG leaning against his shoulder was scanning the street. On their way to Karzai's guest room, the three Americans wove around small circles of Afghans sitting on the ground and talking quietly.

Pausing outside the door, Amerine said to Fox, "I won't stay, sir. He's very personable, very intelligent, and speaks perfect English. He has his hand on the pulse of everything going on—he has extremely reliable intelligence. If I can make one suggestion?"

Fox nodded.

"Stay with the G-chief, just like in Robin Sage,"* said Amerine. "I can't emphasize enough how important that training was. Karzai appreciates being advised and won't think it overbearing. I've been joined at the hip with him since we got here."

"Thank you, Captain," said Fox.

The Americans entered the room, and all conversation in the large circle halted, the eyes of the tribesmen following Fox and Bolduc as Amerine led them to Karzai's usual spot near the western wall. Amerine made introductions and Karzai stood to shake hands. Two of the Afghans seated to Karzai's left moved over, creating an opening in the circle.

As Amerine left, he heard Karzai say, "Please sit. Tea?"

/

While Fox and Bolduc spent their first hours with Karzai and his tribal leaders, sixteen delegates, representing the four major Afghan tribes—Uzbek, Tajik, Hazara, and Pashtun—gathered at a luxury hotel outside Bonn, Germany.

This historic meeting of traditionally hostile groups had been convened by the United Nations to discuss the future of Afghanistan. They'd been brought together by their common hatred for the Taliban and a desire to replace the regime with what the U.N. called a "broadly based" government representing Afghanistan's diversity. The lofty goal of this consortium was to let the Afghan people decide their own democratic government—one that would satisfy all the ethnic factions, or at least keep them from fighting another civil war.

Those in attendance included representatives from the Northern Alliance, which at the time controlled most of Afghanistan, and

---

* Robin Sage is a training exercise conducted by the John F. Kennedy Special Warfare Center at Fort Bragg, North Carolina, for U.S. Army Special Forces candidates. It is the crux of eighteen months of training that soldiers must satisfactorily complete before being presented with their green berets, during which they fight a realistic unconventional war, complete with guerrillas and enemy regime troops.

the Rome Group, a delegation of exiles loyal to former king Zahir Shah, of which Karzai was part. Diplomats from Russia, the European Union, all six of Afghanistan's neighboring countries, and the United States, represented by James Dobbins, were not allowed in the meeting itself, but had flocked to the hotel in order to meet with the delegates and each other.

Following opening remarks from Germany's minister of foreign affairs, the U.N. special representative to Afghanistan, Lakhdar Brahimi, explained that each representative group present would have the opportunity to make a statement. But first they would hear from Hamid Karzai, who was in Tarin Kowt sitting beside Lieutenant Colonel Fox when the expected call came through.

"Excuse me," Karzai said to Fox as he answered the phone.

He spoke in Pashto, his words coming in clear over the speaker in Bonn: "We are one nation, one culture. We are united, not divided. We all believe in an Islam that is a religion of tolerance."

For nearly five minutes, Fox listened to Karzai's melodic voice as the tribal leaders present nodded repeatedly in affirmation.

"This meeting is the path toward salvation," Karzai concluded. "The interim authority you seek to organize there in Germany is a means of getting to a Loya Jirga."

Dobbins was in his suite at the hotel in Bonn. He had yet to speak with Karzai, but in his meetings with the regional players, Karzai was the only name that was consistently mentioned as someone capable of bringing the country together.

"Among the international representatives was a strong concensus in favor of Hamid Karzai," Dobbins would later recall in his memoir. "Virtually every foreign official with whom I had met in the past month, including the Pakistani, the Indian, the Russian, the Iranian, the Turkish, and European delegates had mentioned his name unprompted. The unanimity of international support for Karzai was largely [Northern Alliance representative] Dr. Abdullah's doing. He and Karzai had served together in an earlier coalition government in Kabul [closely following the Soviet occupation]. He knew Karzai as a moderate, personable, conciliatory figure of the sort who might be able to hold a fractious coalition together."

An endorsement for Karzai at Bonn from Iran's foreign minister—which staunchly opposed the United States' foreign policy—surprised Dobbins. More astounding had been the nod for Karzai from the Pakistani intelligence chief, whom Dobbins met in Pakistan two days after Karzai had secretly left J-Bad to infiltrate Afghanistan with ODA 574.

It seemed that everybody Dobbins spoke to respected Karzai, who as an émigré statesman had been lobbying on behalf of his country for years. While Dobbins recognized that Karzai could not have achieved his current military credibility in Afghanistan without the United States, he was coming to realize that the man's political and diplomatic reputation was purely self-made.

/

"Congratulations," Amerine said as he sat down later that afternoon with Karzai.

With Mike and Brent showing Bolduc, Fox, and Smith around Tarin Kowt, Amerine was the only American in the room. He appreciated how the circle of Afghans barely paused to acknowledge his presence; he had indeed become a fixture here.

"Lieutenant Colonel Fox told me you addressed your countrymen in Germany."

"Yes. I hope they could understand me." Karzai coughed. "I'm not feeling well."

"You need more sleep, Hamid," said Amerine.

"There is no time," said Karzai, nodding at a young man, who poured two cups of tea for them. Karzai lifted a cup to his nose, and inhaled the rising steam. Amerine sipped his. Neither of them spoke while they drank two more cups of tea, then Amerine said, "I'm going to brief Lieutenant Colonel Fox shortly about tomorrow's movement to Petawek and I need to confirm that the vehicles will be ready just after sunrise—ours assembled on this street and the rest at the edge of town."

"I will see to it," Karzai said, leaning forward when Amerine smoothed his creased and wrinkled survival map before them on the carpet.

One of several small villages spread along the foot of the mountains that bordered Kandahar and Uruzgan provinces, Petawek was fifty miles southwest of Tarin Kowt. It was a remote truck stop for traders, with a population of one thousand Pashtun. The drive to Petawek would take them over multiple mountain ranges, across deserts and high valleys, and through deep canyons—extremely rough and wild country that Karzai said the Soviets had learned to avoid after a few devastating ambushes.

Karzai had been negotiating with the tribal leaders of the districts, towns, and villages along their intended route; on Amerine's map these were represented by a swath of circles, like stepping-stones all the way to Petawek. If they could safely connect those dots—and Karzai had assured them a clear drive—they would reach Petawek within ten hours.

"Do you still feel the time is right to move?" Amerine asked.

"Yes. From what I know today, tomorrow is a good day."

"Then tomorrow it is," said Amerine, folding up the map.

"Oh, something funny," said Karzai. "One of your men, the one who calls me Mr. K . . ."

"Sergeant Magallanes? Mag?"

"Yes, Mag. He asked me earlier if I would sign Afghan money for him, as gifts for his children. He said, 'You're going down in history, Mr. K, and I'd like some proof that I was there for the ride.' Something like that."

The two men laughed. "So, does this mean you're an official candidate?" asked Amerine.

"There is still nothing *official* in Afghanistan," Karzai said, "but the invitation to speak today . . . hmmm." He changed the subject. "How many children *does* Mag have, Jason?"

"How many afghanis did he have you sign?"

"Forty!" said Karzai.

"Not *that* many." Amerine chuckled. "If you become the leader of Afghanistan, Hamid, what will we call you?"

"Let's not talk of such titles," Karzai said. He shivered and pulled his blanket up around his shoulders. "Today we are just friends."

"Stay warm, then, my friend," said Amerine, getting up to leave.

On his tour of Tarin Kowt, Lieutenant Colonel Fox had been introduced to Karzai's "fighters," some of whom were armed with ancient flintlock rifles and, in one case, a pitchfork. What he'd seen didn't even qualify as a militia. He envisioned the thousands of faithful Taliban prepared to defend Kandahar and thought, *Okay, I've got one ODA and this small force of Karzai's well-meaning friends up against hardcore Taliban—I'm not sure how I'm going to do this.*

Toward the end of his first day in Afghanistan, Fox returned from Karzai's compound and joined Amerine and JD, who were discussing the convoy they were set to lead toward Kandahar the following morning.

"I'm delaying things a day or two," Fox said. "Just talked it over with Hamid, and what I'm going to do is have him send an advance recon, three-man element to drive our route to Petawek twenty-four hours ahead of our main party to make sure it's clear—obstacles, mines, that kind of thing."

Amerine noticed JD raise his eyebrows. They were both thinking the same thing: *Fox has been on the ground for less than twenty-four hours and he's already making decisions without bothering to consult with us?*

"Sir, we need to get the guerrillas moving south," said Amerine. "Hamid has to mass them just in time to move, since the town can't support a large force. Delays like this can cause the whole machine to seize up and—"

"We aren't going south without more recon and a more solid plan," Fox said definitively.

Once Fox had left, JD said, "Guess he didn't like our plan."

"I guess not. He wants things tight in an environment that is all about controlled chaos. On the other hand, I might be too comfortable playing it loose with our guys."

JD smiled. "We made it this far by playing it loose."

That night an F-18 recon flight picked up seven vehicles heading north from Kandahar. It fit their definition of an enemy convoy, but when Alex plotted the location on the map, he saw that they were moving along a mountainous segment of the road. Amerine told Alex to hold off bombing and to continue monitoring the convoy, saying, "This one feels like it might be another bottleneck."

JD and Bolduc were in the room when Amerine made his decision. "Civilians are always at risk in war," Bolduc said, coming over to peer at the map. "You can't let that dictate your operations. You still have to be aggressive."

Not including the Battle of Tarin Kowt, Amerine had authorized the bombing of at least forty-seven vehicles over the previous nine days. He had refrained from bombing twelve vehicles (and one encampment of refugees) during the same period. Using conservative estimates—eight men per vehicle—they'd killed at least 376 enemy combatants.

"We've been bombing convoys every day since we got here and haven't killed any civilians yet," said Amerine. "I'm not going to start being a cowboy now."

After a moment of uncomfortable silence, Bolduc walked out of the room.

"Water off your back, sir," said JD. "If something doesn't feel right, that's the beauty of this command structure. Bolduc said it himself this morning—they are here to advise Hamid and provide top cover for us. Mulholland is leaving the fighting to us."

The convoy ultimately passed through the bottleneck but remained in tight formation, continuing across the desert as a unit. As it approached Uruzgan Province, Amerine cleared the pilot to engage. All seven vehicles were destroyed.

Shortly after noon three days later, a light rain was falling while the Americans loaded weapons and gear into four trucks parked in a row across the street from their compound, preparing to move to Petawek. The low cloud cover currently made aerial reconnaissance of their route almost impossible.

"Are we going to have any problem getting air?" Amerine asked Alex, who was setting up his radio in the back of their truck.

"Too early to tell," said Alex.

The fact that the advance recon Fox had insisted upon had driven through Uruzgan Province without incident two days before meant little for today. In order for the movement to be as simple as possible, Amerine had wanted to condense their forces into a single convoy that would have a small footprint and allow him tighter control of the guerrillas. Fox saw things differently, adjusting Amerine's plan so that the convoy would move in two separate units.

The first, smaller section, acting as forward security, would be led by an Afghan named Bashir—whom Bari Gul had vouched for—and three trucks full of his men, followed closely by Amerine's vehicle, carrying Mike, Alex, and Seylaab. Mag's truck, with Wes, Ken, and Victor, would trail five minutes behind Amerine with three more trucks of guerrillas.

Forty-five minutes behind Amerine, the main part of the convoy would be headed by Bari Gul and his three trucks of guerrillas, then JD's vehicle carrying Dan, Brent, and Ronnie, followed by the shuttle bus with Karzai—and Fox, Casper, and the rest of the spooks. Another twenty vehicles loaded with Afghans would bring up the rear.

ODA 574 had listened to Fox's revised plan the day before in concealed bemusement. The team had already experienced the undisciplined nature of the guerrillas and doubted they would adhere to the complicated parameters of the movement, but Fox was adamant. "Let's just roll with it," JD whispered to Amerine during the brief. "The guerrillas will dictate how it ends up."

Now, shortly after 2 P.M., Amerine's and Mag's vehicles were sloshing through muddy streets toward the southern edge of Tarin Kowt. In spite of the gloomy weather the roads were festooned with the national flag of Afghanistan; children carried them as they ran through puddles, keeping pace alongside the vehicles. Karzai's movement to Kandahar was no secret.

Just before the town gate, the old man who had refused to accept Karzai's name as credit for gas the week before stood in front of his pumps, lifting his fist in the air and cheering the convoy on. At the

ODA 574 at an impromptu farewell ceremony the day after 9/11/2001 at the paratrooper base in Kazakhstan. L to R: Amerine, Allard, JD, Mike, Bob (a temporary medic), Mag, and Brent. (*ODA 574 archives*)

JD, flanked by Victor (L) and Brent (R), presents a toast to the Kazakhs on behalf of ODA 574 later that evening. (*ODA 574 archives*)

Dan (R) shakes hands with a Kazakh lieutenant pre-9/11. (*ODA 574 archives*)

Colonel John Mulholland, commander, Fifth Special Forces Group (*Kelley family archives*)

Major Chris Miller, ODA 574's company commander who was sent to SOCCENT on September 17, with instructions from Mulholland to "Get Fifth Group into the fight." (*Miller family archives*)

Chief of plans at SOCCENT in 2001, Major Bob Kelley, who with the other "True Believers" pushed for unconventional warfare in Afghanistan from the first crisis action planning meetings. (*Kelley family archives*)

From Fort Campbell, Kentucky, the team deployed to this "isolation" facility at forward operating base "K2" in Uzbekistan. (*ODA 574 archives*)

The last photo of ODA 574, taken upon arrival at K2, before the team went to war. Top row: Victor, Mike, Dan, Wes, JD, Ken. Front row, kneeling: Ronnie, Brent, Amerine, Mag. (*ODA 574 archives*)

J-Bad, Pakistan: the aircraft hangar where the AFSOC operations center was located. The larger building to the left was the Pakistani general's headquarters. The building in the center background was the "safe house" where ODA 574 planned the bulk of the insurgency with Karzai. (*USAF/TSgt. Scott Reed*)

Amerine with Lieutenant Colonel Steve Hadley at J-Bad, a few days into the planning. (*Hadley family archives*)

Hamid Karzai, a former Afghan statesman, still relatively unknown on the international stage, during the planning of his insurgency, early November. (*ODA 574 archives*)

During the infiltration, each team member was given a "Blood Chit" similar to this, which read in seven local languages: "I am an American and do not speak your language. I will not harm you! I bear no malice towards your people. My friend, please provide me food, water, shelter, and necessary medical attention. Also please provide safe passage to the nearest friendly forces of any country supporting the Americans and their allies. You will be rewarded for assisting me when you present this number to American authorities."

The men of ODA 574 on November 15, the day after the infiltration at Haji Badhur's Cove, with their CIA counterparts, including Casper, Mr. Big, Charlie, and Zepeda (faces blacked out). (*ODA 574 archives*)

ODA 574 with Bari Gul's guerrilla fighters during the battle damage assessment on November 18. Bari Gul is to the left of Amerine (center back row); Seylaab is to the right of Amerine.

The "living room" at the team compound in Tarin Kowt, late November. (*ODA 574 archives*)

Ronnie with one of the guerrillas at the team compound at Tarin Kowt. (*ODA 574 archives*)

Dan, sighting his carbine on a knoll in Tarin Kowt just prior to departing for Petawek. (*ODA 574 archives*)

Mag with guerrillas in Tarin Kowt. (*ODA 574 archives*)

Mike with Bari Gul (to Mike's right) and his men while formulating the team's evasion plan at Tarin Kowt.

Alex and Amerine leaving Tarin Kowt with the convoy on November 30. (*ODA 574 archives*)

The children of Petawek. (*ODA 574 archives*)

Nelson Smith with local at Petawek.
(*ODA 574 archives*)

Karzai in his command post at Petawek with Fox (barely visible), Bolduc, and Amerine—reviewing their route to Damana and Shawali Kowt on December 2. (*Rambo 85 archives*)

ODA 574 with Karzai and headquarters staff on the morning of December 3 before departing Petawek. L to R front: Alex, Bolduc, Mike, Mag, Dan. L to R, standing: Ronnie, Wes, Ken, Victor, Karzai, Brent, Fox, Smith, Amerine, JD. (*Gilbert "Mag" Magallanes*)

The convoy leaving Petawek, with the mountains of Uruzgan behind them and Mag at his machine gun in back of the center truck, heads toward Kandahar Province. (*ODA 574 archives*)

Shawali Kowt medical clinic—which became the casualty collection point for the wounded on December 5—as seen while looking northwest from atop the Alamo. (*ODA 574 archives*)

The bridge over the Arghandab River as seen looking southwest from the Alamo over the rooftops of Shawali Kowt. (*ODA 574 archives*)

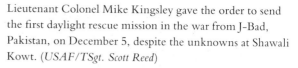

Lieutenant Colonel Mike Kingsley gave the order to send the first daylight rescue mission in the war from J-Bad, Pakistan, on December 5, despite the unknowns at Shawali Kowt. (*USAF/TSgt. Scott Reed*)

Captain Paul Alexander, copilot on Knife 04. (*AFSOC archives*)

Dual-hatted Lieutenant Colonel Hadley was both the air mission commander for the rescue efforts and lead trauma physician on Knife 03. (*USAF/TSgt. Scott Reed*)

Captain Steve Gregg, pilot and aircraft commander of Knife 03. (*AFSOC archives*)

Staff Sergeant Scott Diekman, the tailgunner on Knife 03. (*AFSOC archives*)

Knife 03 and Knife 04, low level and broad daylight over Afghanistan, early December. (*USAF/ TSgt. Scott Reed*)

The CCTs and PJs surround Hadley after the mission at Camp Rhino on December 5. (*Hadley family archives*)

Cubby and Allard with the Alamo in the background on December 7. (*Wojciehowski family archives*)

Karzai walking in the desert of Uruzgan Province on December 3. Two days later, he would narrowly escape death and be named the interim leader of Afghanistan. (*ODA 574 archives*)

Karzai being sworn in as interim leader on December 22, 2001, in Kabul. (*Hadley family archives*)

Captain Amerine's mentor, Dennis Holloway—shown here outside of Kuwait City on January 18, 1991, during Operation Desert Storm—walked him through the Trees of the Dead at Gabriel Field when Amerine was still a cadet at West Point. (*Holloway family archives*)

The Trees of the Dead, Gabriel Field, Fort Campbell, Kentucky, 2008. (*Bruce Watts*)

gate itself was the massive artillery piece that ODA 574 had found in the valley below Tarin Kowt Pass. Someone had hauled it back to town and aimed it south toward Kandahar. Outside the gate, at least thirty idling vehicles were on both sides of the road. Some drove about in the mud as if impatient to get moving, but the majority were parked facing the road and crammed with guerrillas, RPG launchers, and AK-47s.

Bashir, in the first of three trucks, waved to Amerine and pulled into place in front of the captain's truck; three more trucks fell in place behind Amerine and just ahead of Mag. As a group—seven Green Berets in two extra cab trucks and sixty guerrillas packed into six king cab trucks—they headed toward the labyrinth.

That was unbelievably organized, thought Mike, watching Tarin Kowt shrink away in the rearview mirror.

/

While Amerine's lead element began to ascend the road toward Tarin Kowt Pass, the main element met up with the twenty remaining guerrilla vehicles waiting on the edge of town. The rain had stopped and the roads were nearly dry when Bari Gul's truck took its place ahead of JD, followed by the shuttle bus. As Karzai's bus passed, the cobbled-together militia honked their horns and cheered for him.

The first few miles went well.

Hey, thought Fox as they drove around the cemetery and into the labyrinth, *this is not too bad. We're moving, the skies are clearing, air cover will be back up shortly. We're heading south.*

They traveled past ODA 574's original position overlooking Tarin Kowt Valley, down the long traverse, and onto the valley floor. Then, as if someone had waved a green flag, cars and trucks veered out into the desert and swooped back, falling into place alongside Karzai's shuttle bus to wave at him. More trucks came in from the sides of the valley, as if they'd been lying in wait. The unsettled Americans couldn't tell who was going and who was coming. An approaching truck full of men waving AK-47s could have charged ahead, spun around, and returned—or it could be a bunch of suicidal Taliban.

This, thought Major Bolduc, *is a freakin' disaster.*

For Fox's communications sergeant, twenty-five-year-old Nelson Smith—who had just graduated from language school and was about as fresh to Special Forces as they come—the confusion was more a distraction than a worry. This was his first look at the countryside beyond Tarin Kowt, where Bedouins and goatherders roamed the land. He saw steel-armored wreckage of modern warfare rusting near the ruins of ancient earthen fortresses. At roadside stands, Frisbee-sized disks of flat bread cooked in traditional clay ovens hung from Coca-Cola signs riddled with bullet holes. On long sections of road, if it weren't for the smell of exhaust, the sounds of laboring engines, and occasional gunfire from the exuberant Afghans, he imagined the country looked as it did when Alexander the Great fought his way through these very mountains and deserts. Beyond Tarin Kowt Pass, villages appeared out of nowhere, like rest stops along an interstate highway. "Here comes another Cracker Barrel," Bolduc proclaimed to Smith as these choke points forced the guerrillas' vehicles to briefly converge.

At dusk, the main group approached the lead group, now parked haphazardly on the shrubby, rolling terrain. At this unplanned stop, the dust settled while guerrillas from both elements of the convoy got out of their trucks, unfurled carpets, and knelt down to pray—their only synchronized movement of the entire day.

"So much for our forty-five-minute lead," said Alex.

From the bed of the same truck, Mike coined what would become a regular saying for the men of ODA 574: "Fucked up as an Afghan convoy."

The Americans waited as the Afghans prayed, rolled up their carpets, and returned to their vehicles.

"Okay, let's roll," Amerine said to Bashir, who was walking toward him. Seylaab translated Bashir's response as the guerrilla handed a stack of flat bread to Amerine. "No, we will leave soon. Now we eat."

An hour and a half later, the lead section of the convoy edged slowly into the night, crossing the open desert of southern Uruzgan Province. Then the road narrowed and climbed into the mountains, where a sheer drop on one side and a rock wall on the other forced the convoy into order. In the open air of the truck bed, Amerine craned his neck to look up at the rock face above them. He imagined the anxiety the Soviet patrols must have felt in these craggy canyons, tailor-made by Allah to conceal the faithful as they terrorized the infidels passing through them. He understood now why the Soviets had for the most part avoided Uruzgan, and was thankful that Karzai had persuaded the clans in this region to allow them safe passage.

Some eight hours after they left Tarin Kowt, the road widened and the mountains parted like curtains on a massive stage to reveal a vast desert. At 10 P.M., the convoy, having come together as one in the mountains, reached Petawek. Situated on the fringe of the foothills at the southern edge of Uruzgan Province, the village was bisected by the Kandahar Road, which continued south into the desert.

More than half of the guerrillas parked their vehicles north of the village, up against the mountains they'd just passed through, guarding their rear. Karzai's shuttle bus followed Bari Gul's and JD's trucks to a compound in the more densely populated section of the village on the right side of the road, and Amerine's trucks pulled up and parked alongside JD's. As Karzai was greeted by a village elder and escorted into the compound's courtyard, the Americans formed their usual defensive perimeter.

"This will be Karzai's headquarters," Fox said, approaching Amerine and JD. "He's going to meet with the locals and bed down. We'll discuss the movement tomorrow. I want your team on the hill over there, to guard the town." He gestured toward some high ground a few hundred yards to the east that overlooked Kandahar Road and the desert to the south.

Amerine watched Casper and his men unload their gear from the shuttle bus and move into Karzai's compound. "You don't want us in there with Hamid?" he asked Fox.

"No, I don't. Get your men moving. I'll be sleeping out there with your team."

ODA 574 drove away from Petawek and parked on a flat-topped

ridge, facing their vehicles back toward the road and the village. Two hundred yards from the nearest buildings and three hundred yards from Karzai's compound, nothing stood between them and Kandahar Province except sand, until Bari Gul and his men arrived and set up a perimeter around the Americans as they had done in Tarin Kowt.

Amerine scanned the surroundings with his NODs. The village sat on an arid, rocky plateau of rolling hills covered with patches of scrub brush. Their observation post was located where the plateau descended abruptly to the edge of a desert that extended to the horizon. As with Tarin Kowt, aerial reconnaissance would be their only early warning if Karzai's spies failed to warn them of an attack.

"Sir," JD said quietly to Amerine, "let me get this straight. We're three hundred yards from Hamid, the C-team is out here with us doing nothing—shouldn't somebody be with the G-chief?"

"I brought that up with Fox," said Amerine, "but he appears to have a reason for being out here with us."

"Maybe you should consider keeping a split team in the compound, so we know what's going on—kind of slide back into your old liaison job if they aren't going to do it."

"They haven't even been here a week. Let's give them a chance to do their job before we start working around them."

"Fair enough," said JD.

"Come up with a plan for us to drive back and grab Hamid if we get attacked," Amerine said. "I'm going to check on the recon flights and see if anything is going on."

"I'll put the team at fifty percent tonight," JD said. "See that glow out to the south?"

"Yeah," said Amerine, watching as a surface-to-air rocket, tiny in the distance, rose from the darkened void well beyond the horizon. The streak hung there, then evaporated into the blackness.

"That's Kandahar."

"Say hi to the Christmas present," Mag called out as Amerine and Mike, on their way to meet with Karzai in his new command post, trotted down from the top of the hill where ODA 574 had spent the night.

"Christmas present?" Amerine turned, looking back up the slope at Mag.

"It's December first, sir. Right now we're Santa Claus. Mr. K's the Christmas present. We gotta deliver him to Kandahar before Christmas."

"Where do you come up with this stuff?" said Amerine, shaking his head.

"Sir, it's just how my mind works," said Mag. "You always have to have a goal." Mag's singing followed them down the hill: "Feliz Navidad . . . Feliz Navidad . . . I want to wish you a Merry Christmas . . ."

An hour later, Amerine and Mike returned to the team's perimeter with Fox and Bolduc, who had met with Karzai earlier, in tow.

"We'll be here another night," Amerine told JD. "Hamid refuses to move forward until we get another lethal-aid drop and some humanitarian aid for this village and his men."

"I'll get Dan on it," said JD.

Amerine gestured toward Fox. "The colonel is putting together the list for Santa Claus right now." He winked at Mag. "He'll run it past you."

They were out of earshot of Fox and Bolduc when JD said, "Have you figured out why the lieutenant colonel has us all the way out here?"

"I don't know," said Amerine. "But Casper has gotta be happier than a pig in shit since Fox is apparently staying with us."

"So, what's the plan for today?" asked JD.

"You want to take a recon element out?"

"I'm afraid I got some of what Miles had. I'll be fine, but if you don't mind, I'll stay here to make sure this hill doesn't go anywhere."

"Okay," said Amerine. "I'll grab Seylaab, have him get Bari Gul's men moving. Then I'll take Alex and Mike south and recon to that ridgeline out on the horizon." Amerine indicated a dark streak in the distance where hills could be seen rising above the cream-colored desert. "You get the guys organized for the supply drop tonight. Once we get all that sorted out, we'll plan the next push forward."

Four trucks headed south on the main road out of Petawek, the first three carrying Bari Gul and his men while Mike drove Amerine, Alex, and Seylaab in the fourth. The recon route descended from an arcing line of leafless trees that marked the outskirts of Petawek and into a broad expanse of desert. Here the road was barely discernible beneath a layer of powdery sand that had been swept smooth by the wind. About ten miles away, the hills that were their destination crouched in front of distant mountains.

Halfway across the valley, the Americans looked back toward Petawek: Set against the mountains, with only north and south avenues of approach, the village would be easy to defend. Even if an enemy convoy managed to slip through Karzai's network of loyal Pashtun villages or conceal itself from aerial recon, it would still have to cross eleven miles of open desert.

After twenty minutes, the trucks rose out of the valley and turned off the road onto hard-packed red clay dotted with angular rocks. Reaching a saddle between two peaks, the men parked and got out. To the south, the mountains obstructed their view; to the east, they could make out the main road as it left the desert and threaded south through the mountains.

Amerine, Mike, and Alex stood around a map spread out on the hood of their truck and estimated this range to be about fifteen miles across from north to south. Beyond, the terrain sloped down gentle foothills that fanned out onto a vast high-desert plain on which sat Damana, their next destination. The farming community was still under the control of the Taliban owing to its proximity to Kandahar, fifteen miles farther south.

"These mountains are where Hamid expects to encounter Taliban patrols," said Amerine. "But the larger forces are right on the outskirts of the city."

"Do we have any idea how many?" asked Mike.

"Tens of thousands, down from the hundreds of thousands thought to be in Afghanistan when we started."

"Which means we don't have a clue," said Alex. "I'll get more recon up tonight. Really have them work these mountains, so we don't get surprised by anything."

"Shit," said Mike, looking at a puddle forming on the ground. "Radiator's leaking."

"Call Triple A," Amerine said with a grin.

Bari Gul walked over, crouched down, and peered under their vehicle. He beckoned over one of his men, who raised the hood, uncapped the radiator, and poured in a pouch of chewing tobacco.

"He says this will close the leak," said Seylaab. "It should get you back to town, but then you will need a better repair, or a new truck."

"Tashakor," said Amerine, thanking the man in Pashto.

Mike was scanning the desert to the east, between them and the road back to Petawek. "Is that what I think it is?" he said, lowering his binoculars and pointing to two parallel indentations traversing below a ridgeline.

Amerine could see the marks without binoculars. "Tank tracks," he said.

"The ground is rock hard," Mike said. "No telling how old they are, but there certainly weren't any tanks in Petawek."

"Let's get out of here," said Amerine. "Alex—we got air?"

"Yes, we do. I'll bring one this way for another look."

To Seylaab, Amerine said, "Ask Bari Gul if he knows anything about tanks."

Seylaab translated, then said, "He doesn't. Should we go?"

"Yes. Tell him to be careful," said Amerine, glancing at the radiator fluid still dripping from their truck before he climbed into the passenger seat.

"Imagine being chased by a tank, then our truck breaks down," said Mike as he got behind the wheel.

"That is *not* a story I want to tell my grandkids," said Amerine.

As the convoy descended the hill in the direction from which they'd come, the men heard the sound of an engine through their open windows. They halted. A large cloud of sand was being kicked up on the main road a couple hundred yards away—whatever created it was hidden from view by a small rise, but it was big.

"Oh fuck," said Amerine. "Get me some elevation."

They backed up, parking behind a dune to wait. Finally, a giant yellow bulldozer came into view, clearing sand the way a plow clears snow.

"Well, that was fun," said Mike.

"Let's go back and get a new truck," said Amerine. "We can tell JD we fled in terror from an Afghan in a bulldozer."

Even before he entered Karzai's headquarters to request a new truck, Amerine knew something was up when he heard the tribal leaders inside talking excitedly. The small receiving room was packed with Afghans sitting shoulder to shoulder and knees to backs, filling every inch of the floor like a human carpet. Karzai was against the far wall, facing men who looked serious, even angry, waving their hands and fists in the air and speaking all at once. When he noticed Amerine, Karzai lifted his hand and the crowd parted slightly, providing a five-inch-wide pathway that Amerine pushed through.

"What's all the excitement about?" Amerine asked.

"Word arrived from Germany," said Karzai. "I'm being considered for interim leader."

Uncertain what this meant, Amerine said, "Interim leader of . . ."

"Afghanistan," said Karzai, who chuckled when Amerine's eyes widened in surprise. "That was my reaction as well. In Bonn, they have identified a list, and my brother tells me I'm favored to lead the interim government—a whole new administration. The process will lead to a Loya Jirga, then the writing of a new constitution and, in a couple of years, elections for president."

"Congratulations," Amerine said. "Sounds like democracy. But your men don't appear to be celebrating."

"They are angry because there is a rumor that the supporters of King Zahir Shah are lobbying for him to add his name to the list of candidates to be considered. They fear that with his popularity, it would block my chances." The phone Karzai was holding in his hand rang and he took the call, talking loudly over the din in the room.

Amerine had known that Karzai would play an important role in bringing the tribes together in support of a post-Taliban government, but his tireless lobbying for the Loya Jirga had seemed to overshadow even himself as a consideration for the top slot in any future government. Now Karzai was the front-runner. *Do I call for a helicopter and evac him out of here?* Amerine wondered. *No, we need Hamid to press the Taliban to surrender. Is there anybody else? No, this army will disintegrate without Hamid. I can't even get a truck without him.*

When Karzai got off the phone, Amerine said, "Sorry to jump right into business, but I need a new truck."

"You will have one before nightfall," said Karzai.

Amerine left a few minutes later with a smile on his face, but it faded as he continued to dwell on the dangers ahead. If the Taliban were to focus on killing one person to thwart the campaign, Karzai would be their prime target.

Approaching Fox at ODA 574's observation post, Amerine told him the news. "You might want to get down there and talk to him," he said.

Fox and Bolduc went straight to Karzai's headquarters, and JD called the team together.

"All right," Amerine said. "This mission just got a whole lot bigger." He gave a rundown of what was happening in Bonn, then continued: "Our job is to get Hamid to Kandahar and force the Taliban to surrender. Even though he is being considered for interim leader, we are not his bodyguards. We still need to take him to the fight."

That evening, Amerine, Fox, Bolduc, and Karzai gathered around a map in the lantern-lit receiving room, now nearly empty except for Karzai's standard entourage.

They'd been in Petawek for less than twenty-four hours and already Karzai was receiving updated intelligence from Afghans fleeing Kandahar Province in expectation of a battle. Some of the Taliban defectors who had abandoned their posts were holed up with friends or relatives in nearby villages, Karzai told the Americans; the air strikes over the past two weeks had definitely dissuaded Taliban movements north into Uruzgan Province, and only small patrols limited to one to three vehicles were pushing north of the Arghandab River, the main waterway that wraps around the northern and western outskirts of the city of Kandahar.

Supporters of Karzai had come to Petawek from Damana, Pashtun farmers who informed Karzai that the Taliban troops stationed in their village were gone. Damana was now being "watched" by smaller Taliban patrols that came from the direction of Kandahar, crossing the Arghandab on a bridge at the town of Shawali Kowt,[5] which was three miles south of Damana and ten miles from the city center of Kandahar. According to these reports, it seemed logical to assume that the Taliban would defend Kandahar along the river and specifically at this bridge, the only one for miles.

"We need to control that bridge," said Amerine.

Fox nodded in agreement.

"How big is Damana versus Shawali Kowt?" Amerine asked Karzai.

"Shawali Kowt is almost a town, stretched along the northern bank of the river. Damana is barely a village. Very few people. Hundreds, versus one or two thousand in Shawali Kowt."

"We will move as before, with your forward element seizing Damana in advance of the main body of the convoy," Fox said to Amerine. "From there, I want you to move out to this hill southwest of the town." A tightly wound circle of lines on the topographical map indicated a small but steep hillock, perhaps two hundred feet high and a quarter mile beyond Damana in the direction of Shawali Kowt and the bridge.

"We need to seize Shawali Kowt and take the bridge," said Amerine, voicing his reservations. "That's the only way to secure and hold Damana. A major road from Kandahar leads straight to the bridge, so we have to consider it the main avenue of approach for any Taliban coming north to attack."

Though Fox understood the bridge's strategic importance, he felt that pushing so far in one day was overly ambitious, and he was more comfortable with the closer goal of the hillock.

"For now, plan to look at the hill beyond Damana," Fox said. "If you can see the whole area from there, it can serve the same purpose."

Amerine nodded. "Will do—I'll go brief the men."

Around midnight, more weapons and supplies drifted down from the sky beneath big, billowing parachutes, except for one that "burned in" like a missile and smashed into the ground after its chute failed. ODA 574 prepared for the free-for-all that had occurred at the team's first airdrop, but the guerrillas hefted the crates into the beds of a few trucks and drove them back to town without incident. Within a half hour, the crates had disappeared into Karzai's compound.

At 5 A.M., Mike, Ronnie, and Brent crawled from their sleeping bags and walked over to Karzai's compound to check the damage to the weapons that had been in the crate with the failed parachute. Soon their hands were coated with Cosmoline—the sticky, oily-smelling rust preventive used to protect guns in long-term storage. The weapons sergeants spread a jumble of broken AK-47s and PKM machine guns on blankets and began to salvage parts. As the sun rose higher, the three men had a growing number of assault rifles and machine guns assembled from what was still usable, and the sharp crack of AK-47 fire echoed off the mountains as they test-fired the weapons before distributing them to the locals along with food, clothing, and blankets.

Out at the hilltop observation post, the rest of the team was taking turns on watch. Amerine was writing notes in his journal when Alex said, "We've got company."

Standing up quickly, Amerine looked to the south.

"No," said Alex. "Over there."

Charlie the spook was approaching from the village, and Amerine walked down off the hill to greet him.

"Hamid wants to see you," Charlie said.

"On my way," replied Amerine, who grabbed his M4, pulled on his load-bearing vest, and went over to Fox, who was sitting on the tailgate of JD's truck. "Hamid called for me," Amerine said, "so I'm heading over to see him."

"Let me know if anything is going on," said Fox.

"Will do."

Amerine and Charlie entered Karzai's headquarters just as four Afghans were leaving, each of them staring solemnly forward, walking in a line like condemned men. Had it not been for their grave expressions, Amerine would have thought they were his own guerrillas.

"Jason, I have information about a Taliban headquarters and weapons depot," said Karzai. "The men you just passed are Taliban deserters. They say there are hundreds of fighters gathered in a walled compound near a madrassa on the edge of a town south of the Arghandab River."

On his map, Karzai pointed out the location roughly a mile beyond the bridge at Shawali Kowt. According to the deserters, the town remained staunchly Taliban.

Dan had been giving Amerine hourly intelligence reports. The Marines were still at Camp Rhino, with a few manning checkpoints on the roads heading into Kandahar from the south. The ODA with Sherzai had begun to disrupt enemy traffic on the roads well outside the city. These American emplacements had a common goal of bottling up the Taliban inside Kandahar, the initial stages of an expected siege. Both the Marines and Sherzai were following Task Force Dagger's adamant directive to stay out of the city.

"So this information from these men is a peace offering?" asked Amerine. "Now they are on our side?"

"Yes."

"Do you trust them?"

"I don't think they are lying."

"Then we should direct our bombers there and destroy it?" Amerine asked.

By now Amerine felt he could read Karzai for signs of doubt—a slightly raised eyebrow or change in posture. He had noticed this when he told him about the encampment that proved to be refugees. This time there was no hesitation. If they didn't strike the enemy now, they would likely meet them, along with all those weapons, on the road to Kandahar.

"Then I believe we should move tomorrow," said Amerine. "After this strike, there's no reason to wait here another day."

Satisfied with the airdrops, Karzai concurred. "Tomorrow morning we depart for Damana."

Returning to the observation post, Amerine headed straight to Dan and Wes, who sent SITREPs to Task Force Dagger and brought up satellite imagery of the intended target on their laptops; Alex directed aerial reconnaissance aircraft to the area. Amerine then informed Fox and Bolduc of the new developments, and the three of them were looking at the maps on Alex's computer when recon pilots radioed that they had "eyes on" the enemy compound. Their report fit the description the deserters had provided, including the two adjacent outbuildings purportedly being used as large weapons caches. A great many vehicles were scattered in the area, a pilot said, "like grazing sheep."

Since the target was located near the edge of a populated area, this strike held the greatest risk for collateral damage that Amerine had authorized, and he sought Fox's opinion. Fox, with a nod from Bolduc, agreed: It was risky but necessary.

ODA 574 monitored the situation for the rest of the day, learning from the pilots that a steady stream of people was coming and going from these small buildings; it appeared that Taliban fighters were stocking up.

After sunset, most of the guerrillas and many of the locals from Petawek gathered between Karzai's compound and ODA 574's observation post, sitting on blankets or on the tailgates of trucks, their gazes fixed south as if waiting for a drive-in movie to begin. Word had spread that the Americans were attacking a Taliban position, and they were here for the show.

Finally, Alex said, "The bomber is vectored in—the pilot's at the right place."

Amerine cleared the target hot.

Within ten minutes, the horizon glowed from the explosions thirty miles away. Some cheers rang out among the Afghans, but at this distance, the ensuing fire was only an orange glow. Apparently unimpressed, many of the guerrillas retired to their encampments.

The Americans remained fixated. Another explosion blipped on the horizon. Then another. These secondary blasts were from the cached weapons: stores of grenades, RPGs, perhaps even surface-to-air missiles. They continued sporadically, alleviating Amerine's concerns that the deserters might have fed them bogus intelligence.

He marked the location on his map with an X, then pulled out his black journal, describing the explosions and distant glow as "death on the horizon."

Dawn broke clear and cold on the third of December. The guerrillas were scattered among their vehicles, carpets rolled out on the hardened soil where they had been praying toward Mecca moments before. An hour later, carpets rolled up, MREs eaten, third cups of tea or coffee drunk, most of the bipeds in the vicinity were still sitting on their asses—another late start. "It's Afghan Standard Time," Mike said to Wes. "It's a disease."

Amerine was going over the day's route with Alex when he saw Dan trotting down off the hill toward Petawek, alone. He watched Dan walk straight to Karzai's compound and talk to the guerrillas guarding the door, who stepped inside and conversed with one of the CIA spooks before allowing Dan inside.

How things had changed: Now the team was going through Afghan bodyguards or the CIA to speak with Karzai. Amerine looked over at Fox and Bolduc, who had been spending nearly all their time out at ODA 574's post, ignoring the golden rule of guerrilla warfare: Always stay with the G-chief.

Half an hour later—or three cups of tea, Amerine guessed—Dan and Karzai emerged from the compound and strolled up to the observation post, Dan looking like a woolly mountain man and wearing his Red Sox cap, and Karzai, beard neatly trimmed, wrapped in a tan blanket. The two men approached Amerine, who noticed that although Karzai's eyes were as clear and alert as ever, they were rimmed with dark circles from lack of sleep.

"I asked Hamid to come out for a team photo before we push out," Dan said with a grin. "Thought this was a good time for it."

"Good idea," said Amerine with a nod to Karzai. "Get everybody together."

As ODA 574 gathered around Karzai for the picture, Fox and Bolduc came over and stood directly in the middle of the group; appearing apologetic, Nelson Smith shuffled to the back.

Mag set up his camera on the tailgate of a truck, set the timer, then ran back to a space between Mike and Dan, kneeling in the front row.

"Let's take one more," said Ken said after the camera clicked. "This time with just the guys who were here from the beginning."

There wasn't a man on ODA 574 who didn't smile at Ken's suggestion.

It was almost twelve, and the team's three vehicles—including a new truck, purchased from a local to replace Amerine's—were loaded and ready to join the guerrilla convoy already assembling. They would continue in the same formation used since leaving Tarin Kowt.

ODA 574 gathered for a final huddle, and Amerine recapped the plan they'd been preparing for the day's movement to Damana, twenty-five miles away.

"I don't expect the hill west of Damana to yield anything," Amerine said, "so get your heads focused on Shawali Kowt. We'll make contact with the enemy today. If we have to take Shawali Kowt, it isn't going to be easy. But that town and that bridge are the key to defending the entire area."

"Enough fun and games," said JD after a long pause. "Let's saddle up."

While the rest of the men moved out to their vehicles, Amerine took JD aside and said, "We're going to run into something out there today. If things go to shit and I give you the word, get Hamid's ass out of there. Get him airlifted to Pakistan or back to Tarin Kowt, whatever it takes. We'll find our way back to you; don't try to come for us. Your job is to keep Hamid alive."

"I hear you, but we're not going to leave you behind," JD said, tugging the bill of his Harley-Davidson cap downward.

"You're going to have to trust that I will call for you to come help if there is anything you can do. Remember, Hamid Karzai is about to become the leader of this country's government. You are protecting the future of Afghanistan."

CHAPTER NINE

Death on the Horizon

Unlike the northern capital, Kandahar does not lie in the shadow of lofty hills; but about three miles off, from the north, westward, to the south, there runs a bare serrated range, with many a fantastic peak and clearly-cut block showing against the sky-line. To force a passage in this direction, through thickly sown villages and gardens and vineyards, was no child's play. Without masses of well-trained infantry the attempt could not have been made at all.

—Lieutenant Charles Gray Robertson, 1881[1]

The convoy pushed out from Petawek at the crack of noon, the men waving good-bye to the children for whom, over the last few days, they had provided a distraction from the tedium of village life. Nelson Smith, a new father, had been particularly taken with these beautiful children and was astounded at how weathered they were by the desert wind and sun, even at just two or three years of age. In some cases they already had wrinkled hands and crow's-feet forming at the corners of their eyes.

"I wish I could put one of these kids in my rucksack and take him home," Smith told Mag. "Could probably give him a cracker every once in a while and he'd be happy as a clam."

Before they departed, Fox had emphasized to Karzai the importance of an orderly convoy; they couldn't afford another off-road rally this close to Kandahar. Karzai's followers were to stay behind the shuttle bus. If they wanted to swarm around the desert in the rear, that was fine. Showing great restraint, the guerrillas maintained order as the line of vehicles crossed over into Kandahar Province without so much as a speed bump marking the sandy border and climbed into the mountains where Amerine and his split team had mistaken the bulldozer tracks for a tank's.

Caves, overlooks, and fighting positions—foxholes and trench lines—abounded on both sides while the convoy moved cautiously down the rough road, but the positions were unoccupied. Word of Karzai's victory had reached the province, where local tribal leaders had opened channels through which they were now traveling unopposed. They were less than twenty-five miles from Kandahar with no sign of the enemy, only an occasional farmer walking along the road, carrying firewood or a sack of dried goat dung. Every so often, the outline of a camel in the distance alerted them to a Bedouin camp.

Around 3 P.M., the lead element crested the far side of the range, and the terrain smoothed out before them: an arid landscape striped by belts of vegetation—some green, but mostly the burnt hues of autumn; the few villages in the valley below looked like handfuls of pebbles strewn among the brown and tan fields. There was nothing to suggest that a thriving metropolis lay only fifteen miles beyond the sharp peaks jutting like the serrations of a saw blade on the far side of the valley.

The road swept down through the foothills of the range until Damana appeared abruptly on the plain below: a dozen scattered mud huts and a few compounds surrounded by hundreds of acres of farmland. From here, Amerine could see the hillock Fox was interested in occupying as a new command post. It was too rugged and steep, seemingly impassable and thus unsuitable as a vantage point.

Just as the guerrillas' vehicles rolled into town, two trucks pulled out from behind buildings on either side of the road ahead of them and turned away from the convoy. Mike slowed his truck. Through binoculars, Amerine could see men in the cabs, but the beds were empty; he suspected it was a Taliban patrol. The trucks sped south over a rise, and Alex, who had jets waiting overhead, glanced at Amerine, awaiting his orders. Amerine shook his head. The men had not opened fire and might only be frightened locals.

Mag and his guerrillas were right behind Amerine. Amerine instructed twenty guerrillas to secure Damana for Karzai's segment of the convoy, then radioed Mag to follow him toward Shawali Kowt. The two trucks full of Americans, along with thirty guerrillas in three trucks led by Bashir, emerged on the south side of Damana. From here they could see Shawali Kowt, three miles farther south and, on its western edge, the bridge over the Arghandab River; to get there, however, they had to pass through Shawali Kowt. As Amerine's truck followed Bashir's men, a soldier's intuition warned him that bullets were about to fly.

In the back of the vehicle, Alex learned from aerial recon that the two trucks fleeing Damana had turned off the main road and continued south along another track toward the more densely populated eastern side of Shawali Kowt, about a mile upriver from the bridge. The guerrillas took this same road, followed by the Americans, while the pilots reported that the vehicles had now pulled into Shawali Kowt and parked among its densest cluster of buildings. (See map on p. 354)

The north side of the town, facing the desert, was protected by a berm ranging in height from ten to twenty feet, a natural barrier that had been created by episodic flooding of the river. This was the only thing standing between the lead of the convoy and Shawali Kowt. A hundred yards ahead of Amerine's truck, the guerrillas pulled over to the west side of the road seventy-five yards short of a wide gap in the berm, and parked their vehicles facing back toward Damana as if preparing to retreat.

"That can't be good," said Mike.

Jumping out of the trucks, the guerrillas ran toward the embankment.

"At least they didn't just drive into town without taking a look," said Amerine.

Mike slowed the truck but continued to creep forward, catching glimpses of the town through the notch where the road split the berm. There was no gate, no guard tower, no machine-gun emplacements—and no people. Unlike the guerrillas, he parked the truck facing forward, which allowed Amerine, Mike, Alex, and Seylaab to watch the Afghans scrambling up the berm. Seylaab pointed out a barely visible white flag waving from the top of a distant roof. "Taliban," he said, just as the guerrillas peered over the berm. Automatic weapons fire erupted from the town, and some of the Afghans flattened themselves to the ground.

"This town is not clear," Alex calmly said into his radio on the local channel. Switching channels, he went to work, calling out "troops in contact" to the F-18 Hornet pilots flying overhead.

A quarter of a mile behind them, Mag was riding in the back of the second American truck, with his M4 rifle, a half-dozen RPGs, and a PKM machine gun that Brent had salvaged. Nothing gave Mag more confidence than a perfectly operating weapon with unlimited ammo, and this PKM had purred when he'd tested it out in the desert just after leaving Petawek.

A rocket suddenly streaked into the sky at one o'clock from their position, and Mag gripped the machine gun tightly, swinging it to his nine o'clock and three o'clock, anticipating an ambush. They cleared a gradual rise. Before them, a wide, sloping plateau descended six hundred yards to Shawali Kowt. Beyond the town, the yellow and orange of what appeared to be orchards stretched along the banks of the Arghandab, which at this time of year was a muddy ribbon of earth. On the other side of the riverbed, mountains shot up from the valley floor.

Ken turned the truck sharply to the right and parked behind a low rise, and the Americans grabbed their weapons and hurried into a roadside ditch.

"What's going on up there?" Ken said into the radio. "What's the status up there? You in contact?"

Far ahead they could see Amerine's truck—facing away from them—and, in front of it, the guerrillas' vehicles facing toward them. The Afghans were on a twenty-foot-high section of the berm that ran east–west for a mile. Machine-gun tracers arced from the town toward the berm like a line of sparks. Amerine's voice came through the radio: "Our guerrillas are in contact north of the town with an unknown number of enemy using small arms and RPGs."

The main body of the convoy was closer to the lead element than it was supposed to be. The trucks had just reached Damana when gunfire crackled over the Americans' radios. "The town is not clear," both JD's and Fox's men heard Alex say, and Smith, who was driving JD's truck, came to an abrupt stop, halting the convoy.

JD, Fox, Bolduc, Ronnie, and Dan jumped out and spread a map across the vehicle's hood while Smith set the parking brake, grabbed his rifle, got down on one knee, and covered the left flank. After studying the map for a few moments, Dan radioed a SITREP to Task Force Dagger.

"I need to get forward and see what they're up against," JD said to Fox. "You coming or staying with Karzai, sir?"

Bolduc was itching to get forward, too. Like Fox, he was supposed to stay with Karzai, but both men considered the CIA to be Karzai's bodyguards. "Sir," Bolduc said to the lieutenant colonel, "we gotta get up there and help out."

With a last look at the map, Fox gave the order: "Let's move!" Smith got back behind the wheel, the sound of explosions in the distance accompanied by nonstop machine-gun fire over the radio.

Not far behind, Karzai's bus was idling with the rest of the convoy, Afghans and CIA guarding its rear, front, and flanks.

"Should we send more men forward with them?" Karzai asked Casper.

"I don't know," said Casper. "We'll monitor the situation. For now, let's get you off the road."

"Enemy strength unknown." Alex completed his brief of the situation to the pilots standing by while Mike looked to Amerine for an order.

"Stay here with Alex," said Amerine. "I'm running ahead to see what we're up against. Get ready to pull back to Damana."

Pushing the door open, Amerine pulled Seylaab out with him and sprinted toward the berm.

"Hey!" shouted Mike. Seylaab and Amerine turned in unison, and Mike tossed the interpreter his rifle. "You might want this."

As he ran forward, Amerine saw the reddish-orange flame of an RPG arcing high overhead and heard the whoosh of more in flight. Looking up, he saw one RPG fly steeply into the sky, then hit its apex and angle back toward earth. The trajectory was off to the west and the explosion was far beyond their vehicles. The Taliban were pointing the rockets up in the air like artillery rounds, using the road to Shawali Kowt as their target.

"We are being engaged by mortars," radioed Ken.

"Negative," Amerine radioed back. "Those are RPGs."

Bashir's guerrillas had begun to head back down the berm toward their parked trucks, and Amerine ran toward them, waving his arms and shouting, "Stop! Stop!" Beside him, Seylaab belted out something in rapid-fire Pashto and mimicked Amerine's movements. The guerrillas continued their retreat.

"Stop!" Amerine continued to yell, gesturing frantically. "Stop!"

At last they did, though appearing ready to bolt again at any second. Panicked American voices came over Amerine's radio. "All elements hold tight," he radioed back. "And keep the net* clear. I'm reconning the town."

Stay where you are! Amerine waved at the guerrillas again. *Stay right there!* Crouching low, he climbed the berm while sticking foam plugs in his ears. When he reached the top, he dropped on his stomach and edged forward to survey Shawali Kowt.

"What's going on up there?" Ken said over the radio. "Are you in contact?"

Lying prone beside Ken, Mag said, "No fucking shit, Ken, they're in fucking contact. Ask them which side they want support on."

It seemed to Mag and Wes that Ken was more concerned with the RPGs falling just ahead of their position than the fact that their lead vehicle was in contact with the enemy. The gunfire increased, and more RPGs ripped across the clear sky.

---

* The radio network that linked the team with Task Force Dagger, air support, and quick reaction forces for medevac or search-and-rescue.

"Ken!" Mag yelled when the medic repeated his question into the radio. "Shut the fuck up. We're out of range of the RPGs. Ask them which side do they want support on? Right or left?"

"They're exploding right in front of us!" Ken said. "We need to know what's going on up there before we move forward."

The explosions stopped a couple of minutes later, and Mag got Ken back into the truck. Wes slid behind the wheel and peeled out, the truck lurching forward, then accelerating down the road toward Shawali Kowt.

As soon as Amerine crested the berm, he could see where the RPGs were being fired from. Three Taliban stood among what looked like the decomposing ruins of an earthen wall on top of a wide twenty-foot hill about two hundred yards south of his position and just east of Shawali Kowt. They launched another RPG. More armed fighters with AK-47s were running in streets that angled between the buildings below him.

Amerine glanced back. The only way to get the guerrillas into the fight was to lead by example. Taking aim at one of the Taliban on the hilltop with his M4 carbine, Amerine squeezed off a round, then another, adjusting for the distance.

Withering gunfire raked his position, and an RPG exploded in front of him, showering him with dirt and rocks. Chuckling at his mistake, Amerine rolled halfway down the berm and stopped at the feet of the guerrillas.

"Tracers—bad fucking idea," he said to the uncomprehending Afghans. Blood streamed down the bridge of his nose where his weapon had apparently hit him in the tumble down the slope. Bewildered, the guerrillas watched as the laughing, bleeding American changed out his ammo clip for one *without* tracers. On the way from Tarin Kowt, Amerine had kept loaded a full magazine of tracers, an old infantry technique leaders use to mark targets for their soldiers—which would have proved helpful if the convoy had been ambushed. In this situation, tracers were suicidal.

"Tell them to follow me!" Amerine shouted to Seylaab before charging back up the embankment to a new position twenty-five yards to the right of where he had fired the tracers.

A few Taliban walked cautiously out from the town toward the berm. Behind them, a dozen or more armed men followed, the closest spraying gunfire across the top of the embankment, where Amerine remained invisible to them. He slid his M4 into position and opened fire.

The Taliban returned fire with wild bursts of ammunition and scattered. A few fell to the ground and were still; the rest fled in confusion, running and diving for cover behind buildings. Scanning the town, Amerine swung his carbine east to the hill, where there were now only two Taliban, both firing at him with AK-47s. *Did I hit the guy with the RPG, or did he run out of rounds?* Amerine wondered, taking aim at one of the two. He shot three rounds, and the man dropped out of sight behind the wall. Keeping his weapon in the direction of the hill, Amerine glanced toward Shawali Kowt. The street was completely empty.

Several shots kicked up dirt along the berm and Amerine noticed movement to his right. He turned and shot twice at a lone figure sprinting toward him and the berm, clutching an AK-47. In the silence that followed, Amerine could just hear the sound of the body hitting the dirt less than fifty yards away, and he stared at it for a moment, realizing that the guerrillas, who were now hunched down beside him, had been watching but not shooting their rifles. A few armed men hid around the corners of buildings and sprinted at intervals across the streets.

"Tell them to shoot!" Amerine yelled at Seylaab.

⚔

Mike didn't want his captain to be alone up there on the berm, but he knew his position, two hundred yards back with Alex, was crucial. Alex was their link to airpower, and if they were overrun, airpower would cover their retreat. That was why Amerine had ordered him to stay put, but Mike could see that the guerrillas weren't being much help and would most likely abandon Amerine if the enemy came rushing over the berm. This was the heat-of-battle reasoning behind Mike's split-second decision: *I gotta get up there with the captain.*

"I'm going," he told Alex, who had every pilot in Afghanistan headed their way. "If you see us getting overrun, put air on us and get the hell out of here."

Mike sprinted forward twenty yards, hearing bullets whizzing overhead. *Holy shit, this is for real!* he thought. *Oh, fuck. I'm scared as shit. Oh man, they're really shooting—I can't believe this. This is funny. No, this is not funny. I need to kill these motherfuckers; I need to go that way, toward them.*

He paused twenty yards out. Directly ahead of him was a "fatal funnel," where he would be exposed for at least a hundred yards without cover. "Fuck this," he said out loud. He ran back to the truck.

"These fuckers are trying to kill us!" he shouted at Alex, and they both laughed. "This is a bad fucking place to park. We'll have more cover ahead, closer to that berm."

The guerrillas did not react as Amerine shouted at them to attack; they just stared at the retreating Taliban. Amerine kept shouting, "Shoot! Attack!"

Misinterpreting Amerine's order, Seylaab stood up on the crest of the berm, yelled something in Pashto, and charged down toward Shawali Kowt with a guttural roar, spraying bullets wildly from his AK-47, his bright aqua robe flowing behind him. As surprised as Amerine, the other guerrillas immediately sprinted after him, and Amerine followed, laughing.

Mag's vehicle pulled up to the berm just as Amerine disappeared over it. He climbed up the embankment to see Amerine and the guerrillas running forward despite the gunfire ringing through the air. *What in the hell does the captain think he's wearing?* thought Mag. *Bulletproof everything?*

As Amerine ran, he grabbed three guerrillas and diverted them to their left toward the hill, where he was certain he'd shot the Taliban with the RPG. He was motioning for them to get up there when he saw an old man walking slowly and deliberately toward the body of the Taliban whom Amerine had shot.

The AK-47 was in the dirt in front of the body, and Amerine moved forward, grabbed the weapon, and tossed it to a guerrilla behind him. The older man did not hesitate in his stride. He kneeled down, pulled the limp body onto its back, scooped his hands under what Amerine now saw was a teenager, and carried him back to the town. Amerine continued to watch over his shoulder as he began to climb up the berm, pausing when the man pushed open a door painted turquoise and disappeared into a building.

Most of the guerrillas had followed Seylaab, with Bashir just behind, into the streets of Shawali Kowt. When bursts of AK-47 fire echoed off the walls of the buildings, Amerine knew he had no hope of keeping control of the guerrillas; he needed to bring forward more fighters from Karzai's position in Damana, set up a command post, and clear and occupy the town.

Amerine ran to the top of the berm, crouching beside Mike, whose truck was now parked below.

"What the hell happened to you?" Mike said when he saw the blood drying on the bridge of the captain's nose and smeared down his cheekbones.

"Not sure," said Amerine, wiping at his nose. He looked at the smudges on his fingers, which were numb with adrenaline.

More guerrillas streamed over the berm and headed into town, where gunfire could now be heard to the south near the river. Out of breath, JD and his split team joined Amerine and Mike.

"Where in hell did *you* come from?" Mike asked.

"There was a lot of panic on the radio, sir," JD said to Amerine. "I know you said not to come forward unless you requested, but it sounded like you guys were in the shit. Did you get that fucker with the RPG?"

"I think so. Those are our guerrillas out there now." Amerine pointed at the hill.

"Over *there*?" Mike said. "That's a couple hundred yards."

"Looks like good real estate," said JD.

At the base of the embankment, Alex shouted up from the bed of the truck where he was working his radio, "Standing by with air!"

"Looks like we spooked them," said Mike.

"For now," said Amerine. "Let's get out to that hill."

/

The hill that had been occupied by the Taliban with the RPG rose twenty feet above the barren terrain sixty-five yards east of Shawali Kowt, a lone, elongated lump— like a whale surfacing from the desert floor—forty yards long and fifteen yards across at its widest spot. It was tallest and widest at the "head," which faced northwest, toward town, as if the whale were swimming away, at a sharp angle from the Arghandab River, and tapered in both height and width toward the "tail." A mortar pit surrounded by a low earthen wall was located where the blowhole would be on a whale's head—a position the team suspected the Soviets had once occupied to lob mortars at the Pashtun Mujahideen. The hill was scarred with foxholes, shallow trenches, and the crumbling mud walls of a structure that had seen centuries of war.

This, the highest point in the immediate area, offered the best perspective of Shawali Kowt and the orchards and fields that began eighty yards to the south and stretched half a mile to the river, which flowed from east to west. Along the near side of the river, a quarter of a mile to the east, the men could see a small village that appeared to be deserted.

A half mile downstream to the west, about half the distance to the modern concrete-and-steel bridge, more than a hundred Taliban kicked up dust as they climbed the far bank of the dry riverbed and escaped to the other side.

Bashir, Seylaab, and thirty other guerrillas had flushed the Taliban out of the orchards and forced them across the river. The guerrillas were still firing their AK-47s from the trees.

"There's a cluster of them regrouping!" Mike yelled.

"We've got air, sir," Alex said. Amerine took a quick head count. His entire team was now either on the whale hill, on the berm, or with the trucks parked below it. Bari Gul, who had driven from

Damana, was walking toward the hill; his guerrillas had parked in a semicircle beyond the team trucks and were covering their rear and eastern flank.

"We've got a vehicle," Mag said. Raising his binoculars, Amerine saw a green sedan tearing down the road paralleling the opposite bank, approaching the fleeing Taliban from the direction of the bridge. It stopped next to a group of them.

"Put a bomb on that fucking thing," said Amerine.

Alex talked an F-18 onto the vehicle. "Weapon away," he said.

Despite the language barrier, Bari Gul understood what was about to happen and began to shout out one of the few English words the Americans had heard him utter: "Taxi! Taxi!" He frantically pointed at the vehicle. "Taxi! Taxi!"

Amerine looked again. The Taliban were gathering around the car, which had a small sign on the door he had missed before. "Shit!" he said, turning to Alex. "Anything you can do about it?"

"I'll try," said Alex, who calmly radioed the F-18. "Pilot's walking it away," he told Amerine seconds later.

The pilot, controlling the 500-pound laser-guided bomb, moved the crosshairs of his targeting system a fraction to the north and the bomb exploded harmlessly in the dry riverbed with a teeth-rattling boom. As soon as it hit, six Taliban poured out of the taxi even while the mob of men continued to crowd around it.

"They're armed," Mike said.

"Reengage." Amerine gave the order to Alex, then told JD to send SITREPs to Task Force Dagger and to Fox, who he assumed was back in Damana. "And let Hamid know what's going on. Then get our guerrillas into a perimeter on this hill."

"Roger that. Wait a minute," said JD. "You can tell Fox yourself. He's here."

"What?!" said Amerine. "Who the fuck is with Hamid?"

Fox, Bolduc, and Smith had parked their truck at the base of the hill and were running up it. Shaking his head, Amerine peered back through his binoculars in time to see the taxi blow up in a black cloud. The remaining Taliban scattered into the orchards and fields across the river.

Amerine turned his attention to the bridge. Taking and controlling both sides of the structure would require a complex plan, and Amerine wasn't sure the guerrillas were capable of carrying it out. Then he noticed a prominent hill topped with the crumbling ruins of a fort rising from the fields two hundred yards northeast of the bridge, on their side of the river. It was the perfect overlook. From there, ODA 574 would be able to control the bridge—the next best thing to seizing it.

"Hey, sir," Amerine said to Fox, who was now standing beside him, "there's our bridge."

Fox lifted his binoculars.

"Our guerrillas are too scattered to get to it before dark," said Amerine. "I'm going to consolidate here and attack it tomorrow."

"There are some people on the hill," said Dan. "You gonna take a leader's recon out there?" He raised his eyebrows up and down rapidly.

"I think we can see all we need to know from here."

"Should we drop something on it?" asked Alex.

"Can't really tell *who's* on it," said Amerine. "I don't see any weapons. Besides, we need to occupy those ruins. We don't want any unexploded ordnance sitting around."

On top of the hill shaped like a whale, JD placed the team in a security perimeter, starting at the higher and wider western end and working his way east. The circular mortar pit became the command post, the earth inside of it stained with the blood of the RPG-firing Afghan that Amerine had shot.

Awaiting orders, the guerrillas, including Bashir and his men, were sitting in small groups between the hill and the berm. Nobody had seen Seylaab since he'd led the charge into town, so the Americans could barely communicate with the Afghans.

"Get a perimeter around this hill with Bari Gul's men," Amerine told JD. "We'll be staying here tonight. I'm going to run over and see if those guerrillas know where Seylaab went."

"We'll co-locate our command post with yours," said Fox.

"You aren't heading back to Damana to be with Hamid?"

"No, I think we need to be out here."

"Okay, sir." Amerine walked out of the mortar pit with JD.

"So, they're staying?" said JD.

"Yeah," said Amerine. "I think we need to do what you suggested back in Petawek and establish a liaison with Hamid again. If they aren't going to do it, we will."

"But tomorrow we have to take the bridge," said JD. "That's going to require the whole team."

"Once we're in control of the bridge, we'll send Dan and Mag up north to be our link to Hamid. Now I need to find our interpreter so we can tell all these guerrillas what we're planning to do."

A truck with some of Casper's men pulled up to the north side of the hill, while Amerine headed in the direction of the nearest building, where several familiar guerrillas had gathered. Seylaab was not among them, so he moved to another group seated along a wall and repeated Seylaab's name until a man stood and pointed toward the center of town.

Okay, thought Amerine, *Seylaab is playing Rambo. Hopefully he'll remember he's our interpreter and get his ass back here before dark.*

As he turned back toward the hill, an impulse drew him to the spot where the Taliban had fallen, the lone teenager charging from town that Amerine had shot. Amerine numbly watched some guerrillas pick up blood-covered rocks and put them in their ammo pouches for souvenirs. He needed no physical token to remember this brief battle, which was already replaying itself in his mind.

"Hey, Captain!"

Zepeda came around the corner of the building and stopped a few yards from the stain on the ground where the young Taliban had fallen. "Not the best idea being out here alone."

"I was looking for my interpreter," said Amerine, heading back toward the hill with the spook.

"Heard you shot someone on that hill over there," Zepeda said.

Amerine nodded. *And also a teenager* he kept to himself.

"Your guys are claiming it was a two-hundred- or three-hundred-yard shot," Zepeda said as they crossed the street where Amerine had fired on the large group of Taliban. "Jesus, lot of blood down here too. How many guys did you shoot?"

"Not sure. Turned them around, though."

At the top of the hill they found another of Casper's men named Mr. Big talking with Ronnie and Mag near a sticky-looking puddle inside the mortar pit.

"It goes this way," said Mag, following streaks of blood that headed off the backside of the hill and toward the river. "Looks like his buddies dragged him into those orchards."

"Welcome to the club," Mr. Big said quietly to Amerine, who gave him a puzzled look.

"The man-killer's club." He winked and slapped Amerine roughly on the shoulder.

Unsure how he felt about being a member of this particular "club," Amerine went to check the perimeter, taking stock of the fortifications on the northern side of the hill. At the far end, Bari Gul was standing with his guerrillas and some locals, staring at the seemingly deserted village along the river to the east.

"Taliban," said Bari Gul, pointing to the village. Then, to convey the number, he stabbed the air repeatedly: "Taliban, Taliban, Taliban, Taliban, Taliban."

Amerine nodded. "I get it; many Taliban."

Using binoculars and hand motions, Bari Gul singled out a compound with a large building inside. He pantomimed bombs dropping from the sky.

Karzai had warned Amerine about Afghan-style retribution, that they would gladly bomb everything in sight to settle old scores. While Amerine was confident he could rely on Bari Gul in battle, he didn't know if he could trust his judgment in this situation, especially since he seemed to be getting his intelligence from locals Amerine didn't recognize. He would have to check with Karzai.

"No bombs," he said, shaking his head.

Just before dusk, an excited Seylaab returned to the hill and recounted his adventure to Amerine: of chasing the Taliban through the streets, of capturing a Taliban flag as a gift for Karzai, of chasing them into the orchards with Bashir and his men. At this point, he began to make sounds like gunfire, then rattled off the rest of what must have been a hell of a story—in Pashto.

Amerine let him finish before steering him over to Bari Gul's position, where he was watching the village to the east; people had been spotted occasionally walking between the buildings. After fifteen minutes of Seylaab's interpreting, it became clear to Amerine that the building they wanted to bomb *had* been a Taliban refuge, but Bari Gul's men couldn't agree on whether that was last month, last week, or yesterday. Still, Bari Gul and the locals wanted it bombed.

Again Amerine refused, telling Bari Gul that unless they could visually identify armed men or believed the building to harbor an immediate threat, they would have to wait until he discussed it with Karzai.

By dusk, half of the three hundred guerrillas had come forward to Shawali Kowt, leaving the other half with Karzai and the spooks in Damana. Trucks were, as usual, parked haphazardly everywhere. Between the vehicles, these Afghans sat in large circles, laughing and at ease, occasionally firing off bursts of celebratory gunfire to punctuate their revelry.

Fox and Bolduc settled into ODA 574's command post in the mortar pit, telling Amerine that they were "coordinating with the CIA" to handle Karzai. Meanwhile, Smith had backed his truck up to the nearest building—a deserted medical clinic—which JD had designated as the team's sleeping quarters, and was unloading his radio equipment.

Anticipating a counterattack, Amerine set security at 50 percent, and JD and half of the team headed down to the medical clinic to get some sleep. Amerine watched them cross the hundred yards of open ground, smiling when he saw that the pole from which the white Taliban flag had been hung was now flying the flag of Afghanistan. At 6:30 P.M. it was dark enough for the rest of ODA 574 on the hill to don their NODs and hunker down into the fighting positions they'd chosen to cover their assigned zones. Mag put his go-to-hell pack in a shallow trench facing the river, checked his weapon, and, before sitting down, trotted a few yards away to investigate a shadow he'd noticed two-thirds of the way down the slope.

"We've got a bunker over here!" he called out to Amerine.

"How the hell did we miss this?" Amerine said, joining Mag. He stared at the opening of what looked like a cave just below the trench line marking their security perimeter.

"It doesn't look like it can go very deep," said Mag.

"You want to lead or cover?"

"I'll cover you, sir," Mag said with a smile.

They walked down to the large opening and, without making a sound, turned on the lasers mounted on their carbines. Mag knelt on the slope above, while Amerine crouched on one side of the entrance, which was a couple of feet wide and high enough to allow him to walk upright, his beam lighting the interior earthen walls in an infrared glow.

Cautiously, Amerine peeked around the corner and scanned the recess fully, his laser tracking quickly from one side of the bunker to the other. The small space was empty, except for a beat-up carpet on the dirt floor. Calling out "All clear," he entered the bunker. Mag followed.

On cue, three of Bari Gul's men came in behind them, carrying blankets and flashlights that blinded Amerine and Mag, who quickly pulled off their NODs. The Afghans smiled at the Americans.

"Guess they found a home for the night," said Mag.

With half of ODA 574 asleep in the next room, Smith worked by the glow of his open laptop to orient the satellite antenna out the open window of the clinic and into the night sky. When the computer was dialed in, he sat back in a folding chair and surveyed his work space. His M4 carbine was propped up against the wall, his rucksack was on the floor beside him, and six inches to the right of the keyboard was his "spitter," an empty water bottle for the big dip of Skoal packed behind his lower lip.

As he began to type out a message to Task Force Dagger, the stillness was shattered by machine-gun fire. Out the window he could see tracers lighting up the sky—originating from the bridge and heading in his direction.

Fumbling in the dark, Smith stuffed his equipment back into his rucksack, ran outside, heaved the pack into his truck's bed, and slammed the tailgate shut. He heard something to his right and smelled hashish. Pulling on his NODs, he peered around the side of the medical clinic and saw three guerrillas on their haunches, the embers of their hash pipe glowing through his night vision.

Over the machine-gun fire somebody yelled out from the hill, "All right, everybody get up here. This is it. This is the Alamo!"

Come on, everybody, let's get high. Smith sang his own impromptu version of the Vietnam War–era hit by Country Joe & the Fish, steadying his nerves as he got in the truck and drove the short distance to the hill. *Whoopee, we're all gonna die.*

/

JD and the rest of the sleeping members of ODA 574 were awake, armed, and up the hill—spontaneously dubbed the Alamo—three minutes after the first gunfire shattered the silence.

Alex was on the radio calling out "troops in contact"; Dan was sending word to Task Force Dagger. The guerrillas parked near the Alamo were running for their trucks in a frenzy, tossing supplies in the backs, leaping in, and spinning their wheels as they tore out through the berm and north into the desert toward Damana.

"What do we have?" JD asked Amerine, who was watching tracer fire from enemy guns streaking across the bridge a little over a mile to their west.

"Counterattack is in progress. I'm seeing dozens of enemy dismounts [foot soldiers] pouring across the bridge, around fifty so far and more coming. They're firing something big at what must be another group of our guerrillas retreating from the bridge toward Damana."

"We have guerrillas by the bridge?" JD said.

"I don't know which other trucks would be getting fired at." To Dan, Amerine said, "Try to get commo with Hamid."

"Who am I supposed to call?" asked Dan with a glance at Fox and Bolduc.

"Try the CIA," said Amerine.

"This is fucked up, sir."

"Do your best," said Amerine. "We need to let them know what's coming their way."

The guerrillas' trucks being chased from the bridge by long green streaks of tracer fire turned and came ripping around the backside of Shawali Kowt well beyond the berm. Their headlights and the Taliban tracer fire were suddenly on a crash course with all the trucks that had just retreated from the Alamo. It was a cluster of auto lights and tracer streaks, zigzagging out in the desert.

"What a goat fuck," said Mag.

"Fucked up as an Afghan convoy," said Mike.

"The Taliban might be trying to circle around our rear, sir," said JD.

"I'd rather them surround us here at the Alamo than head north after Hamid," said Amerine. "Damn, who started calling this the Alamo anyway?"

JD laughed.

"Still can't reach the CIA," Dan told Amerine.

He had been trying the CIA's radio for over two minutes, and Karzai's satellite phone was emitting a busy signal. With Fox, Bolduc, and Smith—who was also trying to reach the CIA—on the hill with ODA 574, Amerine had no idea how the 150 guerrillas had been set up to protect Karzai, who he assumed was still in Damana. And since the Taliban were attacking on foot, there were no vehicles for the American jets to bomb. Furthermore, it sounded as if the enemy was firing both light *and* heavy machine guns, suggesting that this was not just a mob but likely an organized unit.

"See the range of those tracers?" Amerine said to Mike. "Doesn't that sound like a Dishka?"*

---

* The DShK (called "Dishka" or, more commonly, "Dushka") is a Russian 12.7 x 108 mm gas-operated, air-cooled heavy machine gun that fires 575 rounds per minute with an effective range topping 2,200 yards, which put the Alamo within range from the north side of the bridge.

"Sure does. Good thing they don't have night vision, because if they wheel that thing down the road a ways, we are in easy range."

"Make sure Bari Gul stays with us," Amerine told JD. "Integrate his men into our perimeter at this end of the hill. Tighten up the lines. We have no idea what we're up against."

JD jogged east toward the other end of the Alamo.

"We've got Spectre inbound," said Alex, referring to a heavily armed AC-130 gunship.*

"I think we're going to need it," said Amerine. Due to its low, slow flight path, the AC-130 would have to return home at dawn when it would become an easy target, but it would probably keep the men alive until then.

Having pantomimed the instructions to Bari Gul—Seylaab was missing again—JD returned to the team while Bari Gul spread his guerrillas out among the American lines of defense, using a flashlight pointed at the ground for guidance. He then approached Amerine, holding his AK-47 at the ready position. Unlike his countrymen, he and his men weren't going anywhere.

With the rest of the guerrillas having fled north, the enemy guns fell silent. This disconcerted the Americans, who had been using the gunfire to estimate the size and location of the Taliban force. None of the attackers had returned to the bridge, which meant there were at least a hundred Taliban on the near side of the river, most of whom had last been seen in the desert beyond the berm, firing toward Damana. But they had also seen some small-arms tracers coming from closer in, on the other side of the berm, suggesting that the Taliban had possibly come back toward Shawali Kowt and surrounded the team's position. It was deadly guesswork; the enemy could be anywhere.

At 100 percent security, ODA 574 covered all avenues of approach

---

* A transport plane mounted with a range of guns on its left-side fuselage—including 25 mm Gatling guns capable of firing 1,800 rounds per minute—and integrated with targeting systems that allow the gunship crews to attack targets with surgical precision. Made famous during the Vietnam War for protecting ground forces and firebases surrounded by the enemy, it is said that no American base protected by one was ever lost.

with their carbines aimed into the night and a supply of RPGs near each man. "Can we set up the mortar tube?" Ronnie asked JD.

"Go ahead."

Ronnie, Mike, and Brent ran to the trucks at the northern base of the hill and grabbed a huge 82 mm Russian mortar, behaving like kids who had just been given permission to launch their new model rocket. They lugged the tube back to the hilltop and began to set it up while Wes, Smith, and some of the guerrillas brought cases of mortar rounds.

"We need to hang a round to get the plate set," said Brent. Together, the three weapons sergeants aimed the mortar toward the bridge, and Brent dropped a round in the end of the super-elevated tube. There was a loud thump when the round launched. No one spoke for several seconds as they listened for the blast.

"Jesus," said Mike.

"A dud?" said Brent.

"Either that or we left on way too big a charge," said Ronnie.

Alex looked up from the digital map on his computer. "We'll have an AC-130 on station in about thirty minutes."

Boom! The mortar exploded in the distance.

"Not a dud," said Brent.

"We have a problem," said Amerine, who was standing next to Alex scanning the berm that wrapped around the northern side of Shawali Kowt. "The guerrillas left some of their own behind, and now they're up on the berm and who knows where else."

"That's gonna make it tough for the gunship to know where to shoot," said Alex. "Especially if we get attacked from the north."

Amerine nodded. "Sir," he said to Fox, who was still trying to get through to Karzai on the radio. "I'm sending out a recon element to bring back some of our guerrillas. I don't know how many are out there, but they're going to get cut to shit."

"How many are going?" asked Fox.

"A split team. We won't be gone long—we only have a half hour before Spectre gets on station. Just wanted to keep you in the loop."

It had been five minutes since the Taliban had attacked, and Amerine was expecting them to open fire on the Alamo at any moment.

"Okay, here's the plan," Amerine told JD. "Two jobs. The first is for a split team to go get the guerrillas before the gunship arrives in roughly twenty minutes and mistakes them for Taliban. After the first team returns, a second split team will set up on the berm over there." He pointed north to his original assault position, where Seylaab had led the charge earlier that day. "They're going to keep watch so the bad guys don't sneak up on us."

Perhaps a half mile beyond the berm, a heavy exchange of automatic weapons fire erupted, but the men couldn't see who was shooting or what they were shooting at.

JD checked his watch and said to Amerine, "You take your split team out to get those lost guerrillas. That way you can run the defense when the gunship is on station."

"All right. You reestablish the perimeter. I'll issue a contingency plan before we head out."

Amerine walked over to Mag, who had taken up a position facing north. "Get Mike, Brent, Wes, and Dan," he said. "We're going on a rescue mission."

"Yes, sir!" said Mag.

ODA 574 assembled in the center of the Alamo and conducted a pre-combat inspection of their NODs, the lasers mounted on their carbines, and their radios.

"Good to go," said Mag.

"Okay, five-point contingency plan," Amerine said to the team. "I'm heading out with Mag, Mike, Brent, Dan, and Wes. We'll be gone twenty minutes. If we make contact with the enemy, we'll attempt to defeat him and Charlie Mike [continue the mission]. If we meet a superior force, we'll pop smoke and get back here right away. If you make contact, stay put in this position and we'll return to you. You have nowhere to retreat from the Alamo, so stay here unless you're overrun, then initiate the evasion plan. If you come under attack, keep an eye out for a way for my split team to get back inside the perimeter. If that's impossible, we'll form a second perimeter on the berm and link up when the situation permits. If we're not back in twenty-five minutes and have not made contact, prohibit all AC-130 fires along the corridor from this hill west to the bridge and south of the berm, unless you're engaged with an enemy attack from that direction. Engage everything else freely north of the berm and in every other direction. Time is 2300."

The split team moved north in a wedge, with Brent walking point; Mike, Mag, Dan, and Wes on staggered flanks; and Amerine trailing. "Not so fun being the point man on this little walk," Mike whispered to Dan. They made their way past the medical clinic, then turned west to follow the southern side of the berm. From here they walked toward the bridge with the berm on their right and Shawali Kowt on their left. Sporadic gunfire from the west and northwest led the men to believe that the enemy was staying north of this corridor alongside the berm.

The night was chilly, but Amerine felt beads of sweat forming behind his goggles. He radioed the split team's location to JD, who watched from the Alamo until he lost sight of them behind the buildings in town. With every burst of gunfire in the distance, JD winced, concerned that his boys might have walked into a fight. They had no firm idea how many enemy fighters had attacked or where they currently were.

"AC-130 will be on station in fifteen minutes," said Alex.

Creeping below the base of the embankment, Amerine's split team heard the gunfire getting louder. Suddenly, an Afghan holding an AK-47 at his side came into view on the berm above them. Everyone stopped. The man's body was instantly speckled with the five green dots from their lasers.

"Americans, Americans," Brent called out. Not seeing them, the man half-waved in their direction, keeping his AK-47 pointed down, and the Americans climbed the incline to find four guerrillas sitting in the dirt.

"Come," said Amerine, waving. The guerrillas shook their heads. "They aren't coming," Brent said. "I'm going to crack an IR [infrared] chemlite and leave it here to mark the hill."

As Brent bent the plastic chemlite, the crunching sound of the glass ampoules breaking inside seemed greatly amplified. He shook the tube, the chemicals creating a reaction that caused the stick to emit infrared light through its dark plastic coating.

Brent dropped it next to the Afghans and did his best to explain to them what it was for, hoping they would leave it alone.

"Okay," said Amerine. "Let's keep moving."

⸜

JD checked his watch. The split team had been gone almost fifteen minutes, and the gunfire to the west was getting louder. Then, down by the bridge, they heard the deep rumble of the DShK as it began to belt tracer rounds north and northeast into the desert. If these were local Taliban, JD realized, their families might still be in Shawali Kowt, which stood dangerously close to the Alamo. In that case, they would most likely attack with small arms and RPGs, not the DShK. On the other hand, they might move the heavy Soviet machine gun closer to the Americans.

Finally, Amerine's voice crackled over the radio. "We're on our way back. What's the status of Spectre?"

"It will be on station in five minutes," JD said.

The six men came into view, alone.

"Did you find any of our guys out there?" JD asked when they reached his position on the Alamo.

"Two groups on the berm," said Amerine. "Wouldn't budge, so we marked them with IR chemlites."

"IR chem?" said Alex, putting down his microphone to listen.

"Yeah. Fifteen hundred meters out, the other about seven hundred," said Amerine. "Okay, your turn, JD. Get out to the berm, spot for the enemy, and get your asses back directly if things get hot."

Infrared lights blinking on their shoulders, JD, Ronnie, Victor, Dan, and Brent moved out.

"AC-130 is coming on station now," said Alex.

The roar of the AC-130's four turboprop engines, familiar to the men after years of airborne missions, filled the air as JD's split team quickly covered the 150 yards to the berm and formed a line across the top.

"We are in position," he radioed back.

"What do you see?" Amerine asked.

"The enemy is to the west of us and advancing west-northwest about a klick away. They are well north of the berm."

Alex relayed the four friendly positions—the Alamo, JD's men, and the two groups of guerrillas—to the gunship. Large groups of enemy dismounts beyond the berm were pushing north, he told the pilot, while their own guerrillas were in vehicles. There could be Taliban vehicles in the mix, however, since nobody could be sure that none had crossed the river.

"It's a mess out there; the pilots aren't sure who is who," Alex said to Amerine. "JD spotted a group coming around over there. Watch this."

An infrared spotlight—which the men could see through their NODs—poured down from the Spectre north of JD's position.

JD came on the radio and said, "The enemy is east of that spot about five hundred meters."

"Is Spectre cleared hot?" Alex asked Amerine.

"Yup. Put them to work."

The gunship banked into an orbit over the target, and long streaks of flame, each composed of hundreds of bullets, began pounding a group of twenty to thirty Taliban who had been following a road that ran to Damana.

"They're dead," said Alex.

Behind them, Fox was on the radio finally talking to Casper. "Most of our guerrillas retreated back to you in Damana," Fox said. "We need you to get them to come back down."

And that's why we needed you there, and not here, thought Amerine.

"The enemy is so scattered I have no idea how we're doing," said Alex. "But this is definitely gonna scare the shit out of them."

A moment later, the gunship took out another target farther north.

"Sucks to be the Taliban tonight," said Mag.

About an hour and a half after the initial attack began, the Taliban stopped firing and vanished into the night.

"Gunship isn't seeing anything between Damana and Shawali Kowt," said Alex.

"Start working targets south of the river," said Amerine. "Usual rules of engagement: Look for any convoys coming this way."

It appeared that the AC-130 had forced the Taliban to retreat, but ODA 574 couldn't chance it. They had to assume the enemy was still out there. For hours the men had missed a bunker they were standing on top of. What tunnel systems and camouflaged trenches did the surrounding desert, orchards, and structures conceal? Amerine decided that he'd better keep the team close in case there were any more surprises.

"Wes," he said, "call JD and have him come back."

While the gunship continued to orbit the immediate vicinity, the team stayed at 100 percent security, positioned close to one another along the Alamo's upper slopes, with Bari Gul's men covering the eastern end. IR chemlites scattered down the slopes marked their location for the AC-130.

Around midnight, Smith, who had reassembled his commo equipment near the Alamo's highest point and had spent the last hour sending SITREPs to Task Force Dagger, realized that he'd missed the escape-and-recovery plan. If the Alamo were overrun, he had no idea what to do.

"Sir," he asked Bolduc, "what's the evac plan?"

"Nobody's coming to get us," Bolduc said. "We're staying here."

By four in the morning, the AC-130 had run out of targets after engaging two small convoys on the Kandahar Road, and JD downgraded security to 50 percent. Dan, who had joined Smith at his position, had taken second shift and was rolled up in a ball on the ground, shivering in his sleep. Pulling the poncho liner from his go-to-hell pack, Smith laid it over Dan, tucking the edges between his shoulders and the dirt.

Lying prone at the top of the Alamo, Smith fought to stay awake as he looked down the barrel of his rifle toward the river. Aside from his own chattering teeth, it was mostly quiet, and the monotonous "mrrrr" of the big propeller plane circling overhead began to lull him to sleep. He bit his lip, which silenced his teeth but did little for his eyes, which struggled to stay open. Then the AC-130's guns erupted again, firing at a target to the west and giving Smith one more surge of adrenaline to get him through the shift.

At dawn on December 4, the smoke from cooking fires in Shawali Kowt began to drift across the Alamo, where the sun warmed the men covered in the slime of day-old sweat and dirt. Bari Gul's men were shuffling around the eastern end of the hill, some of them arranging prayer rugs, when Mag opened his eyes.

"Can't believe it's morning already," he said.

"Are you kidding me?" Mike said. "That was one of the longest nights of my life."

In the morning light, the ridgeline across the river was more jagged than Amerine remembered; the contrast between its rusty color and the clear blue sky sharpened its features.

"I see four dudes with RPGs," said Mike, looking toward the bridge with binoculars.

"I've got air," said Alex.

With his binoculars, Amerine saw the four Taliban walking west, toward the bridge, along the road on the other side of the river. There was no need to consult with Karzai; these were enemy combatants nowhere near civilian buildings. But looking over at Fox and Bolduc, Amerine wondered if they had any idea what Karzai was up to in Damana, and if they intended to join him.

"Let's kill those guys," said Amerine, his voice flat. "What do we have, Alex?"

"Clear line of sight. Let's lase them."

Mike was already on it, having set up the SOFLAM—which estimates the distance to a target and marks it for laser-guided munitions—on a tripod. All of the previous bombs had been guided by the aircrafts' own laser marker targeting systems; this was the team's first use of a SOFLAM on this mission.

Within three minutes, Alex had talked an F-18 pilot onto the target's position, confirmed that it was cleared hot by the captain, and chosen a 500-pound laser-guided bomb from the jet's weapons menu. Turning to Mike he said, "Laser on."

"Lasing," said Mike as he pointed the beam at the center of the four-man group.

Seconds later, black smoke and brown dust consumed the men, followed by a loud explosion.

"Damn!" somebody yelled, but otherwise the Alamo was quiet.

The cloud dissipated. Two of the Taliban, bloody and obviously injured, were dragging a body out of sight behind a rise. There was no sign of the fourth man.

Bolduc walked over to Mike to request a SOFLAM tutorial.

Hearing this, Mag muttered under his breath, "OJT" (on-the-job training). The presence of the brass continued to irritate him, and it only got worse a half hour later when JD informed ODA 574 that the rest of Fox's staff would arrive that night.

Since their first day in Petawek, Fox had been coordinating to get his battalion staff in-country. They had solved the transportation problem by purchasing two new Toyota Tundra king cab trucks in Pakistan to be flown in with the men.

"How many more guys are coming?" Mag asked Amerine, taking advantage of a moment when Fox and Bolduc had moved out of earshot.

"Twelve. It's not the entire battalion staff, just a command-and-control group."

"Any ODAs coming with them?"

"Not that I've heard about," Amerine said.

"Twelve battalion staff on this tiny hill is twelve too many," said Mag. He suddenly realized that Smith was only two feet away, trying to ignore the conversation. "Shit," said Mag. "No offense."

Smith shrugged. "None taken," he said.

/

Shortly before one o'clock that afternoon, the guerrillas who had fled to Damana returned to Shawali Kowt, honking their trucks' horns and holding their weapons overhead as though they had won the night's battle. The men of ODA 574 watched in numb amusement, too tired to be angry at them for running away the night before. The fact that the guerrillas were able to return supported the evidence from aerial recon that their attackers had either been killed by the AC-130 in the desert between the two towns or escaped back to the southern side of the river.

Soon after, Karzai drove in with the CIA team, and Fox trotted down the hill to greet him.

"Looks like we won't have to send Mag and Dan to Damana," said JD to Amerine. "On the flip side, it sure isn't a good idea for Hamid to be down here right now."

"I know, but I would really rather keep him close to us after that mess last night," said Amerine as he watched Karzai and his entourage take over a cinder-block building adjacent to the medical clinic.

When he walked down the hill, Amerine was greeted by the usual group of guerrillas guarding Karzai's headquarters. Inside, Karzai was sitting with his circle of tribal leaders, Fox by his side.

"Hello, Jason," Karzai said.

Amerine sat down. "I need your help, Hamid," he said. "I have to organize a group to take control of the hill overlooking the bridge west of here. This will require a more elaborate explanation than Seylaab can manage, so could you translate? I'd like to get things moving right away."

"Of course. Tell me what men you require."

"I need Bashir. His men did very well yesterday. I will also take my friend Bari Gul."

Seated across from Karzai, Bashir nodded when Karzai spoke to him.

"They will be ready in an hour," Karzai said to Amerine.

⁕

Bashir, Bari Gul, and their men were assembled beside the Alamo, listening to Karzai translate the details of the plan.

JD's split team and Bari Gul's men would establish a "support by

fire" position on the berm a mile west of Shawali Kowt, overlooking ODA 574's new objective—the hill with the ruins—six hundred
yards to their south. Three PKM machine guns with a range of more
than one thousand yards would provide support fire for an assault
team led by Amerine. Once JD's team was in place, Amerine's team
would drive to some compounds they had identified at the base of the
hill. There they would lead Bashir's men in a classic infantry assault to
seize the ruins at its top.

"Four years at West Point and that's all you come up with?" JD
said to Amerine.

Admittedly, it wasn't much; but the simpler the plan, the harder it
would be for the guerrillas to mess up.

As the guerrillas dispersed after the briefing, Amerine took Bashir
by the arm and led him over to Karzai.

"Can you ask Bashir if he's clear on everything?" Amerine asked.
Karzai uttered something in Pashto, and Bashir gave a nod. "He says
his men are ready to take the hill."

"See you on top," JD said to Amerine just before he got in his truck
shortly after 3 P.M. to follow Bari Gul's three vehicles to the western
end of the berm.

Less than a mile down the road from Shawali Kowt, Bari Gul
turned right, passed through a break in the berm, and headed into the
desert. He made a U-turn and drove back to park on the north side
of the berm, concealed from anyone who might have been watching
from across the river. The hope was that their small convoy would
appear as if it were heading back toward Damana.

JD parked alongside the others and hiked up the berm to recon
the position before emplacing his men. He lay prone across the com-
pacted ground at its top, the open desert behind him to the north. In
front of him, to the south, the battlefield stretched across six hundred
yards of farmland to the ruins of a fortress that looked like a sand
castle eroding back into the hill it was built upon. Two hundred yards
beyond that was the bridge across the Arghandab River.

When he sighted down his carbine barrel toward the ruins, JD saw an open, unplanted field, divided at the four-hundred-yard mark by an irrigation canal with a large compound on either side. The nearer one, on the north side of the canal, they'd named "compound one" and was to be the "objective rally point." A wooden bridge barely large enough for a vehicle spanned the canal to "compound two." Past the canal the terrain sloped gradually upward to the ruins, then downward to the orchards along the riverbank. The road that JD's element had taken out of Shawali Kowt turned to the left where the fields ended, skirted the right (western) side of the hill, and continued on over the bridge and to Kandahar. On the west side of the road, about two hundred yards from the bridge, was another set of ruins dubbed "compound three," atop a small rise that the men thought might conceal enemy movement to the west.

Amerine's assault team would leave the road a quarter of a mile before it went left and drive across the field to compound one, then move on foot across the canal to the second compound, where they would stage their assault up the hill. The machine guns manned by JD's team would engage any enemy positions on the hill or in the trenches that existed around it; they would also spot for Taliban hiding in the orchards on their side of the river. If needed, the machine guns could be super-elevated to reach the orchards and ridgeline on the other side of the Arghandab as well.

JD could see no Taliban, anywhere.

The guerrillas lugged the PKM machine guns up the slope, staying quiet and low so as not to silhouette themselves. Soon the guns were in place, tripods dug in and ammunition stacked, with Ronnie, Brent, and Victor standing by as JD arranged Bari Gul's men in a security perimeter.

Dan, who had set up next to the guerrillas amid the boxes of ammunition, called Amerine, speaking in a hushed voice into his radio: "Support by fire is good to go, but we don't see any enemy anywhere."

In an infantry attack, the job of the support-by-fire element is to "soften up the target," that is, kill the enemy defenders on and around the objective by surprising them with overwhelming firepower just prior to the assault team's attack. In this case, the enemy had not shown themselves, which made the assault all the more dangerous.

"This just became a movement to contact,"* replied Amerine, thinking, *Shit, we just lost the initiative.*

"We've got you covered," said Dan.

"Roger," said Amerine. "We're moving out."

---

* An offensive operation in which a unit maneuvers through an area or toward an objective while uncertain as to the location or number of enemy defenders. It becomes a contest of who spots the other first, though the offensive unit is often considered "bait" to flush out the enemy from his hiding places.

CHAPTER TEN

The Ruins

In preparing for battle, I have always found that plans are useless, but planning is indispensable.
　—General Dwight D. Eisenhower

Mike started his truck, shifted into first gear, and eased between the Alamo and the medical clinic onto the dirt road that led west out of Shawali Kowt. He looked over at Amerine in the passenger seat and Alex in the back of his pickup, then focused on Bashir's guerrillas—each armed with an AK-47—in the truck twenty yards ahead. He wondered if their smiles and laughter were born from nervousness, bravado, or the prospect of meeting Allah in the next few minutes.

There were three trucks ahead of Mike's, each with eight guerrillas, and two more close behind. Mag's truck brought up the rear. Standing on top of the Alamo, Fox, Bolduc, Smith, and a handful of Bari Gul's men watched the convoy disappear behind the buildings in town. Karzai's security was now the responsibility of his two hundred remaining guerrillas, who had scattered onto rooftops and along the berm. Inside his command post with Casper's spooks, Karzai was on the phone with reporters, diplomats, the Northern Alliance, his family, and intermediaries of the Taliban, all of whom were probing the statesman for news of his intentions now that he was, as he put it, "just outside Kandahar."

Once the trucks cleared the town center, Mike could see fields on their left, desert and the berm on their right, and the deserted main road that headed over the bridge and on to Kandahar dead ahead.

Passing JD's position on the berm, Bashir's trucks followed the road west, then turned sharply south across unplanted fields toward compound one, the uneven terrain causing the vehicles to spread apart, with wide gaps between them.

When the first truck parked at the compound, the Afghans immediately dismounted and charged toward the hill, not waiting for the rest of the convoy. A second truck stopped, its guerrillas jumping out and running after the first group, followed by the third truck. These ragged clusters of men moved over the rough-hewn timber bridge that spanned the irrigation canal separating compound one from compound two, with Bashir running alongside and making no attempt to stop or organize them.

Bouncing across the field in their truck, Amerine and Mike watched the Afghans sprint over the bridge in a textbook guerrilla attack: lots of gusto and zero organization.

Mike threw up his hand in frustration. "There they go."

"So much for the simple plan," Amerine said.

"You have quite a mess there," radioed JD as Mike parked next to the empty trucks. He, Amerine, and Alex got out and began to run forward.

"Roger that," said Amerine. "We'll go round them up—but it looks like our objective might be deserted after all."

Just as Bashir's lead group was halfway up the hill, unseen Taliban fighters opened fire on the guerrillas. The sharp crack of AK-47s was joined by machine guns; the guerrillas halted, then scattered and ran for cover wherever they could find it—in a ditch, up to the ruins, back behind compound two. At the canal, the Americans paused.

"At least we'll have no problem catching up with them now," said Amerine. "But where the hell is Mag's truck?"

/

Mag, Wes, and Ken had been bringing up the rear when the truck-loads of guerrillas at the head of the convoy had reached the fields and suddenly sped up, leaving a cloud of dust in their wake. Unable to see where they'd turned off the road, Ken slowed the truck.

The hill with the ruins was four hundred yards behind them to their left; the berm with the support-by-fire team was one hundred yards behind them on their right. They had overshot the spot in the fields where the lead element had turned off, and Ken was now steering around a bend in the road that brought them within plain sight of the enemy. Seated in the truck's bed, Mag and Wes heard bullets whiz overhead.

"Out of the truck!" Mag yelled to Wes. Grabbing their rifles, they jumped out as Ken continued to drive, hunched low behind the dashboard, searching for a way to get to compound one that was visible two hundred yards to their left. Behind the slow-moving truck, Mag and Wes used the tailgate for cover as they jogged along in a hunched position.

"We need to turn around and get some solid cover!" yelled Wes. "This truck is a fucking bullet magnet."

"Do you see where the fire is coming from?" Mag shouted back.

"No! Somewhere ahead of us."

Mag yelled to Ken, "Where they at? Where they at?" But Ken didn't respond. The truck almost stopped, and Mag briefly thought Ken was going to get out and use the truck for cover as well, but instead he turned onto a road that looped to their left across the fields toward the rally point and their comrades. Sucking in exhaust and keeping their heads down, Mag and Wes continued to jog with a weapon in one hand and the other gripping the tailgate.

The truck picked up speed until the two men were running to keep pace. They sprinted thirty yards before they had to let go of the tailgate. "Fuck!" yelled Wes as the truck sped away. Mag fell forward, rolled a couple of times in the middle of the road, came to a stop, and shouted "Motherfucker!"[1]

At the support-by-fire location, JD watched the guerrillas who had been charging toward the ruins react to the gunfire. The lead group, including Bashir, broke left and continued their ascent, traversing to the northeast corner of the ruins and disappearing into a crumbling section of the wall. The others scattered to the right, diving into the trench that ran vertically up the side of the slope, parallel to the road that continued onto the bridge: It appeared that this trench line had originally been dug as outer defenses for the hilltop fortress. After approximately ten seconds under fire, the entire guerrilla force had broken its attack and was now hunkered down, out of sight.

JD's split team had identified the positions of the Taliban as soon as they had opened fire, and JD immediately radioed a SALUTE (Size, Activity, Location, Uniform, Time, and Equipment) report to Amerine: "We see two enemy positions by the orchards along the river to the west of the bridge and one enemy position on the ridge across the river to the south of the bridge. They are engaging you guys with small arms and light machine guns. No idea how many there are."

"Roger," said Amerine. "Can you see what my guerrillas are doing on the hill?"

"I have visual on three groups of guerrillas; you own the hill. They aren't really taking much fire, but they sure are keeping their heads down."

To reach the Taliban in the orchards on the near side of the river, and on the ridge more than a thousand yards away on the other side of the river, JD's team pointed their guns into the sky and used plunging fire—shooting the bullets in a rainbow-like arc—at more than 650 rounds per minute. As the bullets landed they kicked up dirt that JD tracked with his binoculars, directing the men to "walk" the fire onto the heads of the enemy.

The Taliban on the other side of the river, who had been firing their light machine guns at the guerrillas, were now staying low or had retreated from their gun emplacements—or were dead—but the Americans continued to rake their positions with bursts of gunfire. There was still enemy AK-47 fire, however, coming from the orchards.

"We're encountering some light resistance," Amerine radioed to Fox back at the Alamo, his calm voice contrasting sharply with the echo of machine-gun fire. "Some of our guerrillas have holed up in the northeast corner of the fort and we're trying to get the rest to move up."

Spitting out the dirt he'd eaten during his somersault along the road, Mag darted behind some low rocks with Wes—the only cover they could find. Bullets were crackling in the air, but all Mag could think about was taking a piss. Lying on his side, he got his pack's waist strap undone and dug below his pistol belt in search of the zipper, his hands fumbling with fear and adrenaline. By the time he unzipped his fly, it was too late; urine was streaming down his legs.

Wes didn't notice— he was too busy trying to scope out the best route to rejoin their teammates without getting shot. He decided on the straight-line approach.

Looking back at Mag, he said "Let's do it!" and started running across the open field toward the compound some two hundred yards away. Mag zipped back up and charged after him. "I am gonna kick Ken's ass," he growled.

A minute later they were at the vehicles, bent over and sucking wind. Mag glanced up to see Amerine beckoning to him; with a grunt, he jogged over, forcing himself not to look at Ken, who was standing beside their truck. Wes joined Mike at the corner of the compound wall, where he was peering around it to the west. There the road met the bridge—the likely avenue for an attack. The last two truckloads of guerrillas were by their vehicles, awaiting orders.

Still breathing hard, Mag knelt beside Amerine next to the canal.

"What happened?" asked Amerine.

"I'll fill you in later. Now's not the time."

"All right," said Amerine, puzzled. "JD's boys are keeping the enemy pinned down. There seem to be positions in the orchards along the river and on the ridge to the south. Our guerrillas are in the ruins and all over this hill. I am going to run forward to compound two and assess the situation, then we'll get the rest of these guys moving."

He radioed JD. "See anything new?"

"Negative."

"Nothing at the ruins?"

"Nothing but our guerrillas keeping their heads down. Looks like they aren't going anywhere."

"Keep that fire coming," Amerine said.

"I'm putting the CCP [casualty collection point] at this wall," Ken called out to Amerine, "with the trucks."

"All right. I'll come back for you in a bit." Amerine turned to Mag. "You're coming with me."*

"If we aren't back in five minutes," Amerine informed the rest of the assault team, "Mike is in charge; try to reach me by radio and give JD a SITREP. Watch that western flank. If you come under direct attack, let me know and we'll come back with some of the guerrillas."

Heads bobbed in unison as the men checked their watches. Crossing the bridge over the irrigation canal, Amerine and Mag arrived at the southeast corner of compound two. Mike and Wes ran to the western side of compound one in time to see a truck speeding across the open ground a half mile to the west. It was well out of range, but Mike went ahead and fired off two grenades from his carbine's launcher that landed far short as the vehicle disappeared into an orchard. Realizing that there could be more trucks out there, and that a full charge from that direction was a possibility, he yelled to Ken, "Radio JD and have him send some of our G's out to that third compound across the road. Have them watch our western flank."

Meanwhile, Amerine and Mag were surveying the sloping hill they needed to ascend in order to reach the objective. The sun was low in the west, casting long shadows that revealed a subtle cleavage near the slope's center all the way up to the ruins.

"Stay here," said Amerine. He walked out about thirty yards into the open, standing at full height in spite of the bullets passing overhead.

"Those are bullets, sir!" Mag shouted.

"Yeah, but they can't see me here!" Amerine yelled back. "I'm in dead space. This is where we'll push the rest of the guerrillas up the hill."

Amerine jogged back behind the wall of compound two. "I want

---

* One of the basics in small-unit tactics is for the team leader to move his men physically on the battlefield: point out where men need to go in person, not over a radio where directions can be misinterpreted, leading to fratricide accidents. This ensures full situational awareness.

to get you and Alex up there so he can put bombs on these assholes shooting at us." He pointed out some high ground directly west of the ruins, which appeared to offer the best overlook for spotting the enemy. "You'll be exposed once you get out there. While you're executing that, I'll get Mike and Wes to help me push the guerrillas up the hill, round up the ones who are pinned down in the trench, and we'll occupy the ruins. Got it?"

"Got it," said Mag, following Amerine back across the canal.

Still watching the western flank with Mike, Wes suddenly said, "Who the hell is *that*?" Looking toward the north, Mike saw a group of guerrillas running south on the other side of the road and into the open desert—led by Seylaab, with his aqua robe flowing behind him. "It's our guerrillas," he said, "and they're with that crazy interpreter."

Mesmerized, both men watched Seylaab bolt across the open terrain directly toward the river and the bridge, in plain sight of the enemy, and run to the top of the small hillock where the eroding walls of compound three were located. With his rifle at his hip, Seylaab emptied his entire clip, on full automatic, in the direction of the bridge.

"I'm telling you," Mike said to Wes, "that guy thinks he's John Fucking Wayne."

Mag and Alex moved out first, crossed the canal to the second compound, and jogged up the dead space, which got them three-quarters of the way up the hill. Then they sprinted at an angle to the west, ascending and traversing the right side of the hill, arriving at the northwest corner of the ruins without drawing fire. At this elevation they could see that the trench continued to the top, running directly to the high exposed ground they would use as an observation post.

Catching their breath for a minute, they did a three-count, darted across the twenty-five yards to the trench, and dove in. Looking uphill, Mag and Alex discovered that they weren't alone: a group of Bashir's guerrillas was sitting against the earthen walls of a deep, circular fighting position, smiling down at them. One, a man in his early twenties, had wrapped himself in an orange blanket, the color the U.S. military had designated to identify friendly forces. Mag laughed. "You want to make damn sure you don't get shot, eh, amigo?" Mag said, tugging on the blanket. The man grinned.

Peering over the top of the trench, Mag and Alex had a clear view of both sides of the bridge and the terrain on the near side of the river. Muzzle flashes were erupting from the edge of the orchard along their side of the Arghandab just west of the bridge; these orchards continued west and jutted north into the desert some five hundred yards downriver. In the desert between their position and the orchard, a Taliban fighter rose from a foxhole three hundred yards out and began to run toward the river. Mag shot a few rounds and the man dove into another hole some four hundred yards out, about the range of his M4. Elevating the carbine, Mag continued to fire while Alex shot M203 smoke grenades from his carbine in the same direction.

The rising smoke acted as markers that Alex used to direct the coming strikes from F-18s. Almost instantly, a jet shot by, heading northwest toward Shawali Kowt. It banked, dropping in elevation, and came back on a western heading, only a mile or two away and screaming directly at them.

"He sees us, right?" Mag said.

"He can't actually *see* us," said Alex, continuing to spot his targets.

"I got a signal mirror here."

Concentrating on talking to the pilot, Alex didn't respond. Mag glanced at the guerrilla with the orange blanket. "Fuck it!" he said, ripping the blanket from the man's shoulders and scrambling over the edge of the trench. Hugging the ground, he spread out the blanket and weighted it down at the corners with rocks. Enemy fire churned the ground around him, and he dived back into the trench.

"Can he see *that*?" Mag shouted to Alex as the aircraft roared past.

A 500-pound bomb exploded a few hundred yards away, shaking the ground. For the first time since the assault began, there was silence. Mag looked toward the orchard. In place of the muzzle flashes, smoke was rising from a patch of blackened earth.

Mike, Wes, and ten guerrillas had crossed the canal to compound two, where Amerine began to orient them on the layout of the hill, including the dead space. He was pointing out where he'd last seen the guerrillas and where Alex and Mag were positioned, when a guerrilla peeked out of a trench only forty or fifty yards up the slope.

"They scattered like mice," said Amerine. "I'm going to get those guys; then we can rally here and move up the hill."

Running across the slope, he jumped into the trench as machine-gun fire raked its top.

Eight guerrillas were seated in the three-foot-wide, four-foot-deep space, smiling broadly, as though they had been expecting Amerine. The oldest, in his late forties, pulled out the small rug he was sitting on and slid it next to him, motioning for Amerine to take a load off. Even in trench warfare, Afghan hospitality persisted.

Amerine thanked him with a slight bow but remained squatting. He waved the guerrillas closer and, following his lead, they cautiously peered over the edge of the trench up the slope, which was being hit sporadically by bullets. Doubting he would be able to make himself understood, Amerine indicated the dead space beyond where the bullets were striking and drew a line with his finger to the ruins. He pointed at himself, ran in place, motioned up the hill, pointed at each of them, and said, "I go up there. You, come."

They seemed to understand—because they shook their heads "no." As if to punctuate their resolve, machine-gun fire raked across the top of the trench. Amerine flinched, then stood tall, which left him exposed from the shoulders up, turned toward the incoming fire, and, with both hands held high, flipped off the Taliban. "Fuck you!" he yelled, before ducking back down.

Another burst of fire showered them with dirt.

The guerrillas cheered and the older man offered Amerine a cigarette. When Amerine declined, the man shrugged and put it into his own mouth, which Amerine took to mean "I'm having a smoke. I'm not going anywhere."

Just then, the bomb that Alex had called in exploded to the west.

In the ensuing silence, Amerine pulled the man with the cigarette to his feet, then crawled out of the trench, staying low for a few yards, and urged the Afghans to follow. One pulled himself out and began to run, and the rest followed, sprinting after Amerine back to the safety of compound two, where Mike and Wes were waiting with the other guerrillas.

"All right, let's get them all to the ruins," said Amerine.

⁄

Still working his radio, Alex turned to Mag and said, "I'm getting a low-battery warning; can you grab me some new batteries?"

"Sure," said Mag, thinking they were in Alex's go-to-hell pack, lying nearby on the ground.

"No," said Alex when Mag reached for the pack. "They're not here. They're down in the truck."

Fuck, thought Mag. But his orders from Amerine were to get "warheads on foreheads," so he put on his go-to-hell pack, picked up his M4, and climbed out of the trench. He bolted across the exposed ground to the corner of the ruins, sprinted down through the dead space, passing Amerine, Mike, and the guerrillas, and didn't stop till he arrived at the bridge over the canal.

Walking over it to compound one Mag studiously avoided Ken, who was still standing by the trucks with a couple of guerrillas. He dug through Alex's pack, grabbed the batteries, and retraced his route, all the way back to the top of the hill.

"Special delivery," he said as he handed Alex the batteries, his chest heaving from the exertion. "Don't let this happen again!" The two men began to laugh.

⁄

"You want to help push these guys up the hill?" Amerine asked Mike, nodding toward the guerrillas waiting alongside the eastern wall of compound two. "Not really," said Mike with a grin as he began to line them up. Wes hung back to cover their flanks as fifteen Afghans followed Mike out from behind the compound onto the open ground. "Let's go! Let's go!" he said, picking up speed. Running now, with Amerine on the right flank, the group moved into the dead space and steadily up the slope. They heard sporadic gunfire but remained unseen to the enemy.

Reaching the northeast corner of the ruins, Mike looked cautiously through a jagged crack in the thick fortress wall, relaxing at the sight of a few familiar guerrillas on carpets with their backs against what had once been the foundation of a room. They were smoking cigarettes, their AK-47s on the ground before them. Noticing Mike, they broke into smiles and waved him over.

Mike led his guerrillas into the center of the rectangular fortress, about twenty yards wide and forty yards long. At the south-facing corners, narrow windows in the remainder of the ramparts allowed them to see all angles of approach from the river. Two guerrillas at the western wall were taking turns emptying their magazines out the window before ducking back inside. A third was loading a PKM machine gun they'd hauled up.

"Mike," Amerine said, bringing up the rear of guerrillas, "establish a security perimeter. I'm going to pull Mag and Alex in here, and then get Ken."

As Amerine climbed back out through the crack in the wall, another bomb hit the orchard to the west. He ran along the wall of the ruins to the northwest corner, where he could see Mag and Alex's position in the exposed trench line, and hopped in without drawing any fire. "We're moving into the ruins. Get in there and set up a command post. Mike is establishing security."

When the next explosion resonated from the orchard, Mag and Alex crawled out of the trench and headed toward the ruins, followed closely by the guerrillas. Inside, Mag laid the orange blanket on the ground near an old bomb crater in which Alex set up the command post. Checking his watch, Mag was jolted by the realization that it had only been a half hour since they'd left Shawali Kowt—probably only twenty minutes since the shooting began. He had experienced time warps in training, but nothing like this. He would have sworn they'd been getting shot at for hours.

The guerrillas joined the fighters Mike had already positioned at the windows, most of them facing the orchards to the west, where a few pockets of Taliban had survived the bombing sorties and were raking the fortress with bursts of light machine-gun and AK-47 fire. On the left side of the western wall, Mike was helping three of the Afghans adjust the sights on the PKM machine gun. Bashir, who was to their right, waved at Mag and, smiling broadly, stepped to a window, sprayed a clip of ammo, and jumped back. Another guerrilla stood at a window in the southwest corner, fully exposed for thirty or forty seconds as he took his time aiming his rifle. This unnerved Mag, who pulled the man away and set him down on the ground.

To avoid creating a pattern the enemy could anticipate, Mag began to move randomly from window to window, watching for muzzle flashes. In sniper training, his instructor had said, "You give me three seconds, I'm gonna put you down." Now Mag repeated in his head, *I'm up, they see me, I'm down,* to keep himself from staying exposed for too long. If he saw flashes, he returned fire with his carbine, sometimes even pumping out a few M203 grenades from his carbine's launcher before moving on to another window.

I'm up, they see me, I'm down. I'm up, they see me, I'm down . . .

Amerine ran down the hill, passing Wes, who was on his way up. He found Ken with some guerrillas between a truck and the wall of the first compound, on standby at the CCP.

"We've got the hill," Amerine said to him. "Have the guerrillas grab the mortar tube and whatever ammo they can carry and come on up. Follow the dead space there." The shadow made by the slope's cleavage was more prominent now that the sun had dropped lower in the sky.

"Someone else should do it, sir," said Ken. "It's better for me to stay here at the CCP."

"I'm telling you again, Sergeant: Get those men and the mortar up the hill. The CCP is now up there."

Amerine grabbed his rucksack from his truck and bolted back to the ruins, joining Alex, who informed him that they were continuing to take small-arms fire from the orchards. "But I think we got most of them," he said, "or they ran, because it has definitely slowed down."

"I'm going to have the guys start moving their gear up from the trucks," Amerine said. He headed over to Mike's position and told him to go down for his rucksack, then joined Mag by a window.

"Still seeing muzzle flashes at the tree line," said Mag. "They're focusing everything they got up here, and it ain't much." Amerine peeked out the window, scanned the trees, and pulled back just as machine-gun bullets pounded into the outer wall, sending a puff of dust floating into the space where his head had just been. Something hit the top of his boot, and he glanced down at an enemy tracer round glowing green in the dirt between his legs.

Mag was still moving from window to window when he turned to see Wes behind him. "Where'd *you* come from?" he said.

"I followed you guys up, pushing guerrillas. What have we got here?"

"Our guerrillas are shooting at something in the tree line at two o'clock, down the hill, across the road—a hundred fifty yards. I'm also seeing muzzle flashes at ten o'clock, over here." The two men spread out along the fortress wall and began shooting out the windows. Within a couple of minutes, they were eight feet apart, converging on opposite sides of the same western-facing window. From the left, Mag peeked out, saw nothing, and pulled out of the opening. Coming from the right, Wes stuck his head into the window.

Mag heard what sounded like the snap of a bullwhip a foot from his head and saw Wes fly backward and land on the ground. At first, Mag thought Wes had realized his error and jumped away as the bullet passed between the two men. Then Wes dropped his gun, sat up, and swiped at the back of his neck, as if a bee had stung him. "What the hell?!" he yelled, looking over his shoulder.

The second he had popped in front of the window, Wes realized his mistake. When the muscle atop his shoulder had exploded in pain, he thought the captain might have walked over and given him a ferocious slap for his stupidity. He turned to see who had hit him, but there was only a guerrilla, five feet away, holding his rifle at his hip and staring at Wes with wide eyes. Only then did Wes understand that he'd been shot.

"Mag! This motherfucker AD'd me!" shouted Wes, accusing the Afghan of accidentally discharging his gun.

"Put the gun down!" Mag ordered the guerrilla, who looked terrified as he sputtered something in Pashto.

"Shoot that motherfucker!" Wes shouted.

"Captain!" yelled Mag over the din of machine-gun fire. "Wes got shot!"

Looking up from the crater where he'd been about to radio JD, Amerine could see Wes sitting on the ground with his legs crossed in front of him. "What did he say?" Amerine asked Alex.

"Somebody got shot?" said Alex.

Amerine ran across the courtyard as Mag grabbed the gun from the guerrilla and shoved him down.

"Where's my medic?" Amerine shouted, scanning the ruins and realizing that Ken had not driven up with the mortar. *He's still back at the trucks*, he answered himself.

He radioed Ken. "Drive your ass up here! Wes got shot. Keep the truck on the north side of the hill in the dead space where I showed you and you'll be fine."

"Oh shit," came the response. "I'll be right there."

Kneeling down beside Wes, Amerine watched Mag—who was an EMT before he entered Special Forces—assess the wounded man. He checked his pulse: It was strong. He unbuttoned the top of Wes's shirt and pulled the collar down a little, revealing a perfectly round hole to the left of his throat—dangerously close to the artery. Trying to keep it lighthearted, Mag said, "You're right, you just got shot!"

He paused to check the guerrilla's AK-47 lying on the ground next to them: The safety was on, no round was chambered, and the barrel wasn't hot. "It wasn't the guerrilla," Mag said, handing the Afghan back his gun.

"Then shoot those motherfuckers," said Wes, pointing out the window.

The guerrilla lay down on his back and stared up at the sky. "I think your guerrilla fainted," Mag said.

"Shoot those motherfuckers," Wes said again.

"Relax, soldier," said Mag, searching for the bullet's exit wound, which he found a few inches down Wes's back to the left side of his spine. He held his fingers over the two wounds, then eased off. A tiny amount of blood dribbled down: Wes's arteries appeared undamaged.

"Wes," said Mag, "you are so lucky. You are so fucking lucky. You're going home, buddy."

"Fuck!" said Wes. "I don't *want* to go home."

Relieved, Amerine stood up. "You got this covered?"

When Mag nodded, Amerine stepped away to first radio JD for a guerrilla escort for Wes, and then Fox with a report: "Everything here is under control; the enemy activity seems to have subsided. Wes is wounded—he got shot through the neck, but he's completely stable. We'll be bringing him down in a minute. Intent is to relocate the support-by-fire element here for the night."

Five minutes later, Ken rushed into the ruins carrying his aid bag. He got out his stethoscope and performed a full medical assessment on Wes; like Mag, he was most concerned with the proximity of the wound to arteries.

As he was being examined, Wes suddenly understood the seriousness of the situation: *God, I'm shot in the freakin' neck,* he thought. *It can't be this simple. Where's all the blood? How much longer do I have? I feel fine. I can't be fine! I'm shot in the freakin' neck!*

"It's all right, isn't it?" he asked.

"Looks good," said Ken. "A lot going on in this area. Don't want to move you unless I'm sure. Let's get you bandaged up."

But when Mag tried to help Wes out of his shirt, he said, "Don't worry about taking my shirt off—just slap something on there."

"No," said Ken, "we've got to get your shirt off to bandage this."

"Don't cut it off. I can get out of it. Then I can walk off this hill."

"You can walk to the *truck*," said Ken. "It's parked over by the northern wall."

Once Wes was properly bandaged, Ken helped him stand, and Wes moved unsteadily to the truck parked in the dead space right below the ruins, supported between Ken and Mag.

"You got my shirt, right?" Wes said, as they helped him lie down in a cradle of rucksacks and gear.

"What is the big fucking deal about your damn shirt?" asked Mag.

"There's a bullet hole in it. That's my souvenir. Don't lose it, okay?"

Mag shook his head. "Don't worry. I'll keep it safe."

Mag drove the truck down to compound one, parked, and climbed in back, where Ken was continuing to monitor Wes.

"Hear that?" Mag said to Wes. It was quiet. Completely quiet. "Sounds like somebody got that motherfucker for you."

When Amerine came off the hill a few minutes later, Wes was still lying in the bed of the truck by compound one, being tended to by Ken. Two of Bari Gul's trucks, sent over by JD, were just pulling up to take Wes back to Shawali Kowt, where a helicopter would medevac him once it was dark.

"You doing all right?" Amerine asked.

"I'm doing all right," Wes answered, groggy from the shot of morphine Ken had given him. "Have fun in Kandahar. Sorry I won't be here to help."

"We aren't going anywhere for a while. When the Taliban surrender, our mission will shift to counterinsurgency—and that's going to be for the long haul. Get fixed up and maybe they'll let you come back and join us."

Wes smiled at that and gave Amerine a thumbs-up.

The sky was shifting to the milky blue that preceded dusk as the trucks drove away and Amerine climbed back to the open courtyard of the ruins. Guerrillas were positioned along all four walls, and at the crater Alex was requesting a Spectre gunship to fly reconnaissance come nightfall. In the southwest corner, a team of guerrillas manned the PKM machine gun pointing toward the bridge. Mike and Mag were in the center of the ruins, directing guerrillas as they set up for the night.

Everything is looking good, thought Amerine as his radio crackled to life. It was Fox. "Okay, we need your honest assessment," Fox said. "How are things there?"

"We're in a good position," Amerine said. "We're solid. Once it gets dark, we'll bring JD's split team over. We control the whole area from this hill."

"Roger," said Fox.

In spite of Wes's wound, it had been a successful day. The bridge was secure, and they controlled everything north of it for several miles. Across the fields, the sun was setting, prompting Amerine to give JD a warning order to prepare his team to relocate to the ruins. Amerine began to discuss the delegation of duties with Mag and Mike: Once ODA 574 was together in the ruins, Alex and Dan would alternate shifts controlling the AC-130, while the rest of the men would switch off on security, using their night vision to keep watch over all avenues of approach.

Another radio call interrupted.

"Texas One Two," said Fox, "I need you to pull your forces off the hill and move to the support-by-fire position."

"Let me reiterate," Amerine responded. "Everything is under control here. I think we really need to stay put. The helicopters bringing in your staff tonight will be landing north of our position. This was the axis of attack last night. We need to control the bridge."

"Roger, understood. Move your men."

Amerine stared at the radio, shaking his head. Fox's order was a cliché right out of Vietnam, where soldiers would sometimes seize terrain from the enemy during the day—incurring great loss of life—only to be ordered to withdraw, thus giving it back to the Vietcong that night. ODA 574 had taken this hill and suffered a single, non-life-threatening casualty. Now the lieutenant colonel wanted to pull the team back? Tactically, this was the only terrain from which to fully control the bridge, and Amerine knew that Fox understood this. The only reason he could guess for Fox's order was that he believed they were too far out front—that it was too dangerous.

Of course it's dangerous, thought Amerine. *Does he understand we're fighting a fucking war here?*

"Bad news?" asked Mike.

"Fox wants us to give up the hill and move back to JD's position."

Mike shook his head, while Amerine thought through his options and concluded that everything was rapidly going to shit. Worst of all, there wasn't a single thing he could do about it. He was a professional soldier, and he would not disobey this order, because it was neither illegal nor immoral. The lieutenant colonel had the tactical authority to move ODA 574 wherever the hell he wanted. If Amerine expected his own men to follow *his* orders, he had to follow those of his superiors—but he didn't bother to hide his displeasure from Mike and Mag.

"Can you believe this shit?" he said.

Mike shook his head again, and Mag said, "This is about as fucked as it gets."

"Yep," said Amerine. "Fucked up as an Afghan convoy."

The assault team—minus Wes—begrudgingly packed up their gear, to the confusion of the guerrillas. Without an interpreter, there was no way to explain why the Americans were walking away from the place they'd fought so hard to occupy.

As the men transferred the equipment from the ruins to their trucks parked at compound one, they noticed a vehicle coming toward them from the direction of the support-by-fire location. It was Casper, being driven by one of Bari Gul's guerrillas.

"Sorry, skipper," Casper said to Amerine, getting out of the passenger seat. "I thought you were too far forward here. It just isn't safe. I was talking to Fox and told him you don't need to be here. Better to pull back because these guerrillas, they'll run if push comes to shove."

Amerine couldn't help himself. He began to laugh, then stifled it. Had Casper spooked Fox into moving the team?

"Sir," Dan said over the radio, "we're standing by here at the support by fire—you're coming to us. Is that affirmative?"

"That's affirmative," said Amerine. "See you in a few minutes."

/

The assault team drove back across the fields just as darkness fell, taking a right turn onto the main road, then a left through the gap in the berm that led to the rear of JD's position. Mike hadn't even killed the engine before Amerine was out the door and stomping up the berm, where Ronnie, Victor, Brent, and Dan had formed a perimeter around the machine-gun emplacements. Though the captain rarely displayed emotion, he was now visibly angry.

"Take a walk, sir?" JD said when Amerine reached him.

"Let's," said Amerine.

They walked a short way down the ridge, where Amerine unloaded a string of scathing curses. JD stood with his arms crossed, nodding his head and listening.

Abruptly, Amerine stopped and smiled. "I feel better," he said. "Would you like to add anything?"

"You about covered it. Do you kiss your mother with that mouth?"

"All right then," Amerine said with a laugh. "Let's see what's next, right?"

Fox was standing on the berm when they got back. "Was he here the whole time?" Amerine asked JD.

"He's been here," said JD. "He came forward with Casper when the shooting started, and he's been hanging back and observing. Bolduc and Smith are back at the Alamo with some G's."

"Thanks for diverting me."

"Part of my job, sir."

"Sorry, Captain," said Fox, stepping up to them. "It just didn't feel right to me. The guerrillas might have left you. We've got good fields of fire on this side of the bridge from here."

Not trusting himself to be civil, Amerine just nodded. He could see that Fox was struggling with what to say: Perhaps he was considering an apology or a further explanation of his decision. Amerine waited in silence.

A call from Smith came through the lieutenant colonel's radio: "Task Force Dagger is ordering Texas One Two to regroup in Shawali Kowt."

"Say that again?" Fox said. "They want the ODA to consolidate back in Shawali Kowt?"

"Roger," said Smith.

"All right," said Fox, taken aback. "But radio them again for clarification. Make sure they understand we're asking the team to pull all the way back to Shawali Kowt."

Fox contemplated how he might challenge this order: *Hey, there's nothing illegal, immoral, or unethical about pulling us back to the town. Maybe they know something we don't know.*

"Okay, this doesn't make any sense," he said to Amerine, "but Task Force Dagger wants all of us to pull back to the Alamo."

In spite of Amerine's simmering anger, he found himself amused by the irony. "No, it doesn't make any sense," he said flatly.

"Well, they're ordering us back," said Fox. "We have to go."

"Yep," said Amerine.

The team drove their trucks to Shawali Kowt in silence and parked at the base of the Alamo. Getting out, the exhausted men leaned against the vehicles, awaiting orders. Nobody on ODA 574 had gotten more than a couple of hours of sleep in the past forty-eight hours, and they were dirty, tired, and bitter about having been pulled off the hill.

"What's the call, sir?" JD asked Amerine.

"Since we don't control the bridge, we're running the same risk of a counterattack. We'll keep the entire team on the Alamo tonight. Reestablish the perimeter and put some of the boys to bed."

While the men retrieved their rucksacks from the trucks, Smith came down from the Alamo to tell Dan he was having trouble reaching Task Force Dagger. Actually, he was unable to reach anybody via satellite, and he thought Dan, who had a reputation for being able to "make commo" when others failed, might be able to figure out what the hell was wrong. Dan followed him back up to the command post on top of the hill.

Remaining where he was, Amerine pulled out his map and erased the circle he'd drawn around the bridge earlier that day. Fox drove up with Casper, avoiding eye contact with Amerine as he walked back up the Alamo.

Soon, Dan returned with JD, who reported that the team was positioned for the night. The net was down—a satellite glitch, Dan informed Amerine. "Smith got the message to pull back from Task Force Dagger. Clear as day, he heard them say, 'Pull back.' Then they lost the connection and could not reconfirm. It's still down—I couldn't make commo."

"Oh, and Bolduc says some Taliban were in the orchards across the river trying to sneak over here." Dan pointed south. "Says it was a flanking maneuver and he took care of it with some guerrillas."

JD snorted. "Did anybody hear about any flanking going on?"

Amerine and Dan shook their heads, as did Brent and Mag, who had come down for more gear. "Fox never mentioned it," said JD to Amerine. "Sounds like bullshit—he's trying for medals."[2]

"Anyway, let me know when commo is back up," said Amerine. To JD he said, "The team needs sleep. We'll go to thirty percent immediately. Make sure they're straight on the alert plan if the Taliban come across the bridge again tonight."

"How do you want to do it, sir?"

"You want me to take first shift, or you?" Amerine asked.

"I don't care," said JD. "Why don't you get some sleep since you're smoked."

"Okay," said Amerine. "Thanks."

Amerine was pulling his sleeping bag out of his rucksack at the top of the Alamo when he was joined by Charlie.

"Just wanted to give you a pat on the back," the spook said. "You've got to be pretty pissed off right now, eh, Jason?"

"Livid," said Amerine.

"Well, I thought I'd fill you in on a few things. First, when the Taliban came over the bridge last night, it wasn't a big coordinated counterattack after all. It was a defensive move on their part, at least at first. Some of your guerrillas crossed the bridge on their own, and the Taliban handed them their asses. That's what started it."

"You know who it was?"

"Haji Badhur," said Charlie. "Him and his men—they came forward from Damana. We think he wanted to pillage those villages on the other side of the river. After he saw you guys spank the Taliban when you first got into town, he thought they'd all retreated. Easy pickings."

"Ha! Sounds completely in character for that pirate," said Amerine.

"Yep. But the bigger news is that Hamid was on the phone all day again, that big conference where the Afghan bigwigs are meeting in Germany, and they're still pushing for him to lead this country after this is all over."

"I can't imagine a better man for the job."

"There's more," said Charlie. "Hamid is expecting a big delegation from Kandahar tomorrow."

"Here?"

"Sometime in the morning or afternoon Mullah Naqib, an intermediary for the Taliban, is coming over from Kandahar to do a face-to-face with Hamid. We're thinking they might be ready to hand over the city."

"Wow." Amerine unbuttoned his cargo pocket, removed the map, and showed it to Charlie, using a red-lensed flashlight to highlight the overlapping circles he'd been plotting, like some bizarre Venn diagram, to document Karzai's campaign. He'd drawn the first circle less than three weeks before, when they'd arrived in Haji Badhur's Cove; after the Battle of Tarin Kowt, Karzai's support had tidal-waved across the tribal belt. Based on Northern Alliance and American victories in the north and overwhelming support for Karzai in the south, Amerine and Charlie deduced that Taliban leaders had realized they were all but finished.

"Wow," Amerine said again. He thought of Wes riding away in the back of the pickup with a hole through his neck. "Wes might be the first SF guy shot by the enemy in this war."

Charlie nodded. "He might be."

"Seven years ago, almost to the day, I had to medevac half my platoon in Panama. That time it was rocks instead of bullets. I swear I'm some kind of widow-maker."

"Ah, that's bullshit," said Charlie. "But I wouldn't mention it to anybody else."

"Oh, I won't."

Amerine sat down on his sleeping bag in a low spot east of the mortar pit, ripped open an MRE pouch, and took a few bites of cold beef stew, washing it down with big gulps of water from his canteen.

"In Somalia I lost a good friend," Charlie said, sitting down next to him. "There was nothing anybody could have done to change that—except maybe to have skipped the war. Wars are always the same. Good people die, get hurt, get crippled. All you can do is what you think is right in the middle of the chaos."

JD walked up. "Security is set," he said, taking a seat on the ground.

"Let's hope it's a quiet night," said Amerine.

"Heard you talking about Somalia," JD said.

"You were there?" asked Charlie.

"Yeah," said JD. "I went home early before my tour ended to attend a medical course, but in Somalia I was the TC* of my Hummer during patrols . . . You know, sat in the passenger seat beside the driver. Anyway, a week after I left, my old crew ran over a mine. It killed the guy that replaced me. Bob Deeks, I'll never forget his name; died on March 3, 1993—three, three, ninety-three. Bothered me for a long time. Still does."

"Somalia," he said after a moment. "What a fiasco. At least now we're in a war that makes some sense."

---

* Military slang for vehicle commander.

The three sat in silence for a while, then Charlie stood up. "Well, if I don't see you later tonight, I'll see you somewhere down the road. I'm heading home."

"Home?" said Amerine.

"Got some stuff going on with my family. It's an emergency. I'm going to hop on one of the helicopters that's bringing in Fox's staff," he said, shaking their hands. "I'll catch you guys later."

After Charlie was gone, Amerine told JD, "Indications are only getting stronger that Hamid will be the interim leader; they're working out the final details tonight in Germany. It's not official yet, but Hamid is almost guaranteed to be named the chairman of a transitional government. The Bonn Conference has created a timeline. Within six months, Afghanistan will have a Loya Jirga and then, in two years, a presidential election."

"So Hamid is going to get his Loya Jirga."

"That's all he wanted."

"God help him if he's elected president," JD said. "He's too good a man for those political games. They'll eat him alive."

Once JD left, Amerine finally lay down in his sleeping bag and was a second shy of nodding off when Dan strode over to tell him commo was up. "You are going to love this: We got a message from Task Force Dagger asking for awards recommendations from all the Fifth Group elements in theater. They want them ASAP."

Amerine sat upright. He had never been to war and he was fairly certain that neither had the people asking for such crap. He would have expected awards to be considered *after* teams redeployed, but here they were requesting a submission from the field, something he hadn't given a thought to—and wasn't going to until they completed the mission.

"Better get moving on that Silver Star recommendation for me, sir," said Dan, grinning. "Oh, never mind: Medals like that are just for you officers."

"When they put out the usual quota system for awards, I'll make sure to keep you at the top of the list," retorted Amerine. "I'm going to rack out for a few hours. Unless something urgent comes through, just save it till morning."

Lying back down, Amerine pushed the notion of awards into the back of his mind, the same place where he'd buried the absurdity of being pulled off two positions within an hour. As he began to doze, he thought of the thing that was most important to him: his men. In the finest tradition of the Green Berets, ODA 574 had pushed unwilling guerrillas up a hill under fire. They'd come together as a team, had taken their objective, and he was proud of them.

/

A couple of hours after Amerine fell asleep, Mag's watch ended, and he found a flat spot just east of the Alamo's command post—a rectangular patch of boot-beaten ground between a trench and a low wall—where he could catch four hours of sleep. The young guerrilla with the orange blanket had been shadowing him all day; now he approached Mag with Seylaab, who translated: "He would like to know how you stop the bombs from falling on you at night." He pointed to the sky, and Mag tuned in to the ominous hum of Spectre's props in orbit at a couple thousand feet. Mag cracked an IR chemlite, set it at the head of his sleeping bag, and let the Afghan look at it through his NODs.

Letting out an "oooh," the man spoke a few words to Seylaab, then hurried down toward the medical clinic.

"He says you're magic," said Seylaab before taking off after the guerrilla.

Mag stretched out beneath his unzipped sleeping bag, which was buffered from the cold, hard ground by a thin piece of foam. His Beretta was on his stomach, his hand on top of that, and his M4 at his side. Boots on, go-to-hell pack ready at his head. Everything was exactly as it was when he went to sleep every night.

He was about to say his evening prayer when the guerrilla reappeared and spread his blanket next to him. Then another young Afghan crowded against his other side. They kept coming, fanning out around him. One put his head on Mag's legs as if they were pillows.

"Wait a minute, I'm not your daddy," Mag said, pushing the man off and attempting to spread them out a bit. With just a few inches of wiggle room between him and ten guerrillas, he began his silent prayer. This time he rambled more than usual, concerned that he'd sinned when he'd shot to kill for the first time in his life earlier in the day. *I'm sorry, Lord, if I was sinning today. Forgive me if I was having fun pulling the trigger, and for looking forward to doing it again.*

Even though Mag was feeling no real threat, he was oddly compelled to end the prayer as he'd only done when his life had been in immediate mortal danger. He didn't question the compulsion, figuring that God knew something was coming.

I know, Lord, I asked you once in the Himalayas stuck in that crevasse, and then when I was sick with giardia, to just get me through and get me off that glacier and get me home. I asked you to save me then, and I didn't walk your path when I got home. This time, Lord, I ain't making no promises. All I'm going to ask you this time, Lord, if anything happens to me, I just want you to watch after my kids, let my family and friends know I love them, and don't let me feel a thing. Forgive me my sins. I accept you as my Lord and Savior.

Amen.

★

CHAPTER ELEVEN

The Thirteenth Sortie

There's a grief that can't be spoken.
There's a pain goes on and on.
Empty chairs at empty tables
Now my friends are dead and gone.
  —Claude Michel Schonberg, "Empty Chairs at Empty Tables"

Just after one in the morning on Wednesday, December 5, Air Force Lieutenant Colonel Timothy Crosby taxied his B-52 down the runway at the U.S. air base on Diego Garcia, an island in the Indian Ocean. He took off, banking north and ascending to a cruising altitude of 40,000 feet. The Stratofortress bomber was part of a squadron of ten B-52s and a half-dozen B-1s that flew out of Diego every day, providing round-the-clock, on-call air support for teams on the ground in Afghanistan. Its five-person crew—Crosby, his copilot, an aircraft navigator, a radar navigator, and an electronic warfare officer—had thousands of hours of flying time between them.

This mission was the crew's thirteenth sortie in Operation Enduring Freedom.[1]

At 3 A.M. in Shawali Kowt, Amerine was waking up after four hours of sleep. JD, hunkered down on watch a few feet away, heard Amerine's sleeping bag rustle. "Top of the morning to you, sir," he said, then gave a status report: Alex had been communicating with the Spectre pilot flying recon, who had detected no enemy movement in the area.

"It's been really quiet," said JD.

Amerine looked around to be sure nobody could overhear him, then said, "I'm going to fire Ken today. He'll go to the C-team, and we'll get their medic, who is coming in tonight with the rest of Fox's staff."

"It's shitty, sir, but it has to be done."

"I'll take my shift after I write up the counseling statement on Ken," said Amerine. "As long as you're feeling all right."

"I'm feeling pretty good, considering," said JD. "Still wired."

Walking along the Alamo's perimeter, Amerine passed Fox, asleep on the ground, as was everyone else except for JD, Wes, and Ronnie. He chuckled when he saw the guerrillas around Mag like a litter of puppies.

Toward the northeastern end of the Alamo he came upon several Afghans huddling by a small fire they'd built in a shallow depression. The guerrillas were still inadequately outfitted for the nighttime temperatures that dipped into the 30s; despite numerous supply drops, few of them had even a sleeping bag. When he got close enough to hear their chattering teeth, he didn't have the heart to make them extinguish the meager flames. In fact, he joined them, sitting off to the side as he wrote Ken up.

The fire broke a cardinal rule of field craft, yet Amerine wasn't concerned. He found the moment oddly nostalgic, remembering bonfires on the beaches of Oahu. His guard was down, he realized, just as it was during Ranger School when he and his fellow students would build fires to mark the completion of a training mission.

He sensed that the battle with the Taliban was over: Sometime after sunrise, probably before noon, a high-level Taliban delegation would be arriving from Kandahar to discuss a peaceful cessation of hostilities. Less than three months had passed since 9/11, yet the United States, with its Afghan rebel allies, was about to topple the Taliban government. And he'd expected it to take six months just for ODA 574 to seize Tarin Kowt.

At 3:45 A.M., four Pave Lows that had originated from J-Bad, Pakistan, touched down in the desert at the landing zone designated

LZ Jamie, a mile and a half north of Shawali Kowt. Sergeant First Class Chris Pickett, a twenty-eight-year-old medic, and Air Force Technical Sergeant Jim Price, thirty-four, were riding in one of two brand-new white Toyota Tundra 4x4s loaded in the cargo bays of the helicopters delivering Fox's battalion headquarters. Price gripped the steering wheel tightly as the Pave Low's ramp lowered, then he flipped on his NODs, turned the key, and steered the truck down and out into a swirling billow of dust and darkness.

A figure suddenly appeared directly in front of him and Price slammed on the brakes. It was Major Bolduc, who used hand signals to direct them south, where three beat-up trucks belonging to guerrillas were parked along the road. Bolduc ran back to the lead truck, which led the king cabs carrying the remainder of Fox's battalion headquarters staff—call sign Rambo 85—to Shawali Kowt.

If Denise Pickett had known her husband was part of a small convoy in the middle of the Afghan desert heading in the direction of Kandahar, she would have been proud but not pleased. Pickett had assured his wife before deploying that, as a medic on Fox's battalion headquarters staff C-team, there was no chance he'd get near the battlefield. "Don't worry about me, honey," he'd said. "Worry about the other guys—the A-teams. I'm with battalion; we don't get into the mix."

Though Fox had also chosen an Air Force combat weatherman, an Army intelligence analyst, and two Air Force TACPs (tactical air control parties), most of the fourteen men of Rambo 85 were Green Berets, personnel from Fox's C-team, many of whom had been shocked in the weeks before this mission when Fox was ordered by Mulholland to start running them through combat drills. They were not a combat unit: The extent of their recent training had been completing—or, as one NCO put it, "fumbling our way through"—a couple of react-to-contact drills, which even the most novice infantry units master before heading into battle.

Now Price, Pickett, and the rest of Rambo 85 were driving through the desert to join ODA 574—one of the teams Pickett had told his wife to worry about.

When Mag opened his eyes the next morning, the first thing he saw in the predawn darkness was a man standing over him, laughing.

"What?" Mag said gruffly.

"Get up," said JD, nudging him with the toe of his boot. He looked around at the Afghans huddled closely around Mag. "You got something you want to tell me about last night, soldier?"

"Yeah," said Mag. "That was a damn cold night."

"Sure was," said JD, holding out a box. "Have one. They're from my wife."

"Well, thank you, Santa, and Mrs. Claus too," Mag said, taking the Rice Krispies Treat.

"This too." JD tossed over a box, and Mag read the return address. "From the love of my life," he said with a grin.

"Battalion showed up in the night and brought the mail," JD said, "and those." He lifted his chin toward the two trucks parked alongside the team's trucks at the base of the Alamo.

Mag held the bar between his teeth while he stuffed his sleeping bag and the shoe box–size package from his girlfriend, Sherry, into his rucksack, hoisted it over his shoulder, and walked away from the sleeping guerrillas to his truck. Mike was there sorting through some gear.

"Hell," Mag said to him, pointing at the white king cabs. "I thought it was all a bad dream, but it's worse. We really did get pulled off the hill—*and* battalion's here."

At a quarter to seven, Amerine and JD stood atop the Alamo watching the headquarters personnel mill about near the medical clinic. The sun glowed on the eastern horizon like a narrow band of orange fog.

"All right," Amerine told JD. "Get Ken. Let's get this over with."

A few minutes later, JD returned with their medic, and the three headed off the Alamo together, away from the rest of the men. JD stood to one side, his arms crossed, while Amerine stared Ken in the eye and said, "I'm relieving you of duty and sending you to the battalion headquarters."

Though Ken's mouth opened in surprise, he said nothing. Without a pause, Amerine read aloud the counseling statement detailing the reasons for his relief, which included his panic in Tarin Kowt and Shawali Kowt and his failure to bring the mortar up to the ruins as ordered.*

Taking the document when Amerine handed it to him, Ken looked it over, angrily shaking his head. At last he signed the paper to confirm he had read it, but he circled the option stating that he did not agree with what the captain had written. Shoving it back in Amerine's hand, he addressed JD. "You're going to let him do this?"

"Grab your gear and move it into the medical clinic," JD said. "Major Bolduc will meet with you and get you settled into Battalion."

With a glare at Amerine, Ken walked away, still shaking his head.

Amerine shifted his attention to the headquarters staff now gathering along the low wall that encircled the command post. He recognized many of them from 5th Group. "A lot of good men here," he said.

"When I got the mail, Chief Reed told me that Bolduc is going to brief the headquarters up there on the Alamo," said JD. "What's our next move, sir?"

"Let the men enjoy their mail, but tell them to be ready to pack up and go as soon as I give the word."

Back on top of the Alamo, Amerine saw Alex lying in his sleeping bag near the command post, talking to two of his fellow Air Force TACPs, including Tech Sergeant Price. They turned their attention to Bolduc when he began to address the headquarters staff, and Amerine grabbed his rucksack and carried it down to his truck. Mag was busy with his own truck—"getting the battle chariot ready," he said—as he performed the daily ritual of cleaning out the air filter, topping off the fuel, and checking the tire pressure. "It will be good to get on down the road," Mag said, motioning toward the Alamo, where a group of curious Afghans had gathered to listen to Bolduc speak.

---

* Amerine was still unaware that Ken had left behind Mag and Wes while fleeing enemy fire.

"What's with the dog and pony show?" asked Mike, walking up.

With a shrug, Amerine leaned back against the truck to watch Bolduc's energetic briefing. JD came over and stood beside him.

"I think we're out of a job," said Amerine.

"Yeah, Bolduc's got troops to lead again," JD said. "Sort of like his own A-team."

"Regardless, the Taliban surrender should come sometime today."

"Don't fool yourself, sir," said JD. "They aren't going to surrender. We're about to go from being insurgents to counterinsurgents."

Bolduc's briefing lasted fifteen minutes. By 7:30 he was ordering some of his men to set up communications in the medical clinic while he directed others to mingle with members of ODA 574 in order to learn more about the area and recent events. Amerine was standing off to the side of the Alamo's command post, waiting for a chance to talk to the major, when Fox walked over after greeting his staff. Just as he arrived, a Pinzgauer crested the berm north of Shawali Kowt and parked on the top. Another one appeared farther west.

Only one unit used these customized fighting vehicles, which are high-speed, go-anywhere tanks on wheels, bristling with heavy machine guns, grenade launchers, and state-of-the-art armaments such as anti-tank rockets and mine-clearing weapons.

"When did Delta show up?" Fox said to Amerine. "Did you know they were here?"

"No idea," said Amerine. "Must have come in during the night."

"Why wasn't I consulted?" Fox said, shaking his head. Amerine watched him trot down toward the medical clinic, then walked over to Bolduc and said, "It's way too crowded up here, sir. If you want this position, I'll move my men somewhere else."

"No," said Bolduc, "we want your team to stay and pull security. Later on we want you to retake the hill, so come up with a plan with Captain Bovee, write an order, and brief me on it before you move out."

"Yes, sir," said Amerine. Though the headquarters had no authority to order ODA 574 to pull security *or* take the hill with the ruins, they could keep the team in place based upon Fox's TACON command authority. Amerine was happy to retake the hill, and he was not about to argue over authority. *I want to get my men as far from here as I can*, he thought.

/

"We're staying put for now," Amerine told Mag back at the trucks. They were watching the guerrillas on the Alamo crowding around the headquarters weapons sergeant, Chris Fathi, who spoke Farsi, Urdu, Turkish, Kurdish, and some Arabic. Word had gotten around that an American spoke the local dialects, and more and more Afghans gathered until more than thirty were pushing in around Fathi, talking over one another and resting their hands on his shoulders. Amerine felt for him—it had taken days for the men of ODA 574 to relax when their backs weren't covered. He also knew that the Afghans were giving him an earful about how the Taliban "are everywhere!"

During the mission, local Pashtun had encouraged ODA 574 to attack homes, buildings, caves, even schools—always stating with certainty that Taliban fighters were inside. As more clans joined Karzai's movement, the false leads and dubious intelligence multiplied until Amerine found it nearly impossible to distinguish reliable tips from bogus information.

Amerine walked from the trucks to the southwestern end of the Alamo, past Fathi and the group of Afghans to where JD sat in the dirt near Dan, reading a letter. Next to him was a small cardboard box, on which lay a four-by-six-inch photo of JD and his family that his wife had sent.

"How's the family?" asked Amerine.

"They're great," said JD, reaching for one of the remaining Rice Krispies Treats. "Here, sir, have one."

"Thanks," said Amerine, taking a bite.

Amerine hadn't gotten a care package or letters. He hadn't provided his family with a mailing address, telling them he would be in touch when he could. He didn't know when he would be able to write and hated the thought of receiving a pile of letters with no way to respond. Even worse, he didn't want that pile of letters going back to his family, unopened, if he was killed on the mission.

Washing down the last of the bar with a swig of JD's lukewarm cocoa, Amerine told him that they'd been ordered to take the hill by the bridge.

"You mean *re*take the hill."

"Exactly," said Amerine, turning to leave. "I'm going to work the plan with Bovee. I don't see us doing things much different from yesterday—we can consider that our live-fire rehearsal. We'll talk later. Enjoy that letter."

"Want another?" JD held up the box.

"You eat them. Then tell the guys what's up."

Amerine walked a few steps over to Dan, who was tinkering with a disassembled radio laid out on a poncho liner.

"Everything going to be working in a couple of hours?" Amerine asked.

"Should be. What's up?"

"We're taking that hill again, so make sure our internal comms are squared away. The radios aren't faring too well, and I'm a little worried."

"You gotta be gentle with them," Dan said, cradling one of the radios in his open palm. "Treat it like a baby." He looked up from behind his bushy beard, cocked his head sideways, and squinted at Amerine. "So, we're going to take the hill again, eh?"

"Looking that way."

"Groundhog Day,"* said Dan. "Any chance I could have Wes's spot?"

"Certainly," said Amerine. Dan was arguably the best marksman on the team. "But make sure JD doesn't mind sending you out with me, and figure out who's going to run commo on his split team."

"Would be good to be up front on the assault."

"It would be good to have you up front. See you in a bit."

Though Amerine doubted the Taliban would attack with a delegation en route to discuss surrender, he would not allow himself to underestimate the enemy. Looking around at the flurry of activity on

---

* A reference to a movie in which Bill Murray's character relives the same day over and over again.

the Alamo—the scene was almost festive, with the guerrillas chatting up Fathi and the headquarters personnel mingling with ODA 574—he thought, *I gotta find Bovee, hammer out this bullshit operations order, and get us moving.*

✗

Pickett was making the rounds, introducing himself as the battalion medic and performing checkups on the members of ODA 574. He approached a man who was grabbing some gear from the back of a truck.

"What do you do?" he asked Ken.

"I'm the battalion medic."

"Wait a minute," said Pickett. "*I'm* the battalion medic."

"Well, not anymore," Ken said.

After confirming this swap of positions with Bolduc, whose idea it had been to give Ken a chance on the headquarters staff, Pickett headed over to his new team sergeant, JD, whom he knew from 5th Group. "Hey, Sergeant, looks like I'm your new medic," he said.

"That's what I got," said JD. "Why don't you put your kit down in that truck. We're gearing up for a mission in a bit; come on back and I'll fill you in."

Feeling a surge of adrenaline, Pickett walked off the Alamo to transfer his gear to one of ODA 574's vehicles. *Boy,* he thought, *is Denise gonna be pissed when she finds out about this!*

✗

Shortly after leaving Dan, Amerine found Captain Dennis Bovee, the headquarters' assistant operations officer, in the command post.

"We have to stop meeting like this," said Amerine with a grin.

Bovee had been with the 101st Airborne Division when it relieved Amerine's battered battalion after the disastrous riots in Panama. Today was December 5, three days before the five-year anniversary of that fiasco.

"Yes we do," Bovee said, smiling. "So, how do you want to work this plan?"

"Let's take a walk. There's a place just up the Alamo where we can see our objective, down by the bridge."

The two captains strolled north along the edge of the Alamo, past the ashes of the guerrillas' fire from the night before, to a section of crumbling wall where they sat facing the bridge and the hill with the ruins a mile to the west.

"Good view," said Bovee.

"Makes a leader's recon pretty easy," said Amerine.

With a flash of fire, a 500-pound bomb exploded on the ridge across the river just south of the bridge, sending up a billow of brown dust and black smoke.

Both men stood up. "What the fuck?!" said Amerine. The Afghans on the other side of the Alamo started to cheer.

"Hold on a minute," Amerine said to Bovee and walked quickly over to the command post. There he saw the headquarters TACP, Price, with his radio and map spread out on the ground before him, and Alex next to him, sitting with his legs in his sleeping bag and eating an MRE. Alex returned Amerine's angry look with an apologetic shrug and glanced over at Fox and Bolduc, five yards away.

Amerine understood immediately what was happening: Bolduc's brief had become the headquarters' air strikes. *The fighting headquarters,* he thought. *Getting a piece of the action.*

Only there was no action and, as far as Amerine could tell, nothing to strike. Combat had ceased the day before, soon after Wes was shot. There hadn't been so much as a bullet fired in the past fifteen hours.

Noticing Amerine, Bolduc stepped over while Fox looked on.

"What's going on, sir?" asked Amerine, choosing words that weren't confrontational but using a tone that clearly was. "What are you doing?"

"I'm orienting my staff, Captain," said Bolduc. "We're engaging Taliban positions on the ridge. I'll get one of the new TACPs linked up with your team sergeant later."

"Well," Amerine said through clenched teeth, "whenever you're done doing whatever it is you're doing, send the new TACP over to JD."

Wes is the lucky one, Amerine thought as he headed to JD's position at the southwestern edge of the Alamo, where forty or more guerrillas had massed to watch the bombing. *He doesn't have to witness this bullshit.*

Reaching JD, Amerine asked if the team was ready to move.

"They're all packed," said JD. "Just holding in place, waiting for the word."

Nelson Smith joined Fathi after the bomb hit. It had taken Fathi only a few short conversations with the Afghans—locals and guerrillas—to determine the locations of numerous enemy positions on the other side of the river. The bomb had been directed at some men the Afghans pointed out—and that the headquarters staff had confirmed with binoculars were armed—coming down the ridge on a trail. No other enemy were spotted.

"So where are the bad guys now?" asked Smith.

"They go inside a cave on that ridge over there," said Fathi, pointing downstream toward the bridge.

"How do they know?"

Indicating one of the Afghans, Fathi said, "He's from that village over there, and he says he knows where they are, and that's where they go. To escape the bombing."

"We should tell Colonel Fox about this," said Smith.

"Just heading that way," said Fathi, accompanying Smith to where Fox was standing alone a few yards away—Bolduc had left the Alamo to pick up his own mail at the medical clinic.

After giving the information to Fox, Smith pointed out the general direction of the cave to Price and Alex, who began to scan the ridgeline with their binoculars. Fox was doing the same. He'd been looking at this ridge all morning and hadn't noticed any caves. *Holy shit*, he thought. *There it is.*

Fox turned to Price and said, "Destroy that cave. Put a bomb on it."

This command was the first instance in Price's six years working exclusively with Special Forces teams that anybody other than an ODA captain, warrant officer, or team sergeant had approved an air strike. It just wasn't done that way in Special Forces, but who was he to question a lieutenant colonel? He'd already crossed Fox once back in Jordan—he had been ordered back to Fort Campbell by his Air Force superiors to refit and prepare to deploy for the war in Afghanistan, but Fox had forced him to stay with the headquarters, citing his need to retain a TACP. When Price reminded Fox that he was the property of the Air Force, he suddenly found himself serving chow in the mess hall at the base where they were staying in Jordan.

Because he hadn't been able to refit at Fort Campbell, Price had borrowed a new type of laser designator called a "Viper" from the battalion's weather specialist, who used it to measure cloud ceilings for his weather reports. The Viper was essentially a pair of binoculars that, paired with GPS, could provide the coordinates for a location with its laser.

Price set the Viper on its tripod and found the cave in its view-finder, but he didn't see any enemy combatants. *They must be inside*, he concluded. Though Fox agreed that the cave looked like a good place for Taliban to hide, none had been spotted there. The only people the Americans could actually see across the river at that time were unidentified—and unarmed—Afghans walking southeast of the cave down the road on the other side of the valley.

But Price's job was not to assess the viability of a target; his job was to put bombs on it when ordered. He radioed the position of the cave to an F-18 pilot, reading off the GPS latitude and longitude coordinates from the Viper: "North 31, 46, 29 decimal 48; east 65, 45, 46 decimal 92." Next he used a topographic map to estimate its elevation at 4,000 feet, about 700 feet higher than their position on the Alamo. Then he talked the pilot onto the target with various features, including the dry riverbed and the bridge. With all the required information received, the F-18 pilot began his attack, releasing the second 500-pounder of the morning.

Around 8:30 A.M., Lieutenant Colonel Crosby guided his B-52 into Afghan airspace. It had been seven hours since he'd taken off from

Diego Garcia, on course for a preassigned orbit point in the north. Following protocol, Crosby checked in with a combat flight controller, who redirected him to a developing situation in the south, near Kandahar. The pilot tuned his radio to the channel on which Tech Sergeant Price was working an F-18 using Fox's battalion headquarters call sign, Rambo 85.

Once over Kandahar, the B-52 entered a clockwise orbit at 40,000 feet, above the "meat block" altitude: within range of surface-to-air missiles and anti-aircraft artillery. The weather was perfect for flying: mostly clear, a fifty-knot wind from the west, with only light scattered or broken cloud cover below them. Upstairs at the controls, Crosby and his copilot could see their arcing contrail as well as most of the city, but not the F-18 or the location from which Price was calling in air support.

⚔

Amerine returned to the wall and sat beside Bovee, trying to control his anger.

Another bomb exploded on the ridgeline west of where the first bomb had hit, closer to the bridge. Lifting his binoculars, Amerine scanned the area: smoke and dust. *What in the hell are they bombing over there?* he thought. There were no people, no fortifications, and there had been no more gunfire. In other words, there was no threat.

"Anyway," said Amerine. "Let's talk about attacking the hill."

⚔

Over the next fifteen minutes, two F-18s dropped three more 500-pound bombs, none of which hit the cave. Out of weapons and low on fuel, their pilots told Price they were returning to their carriers to rearm.

Price was puzzled. Why hadn't the F-18s been able to hit the cave? One of the bombs had landed in the riverbed *three hundred yards* short of the ridge. The frustrated pilots did one more pass—lower this time—and were finally able to get a clear visual of the cave with their jets' targeting system. One asked Price if he would like him to radio for additional planes; Price said that a B-52 was checking in and would put a JDAM* on the cave. The pilot then told Price that the original coordinates appeared to be a couple hundred meters off the target—if Price were to give the same coordinates to the B-52 crew, their JDAM would also miss. A minute later, the F-18s were gone.

Concluding that the pilot had a better perspective than he did from his position on the Alamo, Price decided to try to generate a new set of target coordinates for the B-52. First, though, he would have to recalibrate the Viper, whose internal magnetic compass he suspected was slightly off.

/

Emerging from his command post west of the medical clinic, Hamid Karzai pulled a tan woolen blanket tightly around his shoulders to ward off the chill. The walls of the cement building were so thick they had muffled the explosions from the half-dozen 500-pound bombs dropped in the previous twenty minutes.

Assuming that the large group of men gathered atop the Alamo had been drawn there by the sun, Karzai decided to join them to warm himself before meeting with the Taliban liaison Mullah Naqib, whose arrival he anticipated later that morning. Unaware of the bombing across the river, he walked briskly toward the hill, flanked by his ever-present Afghan and CIA bodyguards.

/

Still circling high above Kandahar, the crew of the B-52 had learned from listening to the radio traffic that the target was an enemy cave near the American position.

Finally, Price checked in with Crosby. "This is Rambo Eight Five," he said. "Say lineup."

"This is Aetna Seven Nine," said Crosby, who proceeded to give

---

* Joint Direct Attack Munition is a guidance system kit bolted onto unguided 500- or 2,000-pound gravity "dumb" bombs.

Price a brief detailing his mission capabilities—how long he could stay in the area and in what format he would like to receive the coordinates—then read the B-52's available weapons menu. Today's special: a full load of 2,000-pound JDAM bombs.

Price looked over at Fox and his staff a few feet away; ten yards beyond them the mob of Afghans, all eyes and a few pairs of binoculars fixed on the ridgeline, waiting for him to destroy the enemy cave. It was time to try a JDAM.

While JDAM technology had been around since the Gulf War, it hadn't been used for close air support before Operation Enduring Freedom; that is, ground forces had never called in a JDAM bomb to hit targets in proximity to their position. Still, Price considered it a fairly straightforward weapon: A target's coordinates are entered into its guidance system, and the bomb goes where it's told.

But since the JDAM had not been used for close air support, Price and the other forward controllers in Afghanistan had yet to be trained in the procedure to deliver the coordinates to the bomber crews who would program the data into the weapon's guidance system. Officially, there had been zero training available, period, on the employment, tactics, techniques, and procedures for utilizing the weapon in this manner. This was, for Price, on-the-job training.

Crosby informed Price that he had two types of JDAM to choose from: one that burrows into the ground before detonating and another that detonates upon impact with the target or just above its surface. Since the target was a cave, Price selected the penetrating warhead. Then he told Crosby to stand by.

Crosby and his B-52 crew went into orbit safely above Shawali Kowt, assuming that the reason Price could not immediately provide coordinates was that his Special Forces team was engaged with the enemy. As the B-52 crew awaited further instruction, Price followed the Viper's directions for recalibrating off its current location, using the built-in compass to guide him as he held the laser at a 45-degree angle to the ground and fired the device to the north, then south, then east, then west. When he finished, he noticed that the GPS showed a low-battery warning, so he installed new batteries. With the Viper recalibrated, Price pointed the laser at the cave and "shot" the location in order to generate a new set of latitude-longitude coordinates—north 31, 46, 53.33; east 65, 47, 07.43—that he relayed to the B-52.

The bomber crew also requested the coordinates of Price's location, which he refused to provide. He had heard that providing friendly coordinates was the fatal mistake in the Mazar-e-Sharif incident nine days earlier when Lieutenant Colonel Queeg's headquarters staff had called the bomb in on itself. Standard operating procedure dictated that you didn't give your own coordinates while calling in close air support, in order to avoid your location being confused with that of the target. All Price would tell Crosby was that the friendly position was 2,000 yards east of the cave, a distance that put them out of the JDAM's powerful blast radius.

When everything was set, Price said to Fox, "Weapon ready, cleared hot?"

"Clear," said Fox. "Drop it."

Coming in on a south-southwest heading, the crew of the B-52 announced, "Weapon away," then banked right to await a report from Price.

⁂

On the Alamo, Amerine sat with Bovee twenty yards northeast of the command post, oblivious to the contrail—barely visible against a dark blue sky—of the B-52 that had been circling high above.

He had just finished explaining to Bovee the plan to retake the ruins. "We just need to figure out how you want to present all this to your boss," Amerine said.

While Bovee considered this, Amerine looked over his shoulder and saw Brent and Victor standing near the command post with Staff Sergeant Cody Prosser, a twenty-eight-year-old Army intelligence analyst who'd come in with the headquarters, and whom Amerine knew well from recent deployments to Kuwait. Brent was brushing his teeth while Victor and Cody shared a laugh about something. Turning his head, Amerine stared at the hill to the west. He still couldn't believe that he and his men weren't there right now.

That was Amerine's last thought.

There was a hot and blinding flash. The explosion sounded like a thunderclap and felt like a paralyzing kidney punch that sucked the air out of Amerine's lungs and tossed him through the air. He hit the ground on the other side of Bovee. Stunned but conscious, he started to roll down the slope, stopping several yards away. He heard himself saying, "I'm okay . . . I'm okay . . . I'm okay . . ."

Less than a minute before the explosion, Dan had walked up to JD, who was telling headquarters Chief Warrant Officer Terry Reed about Wes.

"JD tells me your junior got shot yesterday," said Reed. "Sorry to hear that."

"I've always been a senior and never had a junior working under me," said Dan. "I get a junior, what happens? He gets shot. You watch, I'll be next."

Leaving Dan and JD, Reed wove his way through the Afghan spectators along the southern edge of the Alamo. He noticed a pair of binoculars on the low wall of the command post near Fox, and was reaching down to pick them up when the blinding flash turned everything white.

Mag had been standing at the trucks with Mike, who had just tied down a couple of gas cans in the bed of one, closed the tailgate, and grabbed a canned ham that his wife and kids had sent him. "I'm gonna eat this sucker for Ramadan tonight," he told Mag. Digging into a can of Copenhagen, Mag put a huge dip in his mouth and shared some with Mike, who then began to walk up the hill toward Brent, Victor, and Cody Prosser. He had taken four or five steps when he was consumed by a wall of flames.

Brent was brushing his teeth and listening to Prosser and Victor talk about home. Since arriving in-country, ODA 574 had been completely isolated, and Prosser was the first person they'd been able to grill for news. Brent spit out his toothpaste. The next thing he knew, he was facedown in the dirt a few yards away, a burning sensation covering his entire body. The ringing in his ears muffled all other sound. Smoke billowed around him. He pushed up onto his knees and felt overwhelmingly sick. Everything went brown as he fought to stay conscious.

Twenty yards down the slope from Brent, Amerine was sprawled on his stomach near Bovee. Black smoke was blowing overhead, darkening the sky that a moment before had been a deep, clear blue. Dust swirled everywhere, the acrid smell of explosives was thick in the air, and Amerine experienced an overwhelming sense of triumph in surviving the blast. He wanted to shout out "Fuck you! I'm still alive!"

But then it began to rain down around him—rocks, sand, and scraps of human flesh, followed by pieces of clothing and paper. The explosion, he realized, had been more powerful than an attack by mortar or artillery—the only weapons he believed that the Taliban in this area possessed. Whatever hit them, he knew, could only have come from an American aircraft.

As he struggled to his feet, it felt as if somebody took a baseball bat to his left leg. He looked down and saw a few small holes on his upper thigh, the largest the size of a penny, and realized he'd been hit by shrapnel. He could hear muffled noises in his right ear but nothing in his left. Lying on his back a few feet off, Bovee looked stunned.

"You okay?" Amerine asked.

"Yeah, yeah," said Bovee, rolling to his side and pushing himself up to a sitting position.

Leaving Bovee, Amerine ran up the Alamo through the smoke and falling debris to find Brent and Victor on their hands and knees trying to get up off the ground. Blood dotted Victor's face and trickled from his ears, but he appeared to have no major injuries.

"This is the rally point. Stay here. I'll be back," Amerine yelled to them before scrambling over the crest of the Alamo and stumbling upon a burned, decapitated body. He allowed himself a single thought: *That's the most horrible thing I've ever seen*, then he ran forward another ten yards to the command post. Here, the metallic, sulfurlike smell of the bomb was overpowered by the stench of burned flesh and hair. Within the low walls, ten bodies were woven together into a mass of limbs, heads, and torsos covered by a thin coat of gray dust. Amerine couldn't tell where one began and the other left off, and he focused on the one member of his team he could identify—Alex, drained of color and motionless. *Dead*, Amerine thought. *All of them.*

There was movement at the edge of the bodies, which had been pushed up against the wall like debris left by the tide. Fox suddenly sat up from the heap of bloody gore, pushing the torso of a dead Afghan off his chest. He sat there, staring forward.

"Sir!" Amerine yelled, but Fox was swaying, with a confused expression and showing no indication that he'd heard Amerine.

I need to get help, Amerine thought, sprinting off the Alamo and past the team's trucks—where more Americans were strewn about on the ground—heading toward the berm where he'd last seen the Pinzgauers. As he rounded the northeast corner of the medical clinic, still in the smoky perimeter of the blast site, he nearly collided with a Delta operator coming his way. "What the fuck happened?!" the soldier said.

"We just got hit by friendly fire. Everybody is down. We are combat ineffective. I need everyone with medical training you can spare to help the wounded, and I need you to call for medevac—the Marines at Camp Rhino are closest. I also need you guys to set up a perimeter and secure the area."

The Delta operator stared at him, then said, "Yes, yes, roger that." He turned toward his unit, housed in an abandoned compound near the berm, while Amerine ran back up the Alamo, mentally going over a checklist: *Okay, Delta is sending over their medics and calling for medevac. Now I need to account for my men, get a casualty collection point established, move the wounded, and triage the casualties. Marines should be here in less than an hour.*

When Mike came to, he was sprawled facedown in the dirt. He couldn't feel his body or hear anything over the ringing in his ears, and when he tried to look around, the world was blurry.

He moved his head slowly to the right, resting his left cheek on the ground. His right arm came into focus, limp at his side. It took him a moment to remember that his hand wasn't supposed to be twisted back against the inside of his elbow. *Oh, compound fracture, that's bad,* he thought. Turning his head, Mike regarded his left arm, which was broken in a 90-degree angle between the shoulder and elbow. *Oh, that's really bad,* he thought. Unable to use his arms, he pushed his forehead against the dirt, raising his chest up a foot with his abdominal and back muscles. That was when what looked like a gallon of red paint dumped out of his body onto the ground, and he noticed the gaping wound on his chest. "Oh my God! Oh my God! Oh my God!" he said.

Feeling himself start to pass out, he struggled to keep his head to the side, thinking, *If I put my face down in this puddle of blood, I'll drown.*

/

Smith had returned to his truck to get new batteries for his radio when the explosion slapped him to the ground between two vehicles like a flyswatter smashing a fly. Everything went black as night. He stood up and grabbed at his arms, legs, body, making sure he was alive. The darkness quickly became a rusty orange haze, and Victor emerged through the thinning smoke, moving slowly toward him. Blood streaked down his cheeks.

"What the hell happened?!" Smith shouted.

"No idea . . . incoming artillery? Let's go this way!"

They headed for the northeast end of the Alamo, where the smoke was less dense, and threw themselves into an old bomb crater.

/

Brent didn't remember Amerine telling him to stay where he was, because he was barely conscious at the time. When Amerine ran off, he tried to stand and fell back down. He remained on his hands and knees, fighting the urge to throw up. It passed and he sat down, patting his hands over his body, which seemed to be mostly intact. The uniform covering his lower body looked as if it had gone through a cheese grater, the shrapnel imbedded in his legs feeling hotter and more painful as the shock wore off. Assuming that they'd been attacked, Brent grabbed an AK-47 on the ground next to him and crawled behind a section of the eroding wall. He checked to see if the weapon was loaded, pushed up to his feet, and stumbled through the drifting smoke in search of a better fighting position.

Kneeling together in the crater, Smith and Victor called out when they saw Brent stumbling around, unaware that half of the AK-47 in his hands was gone. He dived into the crater between them, and the three men began scanning the smoke for signs of a Taliban attack.

After a couple of minutes, Brent said, "My legs are feeling kind of numb—and my back." Smith pulled up Brent's shirt to reveal a round, nickel-size hole in his lower back, deep and blackened; his torso and both of his legs were peppered with smaller burns and lacerations.

"Oh jeez, you're hit, man," Smith said.

"Who's hit?" asked the battalion sergeant major, Ray Reid, who appeared out of the cloud and knelt down by the edge of the crater for a closer look at Brent's wounds. "Let's get him off the hill so we have a wall behind us," he said, and Victor and Smith helped support Brent down to the side of the medical clinic.

"Set him down," said Reid, then he yelled out in a deep voice that carried across the Alamo: "This is the CCP!"

/

As Amerine ran back up to the command post, he heard Reid's shout. At the top of the Alamo a short distance from the mass of bodies, he found Fox kneeling beside the headquarters combat weatherman, Staff Sergeant Craig Musselman, who was lying on his back and moaning, his hands covered in blood and his heels kicking at the ground. Fox's rucksack was open beside him, and he was pressing a bandage over Musselman's right eye, trying to stop the blood that was flowing down his cheeks.

"You hit, sir?" Amerine shouted to Fox, whose face, hair, and the front of his uniform were coated in red. Fox looked at him through the smoke, pointing at his ears. Amerine yelled the question again.

"I'm all right," said Fox. "This isn't my blood!"

"Delta is calling for medevac and setting up security. We gotta get these guys down to the medical clinic."

Mr. Big, Zepeda, and another CIA spook hurried up, carrying aid bags. "How can we help?" asked Mr. Big.

"Help our guys," said Amerine. "We're just getting started. Help anyone you can find."

Amerine heard the distinct whoosh of a rocket from somewhere inside the smoke enveloping the Alamo, then saw an RPG's glow rising into the air. Somebody yelled, "Incoming! We're under attack!" More ammunition started to cook off, sounding like firecrackers. Looking down at the trucks, he saw piles of RPGs engulfed in flames. He ran back down the slope to extinguish them. That was when he noticed legs poking out from underneath the truck parked closest to the blast. The right side of the vehicle was dented and punctured by shrapnel, its windows were blown in, and the passenger side of the cab was collapsed and bent inward as if a wrecking ball had clobbered it.

Kneeling down, Amerine saw that the legs belonged to Dan.

Amerine knew he was dead by the extent of his abdominal wound. As he stared in disbelief at Dan's face, the periphery faded into a blur until a series of whooshes right beside the truck jolted him back to his surroundings. He looked up, then shielded his face with his arm as three RPGs ten feet away blasted off in different directions.

RPGs lay on the ground around the trucks, their cloth carrier bags on fire. The safety cones were still on these rockets, keeping them from detonating, but the burning bags were heating the propellant and causing the RPGs to fire off as lethal projectiles. The guerrillas were notorious for removing safety cones, so it was possible that some of these rounds were live and would explode on impact. Amerine stood up and spun around, taking in the scene: Smoke and dust still hung in the air; men were staggering aimlessly or sitting down, confused. Delta operators were arriving on the scene, running toward the Alamo, and a Pinzgauer had rolled out of Shawali Kowt and parked with its machine guns pointing south and west to cover those flanks. Twenty or thirty yards to the west of the truck, a leg in American camouflage lay in the dirt, as if it had been ripped off a toy soldier.

Another RPG took flight, and again a voice shouted, "Incoming!"

"We are not under attack!" Amerine bellowed. "Our RPGs are cooking off!" He grabbed the nearest RPG and yanked the rocket out of its burning bag, then another, his bare hands feeling nothing as they reached into the flames again and again.

★

CHAPTER TWELVE

Futility

My subject is war, and the pity of war. The poetry is in the pity.
  —Wilfred Owen

Swirling brown and black hid the Alamo in a cloud billowing sky-ward when Chris Pickett pushed himself up off the ground between the trucks and the medical clinic. He tried to stand, his body swaying on unstable legs. *What happened?!* he thought. *Are we under attack? Did we get mortared?*

Sounds came to him as if through a long tunnel. Over the ringing in his ears, he heard the muted but unmistakable whoosh of an RPG as somebody shouted, "Incoming!"

Pickett stared hard into the dusky fog, thinking, *Run! Run!* He took a step toward the clinic, then stopped. *Okay, where's my weapon?* His M4 carbine was several yards off, its metal bent, the plastic cracked and shredded. Inhaling a long, deep breath, he tasted desert soil and smoke. He heard no gunfire and wondered again if they could be under attack.

A breeze blew over the Alamo and dissipated the cloud for a moment, revealing bodies and body parts everywhere. The smoke closed in again, shrouding the horrific sight. There was another whoosh. Then another. But no explosions.

"We are not under attack!" a voice yelled from somewhere behind the smoke. "Our RPGs are cooking off!"

When the smoke thinned out again after a few seconds, Pickett saw what looked like zombies rising up across the lower slopes of the Alamo, covered in dirt and ash and struggling to keep their balance.

His head throbbed. Crawling his fingers over his scalp to check for injury, he felt the warm, slippery wetness of blood, and probed carefully at the torn flesh and the rough edges of shrapnel imbedded in the back of his skull, which was otherwise intact. He pulled his hand back; it was an oily crimson. The realization that he'd been wounded had an oddly calming effect; it also reminded him of his job. *Okay, you're a medic,* Pickett thought, wiping the blood on his pants. *You've got to start treating these guys.*

Forty thousand feet above, Crosby continued to fly his B-52 in circles. Following more than two minutes of radio silence, he and his crew began to feel anxious. Normally, the ground controller would immediately inform them whether they had struck the target.

Crosby told his copilot to call Rambo 85 and find out what was going on.

After a few unsuccessful attempts to make contact, a Delta operator in Shawali Kowt came on the same local frequency. He informed the crew that he was northwest of the American position, watching smoke billowing up. "Something really big just hit," he said. "I believe they may be under mortar or artillery attack. Do you have more ordnance on board in case we need you?"

"We've got a full load," said the copilot. "What are the coordinates of the American position?"

"Stand by," was the response.

All five crewmen on the B-52 were listening in on the radio when the Delta operator rattled off the numbers. Four of them had heard Price deliver and confirm the coordinates of the cave. Each had recorded the data separately and confirmed that each other's matched up; only then had the target been entered into the weapon. Now the crew rechecked their notes and the computer: The coordinates given to them by the Delta operator were only a few yards away from the ones they'd just programmed into the bomb's guidance system.

"Hey!" the copilot told the Delta operator. "We don't think they're under fire—that appears to be where we dropped our weapon!"

Crosby looked over at his copilot, both men sick with the realization that they'd just hit an American position with one of the most powerful weapons in the world.

"Try to reach them again," Crosby said.

"Any Rambo Eight Five element, this is Aetna Seven Nine. Do you copy?"

With his radio pack between his legs and his microphone in his right hand, Price had been focused on the cave and waiting for the explosion. He had glanced at Alex sitting beside him. The next instant, he was flipping through the air, then there was a flash, and then— nothing.

When Price came to, he was on his back and could not breathe or see a thing. His arm felt dead, as though he'd slept on it, and he had to drag it up to touch his face, which felt hot and tingling. Forcing his lungs to take a big gulp of air, he choked on the gritty earth that was everywhere, packed into his nostrils, his ears, his eye sockets. A coughing fit sent pain shooting through his chest.

A hot wind gusted, clearing the smoke slightly, and he saw that he was covered in dirt from the stomach down. Pushing himself to the side, he was able to sit up. The smell from incinerated bowels was sickening. He looked at the low wall of the command post, and it brought him back to the ridge, the bomb, and the last words he'd heard from the B-52 crewman: "Weapon away."

When Price relayed the order, there were fifty or more Afghans on the Alamo, watching the bombing with most of the fifteen-member headquarters staff. ODA 574's eleven men had been on or near the hill as well. More than seventy men were within forty yards of Price in the moments before he'd cleared the bomber to drop the 2,000-pound JDAM. A bomb that big, he knew, required a buffer space of at least five hundred yards to ensure the safety of friendly forces.

Now this hillside was a wasteland. *What the fuck happened?!* he thought.

He'd told the pilot they were 2,000 yards from the target. He'd been careful not to give their position, providing only what he thought were the coordinates of the cave according to the Viper. Weapons guided by coordinates did not go astray; they went where you told them to go, which meant that he must have given the bomber the wrong coordinates.

In the distance a voice shouted, "This is the CCP!" A dead Afghan a few feet away was sprawled in the dirt with a hole the size of a fist clean through his head. Men were groaning in the smoke around him. Whoever was panting like a dog nearby, Price knew from his medical training, was probably about to die. *I fucked up,* he realized. *I did this . . . Jesus, I fucking did this.*

/

Once the shock began to wear off, Nelson Smith knew he had to get commo running again. Then he remembered that he had left sensitive items—his radio and cipher book—at the top of the Alamo when he'd gone for batteries.

Walking slowly back toward the hill, he nearly stepped on Mag, who was on his side near the lower slope of the Alamo. How had he missed him when he'd run by here just a few minutes before? Had Mag crawled over?

Mag looked up at Smith and spoke like a child: "Don't. Feel. Good." He reached out with a hand that was a dripping mop of shredded bone, flesh, and tendon. Dropping to his knees, Smith gripped Mag's forearm as hard as he could to slow the bleeding and cried out, "Medic!"

/

As Pickett grabbed his aid bag from the bed of one of ODA 574's trucks, he glanced up the rise to where he'd spoken with JD—that entire western slope was now void of anything but drifting smoke. The crowd of Afghans standing there moments before had vanished. As he slung the bag over his shoulder, a hand grasped his bicep. He turned to see Major Bolduc and Sergeant Major Reid standing there.

"Bandage up the doc's head so he can start treating people," Bolduc said to Reid, who reached into Pickett's bag, grabbed a roll of gauze, and wrapped it around Pickett's head. Bolduc started to limp up the side of the Alamo.

"You wounded, sir?" Pickett yelled after him.

"No," Bolduc shouted back. "Just got flattened by the blast, hurt my hip and my ears are ringing, but I'm not hit."

His bandage in place, Pickett ran the twenty yards to where Smith had again called out for a medic. Smith was kneeling beside Mag, squeezing his forearm so tightly that his hand shook from fatigue.

"It's bleeding pretty good, doc," he said. "I gotta get commo up."

"Thanks," said Pickett, replacing Smith's grip with his own.

Lying on his side in the fetal position with his eyes squeezed shut, Mag cried out in pain. Smith hesitated.

"I got it!" said Pickett.

After a few steps, Smith stopped. "His name is Mag," he told Pickett.

"Got it. Go!"

Mag began to kick his legs, as if running in place while holding his injured arm up in the air. Mag's other hand was clamped around the back of his head, and the shoulders and collar of his uniform were soaked with blood and a clear liquid. Glancing at the head wound, Pickett could see a flap of scalp that was peeled off to one side and protruding from beneath Mag's hand. Blood was oozing, but not flowing.

"Keep pressure up there on your head!" he told Mag.

Mag groaned.

Doing his best to hold the pieces in place, Pickett wrapped Mag's destroyed hand and continued up his arm with Kerlix gauze. He fashioned a tourniquet from a cravat, a triangular bandage, and wooden tongue depressors taped together, and tightened it around Mag's forearm, squeezing off the blood flow.

Setting the arm gently down, he eased Mag's other hand away from his head and was shocked to see Mag's brain framed within a jagged hole in his skull. Quickly, Pickett folded the torn scalp over the opening; as he was using a thick pressure bandage to cover it, Mag went limp and passed out. With help from two Delta operators, Pickett carried Mag to the CCP and set him down next to Brent, who was among a half-dozen wounded Americans lying scattered along the eastern wall of the clinic.

"You okay to watch him?" asked Pickett.

"Yeah, yeah," said Brent. "I'm good."

"Watch that arm for bleeding. And if he wakes up, don't let him hurt himself."

/

Cresting the Alamo, Smith came upon the dust-coated bodies piled in what had been the command post. Bovee was checking over Price at one end of the pile, while Fox was on his knees at the other end, searching for signs of life.

Smith's rucksack was protruding from beneath the bodies along a low wall—exactly where he would have been had he not gone for batteries. He walked over and grabbed it, then glanced over the wall. A young Afghan covered in blood and dust was crying, holding the hand of an older, dead Afghan man.

Suddenly Fox yelled, "This guy's alive!"

/

As Amerine finished yanking the RPGs from their burning bags, Karzai, Casper, a Delta operator, and an entourage of armed guerrillas hurried out of Karzai's command post in the building to the left of the medical clinic, one hundred yards away.

Thank God, Amerine thought as he watched Karzai, apparently unharmed, head toward some of the guerrillas' trucks parked near the berm. Returning to the top of the Alamo, Amerine found Fox, Reid, Smith, and a Delta operator carefully separating bodies and laying them side by side. One of them was Alex—alive, but struggling to breathe. His shoulder, which had been ripped open by shrapnel down to the socket, was heavily bandaged, and the midsection of his uniform shirt was torn away, revealing puncture wounds.

Amerine jogged over to Smith, who was helping carry a member of the headquarters staff off the hill. "You have commo up yet?" he asked.

"No," said Smith. "I'm going to set up in the clinic right after we get this guy down to the CCP."

Amerine headed in the same direction as Smith, toward the trucks, where Miles, the Delta operator assigned to Casper's team, was changing an IV bag hooked up to Mike. Mike was on his back in the middle of a huge pool of blood. His face was covered with dust, his lips a pale blue, his closed eyelids drained of color. What hadn't soaked into the earth had run downhill like a tiny creek, forming another puddle where the incline decreased.

"This all from Mike?" Amerine asked.

"Yeah," said Miles. "I'm going to need something to move him, like a door if we don't have any litters."

"Okay." Lowering his voice, Amerine said, "I have to send up a SITREP. What do you think?" He gestured at Mike.

"He's got two compound-fractured arms, one barely still attached. His chest was laid open all the way across, from one armpit to the other down to the ribs. He's got shrapnel everywhere, probably in all his major organs. I'll keep doing what I can, but we better get him on a helicopter real quick."

/

Smith's legs began to shake and his vision blurred. He'd had virtually no sleep for two days, had eaten almost nothing that morning, and was soaked with sweat from the thermal underwear he'd worn the night before. The end of the litter he held started to slip from his grasp, and he wanted to let go, take off his thermals, and sit down. *You piece of shit!* he cursed at himself. *Suck it up! You gotta help this guy and get commo up!*

He made it to the CCP and set the wounded man down. Along the southern wall of the medical clinic, Sergeant Troy Grubb, another commo sergeant from Battalion, was kneeling over Ronnie, who had been blasted with shrapnel and was slipping in and out of consciousness.

"How's he doing?" asked Smith.

"Ah, he's gonna be fine," said Grubb cheerily. Seeing that Ronnie's eyes were closed, Grubb mouthed the words, "Not good."

Grubb's face was covered with small lacerations. "Where were *you*?" Smith asked.

"Inside, setting up my radio, when the windows blew and—"

Commo! Smith remembered and dashed into the clinic. Everything, including the radios, had been knocked to the ground but nothing appeared broken. First, though, he had to get out of his thermals. As he was stripping off the layers, he noticed a Delta operator caring for a wounded Afghan in the far corner of the room. Suddenly the operator ran out the door, and in the relative quiet, Smith heard a repetitive dripping and saw a puddle of blood forming beneath the table where the Afghan lay. The man reached out to him, asking for something in Pashto.

The operator hurried back in carrying some clothes and began tearing them up to make bandages.

"You a medic?" Smith asked.

"Yeah."

"Can I give him water?"

"No!" the Delta operator said, and Smith turned and focused on his radio: "This is Rambo Eight Five. Over."

"I have you, Rambo Eight Five," said a dispatcher at Task Force Dagger. "SITREP?"

"Roger. Don't know if you know what's going on down here."

"Negative, Rambo Eight Five.

"We have massive casualties. Unknown at this time what happened."

The dispatcher told Smith to stand by and keep the line open. While he waited, the room became silent again, and he turned around. The medic was gone. The man on the table was dead.

A few minutes later, Smith was speaking to Colonel Mulholland, which for an enlisted-rank E-5 sergeant is like a White House guard being patched through to the president. Mulholland asked how many were wounded and how many killed; he wanted details of the incident that Smith didn't have. Smith ventured a guess that it might have been a mortar or artillery attack.

"Is your position taking fire now?" asked Mulholland.

"Negative," said Smith. "I'll go find Fox, sir. Lieutenant Colonel Fox. Stand by, sir."

Rushing back outside, Smith narrowly avoided running into Bolduc, who was heading for the CCP; Smith told him the colonel was on the radio and that he needed some numbers and a solid SITREP.

"Start getting me a count, Sergeant," said Bolduc, disappearing into the medical clinic. He swung his head back out. "Everybody. Americans *and* Afghans."

Around the corner, Mr. Big was treating one of fifteen bloody Afghans along the northwest wall of the medical clinic. "I'm doing a count," Smith said. "Do you know how many wounded Afghans?"

"I have no idea," said Mr. Big. "All I know is I'm treating them as fast as I can and they're dying by the second."

It had been ten days since Chris Miller, Lloyd Allard, Tim "Cubby" Wojciehowski, and the rest of their B-team had reinvented themselves as a quick-reaction force at K2 in Uzbekistan. Every member of ODB 570 now kept three separate rucksacks—ranging in weight from fifty to 150 pounds—at the foot of his cot in order to be ready regardless of the nature or duration of the assignment.

After breakfast on December 5, the men were settling into their cots for a marathon viewing of *The Sopranos*. When the thirty-two-inch flat screen illuminated the back of the team tent, Miller strolled over to the "big tent"—the command center for Task Force Dagger—to see if anything had happened overnight. Miller was frustrated at his inability to find an angle that would get his team on the ground—and a little disgusted at himself for looking forward to *The Sopranos*.

This war, he thought, *is passing me by.*

As he neared the tent, an operations officer came bolting out and ran past.

"What's happening?" said Miller, catching the man by the arm.

The officer paused long enough to say, "Uh, sir, something bad happened near Kandahar," then hurried down the road.

The command center was a large rectangular tent lit by fluorescent lights, its desks and aisles clogged with staff officers and personnel, none of whom noticed Miller's presence when he entered. Considering the number of people inside, the tent was exceptionally quiet.

"What's going on?" Miller asked a fellow major seated at a computer.

"Rambo Eight Five and Texas One Two: they've just taken a bunch of casualties. We're—"

Miller didn't wait for the rest.

He sprinted back to ODB 570's tent and, while the team remained engrossed around the television in back, grabbed his gear from just inside the door. Outside, he put on his helmet and M4 rifle, strapped a Beretta sidearm to his leg, threw on a load-bearing vest complete with ammo, grenades, and radio, and rushed back to the command center.

Air Force Lieutenant Colonel Mike Kingsley, the J-Bad air base commander, and his deputy commander, Steve Hadley, had stayed up all night monitoring the infiltration of Fox's battalion staff. The two men never slept when their helicopter crews were conducting missions in Afghanistan.

They'd finally gotten to their cots in a tiny room adjacent to the operations command center in the hangar and had been asleep less than an hour when they were awakened by the frantic voice of the on-call operations officer, Major Dale Reynolds. "Colonel Kingsley, Colonel Hadley, wake up! Sirs! You need to wake up immediately, sirs!"

"What's going on, Major?" said Kingsley, his head still on the pillow.

"They're taking mortar fire at the site we flew into last night. They're requesting immediate medevac."

Both Kingsley and Hadley sprang up. Swinging his legs off the edge of the cot, Hadley began lacing his boots. "Get the word out," he told Reynolds. "We need everybody we've got here in the operations center. Now!"

Amerine finished his sweep of the Alamo, where he'd been unable to locate JD, the only one of his men not accounted for. As he moved toward the CCP, he heard another RPG whistling and watched it crash into the ground five feet from two Americans carrying Chief Reed on a litter. It was almost comical, like a scene from a silent movie, when the men looked over at the rocket, dropped the litter, and ran. Both Amerine and Fox—also on his way to the CCP—sprinted toward Reed, who had balled himself up into a fetal position. Fox grabbed the back of the litter and Amerine the front, the RPG continuing to smolder as they lifted the wounded soldier and rushed him down and around the corner of the medical clinic.

Reed opened his eyes and saw Fox. "Thanks, sir," he said before closing them again.

Stepping away, Amerine paused to take in the scene at the CCP. The chaos and confusion had settled into a surreally stoic rhythm. All the Special Forces soldiers, from both the ODA and headquarters, were trained in combat lifesaving skills and casualty evacuation. Those who were able had gotten to work saving lives, stopping the bleeding of both Americans and Afghans as quickly as they could. Every wounded American had been moved into the CCP, where Jackson, the physician's assistant for Casper's men as well as a former Special Forces medic, took charge. He calmly oversaw Pickett, Nate (another of Casper's medically trained spooks), and the Delta medics, while triaging and treating the Americans and most critically wounded Afghans—whose CCP was simply an extension of the American triage area. Ken, the only other trained medic on scene, was sitting with his back against the wall of the clinic and his arm in a thin makeshift sling, staring off into space. The rest of the walking wounded, including Brent and Victor, were still bleeding as they limped from patient to patient, checking bandages and helping administer IV bags, offering words of encouragement to those who were coherent.

A burst of heavy machine-gun fire rang out from a Pinzgauer somewhere to the west. When no more followed, Amerine decided that it had been a warning to dissuade any enemy that might be in the area from mounting an attack.

With the CCP up and running and the survivors of ODA 574 accounted for, it was time for Amerine to retrieve Dan's body and to try to locate something of JD, who he presumed had been killed with the Afghans at the point of impact.

Between Smith, Delta, and the CIA handling communications, Amerine was certain that at least two calls for medevac had gone up, but he felt duty-bound to call in a last SITREP for ODA 574—even with the entire team down. If nothing else, he wanted to be absolutely sure that Task Force Dagger was aware how bad things were.

Shattered glass crunched under his boots as Amerine walked around the medical clinic and came upon Seylaab holding his AK-47 as though he was standing guard over the rows of wounded Afghans—around fifty, nearly triple the number of injured Americans. He had replaced his aqua robe with a Russian ammo vest, and when he recognized Amerine, he instinctively grinned, then seemed to catch himself and gave a solemn nod.

Amerine returned the nod and stepped inside the clinic, where some papers and MRE boxes were scattered on the floor around an empty table smeared with blood along one edge. Beneath it was a glassy pool of blood. Against the opposite wall sat a desk with a radio, pen, and paper neatly arranged, and an empty chair in front of it, as if waiting for him.

Seating himself, Amerine checked to see that the radio was on the right frequency, then began his transmission:

"Task Force Dagger, this is Texas One Two. SITREP to follow. Over."

/

Major Miller entered the command tent of Task Force Dagger at the moment Colonel Mulholland began to speak into a microphone: "Texas One Two . . . SITREP?"

Normally, satellite communications were broken or fuzzy, but the voice on the other end was clear, as if Amerine were there in the room. "We are not under enemy attack," he said. "We have established security. I have one confirmed KIA; one missing, presumed KIA." Amerine went down the list, "two expectant,* four seriously wounded . . ." He concluded with "Rambo Eight Five will send additional SITREPs on all casualties once they are tallied."

Miller was stunned by Amerine's composure; he might as well have been in a training exercise back at Fort Campbell. It reminded him of a legendary combat commander in the Korean War, "Iron" Mike McKallis, whose higher command learned that the calmer Iron Mike sounded on the radio, the worse the situation was on the ground.

There was a pause after Amerine finished his report, then Mulholland said, "What do you need from us, Texas One Two?"

"I am combat ineffective. We need to be relieved in place by follow-on units."

Turning around, Mulholland spoke to the only person in the command tent wearing a helmet and holding a gun. "Chris, you look like you're ready to go," he said.

"Yes sir," said Miller, "we're good to go."

"Take two A-teams down there with your team and figure it out."

"Roger, sir, we are on our way."

A path cleared in the crowded tent, and Miller ran down it and straight to ODB 570's tent. He burst in, out of breath, and yelled, "Hey, get your shit on—we're going!"

Heads swiveled from *The Sopranos*. A few men started laughing.

"No!" Miller boomed. "I'm serious, get your shit on. We're going *now!*"

Somebody switched off the television. "You're not kidding, sir?"

"Goddamnit, I'm not fucking around! We're going into Afghanistan. Five Seven Four has taken casualties."

***

On the northern outskirts of Shawali Kowt, Hamid Karzai sat on a knoll, his cheek bleeding from a small cut.

---

* Expected to die regardless of medical care.

Five minutes before the bomb hit, he had been making his way to the top of the Alamo when Casper caught up and said that some tribal leaders had just arrived to speak with him. Karzai walked back down the hill and entered his command post. A couple of minutes later, the windows exploded inward and a thunderous blast knocked everyone inside to the ground. Reacting to what they thought was an RPG targeting Karzai, first Casper and then Karzai's Afghan bodyguards immediately piled on top of him, shielding him with their bodies. When no further attacks came, they whisked Karzai to the knoll, where the rocks provided some shelter.

As Karzai had been pulled away from his command post, he'd glimpsed the horrendous scene and knew that many were dead.

While an Afghan bandaged Karzai's cheek, which had been cut by flying glass, a Delta operator joined the CIA-Delta contingent now assigned to him. "What happened?" Karzai asked him.

"Not sure," said the operator, "but it appears they were calling in bombs across the river and one fell short. That's all I know. They're too focused on saving lives right now to give the full rundown."

Karzai was confused. What had Captain Amerine's team been bombing? Were they under attack? Whatever it was had to have been urgent; otherwise Jason would have consulted with him. He had done so on every other occasion since Tarin Kowt.

"I need to see what I can do," Karzai said in Pashto to his personal guard. To the Americans he said in English, "I need to check on my friends."

Heads shook: His protectors would continue to dissuade Karzai from returning to the Alamo until they were certain about what had occurred and that the perimeter was secure.

Fifteen minutes after the bomb hit, Karzai's satellite phone rang. A reporter from the BBC was calling from Bonn, Germany, to inform him that the tribal factions at the conference had come to an agreement.

"Congratulations, sir," she said cheerfully. "You have just been named the chairman of the interim government."

When he was finished sending the SITREP, Amerine stepped back outside the clinic to see Fox and Smith—the highest- and lowest-ranked soldiers on the scene—working side by side, pulling IV kits from the rucksacks of the headquarters personnel, all of whom had been instructed to store at least one behind his backpack's kidney belt. They were making a pile of all available medical supplies outside the CCP, while Bolduc was calling out orders to the headquarters staff.

Casper, who was hurrying toward the CCP, spoke to Amerine as he passed: "The Marines are on the way. We're getting the word out. Shouldn't be long. They're coming from Rhino. Hour flight or less."

Townspeople from Shawali Kowt had emerged to help the surviving guerrillas with the wounded; others were out by the Alamo, stooped over like farmers in a field, picking up body parts. The hill was littered with weapons, clothing, and equipment. A laced boot stood upright. Papers swirled around as the breeze picked up. Amerine knew he should collect the sensitive items—fragments of pages from cipher books, maps, anything having to do with their mission—but that would have to wait until after he had tended to Dan.

The five trucks parked side by side along the northern slope of the Alamo had been perfectly spaced, like a row of dominoes. Now they were askew, lifted up and repositioned by the blast. With a slight limp, Amerine worked his way to the truck farthest right and got down on his knees, which made the shrapnel wound in his thigh burn. *Shit, that hurts!* he thought, then felt guilty for even acknowledging the pain.

Dan was heavy, cumbersome to move, and as Amerine pulled on him, getting most of his upper torso out from under the truck, he imagined Dan opening his eyes and doing one of his favorite impersonations, Bill Murray in the movie *Stripes*: "Chicks dig me because I rarely wear underwear, and when I do, it's usually something unusual."

Tending to his dead friend was the worst moment in the most hellish day in Amerine's life—yet this memory of Dan made him stifle a laugh.

Casper and two Delta operators walked over and silently helped Amerine move Dan onto a poncho, then they carried him over to a small stone hut, away from the wounded, setting him down carefully. One of the Delta operators asked if anyone had a body bag.

"No, I'll use my bivy sack," said Amerine, thinking it seemed less impersonal as they lowered Dan inside the weatherproof covering for the sleeping bag Amerine had slept in throughout the mission, almost as though they were putting him to bed.

Once Amerine had zipped the bag closed over Dan's ashen face, Casper and the two Delta operators left the captain alone.

Kneeling beside Dan, Amerine wanted to say something, but he couldn't find words of his own. He stared up at the sky, a deep blue now that the smoke had cleared, and began to recite "Futility" by Wilfred Owen—about the death of a soldier witnessed by Owen during World War I. Amerine had committed the poem to memory after he'd first read it as a student at West Point.

> Move him into the sun—
> Gently its touch awoke him once,
> At home, whispering of fields unsown.
> Always it awoke him, even in France,
> Until this morning and this snow.
> If anything might rouse him now
> The kind old sun will know.
>
> Think how it wakes the seeds—
> Woke, once, the clays of a cold star.
> Are limbs, so dear-achieved, are sides
> Full-nerved—still warm—too hard to stir?
> Was it for this the clay grew tall?
> —O what made fatuous sunbeams toil
> To break earth's sleep at all?

Reaching the end, Amerine looked away from Dan and began to cry.

CHAPTER THIRTEEN

Rescue at Shawali Kowt

Anytime. Anyplace.
—Air Force, 16th Special Operations Wing motto

At Camp Rhino, less than one hundred miles south of Shawali Kowt, Master Sergeant David Lee, third in command of ODB 540, was in his team's tent when the request for emergency medical evacuation came over the radio shortly before 9 A.M. The 15th Marine Expeditionary Unit, under the command of Brigadier General James Mattis, had occupied the airstrip since November 25. Two days later, Lee and his B-team had arrived; their primary role was as a liaison, coordinating the Special Forces' actions in the area with those of the Marines.

Looking out the door at the parked helicopters—including four Cobra gunships, four transport CH-53s, and six dual-rotor heavy-lift CH-46s—Lee picked up the radio and informed Task Force Dagger that the Marines at Camp Rhino were the closest Americans in a position to respond, a forty-minute helicopter flight away. Meanwhile, Lee's boss—Major Rob Cairnes, the commander of ODB 540—was running across the flat, barren landscape to General Mattis's command post, located in one of the few hard structures on the base, a single-story concrete building. He informed the Marine general, face-to-face, that a presumed mortar or artillery attack on a Green Beret position had occurred and that the wounded needed immediate evacuation from Shawali Kowt. Mattis asked if they were still in contact and wanted more specifics, which Cairnes did not have.

"Well, if they've taken fire," said the general, "and you can't tell me definitively how they got all scuffed up, I'm not going to send anything until you can assure me that the situation on the ground is secure." Mattis went on to explain that there were a thousand Marines at Camp Rhino for him to worry about, and he was not willing to dilute base security and risk sending his air squadron on a dangerous daylight mission just to assist an unknown number of casualties.

Cairnes raced back to consult with Lee and his second-in-command, Chief Warrant Officer Tom Leithead, all of whom were infuriated. They could understand why Mattis wouldn't send all of his helicopters, but no one could fathom why he wouldn't do *something* to help their guys. "Where's the *love* from the Marines?" said another member of the team. "They're supposed to be frothing at the mouth for this kind of shit."

The Green Berets continued to monitor the radio and berate the Marines: "These helicopters outside would be airborne already if it were Marines that were bleeding," said the B-team's communications sergeant.

"You know what," said Lee, who had watched the Marines endure abysmal conditions at the base since they'd arrived. "It's not the Marines. It's Mattis."

"Just heard," said the commo sergeant. "One American KIA, three critically wounded." Still, nobody at Camp Rhino knew the two most critical facts: that this had been a friendly-fire incident, and that the position at Shawali Kowt had not been and was not currently engaged with the enemy.

For the past week, Lee and Leithead had been briefing Mattis and found him a fairly personable guy. *He probably just needs a little prodding in the right direction*, thought Lee. Turning to Leithead, he said, "Let's go have a little talk with the general."

"I'm all for that," said Leithead, and the two hurried to the Marine command post some twenty minutes after Mattis had declined Cairnes's request. Inside, the expressions on the faces of Mattis's staff showed their frustration and embarrassment. One Marine glanced away as they walked past, unable to meet their eyes.

Mattis greeted the two Green Berets at the heavy wood door that led into his spartan concrete-floored office. He held a military-issue canteen cup filled with coffee in his left hand and gestured them inside with the other. After closing the door to a crack, he sat down at a small writing desk where a map was laid out.

"Let's hear it," said Mattis.

"Sir," said Lee, "we've got reports of mass casualties, and word is they expect the numbers to continue to rise. You are the closest American with the ability to respond."

"Do you have an update on how they got all scuffed up? Are they still in contact?"

"With all due respect," said Leithead, "we think that's irrelevant."

"I hear you, but no, I'm not sending a rescue mission," Mattis said. "We. Don't. Know. The situation."

"The situation, sir," said Lee, "is that Americans are dying. And they need your help."

"Look, when I have fighters over the scene so that I've got air superiority, then I'll send choppers. That, or we wait till nightfall."

Exchanging a look with Leithead, Lee said, "That's not good enough, sir."

Standing up, the general cleared his throat. "Sergeant," Mattis called to his sergeant at arms, positioned outside the office. "We're done. Escort these men out of here."

Without another word, Lee and Leithead walked out of the office toward the door to the command post, again passing Marines who wouldn't make eye contact. Behind them, they heard Mattis say, "*Nobody* gets into my office."

Back outside, Lee said, "Who's going to get our guys out of there?"

"Besides here, the only helicopters are at K2 and J-Bad. Uzbekistan and Pakistan. They're at least three hours away, and that's if they're ready to launch."

They looked to their left, at the rows of Marine helicopters parked along the desert airstrip.

"What a joke," said Lee.

Meanwhile, the Air Force at J-Bad was scrambling to launch a rescue mission. All of AFSOC's 16th Special Operations Wing pilots and some of their flight engineers, aerial gunners, para-rescue jumpers (PJs),* and combat controllers convened at the operations center, where Commander Kingsley and Lieutenant Colonel Hadley were frantically putting together the flight plan for a rescue, even though every one of their helicopter crews had just returned from the mission to Shawali Kowt the night before. According to Air Force safety regulations, none of these pilots could legally fly until they'd had twelve hours of "crew rest," including eight hours of sleep.

Hadley broke away from the planning to check on the gathering crew members. They looked like men who had been awake for twenty-four hours straight, which they had. "Mike," he whispered to Kingsley, "they're all fucking exhausted. We have an MC-130** crew that hasn't flown, but we don't have a single helicopter crew that is rested."

Both men considered their options in silence, concluding separately that the only solution was to ignore regulations—which could endanger the rescuers *and* end their own careers in the Air Force.

"We're fucked," said Kingsley.

"I know," said Hadley. "But we *have* to figure out a way to make this happen."

"Sirs!" Major Shawn Silverman, the acting commander of the 20th Special Operations Squadron, burst into the command center. "I heard what's going on. There are two MH-53 crews that just got in for the first rotation of flight crews out of the combat theater."

"They're here already?" said Hadley, who knew that crews would be rotating out over the coming week, but wasn't aware that their replacements had arrived. "What's their story?"

---

* Air Force para-rescue jumpers specialize in rescue missions behind enemy lines. They are trained medics and airmen who also perform ground security for aircraft at landing zones.

** In this case a fixed-wing "fuel tanker" used to refuel the helicopters while in flight.

"One arrived day before yesterday. The other got in last night and hasn't gotten an intel brief or an area brief. Neither knows the routes, procedures, nothing for flying combat missions across the border. They aren't clear to fly into Afghanistan, but I'm certain they are up for anything. Just say the word."

"Where are they now?" asked Kingsley.

"Asleep."

"Wake them up."

Silverman went out the door.

"The PJs' squadron commander is chomping at the bit," Hadley said to the on-call operations officer, Major Reynolds. "Tell him to put together two CSAR [combat search-and-rescue] teams and get them out to the 53s. The aircrews will meet them there."

Reynolds went out the door.

"Steve, we don't know what the situation is," Kingsley told Hadley, "but we'll figure it out on the way. You've been in intel briefs for the past seventy days. You know the routes. You know the missions. You've flown them all. I need you as a doctor and air mission commander."

Though Hadley would have helped any American who needed it, his familiarity with ODA 574 gave him an emotional stake in this mission. Hadley and a few other AFSOC personnel at J-Bad had been involved in every step of the planning for Karzai's insurgency: He'd been Karzai's personal physician at J-Bad; he had treated Karzai's tribal leaders for everything from acid reflux to high blood pressure. And he had shared meals with every member of ODA 574, spending the most time with Amerine, a fellow graduate of West Point. Three weeks earlier, as Amerine left on his mission, Hadley had said, "We've got your back."

"Yes sir," Hadley said to Kingsley. "I'm in. Let's get them out of there."

Air Force Captain Steve Gregg had been in Pakistan only twelve hours when he felt someone kicking his cot. "Sir, wake up!" said First

Lieutenant Paul Alexander. "There are wounded Americans who need our help. We've got a mission right now!"

In five minutes, Gregg, Captain Pat Fronk, and their copilots, Second Lieutenant Marty Schweim and Alexander, were dressed in their tan flight suits with aviator bulletproof vests and running to the command center inside the hangar. There, Kingsley quickly shook each of their hands and introduced them to Hadley, their mission commander, before moving to stand beside a map of Afghanistan tacked to the wall.

"Welcome to the war, gentlemen—here's the situation," Kingsley said. "Americans are requesting emergency medevac north of Kandahar, at the same location our squadron flew into last night. We've got the routes, we know where they are, but that's about it. I know you haven't been briefed on intel, routes, or procedures, and I wouldn't be asking you to fly if you weren't our only option. Lieutenant Colonel Hadley has been in on every intel brief since we got here, and he has flown dozens of missions into Afghanistan. He will brief you en route. Flight time is just shy of three hours.

"From the moment you cross the border, you'll be flying through bad-guy country all the way. This was a mortar attack on an American position; we don't know if our guys are still in contact, but we're assuming it will be hot. As I learn more, I'll relay it to Lieutenant Colonel Hadley. Ground crews are turning around two of the 53s that flew last night; they're already refueled. CSAR teams are getting their gear and will meet you at your aircraft. Godspeed."

Following the briefing, Hadley went directly to the medical unit to request "the most qualified doctor on the base" to be the lead physician in an emergency medical evacuation behind enemy lines that was leaving immediately.

Within moments, he was shaking hands with Doc Frank, a family practice physician. When they left the aid station, each man had with him a basic lifesaving bag that included airways, tourniquets, IVs, chest tubes, a laryngoscope, and various surgical instruments. In addition, they each carried two trauma bags and six units of O-negative blood.

Pointing Frank in the direction of the helicopters, Hadley went in search of Charlie the spook, who had arrived at J-Bad early that morning from Shawali Kowt. He located him in the mess hall. "Got some bad news," Hadley told Charlie. "Your team's position north of Kandahar is requesting emergency medevac."

Charlie stood up, dropped his fork on the plate of a half-eaten meal, and hurried for the door with Hadley. "What the hell happened?" he asked.

"We're not sure, but initial reports say it was a mortar attack. We're going in to pull them out. I know you need to get home, but you're familiar with the layout on the ground. I am asking you as a friend and a soldier to go back in there with me."

"Just let me grab some equipment," said Charlie, leading the way to the spooks' private armory behind the building that had acted as the safe house for ODA 574 and the CIA during the planning of Karzai's insurgency. On a chain around his neck, Hadley kept a key to the cement-walled storage facility; he had standing orders to divvy up the weapons to his staff if the base was ever overrun. He unlocked the metal door.

Loaded carbines and shotguns lined one wall. Crates of exotic weapons, including shoulder-fired anti-tank missiles, were stacked in a corner. In another corner were boxes of grenades and claymore mines, as well as body armor, load-bearing vests, and ammo pouches. Hadley was already carrying his Air Force–issued Beretta M9 sidearm and compact Colt Commando carbine with seven fully loaded thirty-round magazines for each. Charlie selected the same weapons for himself, then added six fragmentation grenades and an extra case of 1,000 rounds of ammo for both men. On the way out, Hadley grabbed three additional boxes of ten hand grenades each for the two helicopter crews.

Jumping into a Humvee, they drove to the two Pave Low helicopters being towed onto the runway.

Every other air mission into Afghanistan had taken several hours or even days to plan. Because helicopters are short-range aircraft, they would need to be refueled in flight at a prearranged location. Since the MC-130s carrying the extra fuel would make easy targets at the low altitude necessary to fill up the helicopters—usually around five hundred feet above ground level—the refueling locations were always far from population centers.

The refueling crews at J-Bad, call sign Ditka 04, were given roughly ten seconds of guidance from Hadley. "We don't know where, we don't know when, and we don't know how much, but we're going to need gas," he said. "Go anchor yourselves somewhere up near these coordinates, and we'll call you when we need you."

By streamlining every aspect of the planning, a cobbled-together rescue mission composed of twenty-four men—two pilots, two co-pilots, four flight engineers, four aerial gunners, six PJs, three combat controllers, a Special Ops physician, one Special Ops pilot/physician, and one spook—was ready for takeoff thirty minutes after the medevac request was received.

Now Kingsley did something he had never done on previous missions: He drove out to see the men off. Parking beside the lead helicopter, Knife 03, he got out of the Humvee and faced Hadley. They had already discussed the fact that there would be no quick reaction force if a Pave Low went down, and every member of the mission was aware that the Soviet occupation had bred in Afghans a particular contempt for helicopter crews. In addition, the Northern Alliance had assured the Americans that any airmen captured by the Taliban would be disposed of in "the Afghan way": castration or disembowelment, followed by hanging or decapitation.

Kingsley and another Pave Low pilot had flown the first Operation Desert Storm air mission into Iraq shortly before 2 A.M. on January 17, 1991, when Pave Lows were the only helicopter with GPS and terrain-following radar capabilities. The two pilots' Pave Lows had guided four Apache gunships from Saudi Arabia nine miles into Iraq, where the gunships simultaneously destroyed Iraq's two main early-warning radar and communications stations. Their successful mission allowed President George H. W. Bush to begin the air bombing campaign and earned Kingsley the Distinguished Flying Cross.

Kingsley knew, probably better than any other helicopter pilot or commander in theater, the advantages of flying over enemy terrain at night. "This is just a reminder in case you hadn't noticed that little yellow ball in the sky," Kingsley told Hadley. "It's daylight, and this is a no-shit very dangerous mission. Get the job done and bring everybody in my squadron home alive."[*]

At the same time, two Air Force Special Operations MC-130 Combat Talon aircraft—known as JMAU (Joint Medical Augmentation Unit), specially equipped for in-flight surgeries and advanced trauma care and with room for fifty litter patients—were cruising at 300 miles per hour toward Kandahar from their base at Masirah, just off the coast of Oman, eight hundred miles to the south. The closest runway to Shawali Kowt capable of accommodating the hundred-foot-long transport planes was at Camp Rhino.

The JMAUs had been requested by Colonel Mulholland immediately after Bolduc's first estimate of the combined American and Afghan casualties in Shawali Kowt: more than twenty-two killed and around seventy wounded. Mulholland now understood the breakdown to be two Americans dead and nineteen wounded, six of whom were in critical condition and one expectant. Of the Afghans, twenty were dead and at least fifty wounded, nine of whom were critical and three expectant.

While the two aircraft were en route to Rhino, Major Miller and his B-team, ODB 570, now tasked as a quick reaction force with the call sign Rambo 70, had been joined by two ODAs plus a forward surgical team at K2 and were just a few minutes into their flight across Uzbekistan, also heading to Camp Rhino. They would then transfer onto what they assumed would be Marine helicopters for the flight to Shawali Kowt, where they would defend the site, assist the wounded, and evacuate them back to Camp Rhino. There the patients would be moved onto the surgical airships that would fly to Oman—the

---

[*] This was the first daytime helicopter mission in the War on Terror.

closest military hospital equipped to receive the casualties. The ODAs would remain in Afghanistan under Fox's command, while ODB 570 would return to K2, back in their tents "in time for dinner," they'd been told.

The team knew that there was one KIA, one MIA presumed KIA, and numerous casualties, and Cubby Wojciehowski was spending the bumpy flight envisioning trauma scenarios in order to prepare himself to treat his former teammates, whom he'd last seen at the back door of the ISOFAC at Fort Campbell a month and a half earlier. As they approached the Afghan border, Lloyd Allard walked back from the front of the cargo hold and squeezed in next to Cubby on the bench. He shook his head a couple of times and mouthed the word *fuck*, then leaned in and with his hand on Cubby's shoulder, yelled over the sound of the engines, "Dan is dead! So is JD!"

Cubby never thought words could pummel a man physically, but that was how he felt—instantly beat down.

"You're sure?" he asked Allard.

"They wouldn't tell us unless they were certain. We gotta just shove this news in a hole, and we'll deal with it later. Right now we need to get in there and see how we can help."

Nodding robotically, Cubby thought about how Dan had tried to cheer him up as ODA 574 planned for the mission without him: "Don't worry, Cub. You don't want to go on this one anyway. We aren't doing anything big. It's going to be boring." Those had been the last words Dan would ever speak to him. JD's final words, he remembered, had been "We'll probably link up with you guys in-country."

Still sitting quietly next to Cubby, Allard also dwelled on that good-bye at the ISOFAC, haunted by the note he'd written on the brown grocery bag with the beer and whiskey he and Cubby had brought the team as a sendoff: "If you find yourself alone, riding through green fields with the sun on your face, do not be troubled, for there is beer."

The actual quote, which Allard had heard with most of the guys on ODA 574 when they'd gone out to see the movie *Gladiator* in 2000, ended: ". . . do not be troubled, for you are in Elysium and you are already dead."

It was 9:30 A.M., one hour after the explosion. The northeast wall of the medical clinic had become the forty-foot-long backstop of the CCP, where the wounded lay on blankets, litters, sleeping bags, and doors that had been ripped off their hinges. Casualties fanned out from the clinic, covering a space roughly the size of a basketball court. The most critical were located toward the center, close to the wall, where they were sheltered from the occasional breeze but still warmed by the sun. The walking wounded had been paired up with critical patients to help the medics monitor their vital signs and keep them talking.

Victor and Brent were sitting between Mike—who was unconscious—and Ronnie, for whom they were feigning a no-worries attitude in spite of their own shrapnel and burn injuries. When Mike woke up, he was barely coherent from the mix of shock, blood loss, and morphine, and struggled to keep his eyes open. "Something's not right," he whispered to Victor. "What happened?"

"We're going home, buddy," said Victor. "We're just waiting for our ride."

Mike passed out again, only to wake up fifteen minutes later and repeat, "What happened?"

Just down from Ronnie, Alex was covered up to his neck by a sleeping bag, his head resting on some wadded clothes. He was pale, his teeth chattered, and his eyes, when he opened them, appeared clouded and faraway. On the other side of Alex, Price kept watch over him, one hand resting on the wounded man's chest.

"How's he doing?" Amerine asked, walking over to Price.

"He's cold. Won't stop shivering. But Doc said his pulse is pretty strong, and they stopped the worst of the bleeding. I'm warming up his next IV." Price lifted up his shirt to reveal the IV bag he was holding against his stomach.

A few feet away from Alex, Mag began to thrash and kick. He ripped out his IV with his good hand while Captain Jeff Leopold, the headquarters intelligence officer, attempted to keep him down by lying over him as he held Mag's head bandage in place. Brent helped by grabbing Mag's legs, and soon Mag relaxed and passed out.

"You just need to rest," Leopold said to Mag, reinserting the IV. "Help is on the way."

Leaning away from Alex so that only Amerine could hear, Price said, "I'm so sorry. I can't figure out what happened, but something got fucked up."

Amerine had worked with Price before and remembered him to be a confident and competent controller. Price was described in a recent evaluation as "a master of his trade, a shining example." But now, an hour after Price had called in the JDAM, Amerine saw only a broken man.

"You did your best," Amerine said.

Tears welled up in Price's eyes. "I thought I did everything right, but . . . I'm so sorry."

"You did your best," Amerine said again, looking down at Alex. "We'll get through this. Concentrate on Alex and forget about that for now."

Opening his eyes, Alex saw Amerine and began making a sound as if clearing his throat. Amerine reached over and held his hand. "You hear me okay?" he asked.

When Alex nodded, Amerine said, "You are going to be fine. I'm going to make sure you're taken care of. Hold on and keep fighting the good fight. I'm grateful for all you did here, Alex."

Alex smiled weakly and closed his eyes.

With Mag unconscious, Leopold kept an eye on another soldier, Cody Prosser, who was also passed out, lying on the other side of Mike with a severe head injury from shrapnel. Unlike the other critically wounded, each tended to by one person, Prosser had three people: a spook standing over him with an IV bag, a Green Beret sitting at his head giving him oxygen, and a Delta medic at his side checking vital signs constantly. Leopold had chosen Prosser, his best friend, for this mission when Fox had requested the best intelligence analyst in the battalion.

Now, as Pickett walked by, Leopold asked if he knew how Prosser was doing, and received the same response he'd already gotten from the other medics: "Not too well, Jeff. We just need to get him to a hospital."

Leopold knew it was much worse than they were letting on. Cody, all of these critically injured guys, needed to get out of here soon or they were going to die.

/

Forty-five minutes after Kingsley had driven out to the runway to see the men off, both helicopters remained on the ground at J–Bad.

They were awaiting final clearance to fly because the encryption of their communications equipment, which was supposed to be changed for each mission, was still configured for the previous night's infiltration. The senior para-rescue jumper, Master Sergeant Patrick Malone, sitting in the lead aircraft, Knife 03, voiced the chagrin of all on board both helicopters when he said, "This is bullshit! What's wrong with the comms we pushed last night?"

The pilots agreed, one of them responding over the internal comms of both aircraft with "Fuck it."

Almost immediately, the Pave Lows were airborne, with Knife 03, piloted by Captain Gregg, flying northwest at top speed three hundred feet above ground level (AGL), and Knife 04, piloted by Captain Fronk, trailing in a staggered-left formation at fifty feet AGL.

"Knife Zero Three," Fronk radioed to Gregg while looking up at the lead aircraft's belly. "Be advised, sir, shooting at American helicopters is a recreational sport here in Pakistan. You might want to drop altitude."

"Roger," said Gregg, bringing his Pave Low down to the same altitude as Knife 04.

Fifteen minutes after liftoff, a Delta combat controller in Shawali Kowt came on the radio asking for an update. "Confirming you are en route?" he asked.

"We are in flight," Hadley responded.

"How long until you get here, sir?"

"Two plus four-five." Two hours and forty-five minutes.

There was a pause, then the operator said, "Sir, Americans are dying. Please hurry. Please."

Hadley leaned forward from where he was standing behind the

pilots. "Fly the most direct route we can, avoiding any towns," he told them. "Pull the guts out of the aircraft."

The pilots recalculated, upping the airspeed from the standard top cruising speed of 120 knots (138 miles per hour) to 130 knots (150 miles per hour) and following a route that would ignore much of the cautionary terrain masking built into the original flight plan.

"Sir," Gregg said to Hadley, "we'll have to play it by ear, but I think we can do it in two hours."

"All right. Keep it low."

Once they hit the Afghan border, the helicopters dropped to twenty-five feet AGL, a safer altitude in terms of surface-to-air missiles: By the time the enemy sees or hears the aircraft, there is no time to calibrate the trajectory on their weapons. They flew the fastest their Pave Lows could fly without risking damage to the airframe.

Thirty-one-year-old Staff Sergeant Scott Diekman had never flown so low or so fast. From his tail gunner position on the open ramp of Knife 03, he looked out the back of the helicopter, which blew up lines of sand as it ripped across the landscape. The pilots tried to avoid settlements but occasionally passed over a Bedouin camp, whose occupants flung themselves flat on the ground or dived into tents.

"Now this is something I never thought I'd see," Hadley said to both crews on the interplane radio frequency. "Afghanistan in the daylight."

Although he sounded calm, Hadley's legs were shaking from nerves. He'd been on numerous missions across the border under the cover of darkness, but without that cloak of safety he felt dangerously exposed. During a lull in the radio chatter, Hadley thought about his girlfriend, Leslie, and wondered if he would ever get the chance to marry her. He thought about the 57 mm anti-aircraft cannons that his pilots had continued to identify on their flights between Pakistan and Kandahar—even after reports that they'd all been destroyed—and the hundreds of Stinger surface-to-air missiles that had not been accounted for since the war with the Soviets.

In the pilot seat in front of Hadley, Gregg looked at the desert landscape rushing toward him; he knew they were the sole aircraft over the entire country flying below 30,000 feet. The last time he'd experienced anything like this had been on September 11, when his was one of only four military helicopters granted special FAA clearance to fly into New York City to help with the search-and-recovery efforts at the Twin Towers. The eastern seaboard had been eerily void of aircraft, the only blips on the radar representing the jet fighters that flew combat air patrols high overhead.

Gregg's orders then had been vague but chilling, just like the one he'd received today: "Go help Americans."

In Shawali Kowt, Amerine had a grim duty to perform: finding something of JD that he could bring home for his family to bury.

Leaving Price and Alex at the CCP, Amerine first stopped in front of the building where the Afghans had been lining up their dead. Adjacent to that was a mound of human remains, which he dug through in search of anything looking like it belonged to an American. He remembered the leg he'd seen, dressed in desert camouflage, but could find no trace of it.

Out beyond the western end of the Alamo, where he'd last seen JD and where he assumed his team sergeant had been at the time of the explosion, Amerine began to search the impact zone. On the southwest slope, no more than thirty yards from the wall surrounding the command post, he found the crater from the bomb. If he hadn't known what he was looking at, he would have walked right past the ten-foot-wide, two-foot-deep gouge in the earth, distinct only because it was coated in white ash. This slope of the Alamo had been blasted clean: There were no body parts, not even any rocks—nothing but the smooth surface of the sandy soil.

But beyond the semicircular blast zone that extended roughly twenty yards in all directions, there were remnants of bodies that had mostly vaporized. Amerine moved slowly outward from the crater as he scoured the ground—littered with blackened shreds of clothing, bits of sandals, and pieces of burnt or bloody flesh—looking for part of a dog tag, a wedding ring, a finger that might identify an individual. Along the way, he picked up scraps of paper containing sensitive information and shoved them in his pockets. With the CCP two hundred yards to his back, the only sound was the constant, muffled whoosh of the wind through his blown eardrums.

Amid the gore, Amerine found some flecks of colored paper—orange, yellow, and pink—from Starburst candy wrappers. JD had stashed a pocketful after the Thanksgiving "turkey" drop to hand out to Afghan children, and Amerine thought that perhaps this confetti indicated the location of his team sergeant's demise.

About seventy-five yards southwest of the crater, he saw what looked like a mask. Stepping closer, Amerine realized it was a man's face, lightly coated with ash and lying on the ground as if it had been surgically removed.

"Bari Gul," he said.

He stacked some rocks to mark the spot and continued his search.

"You're in shock, Captain. You need to come back and sit down."

Amerine turned to see Bolduc. From the medical clinic, the major had been watching as the captain wandered around the impact zone, staring at the ground.

"I'm not in shock," Amerine snapped. "I'm looking for my team sergeant."

In the lengthy pause that followed, Amerine and the major stared at each other. Until now, Amerine had been so focused on the welfare of his men that he had not contemplated the cause of the accident. Now he entertained the idea that Bolduc and Fox were largely responsible. Accidents happen in war and people are fallible, he knew, but this one had been avoidable: The air strikes ordered by the headquarters staff had led to this tragedy. Bolduc was a competent officer who had to have known it wasn't the headquarters' job to be calling in bombs; he had said as much in his speech when he and Fox arrived in Tarin Kowt: "We're here to provide your team with top cover. We're here to advise Karzai."

He glared at Bolduc and realized that his right hand had tightened around the familiar pistol grip of his M4 carbine, his index finger pressing harder than it should against the trigger guard, his left hand gripping the barrel.

Remembering JD's calming voice from the night before—*Take a walk, sir?*—he relaxed his grip. This was no time to cast blame.

"We have to find something for his family to bury," Amerine said quietly, taking a deep breath and refocusing his gaze downward. "I'm fine."

"Understood," said Bolduc. He walked rapidly back to the medical clinic, passing Casper with a nod.

"How are you holding up?" Casper asked when he caught up with Amerine.

"Looking for JD."

"I'll help," said Casper, and together they searched in silence.

Knife 03 and Knife 04 had been tearing across southern Afghanistan for half an hour when two F-14s arrived 2,000 feet overhead and one of the pilots radioed Hadley.

"Knife Zero Three, this is Pearl Four One. We have top cover and are here for the duration."

"It sure is good to have you up there," Hadley said. He proceeded to brief the combat escort pilots on the proposed route. "This is a rescue mission; engage enemy threats only with the intent to protect the helicopters."

"Roger," said Pearl 41, "we copy that—let's go get our boys."

Moments later, Hadley came back over the radio. "Highway One coming up."

Highway One was a major road used by the Taliban to travel between Kabul and Herat via Kandahar. Scanning ahead from the higher altitude, Pearl 41 reported no vehicles. *Lucky timing*, thought Gregg as he and Fronk dropped to ten feet above the desert floor, adjusted their flight path, and crossed over the highway between two dunes, showering the road with sand. Once they were on the other side of the highway, Diekman leaned forward over his machine gun to see if he could spot the jets. "Good to have some top cover!" he yelled over the engines to Charlie, sitting behind him to the left.

Charlie grinned. "Top cover doesn't make you guys any less crazy to be flying here in the middle of the day," he shouted back. "How many missions have you flown across the border?"

"Including this one?"

"Yeah."

"One."

"First mission, broad daylight." The spook shook his head. "You guys *are* freakin' nuts. God bless America."

One hour out from Shawali Kowt, the Delta controller contacted Hadley and reported two Americans killed, one expectant, eight critically wounded. Those on the rescue mission continued to believe these casualties were the result of a battle.

At twenty-five minutes out, the Delta controller radioed again to ask how many wounded the two helicopters could carry. The flight engineers on both aircraft calculated their cargo load capacity, fuel weight, and distance to Camp Rhino. Knife 04 reported they could carry fourteen, while Hadley's Pave Low could take eighteen if they dumped some fuel.

"Three-two," Hadley said. "We can accommodate thirty-two wounded."

"Roger. You're going to need all the room you've got."

Hadley glanced back at the PJs, the surprise apparent on their faces. *This is going to be a lot worse than we thought.*

/

Two minutes before reaching the coordinates for LZ Jamie, Knife 03 released a portion of its fuel in a misty cloud, creating a rainbow that hung in the air. In the helicopter behind, Knife 04's pilot, Captain Fronk, glanced over at his copilot, First Lieutenant Alexander.

"What the fuck are they thinking?" said Alexander.

Fronk shrugged. It was a professional difference of opinion. Considering the unknowns ahead, Fronk and Alexander felt more comfortable with every drop of fuel their tanks could hold.

One minute out from the LZ Jamie, Hadley called Charlie to the front of the helicopter. They could see no friendly forces marking a landing zone. The spook peered over the shoulders of the pilot and copilot and beyond the instrument panels at the terrain rushing toward them: He recognized the cluster of buildings a mile ahead as Shawali Kowt. A quarter of a mile beyond that was the Arghandab River, with the bridge to the west. His eyes widened and he yelled out something. Hadley pushed his radio mic up close to Charlie's mouth so both helicopters could hear what he was saying.

"You're too far south! Don't go over by that bridge!"

"Why?!" Hadley shouted.

"Because that's where the enemy is!"

Just then, Gregg noticed men walking on a road across the river, some carrying RPGs. Knife 03 was already above the river when he banked the helicopter hard to the right, dropped in altitude, and skimmed the tops of the orchard trees. In Knife 04, Fronk had seen a man holding an orange panel, designating friendly forces, and broke formation before the river. In a more relaxed turn, he landed three hundred yards west of the dirt road leading from Shawali Kowt to Damana, a mile and a half north of the CCP. Moments later, Knife 03 landed two hundred yards to the east of the road, opposite Knife 04. Within seconds, both were engulfed by dust.

Amerine felt something like joy pierce his numbness when he heard the sound of helicopters and looked up to see two Pave Lows rip over the rooftops of Shawali Kowt, bank down beyond the bridge, and head back toward Damana.

Amerine glanced over at Casper. Their time was up.

"We'll keep looking," Casper said as they jogged back toward the CCP. Amerine knew he would forever regret giving up the search for JD, but that sentiment would have to wait—along with the sorrow, disgust, and rage he'd suppressed all morning. Right now, he had to bring the rest of his men home.

In the three and a half hours since the bomb had dropped, three more Afghans had died from their injuries. Of the nineteen wounded Americans, only Cody Prosser had not regained consciousness and was still considered expectant.

Amerine approached Bolduc, who was writing on a notepad beside the CCP, to ask about the plan to move the men to the helicopters.

Pausing with his pencil on the paper, Bolduc said, "Fox is working with Hamid to get trucks from the town to take you and your guys, along with my wounded, out of here."

"I can stay," said Amerine. "My leg isn't bad."

"No, I'm going to evac you with your men."

Nodding, Amerine walked to where Mike, Mag, Ronnie, and Alex were still holding on.

"You going with them?" asked Mr. Big, who was labeling tags for the wounded.

"Yeah," said Amerine. "It's the headquarters' show now."

"Here," said Mr. Big, wiring a tan card to Amerine's collar.

Amerine looked down and read CASUALTY on the tag, the details of his injuries already filled in. "So, what club is this?" he asked.

Mr. Big just shook his head.

Vehicles driven by both guerrillas and locals from Shawali Kowt lined up alongside the casualties. His leg now swollen from the shrapnel, Amerine hobbled over to stand by Dan's body as he counted his men being placed in trucks. Then he noticed Karzai for the first time since his entourage had ushered him away after the bomb hit, moving among the wounded with three tribal leaders, a small square bandage on his cheek.

When Karzai saw Amerine, he bowed his head slightly and came over. "I'm sorry about your men," he said. He looked down at the bivy sack. "I was told about Dan and JD. This is . . . ?"

"This is Dan."

"And JD?"

"We haven't been able to find anything," said Amerine. "Did you hear about Bari Gul?"

"Yes," said Karzai. "Some of his men will take his remains to Deh Rawood shortly."

"Bashir?"

"I don't believe he survived. Nobody has seen him."

"And you. Are you okay?"

"Yes," said Karzai, continuing to look around at the wounded. "And you?"

"I'm fine."

The men stood together in the first awkward silence Amerine had shared with Karzai since meeting him in Pakistan a month earlier. Finally, Karzai, who still believed it had been Amerine and ODA 574 who had called in the bomb, looked him in the eye and asked, "How did this happen, Jason?"

Shaking his head, Amerine made the decision not to tell Karzai the details. He had to ensure that Fox and his staff remained close to Karzai as they finished the journey to Kandahar and on to Kabul. The final sacrifice of Amerine and his team would be allowing Karzai to believe that it was ODA 574 who had caused the devastation and the deaths of so many.

"It was an accident," said Amerine.

"Tragic," said Karzai. The two surveyed the casualties. At last Karzai sighed. "I must check the men," he said.

Unable to tell his friend he was leaving—that this was good-bye—Amerine simply nodded, and Karzai walked away. He watched as Karzai moved among the wounded Afghans, speaking encouraging words and covering one shivering man with the blanket from around his shoulders.

Voices shouted out commands: Bolduc and Fox were directing the loading of the wounded Americans, followed by the most critically wounded Afghans, onto the trucks.

Captain Bovee walked over to Amerine. "Time to go," he said.

"We need to get Dan out," said Amerine.

"I've got him. I'll bring him on the next truck. There isn't room on this one."

Amerine moved along the row of vehicles, wincing at the growing pain in his leg as he again accounted for every member of ODA 574: eight men, including Dan. Wes had been evacuated the day before, and as for JD . . . he didn't want to think about it. He had reported JD as "MIA presumed KIA" to Bolduc. The headquarters would resume the search later and, if necessary, a forensic team would be deployed to find something of the man that Amerine had failed to bring home.

From the back of the crowded pickup he'd climbed into, Amerine was watching Bovee and Leopold carry Dan's body to the next truck when Mr. Big came running over from the medical clinic holding a plastic bag. Stopping beside Dan, he hurried to remove what looked like a folded sheet. With both hands, he shook out a new American flag, its colors a vivid contrast to the drab military uniforms and desert sand.

Mr. Big wrapped the four-by-six-foot flag around Dan's body, using safety pins to attach it to the bivy sack. Then he saluted Dan, which was the final vision Amerine wanted of this place. He faced forward, and the convoy started to roll out. But when his truck neared the berm, Amerine was compelled to take one last look.

His first glimpse of Shawali Kowt had been from this road during one of the best days of his life. Forty-eight hours later, his parting view was on the worst day of his life. Amerine's gaze drifted to the Alamo—the whale—whose head bore its newest scar, an ashen crater barely discernable from all the wounds of its previous wars.

CHAPTER FOURTEEN

★

Worth Dying For

Back at home a young wife waits
Her Green Beret has met his fate
He has died for those oppressed
Leaving her his last request.
  —Barry Sadler, "Ballad of the Green Berets"

The moment the rescue helicopters had touched down, Hadley on Knife 03 told Gregg over his radio headset, "You are now the air mission commander. I'm going to shift to doctor."

He followed two PJs carrying aid bags and casualty litters down the ramp, veered to the right into the brownout, and hurried to the road. As the dust cleared, Hadley saw Doc Frank and two PJs from Knife 04 approaching from the other side of the road.

The two groups converged and looked south, toward Shawali Kowt.

"Where the hell are the wounded?" asked Gavin Burns, the lead PJ from Knife 04.

At the helicopters, the pilots had powered down the engines to an idle and remained sitting at the controls. The gunners of each Pave Low also stayed behind their weapons, monitoring three armed Afghans who appeared atop the dunes to the southeast. "I've got three guys with guns two hundred yards out," Diekman announced over the radio. Then he saw a familiar silhouette crest a ridge fifty yards from the armed men. "Looks like there's a Pinzgauer joining us."

"Delta Force," came a dramatic whisper over Diekman's radio. "We're saved." Another voice chuckled.

Delta's presence *was* reassuring, but the gunners remained alert. The three Afghans didn't appear hostile, but if Delta was here, Diekman assumed, so too were the bad guys.

In the direction of Shawali Kowt, dust began to rise on the horizon, then a couple of trucks came into view from behind some dunes a half mile away.

"Here come the wounded!" announced the tail gunner on Knife 04 over the radio. Hearing this, Diekman realized that Delta was providing cover for the medevac convoy.

Hadley, Doc Frank, and the PJs jogged south on the road to meet the vehicles. As they got closer, they saw blown-out windows, dented sides, scoured paint. One minivan's metal roof had been peeled back like an opened sardine can; another truck's door was ripped off at the hinges.

"Holy shit," said Hadley as he and Doc Frank got to the first of the seven vehicles, each carrying two to three Americans. Quickly, they decided to re-triage the patients because they weren't certain they understood the priority system assigned by the medics back in Shawali Kowt, none of whom had arrived in the first vehicles. Hadley and Doc Frank had decided in advance that the wounded requiring "immediate" care would go to Knife 04, Doc Frank's helicopter; "urgent" patients would be divided between both helicopters; and "routine" would go to Knife 03, Hadley's helicopter.

"When you've got your fourteen patients," Hadley said to Frank, "go. Fly as a single-ship mission. Get all the criticals out of here."

PJs passed the two men, running down the row of parked vehicles to check vitals and responsiveness. Stopping at the third in line, Gavin Burns leaned over the tailgate of a truck to check on the man lying in its bed.

"What's your name?" Burns asked, bringing his head close to a face that was deep inside a zipped-up sleeping bag. He heard a muffled groan and realized he recognized the man. *Jesus*, thought Burns. It was Alex Yoshimoto, his good friend from 23rd Special Tactics Squadron, based in Hurlburt Field, Florida. Unzipping the bag, he discovered a large blood-soaked bandage intended for a chest wound but being used on Alex's shoulder. More field dressings covered his torso.

"Alex, it's me, Gavin. Gavin Burns. Do you know where you're at, buddy?"

Alex responded with a slight nod and some mumbling.

For an instant, Burns experienced an emotional surge akin to adrenaline, an overwhelming desire to remain by his friend's side, but then he looked down the line of vehicles.

"Hang tight—we'll get you out of here," Burns told Alex before moving on to another truck, which held Mike, wrapped in blankets and unconscious. He did not respond to verbal or painful stimuli— such as a pinch—his skin was cool to the touch, and the oxygen level in his blood was dangerously low. A quick glance at Mike's wounds reminded Burns of photos he'd seen of great white shark attacks.

This guy is circling the drain, he thought.

When his truck reached the triage area, Amerine staggered out, shouldered his go-to-hell pack, and, holding his carbine at the ready, stepped aside to watch the newly arrived rescue medics work, their clean uniforms in stark contrast to their surroundings. A few hundred yards off each side of the road, the spinning rotors of the two Pave Lows were a blur. Men were running up from the helicopters, carrying casualty litters. He glanced back at the truck behind his, assuring himself that Dan was still there, then hobbled toward the front of the vehicles.

Noticing Amerine, Hadley walked briskly over, pulling the captain into a brief hug.

"It sure is good to see you," said Amerine. "Thanks for coming to get us."

"It's what we do." Hadley skimmed Amerine's casualty card and pointed at Knife 03. "You'll be with me, on that Pave Low."

"I'll wait here—I need to make sure my guys get on. And Dan," he said, motioning toward Dan's body.

"I'm really sorry. He's with us, too. Make sure he gets over to my helo. You feeling all right? Dizzy or anything?"

"I'm fine."

Nobody here is fine, Hadley thought. "What hit you guys?" he asked. "This couldn't have been a mortar attack."

"Friendly fire," said Amerine. "Our own bomb."

"Christ."

The Pinzgauer to the east opened up with a long burst of fire as some PJs and two uninjured headquarters staff began carrying the first vehicle's patients toward Knife 04 three hundred yards away. Hadley ran toward them, shouting, "Go back—get in the fucking vehicles, and *drive* to the back of the helos!"

"Is it safe to drive near the tail rotors, sir?" yelled a PJ.

"Safer than getting shot at!" As far as Hadley was concerned, this was a hot LZ.

"Sir, we've got a slew of Afghan casualties coming up the road in trucks," shouted another PJ. "They're with a bunch of armed men, RPGs and shit. What's the call?"

Hadley grabbed Charlie, who was walking by with a litter, and asked, "Any of those guys coming our way bad guys?"

Setting the litter down, Charlie sprinted down the road with the PJ for a closer look and quickly returned. "I recognize them; they're Karzai's men."

"Are we loading the Afghans?" the PJ asked.

Shit, thought Hadley. Nobody had given him any guidance about that.

In fact, Fox *had* received permission from Colonel Mulholland to medevac Karzai's men, but nobody had told Hadley and he didn't have clearance to take anyone but Americans on board. "Yeah," Hadley decided on the spot. "We'll take everybody we can carry. Get through the Americans and then triage the Afghans."

It took almost twenty minutes to re-triage the nineteen wounded Americans and the most critically wounded Afghans and to transport them and Dan to their respective helicopters.

On Knife 04, the critical patients—Alex, Mike, Mag, and Ronnie, along with four headquarters personnel including Reed and Fathi—were placed in eight of the nine hanging litters, stacked like bunk beds along the sides of the Pave Low's cargo hold. Six walking wounded, including Brent and Victor, sat down between the side gunners on the deck toward the front of the aircraft. Price and Leopold flanked Cody Prosser, who was put on a litter in the center front of the hold.

"How close are you to liftoff?" Fronk radioed Gregg in Knife 03. Although they had been given the go-ahead to fly a single-ship mission, none of the pilots liked the idea. It was far safer, especially over bad-guy country, to fly tandem.

"We're going to be a while," said Gregg. "We're loading Afghans. They keep on coming."

On the tail ramp of Knife 04, Burns was listening in on the radio while treating three critical patients. The most serious was Mike, whose blood oxygen level had remained low at 70 percent; his blood pressure had also dropped, and he was now shivering constantly. Reexamining Mike's bandages, Burns found that his chest wound was seeping blood.

To combat Mike's severe shock symptoms, Burns connected him to his entire fifteen-liter supply of oxygen via a rebreather mask. Then he added new packing to his chest wound, along with two bandages to apply more pressure. Rechecking oxygen levels, he found that Mike still had not improved, and his shivering had intensified.

Fuck, Burns thought, putting another wool blanket on top of Mike. He glanced to the other side of the cargo hold, where fellow PJ Brent Scott was packing Alex's gaping shoulder wound with more gauze, while in the litter below, Mag was desperately giving him the sign for water—as if tipping a glass with his hand. "No water," Scott told Mag, who began to belligerently hit the underside of Alex's litter with his right fist. Noting Mag's extensive cranial bandaging, Burns thought, *Brain injury—guy doesn't know what he's doing.*

Looking toward the front of the helicopter, Burns saw Doc Frank alternating between Ronnie and Fathi, both of whom were hypothermic and in shock. He couldn't believe these guys were still alive. Then Burns heard Gregg, on Knife 03, ask Fronk, "Can you guys carry any more wounded?"

Burns yelled forward, so loudly they could hear him clearly in the cockpit even without a radio: "No! We cannot get anybody else on this aircraft! We gotta go! We gotta go *now*!"

From behind his machine gun, Diekman watched warily as the first two trucks filled with Afghans drove up and parked at the rear of Knife 03. Immediately, more than a dozen armed men jumped out and stood in a group between the trucks, which were carrying two wounded Afghans apiece. Another truck pulled up, and a couple of the Afghans walked toward the ramp and peered into the cargo hold, where a few of the less seriously wounded Americans were sitting.

Moments before, the crew had been alerted that Afghan casualties were on the way, but Diekman's duty was to protect this aircraft, and both training and instinct told him that having these men so close wasn't safe. No Americans were with them, and he couldn't discount the possibility that they could be saboteurs, using the rescue operation to get in close and lob a grenade into a helicopter.

"Permission to leave the aircraft," Diekman said over his radio. "We've got a cluster fuck in progress back here."

A gunner was never supposed to leave his helicopter, but when Gregg looked over his shoulder and saw the number of Afghans near the ramp, he said, "Go."

A few strides beyond the ramp, Diekman realized that he only had his M9 pistol, which to a machine gunner was about as worthless as a peashooter. He turned back to grab his M16 or shotgun and saw that the side door gunner had shifted to the tail gun position and the engineer up front had shifted to the side gun, keeping defenses at 100 percent.

Feeling amply covered from the Pave Low, Diekman didn't bother with his shotgun. He had started to push the crowd back from the ramp when a PJ from the triage area ran up. "Are these our guys?" asked Diekman. "Are we loading them?"

"Yes," yelled the PJ, who bent over a wounded Afghan.

One of the Afghans stood fully upright in the bed of a truck, his head inches from the helicopter's tail rotor, spinning so fast it was invisible. Diekman yanked the man down, pointed out the danger, and indicated that the truck should be parked farther away. He then began to help Knife 03's PJs direct "traffic"—loading the critically wounded Afghans onto the aircraft and placing the worst-off by the tail ramp exit.

From the cockpit, Gregg watched as Knife 04 took off, leaving a trail of dust in its wake as it headed north, then banked and picked up speed heading southwest around Kandahar. One of Gregg's flight engineers came over the radio. "Here comes an American KIA."

"How can you tell?" asked Gregg.

"You need to look to the rear, sir."

Lifting up in his seat, Gregg stared over his shoulder and out of the cavernous cargo hold, where a truck was backing up to the tail ramp. In its bed was a body in what looked like a sleeping bag and covered with an American flag.

Gregg could not fathom how somebody had had the presence of mind to actually pause in the middle of what must have been confusion and chaos in order to wrap the fallen soldier in a flag. *That is patriotism*, he thought, feeling a renewed sense of responsibility to return this American home to his family.

It was 12:25 in the afternoon when Knife 04 rose above the desert, and Mike started to throw up. Burns pulled away the oxygen mask he'd placed over Mike's face and turned his head sideways so he wouldn't choke on the vomit.

Having been unable to locate a suitable vein for an IV, Burns proceeded to slather the center of Mike's chest—just to the side of the bandage—with Betadine. Picking up a large spring-loaded needle, he punched it directly into Mike's sternum and pumped a saline solution directly into his bone marrow.

Over the radio, Alexander announced that the flight to Camp Rhino would take forty minutes. *Forty minutes*, thought Burns, shifting his attention to Reed. *An eternity.* For the next twenty minutes, Burns, Doc Frank, and the PJs continued to monitor vitals and check the airways of their patients, but they didn't remove any bandages on the extensive wounds for fear they'd dislodge a blood clot or disturb whatever it was that had been done by the ground medics to keep these men from bleeding to death for the past four hours.

They were halfway to Rhino when Fronk called Ditka 04 to request their planned aerial refueling. Only a couple of minutes had passed before the tail gunner announced the arrival of the MC-130, a mile out and closing in. "Tally-ho," he said. "I have the tanker."

Amerine waited outside the Pave Low with Dan's body, which had been placed at the bottom of the ramp while the rescue crew loaded wounded Afghans. He had never seen a group of men work so quickly or efficiently, and it appeared that Knife 03 couldn't hold another patient—every hanging litter and almost every inch of floor space was full.

Followed closely by Amerine, two crew members carried Dan up the ramp. As they passed Diekman—who had been tightening the belt on his machine gun's ammo boxes—the tail gunner turned suddenly and bumped into the litter. Immediately, he saw what he'd done and looked at Amerine, who was following them up the ramp.

Meeting his eyes, Amerine quietly said, "Show some respect."

"I'm so sorry," said Diekman.

With a nod, Amerine stepped forward into the helicopter, where the crew had made space for Dan on the floor and were securing him to the hull with webbing. Carefully, Amerine moved among the wounded to stand in the front of the hold, just behind the cockpit.

Knife 03's internal guidance system had behaved strangely during the infiltration the previous night and had stopped working altogether during the medevac ground operations. Now copilot Marty Schweim was figuring out a route the old-fashioned way, on the map covering his lap.

The original route would have taken them west from Shawali Kowt, then well beyond the outskirts of Kandahar, where the Pave Low would turn south to Camp Rhino. It seemed straightforward enough: There were few major roads, the population centers were easy to avoid, and they intended to stay between twenty-five and fifty feet AGL the entire way. They didn't have the exact coordinates for Camp Rhino but knew it was southwest of Kandahar.

The most pressing concern was fuel.

While Schweim studied the map, Gregg radioed the MC-130 that was on its way to refuel Knife 04. "Ditka Zero Four, this is Knife Zero Three. Copy?"

"I have you, Knife Zero Three. What is your status?"

"I'm loaded and will require a Texaco northeast of the planned IP [initial point]. Approaching fuel critical. Will radio our present coordinates as we approach—stand by."

Standing in the center of the hold, Hadley plugged into the helicopter's internal comms in time to hear Gregg say "Texaco," the code word for an emergency aerial refueling at an unassigned location. This surprised Hadley. "How are we that low?" he asked Gregg.

"Sir, remember we dumped fuel on approach to accommodate the extra wounded. We calculated for fifteen minutes on the ground, but we've been here for forty-five."

Hadley had either missed or misunderstood this decision during the flight in. "How critical are we?"

"Eight hundred pounds of fuel," said Gregg. "Fifteen minutes till we flame out."*

Eighteen dirty, bandaged, bleeding casualties surrounded Hadley. All the Americans aboard—Amerine, Ken, Pickett, Musselman, and another TACP from headquarters—were stable. Seven of the thirteen Afghans, however, were critical, and the aircraft was so full that the PJs were kneeling on the hinge of the tail ramp, working on men whose feet were just inches from hanging off the end of the ramp.

"I'm going to have my hands full back here with the wounded," Hadley said to Gregg. "You continue as the air mission commander. I'll be monitoring the radio."

"Roger."

"Okay, tie everybody down," Hadley yelled into the hold as the engines powered up. "We're getting out of here."

---

* In a flameout, one is out of fuel and must land immediately.

Knife 04 was taking on fuel five hundred feet over the open desert far to the west of Kandahar when the crew heard Knife 03 radio the MC-130.

"Ditka Zero Four, we are airborne and coming around the northwest of the city—we are fuel critical. Texaco. I repeat, Texaco. We need you to turn around."

"Knife Zero Four, I'm going to have to cut this short," Ditka 04's pilot radioed Fronk.

"We've got all we need," said Fronk, and the fuel tanker retracted its hose and climbed steeply into a banked turn toward the north.

In Knife 03, Schweim was alternating between glancing at the map and out the cockpit window of the Pave Low, which was cruising at fifty feet AGL. According to the map, they should have been skirting the edge of Kandahar, but instead they were flying over neighborhoods of single-story houses.

"What's the date on that map?" Gregg asked.

"I can't find a date," said Schweim, "but Kandahar has grown since it was printed."

"That's unfortunate." Looking out the two side windows of the cockpit, Gregg could see that these suburbs spread out for miles in all directions. The helicopter was above the most dangerous enemy-held city in the country. *This really, really sucks,* he thought. But with critical patients and critically low on fuel, staying the course was the only option. *The shortest path through a storm is straight ahead.*

He dropped to twenty feet AGL—as low as he could bear to go— and prayed that there wasn't an Afghan in a backyard with a surface-to-air missile.

Diekman gripped his machine gun and watched residents scatter in the Pave Low's wake. Atop one building, a woman was hanging laundry; her mouth opened in a scream as they ripped past.

"Be advised, we are skimming rooftops," Diekman warned the pilots over the radio. "I'm seeing antennas and clotheslines."

Aboard Knife 04 five minutes out from Camp Rhino, Mike regained consciousness and tried to speak. "My feet are cold," he was finally able to whisper to Burns, who realized he'd forgotten to put Mike's socks back on after checking his feet for an IV site. He also realized that Mike's complaining of cold feet was a good sign. Checking his blood oxygen level, Burns found that it had risen to 90 percent. *We just bought you a little time, pal,* he thought.

Fronk announced their arrival to the controller at Camp Rhino, a fellow Air Force CCT who had been assigned to run air traffic with the Marines. Even through the dust, the Pave Low crew could see the two JMAUs parked at an angle off the far end of the dirt runway, but the controller denied Fronk's request to land next to the aircraft. Instead, he was directed five hundred yards away, near the Marine helicopters.

"We will send some trucks to transfer your patients," said the CCT.

"Roger," said Fronk. "Cease all operations while we transfer the casualties."

On the other side of the ramp, PJ Brent Scott had been forced to restrain Mag, who was becoming increasingly disoriented and combative, using a Kerlix bandage to tie the wrist of his uninjured hand to the forearm above his wounded hand. But while Scott tended to Alex, Mag slid the restraint over what remained of his left hand and was using his good hand to continue hitting Alex in the litter above.

As the Pave Low descended, Mag got the strap holding him down unbuckled and tried to rip the bandage off his head, then heaved himself off the litter and onto the deck. There, Scott held him down with both arms on Mag's shoulders and a knee on his stomach while the helicopter flared for landing, then touched down in the dust still floating in the air from the recently arrived JMAUs.

The rescue crew waited, expecting trucks and Marines to come streaming over.

For two minutes they sat in the dust storm, Fronk repeatedly trying to reach the tower. Finally, the CCT responded with "Stand by."

"I'm going to get us closer to the JMAUs," said Fronk. He began to back-taxi the Pave Low, but the dust it kicked up forced him to stop.

Another three minutes passed. "We're wasting time here," Fronk told the crew. "Let's start running bodies ourselves."

Doc Frank and Scott immediately grabbed Mike's litter, ran it down the ramp, and set a pace jogging along the edge of the runway. Fifty yards away, a CH-53 Marine transport helicopter powered up its engine, its rotor stirring up the flourlike dust the men were running through. It lifted off and angled toward them, creating a wind blast that knocked the men down when it passed overhead. Struggling to hold on to the stretcher, which acted like a sail in the rotor wash, they got it to the ground and threw themselves over Mike, whose entire body was pelted with gravel and dust.

Watching from the cockpit of Knife 04, copilot Alexander said, "Are you shitting me?!" He radioed the control tower: "I repeat, cease all operations immediately! This is a medical evacuation. We need assistance. Stop launching aircraft!"

"Is this the fucking Twilight Zone?" Alexander said to Fronk. "Did he not hear what we just said? Did anybody tell him this is a mass casualty evacuation?"

Two Cobra attack helicopters lifted off and followed the CH-53. In the interim, Scott and Doc Frank had picked Mike up and carried him another hundred yards closer to the JMAUs, then lay back down on top of him in anticipation of the blast of air.

"We're getting zero assistance here!" said Alexander.

"Assistance?" said Fronk. "They're a goddamn hindrance."

In back, Burns was choking on the thick dust that had filled Knife 04, but he could make out the silhouette of the airfield's control tower a hundred yards away. Thirteen wounded were still on board, and some of them were facing limb amputations or death if they didn't immediately get to the highly trained general surgeons waiting at operating tables inside the JMAUs a mere five hundred yards off. Five hundred yards of dust storm caused by what appeared to be Marines practicing touch-and-go landings.

He was feeling helpless and contemplating a burst of .50-caliber machine-gun fire to get the controller's attention when a group of men wearing black T-shirts and DCU pants appeared through the brown fog.

"We heard you might need some assistance over here," said the first of sixteen Navy SEALs from SEAL Team 3 on standby at Rhino, where they had been monitoring the tower's radio frequency.

Within three minutes, every casualty was being run over to the waiting surgical teams, even as three more Marine helicopters lifted off and shrouded them in dust.

With just over ten minutes' worth of fuel remaining, Knife 03 was still flying over the southwest suburbs of Kandahar.

Amerine—like the other casualties on board—couldn't hear what was being said over the radio and was oblivious to the dire fuel situation. It was too painful to bend his leg, so he had remained upright, leaning against the divider between the cargo area and the cockpit. Hadley was on his knees next to an unconscious Afghan whose foot was split open, the white metatarsal bones looking like a plastic skeleton that hangs on a door at Halloween. The man's lower leg had been hit by shrapnel, and Hadley's surgically gloved fingers were inside a gaping wound, his other hand digging around with a hemostat. Blood pooled on the colorful blanket beneath the Afghan. Finally, Hadley was able to grab hold of a severed vein with the scissors-like clamp and tie it off with silk suture thread.

There were four PJs on board, every one of whom was likewise too busy caring for three or four patients to give a second thought to the fuel situation. They were dealing with open skull fractures, arterial blood spray, and exposed organs. Every couple of minutes or so, whenever Hadley or one of the PJs felt he might fold under the stress, he would find the strength to carry on by glancing at the flag draped over the American soldier who had given his life.

Out the open back of the Pave Low, Amerine saw a hillside covered with tan buildings; a colorful dome that must have been a mosque; a tree-lined avenue. Just that morning, he had discussed with JD how they would split the team up once they retook the ruins, crossed the bridge, and moved into Kandahar.

So this is Kandahar, he thought sadly. *Wait a minute, why the fuck are we over Kandahar?*

Meanwhile, Diekman scanned the ground for the enemy while glancing constantly up at the sky in search of their Texaco. As tail gunner, it was Diekman's job to spot the fuel tanker as it closed in from the rear—usually at a mile out—and report its approach in increments to the pilots: a three- to five-minute process until the aircraft catches up to the helicopter and the pilot takes over.

As the Pave Low converged with the MH-130, copilot Schweim had been reading their coordinates off his handheld GPS. "We are in the vicinity of north three one, three zero, point four seven; east six five, zero six."

"I see you, Knife Zero Three," said Ditka 04. "I will come to you. Let's keep it low, two hundred feet."

"Did he say two hundred?" Gregg asked Schweim. "Two zero zero?" Schweim nodded.

Not only had the MH-130 slowed to a speed that barely kept it from stalling, if something were to go wrong while refueling, neither aircraft would have altitude in which to react and correct. Gregg generally refueled above one thousand feet, though he had refueled a few times at five hundred feet in training. He was also accustomed to doing it at night, invisible to those on the ground—not in broad daylight, directly above Kandahar, on his first mission in Afghanistan.

The helicopter ascended to two hundred feet, then Gregg suddenly announced to its crew, "I have the tanker—he's coming right at us!"

Both pilots watched in amazement as the hulking MH-130 descended toward them in a shallow dive from a few thousand feet and began a wide arcing turn, at the same time dropping its wing flaps to reduce speed and deploying its fuel hoses.

"They're coming from the *front*?" Diekman said over the radio.

"He's coming around now," said Gregg. "Stand by for a visual."

"Tally-ho, I have the tanker!" Diekman shouted, staring up at the belly of Ditka 04, which slid into place less than one hundred feet above and slightly behind the tail rotor of the helicopter, and immediately sped forward.

"Holy shit, tanker abeam," called out the side gunner a second later.

"Ten minutes to flameout," said Schweim.

At the moment Gregg began to guide Knife 03's fuel boom toward the basket at the end of the tanker's hose, the Pave Low encountered moderate turbulence, causing it to shake and drop. Monitoring the radio, Hadley listened as Gregg missed the first attempt to hit the hose, then again.

"Seven minutes to bingo," said Schweim.

"If you miss again," Hadley told Gregg over the radio, "I'm going to throw you out of the pilot seat and show you how to refuel a helo."

"Got it!" Gregg announced. "We're on."

Thank God, thought Diekman, who had been desperately searching the urban sprawl for some open ground on which to make an emergency landing.

/

The scent of jet fuel filled Knife 03. With the refueling complete, Ditka 04 pulled away from the Pave Low and climbed steeply. Simultaneously, Gregg descended sharply to the helicopter's safety zone, skimming rooftops.

Amerine was feeling the steep descent in his stomach when he noticed a wounded guerrilla—who had joined the team back in Haji Badhur's Cove—attempt to sit up from where he was lying on the open tail ramp. The man had a badly mutilated arm with a makeshift tourniquet, little more than a rag and stick above a gaping wound on his crushed lower arm. Bright red arterial blood was pulsing out of the wound and running down what was left of the Afghan's forearm and onto the deck of the helicopter.

PJs Malone and Schultz, who were looking after the critical patients, stopped the Afghan when he tried to stand and laid him back down on the ramp. Malone applied a new tourniquet, but the blood continued to flow.

"Stop the fucking bleeding *now!*" shouted Hadley, seated between patients near the center of the hold some twelve feet away. Noting that the man did not have an IV, Hadley took an IV bag out of his trauma kit and tossed it to Malone, hitting him in the chest before it dropped to the floor. Malone picked it up and inserted an IV, then readjusted the tourniquet. Nothing was working; the arm was too severely crushed. He looked at Hadley again, shaking his head.

Hadley made a scissors motion with two fingers. "Cut it off!" he yelled. For a second Malone stared at him, puzzled, then Hadley made the motion again, this time against his arm, and pointed at the Afghan. Nodding, the PJ reached into his trauma bag.

At his gun, Diekman focused on the landscape below, trying not to think about what was going on around him. Every time he glanced left or right, he caught glimpses of what looked like a slaughterhouse. But it was impossible to ignore the thick stream of blood flowing down the tail ramp and spraying off into the wind.

He felt a tap on his shoulder.

When he turned his head, the first thing Diekman noticed was the American flag wrapped around the soldier's body; the red and white stripes calmed him. Still gripping the handles of his weapon, he concentrated on what Malone was asking him to do.

After a moment, he realized what that was: The PJ was going to amputate the Afghan's arm, right there on the ramp, and he needed Diekman's help.

/

At Camp Rhino, Master Sergeant David Lee stepped out of ODB 540's command tent and into the dust storm. He was amazed that all three MC-130s—the two JMAUs and one transport carrying Major Miller's quick reaction force from K2—had arrived in quick succession, only minutes before the first helicopter full of casualties.

"They couldn't have planned it better if they'd planned it," he told Leithead, who, along with other members of ODB 540, was hurrying over to the JMAUs, where they would help transfer the wounded.

Lee didn't know that the trucks the CCT in the control tower promised to transport the wounded had never arrived. The B-team's tent was on the opposite side of the runway a couple hundred yards from the Marine helicopter parking area and Knife 04. Because of the brownout, they had lost visual contact with nearly everything on the base.

The Green Berets had been following the rescue operation via radio and, once Knife 04 was en route to Rhino, they passed the information along to General Mattis that the Air Force had evacuated the wounded—without taking any enemy fire. It was then that Mattis released his Marine pilots to fly: The helicopters that had just departed were headed to Shawali Kowt for the wounded Afghans unable to fit into Knife 03 and Knife 04.

On their way to the JMAUs, Lee and Leithead crossed paths with a group of Green Berets—including Miller, Allard, Cubby, and the two other ODAs—jogging toward the two Marine helicopters waiting to transport them to Shawali Kowt. As he and Leithead neared the two planes, where four Navy SEALs were running the last two litters up the ramp and into the belly of one of the aircraft, Lee was awed by the capabilities of the U.S. military to take care of its own in the middle of this remote desert. He was also disgusted by the way Mattis had hesitated—wringing his hands just long enough for somebody else to solve the problem.

Inside the JMAU, every man with an injury—fourteen total—was at a litter station in the middle or rear of the hold, being tended to by teams of trauma nurses. Already the surgeons were working behind hanging curtains in the sterile front of the plane, performing "damage control surgery" on Mike, Ronnie, and Alex. This included tying off ruptured blood vessels, removing shrapnel, and making temporary repairs to internal organs and fractured bones—whatever it would take to get the casualties to the specialized surgeons awaiting them two hours away in Oman.

Outside, off to the side of the airplane's massive ramp, Leopold sat on the ground beside the litter on which his friend Cody Prosser was lying; he was holding Prosser's hand and cradling his head in his lap. Prosser had succumbed to his wounds during the flight and been pronounced dead at Camp Rhino by Doc Frank. He was the third American to die that day.

Blood was still spraying off the tail ramp of Knife 03, now twenty minutes from Camp Rhino, as Diekman kept his right hand on the machine gun to steady himself and placed his left knee on the stomach of the still-conscious but heavily sedated Afghan. He put his other hand firmly against the man's chest and, clenching his teeth, pushed down with most of his weight, pinning him against the ramp while Malone used surgical shears to cut into the severely crushed bone and torn skin and muscle. Diekman grimaced as he watched; the Afghan, whose glassy eyes remained open, didn't even flinch.

Continuing to hold the man down, Diekman looked down the barrel of his gun at the desert rushing past. They'd finally cleared the suburbs and all he could see was blue sky, open land, and Kandahar falling farther and farther behind in their wake. Diekman glanced again at the Afghan just as Malone snipped through the remaining muscle and tissue.* In his headset, he heard Schweim making contact with Alexander, the copilot of Knife 04, already on the ground at Rhino. "We have cross-loaded our casualties into the JMAUs," said Alexander. "They are standing by to head for Oman."

"Copy that, we'll be there shortly," said Schweim. "What are your coordinates?"

Alexander read them off, then said, "You'll see where we're at from ten miles out—just look for the dust cloud rising three hundred feet into the sky."

"What is the frequency for Rhino's tower?"

"You don't want to talk to the tower," said Alexander. "You want to land as close as you can to the two JMAUs. Do *not* land by the helicopters. We'll be ready to help cross-load your patients."

---

* Despite the PJ's best efforts, the man died from his extensive wounds on the final approach to Camp Rhino. All of the remaining critically wounded Afghans medevaced by Knife 03 and Knife 04 survived.

Diekman turned his attention to the front of the hold, where five dirty and bandaged Green Berets were looking around with blank, emotionless eyes. *So that's a thousand-yard stare*, he thought.

Eyes fixed on Dan's body, Amerine was thinking back to nine years before, when he'd walked beneath the Trees of the Dead on Gabriel Field with his mentor, Dennis Holloway.

"I hope you never have to look at these trees and see the faces of the men they represent," Holloway had said. "But if it ever comes to that, you will find comfort knowing that they died for something larger than themselves. You will know in your heart that they died doing something that makes a difference."

As the Pave Low sped toward Camp Rhino, that was what con-soled Amerine. He'd led Dan, JD, his entire team to this end, but what they had fought and died for could not have been more noble.

★

Epilogue

Let us cross over the river, and rest under the shade of the trees.
—Stonewall Jackson's last words

"The Taliban surrendered thirty minutes after the wounded were taken away from Shawali Kowt," President Karzai told me as we sat together in his midtown Manhattan hotel room on September 23, 2008.

He shook his head at the irony. "There was the bombing before that, but the Taliban came anyway. And they said that they would surrender; they brought a letter of surrender to me."

Karzai then confirmed that he had known about the delegation the night before the accident. In an interview at Fort Bragg, North Carolina, the week before, Major Bolduc had told me that although he and Fox knew there was a delegation en route the night before, they didn't trust that the Taliban were surrendering. Bolduc also said that Karzai was the one who had authorized the air strikes on the morning of December 5. I read to Karzai that section of the transcript verbatim: "Ultimately, it wasn't me or Fox that authorized that engagement. It was Hamid Karzai."

"No," Karzai said. "He is wrong. Completely, completely. I didn't even know [they were bombing]. I was, as a matter of fact, going [to the Alamo]. Had I gone that day, had the elders not come, I would be dead now, like Bari Gul, like all those other people."

He looked through the pictures I'd brought, pausing at an aerial photo I'd found of the neighborhood and compound where the team had spent their time in Tarin Kowt. He stopped at the next photo, too: ODA 574 sitting with some spooks on MRE boxes, sipping coffee.

"Do you know this place?" asked Karzai.

"Yes," I said. "It's the compound at Tarin Kowt."

He nodded with a smile. The next photo was of Amerine in the back of a truck, driving away from the compound as the convoy left for Petawek.

"This is Jason," Karzai said, showing the picture to his staff. "Had there been *anybody* else, things would have gone terribly wrong. I have the best memories of that man and his team. He is an exceptional person, extremely polite. You won't see it in him: He's very quiet, but he's very courageous.

"Jason was the best representative of the United States. He came to me one day and said there had been reports of a Taliban get-together . . ." It had been seven years, yet Karzai vividly recalled when the reconnaissance aircraft had identified a possible Taliban helicopter. "Jason said, 'What do you think? Should I authorize [bombing] this?' I said, 'No, let's go and find out.' I sent people, and they found that the camps were refugees from Kandahar. I told Jason and he believed me. Had it been any other person, first, I would not have been consulted. And even if I were consulted, they would have gone ahead, but he didn't . . . If the United States had military officers like Jason in larger numbers, it would be a greater country."

Our scheduled fifteen-minute interview had stretched to nearly an hour when Karzai's spokesman pointed to his watch for the third time, reminding him that Secretary of State Condoleezza Rice was waiting outside.

Karzai walked me to the door, shook my hand, and said, "Please send my regards to Jason and his team. I will never forget those men."

An aide escorted me past security—Afghan bodyguards, U.S. Secret Service, body-armored police, a metal detector, and an X-ray machine—underscoring just how much Karzai's life had changed since *Time* magazine had hailed him as the Great New Afghan Hope when he was sworn in as the leader of Afghanistan's transitional government on December 22, 2001. Six months later, on June 13, 2002, more than 1,500 multi-ethnic delegates from across Afghanistan had convened a Loya Jirga and named Karzai president of the Afghan Transitional Government. Then, on October 9, 2004, he won the country's first free election, becoming the first democratically elected leader of Afghanistan.

"His Excellency loves to talk about the days of the Liberation," the aide told me as I left the hotel lobby. "Now his job is very difficult."

Outside, I paused for a moment to look up at the high rises of Manhattan, where this story began seven years earlier on September 11, 2001. Then I merged into the flow of pedestrians on the crowded sidewalks of Park Avenue. But in my mind, I was still in Afghanistan, sorting through the snapshots of the mission—and thinking about what had become of the men involved.

Shortly after the Taliban delegation arrived in Shawali Kowt to surrender to Karzai, ODB 570, including Cubby, Allard, and Miller, landed at LZ Jamie, the same location that Knife 03 had taken off from an hour before. Even though they had been tasked to get in and out quickly, Mulholland asked them to stay on and assist Fox as a traditional B-team.

As ODB 570 set up a security perimeter on the Alamo, Smith did a final sweep for any remaining papers with sensitive data. It was then that he discovered JD's Harley-Davidson cap, barely visible under a layer of dirt. He collected what few remains he could find in the immediate vicinity and delivered them to Bolduc.

Temperatures dropped to near freezing their first night in Shawali Kowt, and ODB 570—with little beyond their go-to-hell packs and medical equipment—was forced to scavenge the abandoned rucksacks of ODA 574 for extra clothing and sleeping bags. Come morning, Allard and Cubby saw that they were wearing Dan's and JD's clothing.

Two days after the bombing, ODB 570 accompanied Karzai and the uninjured members of Fox's headquarters staff across the bridge over the Arghandab River and into Kandahar, where they received a warm reception from the local population. Allard and Cubby quietly dedicated the day to ODA 574, who they knew should have been leading the convoy to Mullah Omar's palace: their new command post and Karzai's new headquarters.

Several days later, a Green Beret discovered that the palace had been rigged to blow up, its roof imbedded with hundreds of artillery rounds. A bomb squad identified a single wire, buried underground and leading a few hundred yards from the palace to within a few feet of a large battery concealed in a hut; the explosion could have killed Karzai and nearly one hundred Special Forces soldiers. They could only guess that the Taliban assigned to touch the wire to the battery and detonate the bomb had fled.

ODB 570 would remain with Fox and Bolduc and the uninjured headquarters staff for the next four months, providing security for Karzai and fighting pockets of Taliban in and around Kandahar who refused to surrender.

⚔

The surviving members of ODA 574 were evacuated from Camp Rhino to Oman. Wes was at the hospital recovering from his gunshot wound, and was shocked by the arrival of his team, who, as he put it, looked as if they had been "blown to hell." Brent broke down when he told Wes that JD and Dan were dead. Had he not been shot, Wes realized, he probably would have been alongside Dan when the JDAM hit; the bullet he'd taken in the neck likely saved his life.

While the rest of the team flew from Oman to Landstuhl Regional Medical Center in Germany, Mag was taken directly to Walter Reed Army Medical Center in Washington, D.C. Amerine stayed an additional day in Oman so that he could escort JD and Dan back to the United States.

Amerine brought JD home to Elizabethton, Tennessee, where hundreds of police and firefighters from across the state lined the highway along with thousands of citizens. The town honored JD by naming a bridge over the Wautauga River after him—the Jefferson

Donald Davis Memorial Bridge. His family had a bench inscribed with the Special Forces insignia and placed it under a dogwood tree by his grave, where they often find friends, neighbors, and strangers sitting in the shade, paying their respects.

Dan was buried that same weekend in Cheshire, Massachusetts, at a funeral attended by many of his fellow 5th Group Green Berets. The trail across the street from the house where he'd played soldier as a boy was named in his honor—a fitting gesture considering the last line of Dan's death letter to his family: "If you ever get sad and down about this, just open up the front door and listen for the kids down the neighborhood playing Army and think of me."

After extensive surgeries spanning more than a year, Mike—whose right arm had to be amputated below the elbow and who had suffered hundreds of shrapnel wounds and a collapsed lung—returned to Special Forces, where he serves as one of only a few amputees on active duty. When Karzai made his first post-9/11 trip to the United States in late January 2002, Mike sat beside him and First Lady Laura Bush, who had extended the invitation to ODA 574, at the president's State of the Union address.

Ronnie's heart and lungs were punctured by shrapnel, but he recovered and returned to 5th Group less than a year later. He and his wife, also an Army NCO, both deployed to Iraq in 2003. While patients at Walter Reed, Ronnie and Mike attended Cody Prosser's funeral at Arlington National Cemetery, sitting side by side in wheelchairs. On January 29, 2002, Ronnie and Amerine joined Mike at the State of the Union address, where the three men were reunited with Karzai for the first time since December 5.

In the days after the bombing, Amerine had learned, Casper had informed Karzai that Fox and his staff, not Amerine and ODA 574, were responsible for the accident. Following President Bush's speech, Karzai personally thanked the three men from ODA 574, then introduced them to their commander in chief, saying, "Look at what these men sacrificed for both America and Afghanistan. These are some of the bravest men I have ever met."

Alex returned to Hurlburt Field, Florida. While going through rehab, he was visited by then–Secretary of the Air Force James G.

Roche, who asked if there was anything he could personally do for Alex. "Don't let this type of accident happen to anyone ever again" was Alex's reply. Despite being permanently disabled with a shattered shoulder, Alex continues to work in the Air Force Special Operations community as an expert in close air support and combat controller operations. He led the team that pioneered a system designed to help eliminate possible errors by allowing combat controllers to digitally communicate targeting data to attacking aircraft. His assignment with ODA 574 became a model for combat controllers in the Air Force, who continue to be placed with ODAs in both Afghanistan and Iraq.

Although Amerine recommended Alex for the Air Force Cross, the Air Force downgraded the award to a Silver Star because Alex's actions were not deemed sufficiently heroic for that high an honor. Most of the men of ODA 574 were recommended for Silver Stars, but these requests were also downgraded, to Bronze Stars—the same awards given to the members of Fox's headquarters staff. ODA 574 lobbied for the posthumous presentation of Silver Stars to Dan and JD, which were given to their families.

Brent and Victor were the only members of the team who remained on ODA 574 for the invasion of Iraq in 2003. Brent later went on to become a team sergeant. Both are still with 5th Group.

Ken was sent to a different team in 5th Group, retiring in 2002. No disciplinary action was taken following his removal from ODA 574.

Wes returned to 5th Group but left the military after serving a tour in Iraq. He traveled the world as a contracted soldier, going back to Afghanistan in 2006 to work as one of President Karzai's personal bodyguards. The first Green Beret shot in combat in the War on Terror, Wes still has his uniform shirt with the bullet hole.

Mag spent almost two years in hospitals, undergoing surgery and rehab for his traumatic brain injury and to combat a number of other injuries that included loss of part of his vision and part of his left hand, and severe left-side paralysis. Eventually he relearned to walk and dress himself, but he continues to suffer from kidney failure, mood disorders, and migraines. He refused to receive his Bronze Star and

Purple Heart in a hospital, waiting until he was able to return home and stand at attention in a ceremony at the 5th Group block at Fort Campbell. He now participates in Paralympics competitions, recently swimming a mile in open water in a triathlon. In 2008, he discovered the four-leaf clover his daughter had given him in 1990; it had slipped behind some files in a fire vault in his home.

Lloyd Allard retired from the Army after two tours in Iraq. In 2007, he and a staff sergeant from 5th Group, Robbie Doughty—who had lost both legs in Iraq—opened a Little Caesars pizza franchise given to them as part of the Little Caesars Veteran Program, which helps returning veterans transition back into their communities.

Cubby Wojciehowski became a Special Forces warrant officer. He named his son Daniel, after Dan Petithory—"a good, strong name," he said.

Nelson Smith became one of the youngest team sergeants in 5th Group, leading an ODA on multiple tours in Iraq. The other members of the headquarters element—including Terry Reed, Chris Fathi, and Chris Pickett—recovered from their wounds; most returned to 5th Group and took part in the invasion of Iraq.

Chris Miller was involved in the planning for and invasion of Iraq. He was promoted to lieutenant colonel in 2006 after two tours in Iraq, taking command of Fox's old battalion when Fox moved on. Bob Kelley was given an early promotion to lieutenant colonel and selected to command 1st Battalion, 5th Group, in 2003. Under his leadership, 1st Battalion created and led multi-ethnic Iraqi Special Operations units that have played a pivotal role in that war. While many consider him the mastermind behind the unconventional warfare campaign in Afghanistan, he credits the other True Believers, saying, "Success has many fathers."

The Air Force investigation into the friendly-fire bombing on December 5 took almost two years to complete, during which time a rumor circulated around 5th Group that Bolduc had directed the bomb. While the investigative board concluded that Fox's lax supervision—cited as "[i]nadequate command and control interaction between the on-scene ground commander and the terminal attack controllers"—contributed to the accident, the report ultimately blamed Air Force TACP Jim Price, citing procedural errors. Though Price knew he was at fault, the findings of the board never seemed accurate to him.[1]

The GPS device that Price used was never recovered, making it impossible to review the data, but after returning to 5th Group, he was able to re-create the steps he had taken on December 5 and determine exactly what had gone wrong. He had initially tested the Viper—calibrated to store multiple cloud ceilings—by lasing the ground in front of him, a location that was stored instead of being discarded as he had expected. When Price called in the JDAM, he inadvertently used that stored location, directing the bomb to a grid only a few feet ahead of where he was standing on the Alamo. Had he double-checked the target coordinates on the military GPS with his personal GPS, as he had on the previous air strikes, he would have caught the error.

Price served a tour in Iraq as a fully qualified JTAC and controlled his final combat air strike south of Baghdad in April 2004. He retired from the Air Force and now teaches "joint fires and close air support" courses for a U.S. Army school, dedicating his life to helping others avoid the same type of tragic mistake he made.

The penetrating JDAM bomb killed three Americans and wounded twenty-five; it killed an estimated fifty Afghans, including Bari Gul, Bashir, and most of their men. If Price had chosen a surface-detonating JDAM, it's likely that nobody on or near the Alamo would have survived the blast. The crew of the B-52 was cleared of any fault in the bombing incident but would forever remember that horrible morning and the seven-hour flight from Shawali Kowt back to the island of Diego Garcia for its haunting silence.

Investigations into both friendly-fire bombings—of Queeg's headquarters on November 26, 2001, and of Fox's headquarters less than two weeks later—failed to point out that in both incidents, battalion headquarters directed the air strikes in spite of the presence of ODAs who should have been calling in the bombs. No punitive measures were taken for either accident.

During the planning for Operation Iraqi Freedom, Mulholland subtly acknowledged the mistakes made in Afghanistan by making sure that headquarters staff C-teams were utilized according to doctrine, as headquarters providing command-and-control support to combatants, not as combatants themselves. Now a lieutenant general, Mulholland became the commander of the U.S. Army Special Operations Command at Fort Bragg, North Carolina.

Fox and Bolduc were both promoted and presented medals for their actions in Afghanistan. Bolduc was later selected to command a battalion and received an early promotion to full colonel. Fox was given command of a garrison at Fort Bragg. A few months after the bombing, Fox was asked by PBS's *Frontline* whether he second-guessed his decision to call in the strikes on December 5. "Every day," he said. "I'm sure that there was something I could have done better. There was something I could have done to prevent it. Was that cave that important that day? But it's just something I'm going to have to live with for the rest of my life."

General James Mattis, who had refused to send rescue helicopters until hours after the bomb hit, went on to command the 1st Marine Division during the invasion of Iraq. There, in a highly publicized, extremely unusual, and arguably ironic action, he relieved a subordinate, Colonel Joe Dowdy, for hesitating in battle while leading his regiment's drive to Baghdad.

On December 22, 2001, Steve Hadley was invited by Karzai to escort him and his family from Kandahar to Kabul to attend his inauguration ceremony as interim leader. En route, Karzai presented him with his battle flag—the national flag of Afghanistan that he had kept with him throughout the mission with ODA 574—as a personal token of his appreciation for the AFSOC rescue efforts. Hadley still serves as an active-duty USAF pilot-physician and is a renowned trauma expert.

The Air Force Special Operations Command awarded just a few basic air medals for the rescue mission. The vast majority of the officers and enlisted men flying on Knife 03 and 04 that day, including Hadley, were not recognized for their exceptional actions on December 5. But there is not a man from ODA 574 or Fox's headquarters staff who is not indebted to them—as well as the members of Delta and the CIA whose medical skills saved many lives before the helicopters arrived.

Casper, Charlie, Zepeda, Mr. Big, and the other spooks who had worked with Karzai went on to other assignments in the Clandestine Services. Casper became the chief of station for the CIA in Afghanistan for the years following 2001. In many accounts of the war, he is referred to as "Greg" or "Bush," supposedly because of his likeness to George W. Bush.

Since becoming president of Afghanistan, Hamid Karzai has faced growing criticism about his inability to stop corruption within his government and to curb the rise of the Taliban. The reason, according to some Karzai proponents, is the lack of sufficient security forces from the United States and NATO. The shift in focus from Afghanistan to Iraq disheartened many of the men of ODA 574 who had hoped to see Task Force Dagger's brisk victory in 2001 followed by a final coup d'état against the Taliban and al-Qaeda. Instead, they watched international support for Karzai wane.

James Dobbins, now the director of the International Security and Defense Policy Center at the RAND Corporation, told me just prior to the August 2009 presidential election in Afghanistan, "I think Karzai was the ideal man for his time, a figure around whom the international community and the Afghan population could unite, as they did. It's not clear that someone chosen as a peacemaker is equally ideally suited to the job of war making. As yet, however, no more suitable or probable candidate for that position has emerged, making it quite possible that Karzai will have to continue to lead his country through the current conflict."[2]

After Amerine was medevaced to Germany on December 8, 2001, an Army Public Affairs officer asked him to participate in a press conference. Half deaf, with shrapnel still embedded in his leg and his boots stained with the blood of his men, he spoke to the reporters gathered there: "One thing I want to stress is that I do not want to allow this incident to overshadow the good work that my detachment and the headquarters element did over the course of the time we worked in Afghanistan. The mission we were given was a hard one, and I'm proud of the soldiers I served with, both the Americans and Afghans. All the men are heroes, and they should be remembered for what they accomplished during their time in Afghanistan and not as victims in an accident."

Amerine left 5th Special Forces Group in April 2002 to teach in the social sciences department at West Point, his alma mater, and was promoted to major. Before leaving Fort Campbell, he had taken one last stroll around the 5th Group block. He passed the anti-aircraft gun from the Gulf War, the old barracks that housed ODA 574's team room, and the ISOFAC where the men had awaited their deployment to Afghanistan.

Eventually, he arrived at Gabriel Field and walked slowly around the newest additions to the Trees of the Dead: three saplings honoring Master Sergeant Jefferson Donald Davis, Sergeant First Class Daniel Henry Petithory, and Staff Sergeant Brian Cody Prosser—the first Special Forces soldiers killed in the War on Terror.

His final thought as he walked away: *Too much damn shade on this field.*

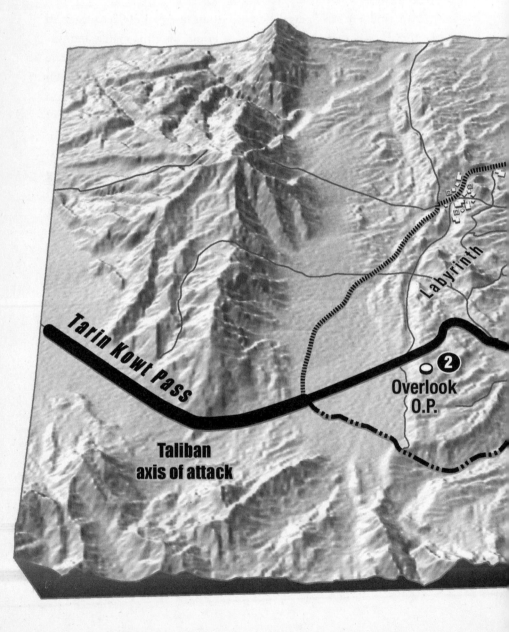

Timeline of events, Tarin Kowt:
Nov. 16 – 17, 2001

Tarin Kowt Pass

Labyrinth

②
Overlook
O.P.

**Taliban
axis of attack**

1 **Nov 16:** ODA 574 arrives at Tarin Kowt.

2 **Nov. 17**: ODA 574 drives to overlook observation post to await enemy. Taliban attacks.

3 **Nov. 17:** ODA 574 falls back to last-stand position on the southern edge of town.

4 **Nov. 17:** ODA 574 moves to labyrinth observation post as night approaches.

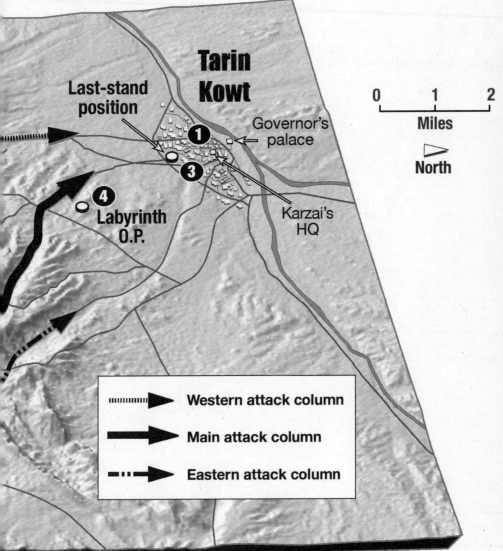

Tarin Kowt

Last-stand position

Governor's palace

Karzai's HQ

4 Labyrinth O.P.

0 1 2
Miles

North

|▷▷▷▷▷▷▷| **Western attack column**

|▶| **Main attack column**

|-■-■-▶| **Eastern attack column**

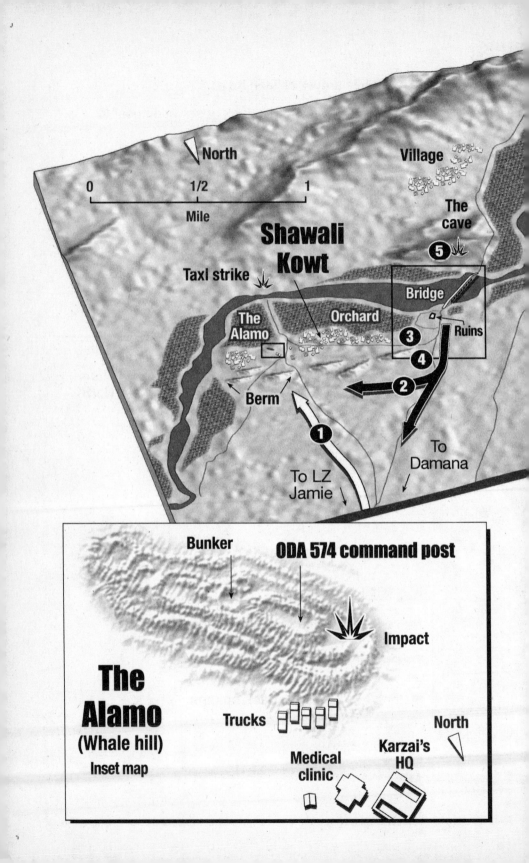

To Kandahar

Arghandab River

Timeline of events, Shawali Kowt: Dec. 3 – 5, 2001

1 **Dec. 3:** ODA 574 assaults Shawali Kowt, forcing the Taliban to retreat.

2 **Dec. 3:** Taliban counterattack.

3 **Dec. 4:** ODA 574 seizes the ruins.

4 **Dec. 4:** ODA 574 ordered to withdraw from the ruins.

5 **Dec. 5:** Fox's HQ directs air strikes from Alamo to destroy cave.

Ruins and bridge
Inset map

Bridge

Arghandab River

Ruins

Orchard

Dead space

Canal

Trench

2

1 Compounds **3**

3

Support-by-fire position

North

4

Enemy position

★

Acknowledgments

As of today, October 27, 2009, 1,494 men and women in the coalition armed forces have been killed in the line of duty fighting the war in Afghanistan (Australia: 11; Belgium: 1; Canada: 131; Czech Republic: 3; Denmark: 28; Estonia: 6; Finland: 1; France: 36; Germany: 34; Hungary: 2; Italy: 22; Latvia: 3; Lithuania: 1; Netherlands: 21; Norway: 4; Poland: 15; Portugal: 2; Romania: 11; South Korea: 1; Spain: 26; Sweden: 2; Turkey: 2; United Kingdom: 223; United States: 908). By the time this book goes to press, that number will have risen. Each of these so-called statistics represents a story of selfless sacrifice, of men and women who are at some level contributing to the collaborative efforts in Afghanistan—all of whom deserve respect and gratitude for their service and ultimate sacrifice.

Thank you to all who have served in Afghanistan, Iraq, and around the world in the War on Terror, which continues to expand today. For those who have lost a loved one, my deepest condolences.

During the course of researching and writing this book, I interviewed the families of several members of ODA 574. I cannot adequately express how honored and humbled I was to sit in your homes and hear the stories of your loved ones. Brent Fowler told me: "As for the wives, they forever have earned their place among the heroes of our SF community. Wives and loved ones are the heart and soul of a fighting man, and I don't think that our military would last without the unsung courage of those holding down the home front and waiting for their soldier to return."

Thank you for opening your hearts to me as I got to know the team: Ron Amerine, Linda Davis, Mi Kyong Davis, Bill and Tammy McElhiney, Judith McElhiney, Barbara and Lou Petithory, Mike Petithory, Nicole Petithory, Sherry Magallanes, Brittany Magallanes.

/

Once I had received the blessing of JD's and Dan's families to tell ODA 574's story, I put the word out to the surviving members of the team via various channels that began with Army Public Affairs and branched out by word of mouth among the Special Forces community. Most of the men of ODA 574 agreed to talk with me, wanting to honor JD and Dan by seeing the story set straight for the history books. That desire and the ensuing interviews are the foundation of this book. Thank you for trusting me with your journals, letters, photos, notes, and memories: Capt. Jason Amerine, Sgt. 1st Class Brent Fowler, Sgt. 1st Class Gilbert "Mag" Magallanes, Sgt. 1st Class Mike McElhiney, Sgt. 1st Class Wes McGirr, Sgt. 1st Class Ronnie Raikes.

While not a living, breathing entity, the mission of ODA 574 was a main—if not *the* main—character in this story. From conception to conclusion, it took on a life of its own. I hope I have accurately captured its essence and, in doing so, honored the men involved.

/

Thank you, President Hamid Karzai, for meeting with me, and thank you to the president's staff, in particular Humayun Hamidzada and Ahmad Razi, for fielding my letters, phone calls, and e-mails.

/

I could not have told the story of ODA 574's mission in such detail and context without the candid and forthcoming interviews granted to me by the following soldiers, airmen, and war planners. Their individual stories are much broader in scope than their portrayal in this book. Thank you:

5th Special Forces Group Rambo 85: Maj. Don Bolduc, Lt. Col. David Fox, Capt. Jeff Leopold, Sgt. 1st Class Chris Pickett, Tech Sgt. Jim Price, Chief Warrant Officer Terry Reed, Sgt. 1st Class Nelson Smith, John Doe 1,* John Doe 2. 5th Special Forces Group Rambo 70: Chief Warrant Officer Lloyd Allard, Maj. Chris Miller, Sgt. 1st Class Tim "Cubby" Wojciehowski.

Others from 5th Special Forces Group: Master Sgt. David Lee, Maj. John Silkman, Chief Warrant Officer Bruce Watts, John Doe 1, John Doe 2, John Doe 3.

U.S. Central Command (CENTCOM): John Doe 1, John Doe 2.

U.S. Special Operations Command Central (SOCCENT): Maj. Robert Kelley, John Doe 1, John Doe 2, John Doe 3.

/

This story would have been incomplete without the interviews granted by the Air Force Special Operations Command (AFSOC) airmen who participated in the rescue mission to Shawali Kowt. Thank you: 1st Lt. Paul Alexander, Tech Sgt. Gavin Burns, Staff Sgt. Scott Diekman, Capt. Patrick Fronk, Capt. Steve Gregg, Lt. Col. Steve Hadley (M.D.), Lt. Col. Michael Kingsley. Also, thank you to Capt. Casey Ward, who flew the AFSOC mission on 9/11 in support of the rescue-and-recovery operation at the Pentagon and World Trade Center.

/

Crucial to all of the interviews with the above active-duty NCOs and officers were many public affairs offices, including U.S. Air Force

---

* All references to John Doe are to sources who wish to remain anonymous.

Public Affairs, New York; U.S. Army Public Affairs, New York; U.S. Military Academy at West Point, New York; and U.S. Special Operations Command 5th Special Forces Group—all of which employ active-duty, reserve, and civilian personnel. Thank you:

Air Force Public Affairs: Capt. Jeff Brown, Maj. George L. Burnett, 1st Lt. Amy Cooper, Tech Sgt. Rebecca Danet, Mathew Durham, Maj. John Elolf, 2nd Lt. Lauren Johnson, Amy Oliver, 1st Lt. Jennifer Pearson, Lois Walsh.

Army Public Affairs: Lt. Col. Clarence Counts, Carol Darby, Lt. Col. Mike Durham, Sgt. Ernest Henry, Lt. Col. Frank Misurelli, Lt. Col. John O'Brien, Lt. Col. Holly Silkman, Bruce Zielsdorf.

Also thanks to Marine Public Affairs officers Maj. Eric Dent and Maj. Cliff Gilmore for your efforts.

The Freedom of Information Act request offices in the U.S. military are faced daily with daunting numbers of requests for official documents. In my case, most of these documents were elusive at best. For your Herculean efforts, thank you: Doreen Agard, U.S. Special Operations Command; Mary Bowling, U.S. Army Special Operations Command; Maj. George Burnett, Assistant Staff Judge Advocate, CENTCOM.

To gain both historical and political insights into Afghanistan—before, during, and after the brief window of time portrayed in this book—I am indebted to the Office of the President of Afghanistan, the Embassy of Afghanistan, Washington, D.C., and the Center for Afghanistan Studies, University of Nebraska, Omaha. Thank you: Director Thomas Gouttierre, Sher Jan Ahmadzai, and Abdul Yaseer.

I am also thankful for the interviews provided to me by: James Dobbins; Nick Mills, author of *Karzai: The Failing American Intervention and the Struggle for Afghanistan*; Michele Mitchell, one of the last journalists to interview Abdul Haq before his death; and Ronald Neumann, U.S. ambassador of Afghanistan, 2005–2007.

A grateful thank you to my family, friends, critical readers, and others who supported my telling of this story: Matt and Sara Baglio, Linda and Raul Balderas, Kevin Blakeborough, Clayton Blehm, Andy and Kelly Blumberg, Jon Boyer, Bill Butterworth, Tracy Bychowski, Mike Carder, Carol Cepregi, Melissa Chinchillo, Debbie and John Cloud, Stephen Coonts, Navy Cmdr. Paul Costello, Scott Coutts, Lee Crane, Craig and Kathy Cupp, Erika and Jason Daniels, Steve Duff, Rachel Elinsky, Aaron Feldman, Mark Fleishman, Bill Forstchen, Dan Green, Kate Hamill, Lori and Rick Hennessy, Shannon Hennessy, Bob Holt, Robin Ingraham, Marilyn Johnson, Jana and Roger Keating, Andrea and Bob Kelly, Mark Kleckner, Jill LaMar, Beth and Brad Lenahan, Anne Loder, Scooter Leonard, Pat Macha, Swanna MacNair, Adam Makos, Garry and Rae Martin, Marcelle and Pete McAfee, Billy McDonald, Ewan Morrison, Tomaya Nakatsugawa, Alden Nash, Mike O'Brien, Eric Parker, Stephanie Pearson, Norman Peck, Marilyn and Paul Phillips, Brian Riley, Kimberly Tilton-Riley, Gregory Saladino, Angela Sampogna, Giovana Savassa, Kate Scherler, Scott Schwarte, Hampton Sides, Navy Cmdr. Jeff Smith, Kathy Spiteri, Brett Stoffel, Kimball Taylor, Wehtahnah Tucker, Madison Tybroski, Mitch Tybroski, Amber Warner, Fred and Judy Warner, Heidi and Jeff Warner, Billy Waugh, Janet Wendle, Charlie Wilson, Natalie Young, Dean and Tyler Zack.

Special thanks to Jonathan Burnham, my publisher at HarperCollins, and David Hirshey, my editor—both of whom saw this as an important story that needed to be told, and got behind the project during a time when book sales on the war in Afghanistan were waning. Assistant editor George Quraishi, my point person at HarperCollins, labored tirelessly on the manuscript, making sure every ambiguity was clarified and spending a great deal of his own time helping me work through many of the most difficult parts of the story. My agent, Christy Fletcher, invoked my confidence as a journalist and a storyteller, reminding me that both can be achieved without forsaking either as long as I stay true to the story. Michael Davis introduced me to the story of ODA 574 and continued to provide encouragement throughout the process. Michael "Scoop" Hennessy allowed his deft research skills to be called upon at the oddest of hours. Dave Merrill created maps and illustrations that are worth a thousand words. Rick Bychowski's and Evan Warner's computer savvy solved many urgent problems, and Evan designed the cutting-edge websites that further the telling of this story. Rita Samols provided meticulous on-call editing, research, and fact-checking from the earliest drafts forward to the project's completion and transcribed more than half—nearly one hundred hours—of the recorded interviews. MX and MJ made sure I took breaks from my computer and always put a smile on my face when I needed it most. And finally, I thank Lorien—my confidante and PIC. I could never thank you enough, but in summary you make me, and my words, look good. Beyond that, you are the glue that holds every other part of my life together.

★

Selected Bibliography

Books

Allard, Colonel Kenneth. *Warheads: Cable News and the Fog of War.* Annapolis, Md.: Naval Institute Press, 2006.

Ashe, Waller. *Personal Record of the Kandahar Campaign by Officers Engaged Therein.* Chestnut Hill, Mass.: Adamant Media, 2005.

Aurelius, Marcus. *Meditations.* Trans. G. Hays. New York: Modern Library, 2003.

Berntsen, Gary, and Ralph Pezzullo. *Jawbreaker: The Attack on Bin Laden and Al-Qaeda; A Personal Account by the CIA's Key Field Commander.* New York: Crown, 2005.

Briscoe, Charles H., Richard L. Kiper, James A. Schroder, and Kalev I. Sepp. *Weapon of Choice: U.S. Army Special Operations Forces in Afghanistan.* Fort Leavenworth, Kans.: Combat Studies Institute, 2003.

Call, Steve. *Danger Close: Tactical Air Controllers in Afghanistan and Iraq.* College Station: Texas A&M University Press, 2007.

Cervantes (Miguel de Cervantes Saavedra). *Don Quixote.* Trans. J. Rutherford. New York: Penguin, 2003.

Chayes, Sarah. *The Punishment of Virtue: Inside Afghanistan after the Taliban.* New York: Penguin, 2006.

Coll, Steve. *Ghost Wars: The Secret History of the CIA, Afghanistan, and Bin Laden, From the Soviet Invasion to September 10, 2001.* New York: Penguin, 2004.

Couch, Dick. *Chosen Soldier: The Making of a Special Forces Warrior.* New York: Crown, 2007.

DeYoung, Karen. *Soldier: The Life of Colin Powell.* New York: Vintage, 2007.

Dobbins, James F. *After the Taliban: Nation-Building in Afghanistan.* Washington, D.C.: Potomac, 2008.

Franks, Tommy. *American Soldier.* New York: ReganBooks, 2004.

Halberstadt, Hans. *War Stories of the Green Berets.* Minneapolis: Zenith, 2004.

Hemingway, Ernest. *For Whom the Bell Tolls.* New York: Scribner, 2003.

Irwin, Will. *The Jedburghs: The Secret History of the Allied Special Forces, France 1944.* New York: PublicAffairs, 2005.

Jalali, Ali Ahmad, and Lester W. Grau. *Afghan Guerilla Warfare.* St. Paul, Minn.: MBI, 2001.

Lamb, Christina. *The Sewing Circles of Herat: A Personal Voyage Through Afghanistan.* New York: Harper Perennial, 2004.

Lawrence, T. E. *Seven Pillars of Wisdom: A Triumph.* New York: Anchor, 1991.

Macrory, Patrick. *Retreat from Kabul: The Incredible Story of How a Savage Afghan Force Massacred the World's Most Powerful Army.* Guilford, Conn.: Lyons, 2002.

Mills, Nick B. *Karzai: The Failing American Intervention and the Struggle for Afghanistan.* Hoboken, N.J.: Wiley, 2007.

Musharraf, Pervez. *In The Line of Fire: A Memoir.* New York: Free Press, 2006.

Priest, Dana. *The Mission: Waging War and Keeping Peace with America's Military.* New York: Norton, 2004.

Rashid, Ahmed. *Descent Into Chaos: The United States and the Failure of Nation Building in Pakistan, Afghanistan, and Central Asia.* New York: Penguin, 2008.

———. *Taliban: Militant Islam, Oil, and Fundamentalism in Central Asia.* New Haven, Conn.: Yale University Press, 2001.

Robinson, Linda. *Masters of Chaos: The Secret History of the Special Forces.* New York: PublicAffairs, 2004.

Scarborough, Rowan. *Rumsfeld's War: The Untold Story of America's Anti-Terrorist Commander.* Washington, D.C.: Regnery, 2004.

Schroen, Gary C. *First In: An Insider's Account of How the CIA Spearheaded the War on Terror in Afghanistan.* New York: Ballantine, 2005.

Schumacher, Gerald. *To Be a U.S. Army Green Beret.* St. Paul, Minn.: Zenith, 2005.

Sinno, Abdulkader H. *Organizations at War in Afghanistan and Beyond.* Ithaca, N.Y.: Cornell University Press, 2008.

Stewart, Rory. *The Places in Between.* Orlando, Fla.: Harcourt, 2004.

Tanner, Stephen. *Afghanistan: A Military History from Alexander the Great to the Fall of the Taliban.* New York: Da Capo, 2003.

Tenet, George, with Bill Harlow. *At the Center of the Storm: My Years at the CIA.* New York: HarperCollins, 2007.

Weiner, Tim. *Legacy of Ashes: The History of the CIA.* New York: Doubleday, 2007.

Woodward, Bob. *Bush at War.* New York: Simon & Schuster, 2003.

REPORTS, ACADEMIC PAPERS, ETC.

Center for Law and Military Operations, The Judge Advocate General's Legal Center & School, United States Army. *Legal Lessons Learned from Afghanistan and Iraq, Vol. I, Major Combat Operations (11 September 2001–1 May 2003).* Charlottesville, Va., 2004

Forrest, Marion L., Ph.D. "Building USAF 'Expeditionary Bases' for Operation Enduring Freedom—Afghanistan, 2001–2002." *Air & Space Power Journal,* 2005

Headquarters, United States Central Command Air Forces. Report of Investigation: 5 December 2001 JDAM Incident Near Sayd Alim Kalay, Afghanistan. Redacted/unclassified version. 2003.

Kelley, Major Robert E. "U.S. Army Special Forces Unconventional Warfare Doctrine: Engine of Change or Relic of the Past?" Naval War College, 2000.

Lambeth, Benjamin S. "Air Power Against Terror: America's Conduct of Operation Enduring Freedom." RAND National Defense Research Institute.

Neske, Chaplain (Major) Robert N. "The Assumption of Adequacy: Operation Safe Haven, A Chaplain's View." U.S. Army Command and General Staff College, 1999.

Ramirez, Armando J. "Thesis: From Bosnia to Baghdad; The Evolution of U.S. Army Special Forces from 1995–2004." Naval Postgraduate School, 2004.

Rubin, Barnett R. "Afghanistan's Uncertain Transition from Turmoil to Normalcy." Center for Preventive Action, Council on Foreign Relations, 2006.

Shienle, Major Duke C. *Liberator or Occupier: Indigenous Allies Make the Difference: A Monograph.* School of Advanced Military Studies, U.S. Army Command and General Staff College, 2003–2004.

Theisen, Lt. Col. Eric E. *Ground-Aided Precision Strike: Heavy Bomber Activity in Operation Enduring Freedom.* Maxwell A.F.B., Ala.: Air University Press, 2003

Wardak, Ali. "Jirga: A Traditional Mechanism of Conflict Resolution in Afghanistan." University of Glamorgan.

★

Notes

Unless noted in this section, all the information in this book is from eyewitness accounts.

Mike McElhiney was one of the first members of ODA 574 I interviewed, and he began, as many of the men did, by asking me what kind of story I wanted to tell. I was ready for the question because I'd already discussed this issue with Dan Petithory's father, Lou. I told Mike, "This story won't be pro-war, it won't be anti-war; it's going to be just the story. I'll tell it the way it happened: how Fifth Group got into the war, how your team got the mission with Karzai, what you guys did on the ground, and what happened on December 5, 2001."

Mike's response: "Sure, I'll talk to you as long as you promise to listen, take good notes, record the conversations, and honor Dan and JD by telling the story the way it happened—because nobody else has gotten it right. If you've read any other books or articles, throw them away. There's so much bullshit out there from reporters who 'quoted' guys on the team who never even talked to them, people who had us firing off rounds when we weren't, blood spattering when it wasn't. Don't make it anything it wasn't—just stick to the ground truth and we'll be good."

You'll notice that there are very few citations in this book. I did not use secondhand reporting—previously published articles or books that covered ODA 574's mission with Karzai—or "hearsay" to describe any of the team's actions and experiences. What you read came directly from the men involved. Conversations and thoughts were based on the notes, letters, and recollections of these individuals.

I did occasionally rely upon quotes and conversations reported by other journalists purely to provide context for the events affecting ODA 574, including quotes by President Bush, CIA Director George Tenet, and Secretary of Defense Donald Rumsfeld. For those instances I provide source material below.

I also read the work of various authors and journalists for my personal understanding of Afghanistan (see Selected Bibliography).

All events reported in this book were described to me by eyewitnesses in exclusive personal interviews conducted over the course of two years: almost 200 hours of conversations (more than 150 hours recorded) with members of 5th Special Forces Group, Air Force Special Operations Command, Special Operations Command Central, Central Command, and family members. The majority of these interviews were with most of the surviving members of ODA 574.

In addition, I relied upon various official reports, including afteraction reports and the investigation of the JDAM incident on December 5, 2001.

Lastly, a few of the notes below expand upon some of the more technical events in the story, as well as potentially controversial ones.

PROLOGUE

1. "Of these, only four served out their 'terms' and died a natural death. The others were dethroned, assassinated, imprisoned, deposed and killed, deposed and exiled, deposed and hanged, beaten to death, and so forth." Editorial by Cheryl Benard, *Los Angeles Times*, February 23, 2009, p. 17.

CHAPTER 1: A MOST DANGEROUS MISSION

1. There are many accounts of the Jedburgh teams available. See especially Will Irwin, *The Jedburghs: The Secret History of the Allied Special Forces, France 1944* (New York: PublicAffairs, 2005).
2. CIA teams are often referred to by the military as OGAs (other government agency). This account references them as CIA or spooks in order to alleviate confusion between ODA and OGA. All CIA and Delta operators in this book have been given pseudonyms.

3. Built for the Vietnam War, Pave Lows have been continuously modified and upgraded ever since. They are the most technologically advanced heavy-lift helicopters in the Air Force arsenal, but that technology is stacked on top of an ancient airframe. The result is that the Pave Lows rarely flew in Afghanistan without some pending maintenance issue.

CHAPTER 2: THE QUIET PROFESSIONALS

1. All sections in the book quoting or describing Colonel Mulholland were reported to me by eyewitnesses to events, not by Mulholland himself—including Major Chris Miller and various members of ODA 574. I also found useful the PBS *Frontline* interview with Mulholland conducted in April 2002.
2. In order to reconstruct Hamid Karzai's background I relied upon various source materials as well as a fact-check of pertinent sections of this book by the Center for Afghanistan Studies at the University of Nebraska, Omaha, coordinated by Sher Jan Ahmadzai. Also especially useful are Christina Lamb, *The Sewing Circles of Herat: A Personal Voyage Through Afghanistan* (New York: Harper Perennial, 2004), and Nick Mills, *Karzai: The Failing American Intervention and the Struggle for Afghanistan* (Hoboken, N.J.: Wiley, 2007).
3. While the rise of the Taliban is well documented, there are variations. I followed most closely the story that ODA 574 learned during their isolation period, from Ahmed Rashid, *Taliban: Militant Islam, Oil and Fundamentalism in Central Asia* (New Haven, Conn.: Yale University Press, 2001).
4. In addition to personal interviews with Major Bob Kelley, the chief of plans for Special Operations Command Central at the time of 9/11, information for this section regarding unconventional warfare was gleaned from a paper written by him in January 2000 for the Naval War College in Newport, Rhode Island, titled "U.S. Army Special Forces Unconventional Warfare Doctrine: Engine of Change or Relic of the Past." The abstract for the paper reads: "As a mission and as a concept, unconventional warfare (UW) is the heart and soul of the United States Army's Special Forces (SF). Since SF was created in 1952, UW operations have been the 'touchstone' for all developments in the organization. Special Forces are the primary force within United States Special Operations Command (USSOCOM) for UW.

   "Doctrine for Joint Special Operations correctly defines a relevant UW mission for U.S. Special Operations Forces. But Army Special Forces doctrine for UW operations focuses on only one aspect of UW—guerrilla warfare. This was appropriate in 1952 for the purpose of organizing partisans in Eastern Europe to oppose the Warsaw Pact. Today, however, guerrilla warfare is the least likely type of unconventional warfare operation to occur. Therefore, SF should now begin to focus on the indirect activities of unconventional warfare: subversion, sabotage and intelligence activities. Special Forces UW doctrine must also be updated to leverage new technological capabilities."

5. The sections in the book when Major Chris Miller volunteers Colonel Mulholland as the JSOTF (Task Force Dagger) commander, and all sections where Miller is at the SOCCENT bunker trying to get 5th Special Forces Group into the fight, are based on interviews with Miller himself. Conversations between Miller and Major Kelley were reported by both individuals.

6. "By the mid-1990s the Air Force had collapsed as a professional military establishment, and remaining aviation assets changed hands over the course of the civil war. Most of the surviving aircraft, amounting to about 40 combat aircraft and various transport planes and helicopters, were under Taliban control. About half the combat planes were Su-20 and Su-22 export versions of the Su-17 fighter-bomber, with the other half including MiG-21 interceptors and ground attack fighters. The Taliban also converted a few ll-39 trainer aircraft to bombers. *The Military Balance, 2000/2001* estimated that the Taliban might have had about 20 MiG-21 and Su-22, and 5 L-39, while the Northern Alliance might have had about 30 Su-17/22, 30 MiG-21 and 10 L-39. Most of the planes were elderly, and many were unsafe to fly. Improvisation and cannibalization provided a few combat aircraft (six or eight) for limited operations." See http://www.globalsecurity.org/military/world/afghanistan/airforce.htm.

CHAPTER 3: TO WAR

1. Taken from interview for the Combat Studies Institute, Operational Leadership Experiences Project Combat Studies Institute, Fort Leavenworth, Kansas.

2. From the U.S. Special Operations Command Official History 1987 to 2007, pp. 87–90, Global War on Terrorism section.

3. Bob Woodward, *Bush at War* (New York: Simon & Schuster, 2003).

4. PBS *Frontline* interview with Robert McFarlane, transcript for *Campaign Against Terror*.

5. Arthur Keller, "Caution: Taliban Crossing," op-ed, *New York Times*, November 11, 2007.

6. Ahmed Rashid, *Descent Into Chaos: The United States and the Failure of Nation Building in Pakistan, Afghanistan, and Central Asia* (New York: Penguin, 2008), p. 88.

7. During my research to understand the difference between the two types of forward air controllers in the Air Force—CCTs, like Alex Yoshimoto, and TACPs, like Jim Price—I spoke with an Air Force Public Affairs officer who simplified it a bit.

"Don't get me wrong," she said. "Both TACPs and CCTs are elite airmen who work alongside ground troops—both conventional and Special Operations forces. A CCT's career field covers a wider range of capabilities." She explained that CCTs are also certified Federal Aviation Administration air traffic controllers, who can, and have been known to, open and run airfields seized behind enemy lines. Both CCTs and TACPs are highly trained, and "to confuse matters more, both can be JTAC [Joint Terminal Air Control] certified, which broadens their capabilities even further to include calling in close air support from both fixed-wing and rotary-wing [helicopter gunships] aircraft; forward firing weaponry [missiles]; artillery from ground units; and sea-based weapons platforms [artillery and missiles from ships at sea]."

As one team member put it, Alex and Price were "the guys who will call shit in when we need it."

In his book *Danger Close*, Steve Call describes in detail who these men are and what they do. Many consider the CCTs and TACPs "America's secret weapon." See *Danger Close: Tactical Air Controllers in Afghanistan and Iraq* (College Station: Texas A&M University Press, 2007).

8. Gary C. Schroen, *First In: An Insider's Account of How the CIA Spearheaded the War on Terror in Afghanistan* (New York: Ballantine, 2005).

CHAPTER 4: THE SOLDIER AND THE STATESMAN

1. Though Pakistan's president, Pervez Musharraf, fervently denied that he was strong-armed into providing these basing rights, Secretary of State Colin Powell had delivered to him the Bush party line: "You are either with us or against us." Under a "leasing" agreement with high rent and numerous conditions, the United States was also granted a narrow flight corridor into and out of Pakistan, to be used only for logistics and aircraft recovery; no attacks could be launched from within Musharraf's country. See Pervez Musharraf, *In the Line of Fire: A Memoir* (New York: Free Press, 2006).

2. Woodward, *Bush at War*.

3. Robert McFarlane, "The Tragedy of Abdul Haq," *Wall Street Journal*, November 2, 2001.

4. James F. Dobbins, *After the Taliban: Nation-Building in Afghanistan* (Washington, D.C.: Potomac, 2008).

CHAPTER 6: THE BATTLE OF TARIN KOWT

1. Every member of ODA 574 was issued a detailed, topographical Joint Operations Graphic "pilot survival map," generally carried by pilots in the event they are shot down or crash behind enemy lines and must evade the enemy. Special Forces in Afghanistan used any number of maps, but many found this survival map the most useful for referencing such things as terrain, roads, waterways, and mountains. Names of villages, road locations, bridges over waterways, and other features on the map, however, differed greatly from what the men discovered once on the ground.
2. "Under Operations Safe Haven and Safe Passage nearly 7,300 Cubans were transported from Panama to Guantanamo Naval Base between 01 February 1995, the date the movement began, and 20 February 1995. The mission of the transfer operation was to move the Cuban migrants from Safe Haven camps in Panama to Guantanamo in a safe, orderly manner." See http://www.globalsecurity.org/military/ops/safe_haven. htm.

CHAPTER 7: CREDIBILITY

1. Maura Reynolds and Alissa J. Rubin, "Response to Terror: The Front Lines," *Los Angeles Times*, November 25, 2001.
2. U.S. Army Special Operations Forces in Afghanistan, *Weapon of Choice: ARSOF in Afghanistan*, official history, Combat Studies Institute, Fort Leavenworth, Kans., p. 157.
3. While I interviewed James Dobbins personally, much of what I gleaned or quoted can be found in his book *After the Taliban*. The book also provides an overview of the process at Bonn.

CHAPTER 8: MADNESS

1. The U.S. Army was unable to deliver this situation report, in spite of a Freedom of Information Act request. As such, the content is paraphrased, but deemed accurate by team members who read the original.
2. Tommy Franks with Malcolm McConnell, *American Soldier* (New York: ReganBooks, 2004), p. 309.
3. *Weapon of Choice*, pp. 158–66. To further understand the uprising, and how a headquarters element ultimately called in a bomb on its own position, I interviewed members of ODAs operating in northern Afghanistan at that time who confirmed that they had requested to return to the

prison to help with the rescue efforts but were told by Queeg's headquarters staff that they were not needed.

4. From September 27 to October 31, Fox had led a training exercise in Jordan. Upon completion, the battalion was ordered to hold in place, at El Jafr air base in Jordan. A week later, Fox was told to pick fourteen members of his battalion staff who could function as a nimble command-and-control group to execute missions into northern Afghanistan. From Jordan, Fox and his fourteen-member SOCCE staff were sent to Uzbekistan aboard a commercial airliner, then made their way to K2 on a public bus. Two and a half days later, they were in Pakistan for Thanksgiving, on standby at J-Bad until they joined ODA 574 and Karzai.

5. While some called the town Shawali Kowt (it is also the main town in Shawali Kowt District), others called it Sayd Alim Kalay, which was the name used in investigations conducted by the U.S. military. I chose Shawali Kowt, the name used by Amerine and Karzai.

Chapter 9: Death on the Horizon

1. Charles Gray Robertson, *Kurum, Kabul, and Kandahar* (1881; rept. Elibron Classics), pp. 209, 210.

Chapter 10: The Ruins

1. Mag's and Wes's accounts of being left behind by Ken were nearly identical. Despite numerous attempts, I was never able to get Ken's version of the story to see if he might have thought they were both in the back of the vehicle when he sped off. Neither man confronted him later that night, and he never apologized. Numerous people told me that it was Ken's job to make sure his passengers were in the vehicle. Ultimately, both Wes and Mag assumed he had simply panicked and lost all situational awareness.

2. While nobody on ODA 574 knew anything about Bolduc's thwarting of an enemy flanking maneuver on the late afternoon of December 4, 2001, I was able to find one semi-witness to the events. Nelson Smith confirmed that Bolduc did take a number of guerrillas with him down off the Alamo (while the battle for the ruins by the bridge was in full swing) toward the river after verbalizing his suspicions to Smith that there might be enemy coming across it, something Bolduc inferred from some intercepted radio traffic. A few minutes later, while Nelson was trying to set up a hasty defense of the Alamo with the remaining guerrillas in the area, he heard gunfire coming from the direction of the river.

Bolduc later called it a flanking maneuver by the enemy. ODA 574 was dubious of the story because in the unanimous opinion of all team members I interviewed, if there had been such a flanking maneuver by the enemy in progress while the men were engaged in combat at the ruins, they should have been informed about it immediately, as they were the ones potentially being flanked.

In my interview with Bolduc, he told me that he saw a group of armed Afghans (estimated at thirty) coming out of an orchard across the river, and opened fire on them as they made their way onto the dry riverbed. The guerrillas he brought along joined in, and the Afghans retreated into the orchard. When I interviewed Fox (who had moved forward to JD's support-by-fire location at the time), he said that he hadn't heard about Bolduc's combat back near the Alamo until Bolduc told him about it in person a couple of hours later, once Fox had returned to the Alamo. Bolduc's own version of the account has been documented in *Weapon of Choice*, pp. 176–77.

CHAPTER 11: THE THIRTEENTH SORTIE

1. The facts, quotations, and sequence of events used to describe the B-52's mission were taken from the recorded transcripts of the official Air Force Accident Investigation, in which all five crew members were questioned under oath. See Report of Investigation: 5 December 2001 JDAM Incident Near Sayd Alim Kalay, Afghanistan (redacted/unclassified version), 2003.

EPILOGUE

1. After remaining anonymous to the public ever since the accident occurred, Jim Price allowed me to use his real name and to hear his account of the events. Since the technical aspects of what went wrong have been simplified herein, and because what truly went wrong was never discovered in the investigation, some further explanation is warranted.

Price ultimately discovered his error on a field exercise supporting 5th Group ODAs in August 2002, after a Special Forces operator questioned Price about an odd "gross deviation error" on his GPS screen. Price shut down the exercise and after a couple of hours tinkering with the device, discovered "deliberate" and "hasty" modes in the software.

On the morning of December 5, 2001, Price had calibrated the Viper laser range finder after talking with the F-18 pilots. One of the calibration points was the ground in front of him that he had lased. Because the

Viper had been borrowed from the weather detachment and configured to measure cloud heights, its software was set on "hasty" mode, which allowed Price to scroll past a "gross deviation error" message warning him that the coordinates were too close to his current location. Had the software been set on "deliberate" mode—the proper configuration for close air support—the device would not have allowed him to pull up a coordinate in the immediate vicinity. The software also stored only ten sightings and would not overwrite the final target sighting, so it stored his test location rather than discarding it as he had expected. When Price called in the bomb, he inadvertently used that stored location, directing the bomb to a coordinate only a few feet ahead of his position. Had he double-checked the target coordinates on the military GPS with his personal GPS, he would have caught the error.

A warning report was ultimately issued throughout the military on January 16, 2003, that stated the equipment Price was using created a "fratricide risk": "There is a potential of fratricide when using the PLGR II or the V-PLGR with a Viper/Vector LRF while in 'Hasty' or 'Deliberate' LRF mode." Also, "As a result, munitions may be called on an Operator's position when using the [equipment] set to 'Hasty' LRF mode."

2. By mid-September 2009, the votes had been cast in Afghanistan's second democratic presidential election, and the Afghan Independent Election Commission determined that Karzai had achieved the necessary votes to defeat his closest contender, Dr. Abdullah, and would remain president for a second term. His victory, however, was tainted by allegations of electoral fraud and ballot stuffing. A subsequent investigation reduced his total votes from 54 percent to 49.7 percent, .3 percent short of the votes required to avoid a runoff. A runoff election was scheduled for November 7, 2009, between Karzai and Abdullah, the Northern Alliance leader who had first endorsed Karzai's interim leadership in November of 2001, two days following the battle of Tarin Kowt. On October 25, 2009, correspondent Fareed Zakaria interviewed Karzai on CNN, asking the incumbent president whether or not he had been pressured into accepting the runoff. Karzai responded that to not accept the runoff was to "insult democracy" based upon the evidence of vote rigging. He added that it was required "For peace, for stability, for the future of democracy in Afghanistan, and for the future of institutional order in Afghanistan."

On Sunday, November 1, just a few days before this book went to press, Abdullah dropped out of the race, and the following day the Independent Election Commission proclaimed Karzai the victor. He will lead Afghanistan for a second five-year term as president.

Journey of ODA 574:
Sept. 11, 2001 – Dec. 5, 2001

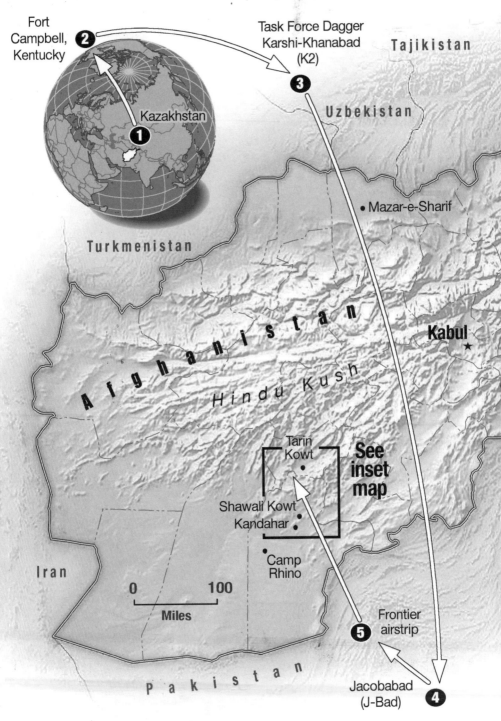